# THE THEORY OF ENGINEERING DRAWING



MAXWELL PRESS

# THE THEORY OF ENGINEERING DRAWING

ALPHONSE ANDREW ADLER B.S., M.E

Member American Society of Mecahnical Engineers;
Instructor in Mechanical Drawing and Designing,
Polytechnic Institute, Brooklyn, N.Y.

MAXWELL PRESS

Chennai Trichy New Delhi

MAXWELL PRESS

This edition has been published in india by arrangement with Carson Books, UK

ISBN 978-93-5528-053-4

**Maxwell Press**
No. 44, Nallathambi Street,
Triplicane, Chennai 600 005



MJP 1304



Publisher : C. Janarthanan

# Publisher's Note

The legacy of a country is in its varied cultural heritage, historical literature, developments in the field of economy and science. The top nations in the world are competing in the field of science, economy and literature. This vast legacy has to be conserved and documented so that it can be bestowed to the future generation. The knowledge of this legacy is slowly getting perished in the present generation due to lack of documentation.

Keeping this in mind, the concern with retrospective acquiring of rare books has been accented recently by the burgeoning reprint industry. Maxwell Press is gratified to retrieve the rare collections with a view to bring back those books that were landmarks in their time.

In this effort, a series of rare books would be republished under the banner, "Maxwell Press". The books in the reprint series have been carefully selected for their contemporary usefulness as well as their historical importance within the intellectual. We reconstruct the book with slight enhancements made for better presentation, without affecting the contents of the original edition.

Most of the works selected for republishing covers a huge range of subjects, from history to anthropology. We believe this reprint edition will be a service to the numerous researchers and practitioners active in this fascinating field. We allow readers to experience the wonder of peering into a scholarly work of the highest order and seminal significance.

**MAXWELL PRESS**

# PREFACE

ALTHOUGH the subject matter of this volume is, in large measure, identical with that of many treatises on descriptive geometry, the author has called it Theory of Engineering Drawing," believing that this title indicates better than could any other, the ultimate purpose of the book. That texts on descriptive geometry appear with some degree of frequency, with but few, if any, additions to the theory, indicates that teachers are aware of certain weaknesses in existing methods of presenting the subject. It is precisely these weakness that the present work aims to correct.

The author emphasizes the fact that the student is concerned with the representation on a plane of objects in space of three dimensions. The analysis, important as it is, has for its primary purpose the development of methods for such representation and the interpretation of the resulting drawings. It is nowhere regarded as an end in itself. The number of fundamental principles has been reduced to a minimum; indeed it will be found that the entire text is based on the problem of finding the piercing point of a given line on a given surface, and a few additional operations. The accepted method of presenting the subject, is to start with a set of definitions,to consider in detail the orthographic projection of a point, and then, on the foundation thus laid, to build the theory of the projection of lines, surfaces, and solids. Logical and beautiful as this systematic developmeen may be, it nevertheless presents certain inherent difficulties, chief of which is that the student is confronted at the outset with that most abstract of all abstractions, the mathematical point. In this volume the order of presentation is reversed and the reader is asked to consider first some concrete object, a box, for instance, the study of which furnishes material of use in the later discussion of its bounding surfaces and lines.

The " Theory of Engineering Drawing is divided into four

parts. Part I treats of oblique projection, orthographic projection, and a special case of the latter, axonometric projection. The student is advised to give special attention to the classification at the end of this section, because it gives a complete outline of the entire subject. Part II contains a variety of problems of such nature as to be easily understood by those whose training has not extended to the more highly specialized branches of commercial or engineering practice. Part III considers convergent projective line drawing, more familiar under the name of perspective. Part IV has to do with the pictorial effects of illumination, since a knowledge of shades and shadows is frequently required in the preparation of complicated drawings.

No claim is made to originality of subject matter, but it is not possible to acknowledge indebtedness to individual writers, for the topics discussed have been widely studied, and an historical review is here out of place. The author wishes, however, to express his sense of obligation to Professor William J. Berry of the Department of Mathematics in the Polytechnic Institute of Brooklyn for his criticism of Chapters IX and X, and other assistance, and to Mr. Ernest J. Streubel, M.A., of the Department of English for his untiring efforts in preparing the manuscript for the press.

Polytechnic Institute of Brooklyn,
October, 1912.

# CONTENTS

## PART I

## *THE PRINCIPLES OF PARALLEL PROJECTING-LINE DRAWING*

### CHAPTER I

### INTRODUCTORY



### CHAPTER II

### OBLIQUE PROJECTION



### CHAPTER III

### ORTHOGRAPHIC PROJECTION

## CHAPTER IV

## AXONOMETRIC PROJECTION



---

# PART II

# *GEOMETRICAL PROBLEMS IN ORTHOGRAPHIC PROJECTION*

## CHAPTER V

## REPRESENTATION OF LINES AND POINTS

## CHAPTER VI

## REPRESENTATION OF PLANES



## CHAPTER VII

## ELEMENTARY CONSIDERATIONS OF LINES AND PLANES



## CHAPTER VIII

## PROBLEMS INVOLVING THE POINT, THE LINE, AND THE PLANE

## CHAPTER IX

## CLASSIFICATION OF LINES

## CHAPTER X

## CLASSIFICATION OF SURFACES



## CHAPTER XI

## INTERSECTIONS OF SURFACES BY PLANES, AND THEIR DEVELOPMENT

## CHAPTER XII

## INTERSECTIONS OF SURFACES WITH EACH OTHER AND THEIR DEVELOPMENT

# PART III

## *THE PRINCIPLES OF CONVERGENT PROJECTING-LINE DRAWING*

### CHAPTER XIII

### PERSPECTIVE PROJECTION

# PART IV

## *PICTORIAL EFFECTS OF ILLUMINATION*

## CHAPTER XIV

### PICTORIAL EFFECTS OF ILLUMONATION IN ORTHOGRAPHIC PROJECTION



## CHAPTER XV

### PICTORIAL EFFECTS OF ILLUMINATION IN PERSPECTIVE PROJECTION

# PART I.

**101. Nature of drawing.** Drawing has for its purpose the exact graphic representation of objects in space. The first essential is to have an idea, and then a desire to express it. Ideas may be expressed in **words, in pictures,** or in a combination of both **words and pictures.** If words alone are sufficient to express the idea, then **language** becomes the vehicle of its transmission. When the idea relates to some material object, however, a **drawing** alone, without additional information may satisfy its accurate conveyance. Further, some special cases require for their expression a combination of both **language and drawing.**

Consider, for purposes of illustration, a maple block, 2 inches thick, 4 inches wide and 12 inches long. It is easy to conceive this block of wood, and the mere statement, alone, specifies the object more or less completely. On the other hand, the modern newspaper printing press can not be completely described by language alone. Anyone who has ever seen such a press in operation, would soon realize that the intricate mechanism could not be described in words, so as to make it intelligible to another without the use of a drawing. Even if a drawing is employed in this latter case, the desired idea may not be adequately presented, since a circular shaft is drawn in exactly the same way, whether it be made of wood, brass, or steel. Appended notes, in such cases, inform the constructor of the material to use. From the foregoing, it is evident, that drawing cannot become a universal language in engineering, unless the appended descriptions and specifications have the same meaning to all.

**102. Science and art of drawing.** Drawing is both a **science** and an **art**. The science affects such matters as the proper **arrangement of views** and the manner of their **presentation.** Those who are familiar with the mode of representation used, will obtain the idea the maker desired to express. It is a science, because the facts can be **assimilated, classified,** and **presented** in a more or less **logical** order. In this book, the science of drawing will engage most of the attention; only such of the artistic side is included as adds to the ease of the interpretation of the drawing.

The **art** lies in the skilful application of the scientific principles involved to a definite purpose. It embraces such topics as the **thickness** or **weight** of lines, whether the **outline** alone is to be drawn, or whether the object is to be **colored** and **shaded** so as to give it the same appearance that it has in nature.

**103. Magnitude of objects.** Objects visible to the eye are, of necessity, **solids,** and therefore require the **three principal dimensions** to indicate their magnitude—**length, breadth,** and **thickness.** If the observer places himself in the proper position while viewing an object before him, the object impresses itself on him as a whole, and a mental estimate is made from the one position of the observer as to its form and magnitude. Naturally, the first task will be to represent an object in a single view, showing it in three dimensions, as a solid.

**104. Commercial application of drawing.** It must be remembered that the function of drawing is graphically to present an idea on a flat surface—like a sheet of paper for instance—so as to take the place of the object in space. The reader's imagination supplies such deficiency as is caused by the absence of the actual object. It is, therefore, necessary to study the various underlying principles of drawing, and, then, apply them as daily experience dictates to be the most direct and accurate way of their presentation. In any case, only one interpretation of a drawing should be possible, and if there is a possibility of ambiguity arising, then a note should be made on the drawing calling attention to the desired interpretation.

## QUESTIONS ON CHAPTER I

1. In what ways may ideas be transmitted to others?
2. What topics are embraced in the science of drawing?
3. What topics are included in the art of drawing?
4. How many principal dimensions are required to express the magnitude of objects? What are they?
5. What is the function of drawing?
6. Is the reader's imagination called upon when interpreting a drawing? Why?

# CHAPTER II

## OBLIQUE PROJECTION

**201. Nature of oblique projection.** Suppose it is desired to draw a box, 6″ wide, 12″ long and 4″ high, made of wood ½″ thick. Fig. 1 shows this drawn in oblique projection. The method of making the drawing will first be shown and then the theory on which it is based will be developed. A rectangle **abcd**, 4″×6″, is laid out, the 6″ side being horizontal and the 4″ side being vertical. From three corners of the rectangle,

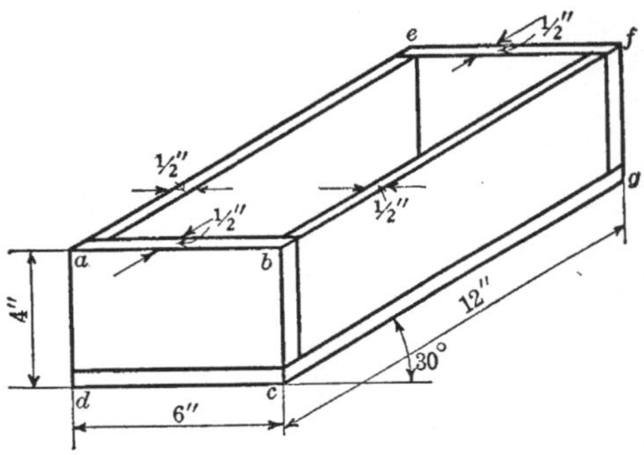


Fig. 1.

lines **ae**, **bf**, and **cg** are drawn, making, in this case, an angle of 30° with the horizontal. The length 12″ is laid off on an inclined line, as **cg**. The extreme limiting lines of the box are then fixed by the addition of two lines **ef** (horizontal) and **fg** (vertical). The thickness of the wood is represented, and the dimensions showing that it is ½″ thick indicate the direction in which they are laid off. The reason for the presence of such other additional lines, is that they show the actual construction.

The sloping lines in Fig. 1 could be drawn at any angle other than 30°. In Fig. 2, the same box is drawn with a 60° inclination. It will be seen, in this latter case, that the inside bottom of the box is also shown prominently. It is customary in the application of this type of drawing, to use either 30°, 45° or 60° for the slope, as these lines can be easily drawn with the standard triangles used in the drafting room.

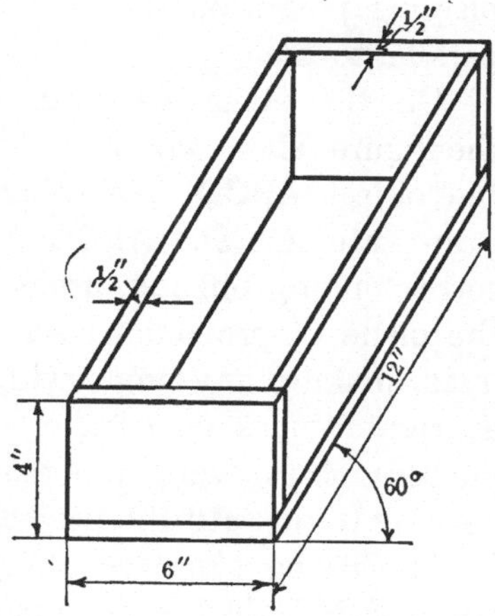


FIG. 2.

**202. Oblique projection of lines parallel to the plane of projection.** In developing the theory, let **XX** and **YY**, Fig. 3, be two planes at right angles to each other. Also, let **ABCD** be a thin rectangular plate, the plane of which is parallel to the plane **XX**. Suppose the eye is looking in the direction **Aa**, **inclined*** to the plane **XX**. Where this line of sight from the point **A** on the

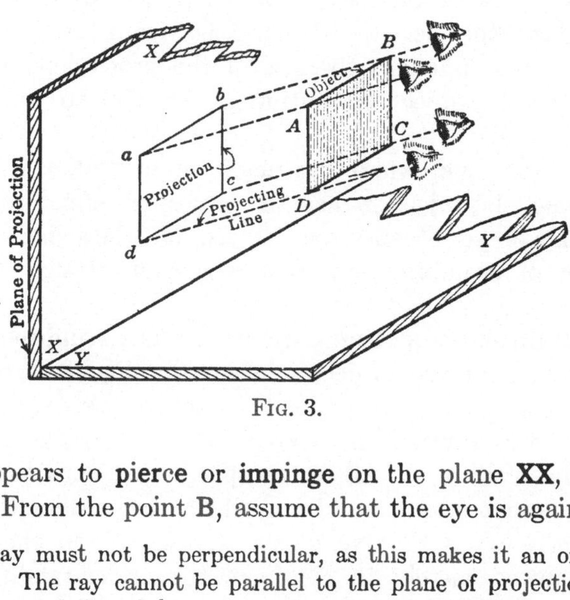


FIG. 3.

object appears to **pierce** or **impinge** on the plane **XX**, locate the point **a**. From the point **B**, assume that the eye is again directed

* The ray must not be perpendicular, as this makes it an orthographic projection. The ray cannot be parallel to the plane of projection, because it will never meet it, and, hence, cannot result in a projection.

toward the plane **XX**, in a line that is parallel to **Aa**; this second piercing point for the point **B** in space will appear at b. Similarly, from the points **C** and **D** on the object, the piercing points on the plane will be **c** and **d**, **Cc** and **Dd** being parallel to **Aa**.

On the plane **XX**, join the points **abcd**. To an observer, the figure **abcd** will give the same mental impression as will the object **ABCD**. In other words, **abcd** is a **drawing** of the thin plate **ABCD**. **ABCD** is the **object** in space; **abcd** is the corresponding **oblique projection** of **ABCD**. The plane **XX** is the **plane** of **projection**; **Aa**, **Bb**, **Cc**, and **Dd**, are the **projecting lines,** making any angle with the plane of projection other than at right angles or parallel thereto. The plane **YY** serves the purpose of throwing the plane **XX** into stronger relief and has nothing to do with the projection.

It will be observed that the figure whose corners are the points **ABCDabcd** is an oblique rectangular prism, the opposite faces of which are parallel because the edges have been made parallel by construction. From the geometry, all parallel plane sections of the prism are equal, hence **abcd** is equal to **ABCD**, because the plane of the object **ABCD** was originally assumed parallel to **XX**, and the projection **abcd** lies in the plane **XX**. As a corollary, the distance of the object from the plane of projection does not influence the size of the projection, so long as the plane of the object is continually parallel to the plane of projection.

Indeed, any line, whether straight or curved, when parallel to the plane of projection has its projection equal to the line itself. This is so because the curved line may be considered as made up of an infinite number of very short straight lines.

**203. Oblique projection considered as a shadow.** Another way of looking at the projection shown in Fig. 3 is to assume that light comes in parallel lines, oblique to the plane of projection. If the object is interposed in these parallel rays, then **abcd** is the shadow of **ABCD** in space, and thus presents an entirely different standpoint from which to consider the nature of a projection. Both give identical results, and the latter is here introduced merely to reenforce the understanding of the nature of the operation.

**204. Oblique projection of lines perpendicular to the plane of projection.** Let **XX**, Fig. 4, be a transparent plane surface, seen edgewise, and **ab**, an arrow perpendicular to **XX**, the end a of the arrow lying in the plane. Suppose the eye is located at **r** so that the ray of light **rb** makes an angle of 45° with the plane **XX**. If all rays of light from points on **ab** are

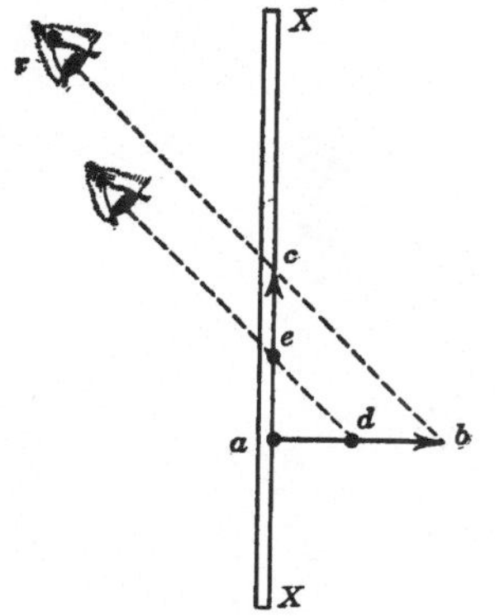


FIG. 4.

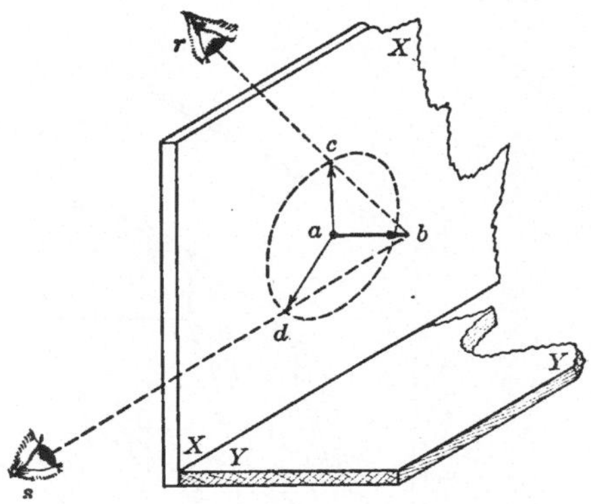


FIG. 5.

parallel to **rb**, they will pierce the plane **XX** in a series of points, and ac, then, will become the projection of **ab** on the plane **XX**. To an observer standing in the proper position, looking along lines parallel to **rb**, **ac** will give the same mental impression as the actual arrow ab in space; and, therefore, ac is the projection of **ab** on the plane **XX**. The extremities of the line **ab** are hence projected as two distinct points **a** and c. Any intermediate point, as **d**, will be projected as **e** on the projection ac.

From the geometry, it may be noticed that ac is equal to **ab**, because **cab** is a right angled triangle, and the angle **acb** equals the angle **cba**, due to the adoption of the 45° ray. Also, any limited portion of a line, perpendicular to the plane of projection, is projected as a line equal to it in length. The triangle **cab** may be rotated about ab as an axis, so that c describes a circle in the plane **XX** and thus ac will always remain equal to **ab**. This means that the rotation merely corresponds to a new position of the eye, the inclination of the ray always remaining 45° with the plane **XX**.

The foregoing method of representing 45° rays is again shown as an oblique projection in Fig. 5. Two positions of the ray are indicated as **rb** and **sb**; the corresponding projections are **ac** and **ad**. Hence, in constructing oblique projections, the lines that are parallel to the plane of projection are drawn with their true relation to each other. The lines that are perpendicular to the plane of projection are drawn as an inclined line of a length equal to the line itself and making any angle with the horizontal,

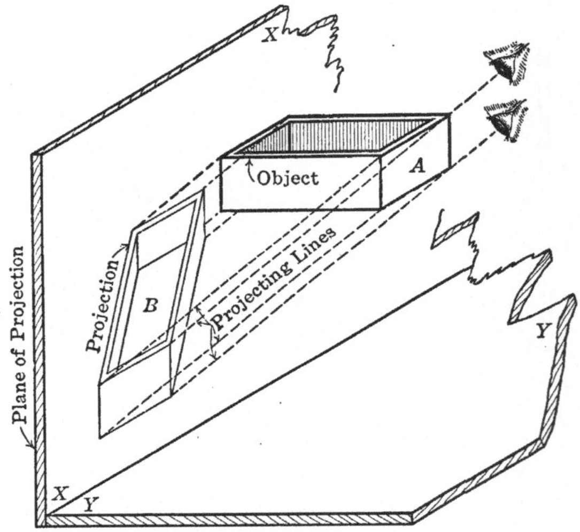


FIG. 6.

at pleasure. Here, again, the plane **YY** is added. The line of intersection of **XX** and **YY** is perpendicular to the plane of the paper, and is shown as a sloping line, because the two planes themselves are pictured in oblique projection.*

**205. Oblique projection of the combination of parallel and perpendicular lines to the plane of projection.** Fig. 6 shows a box and its projection, pictorially **indicating** all the **mental steps** required in the construction of an oblique projection. The object (a box) **A** is shown as an oblique projection;

* Compare this with Figs. 1 and 2. The front face of the box is shown as it actually appears, because it is parallel to the plane of projection (or paper). The length of the box is perpendicular to the plane of the paper and is projected as a sloping line.

**its projection B** on the plane of projection appears very much distorted. This distortion of the projection is due to its being an oblique projection, initially, which is then again shown in oblique projection. From what precedes, the reader should find no difficulty in tracing out the construction. Attention may again be called to the fact that the extremities of the lines perpendicular to the plane of projection are projected as two distinct **points.**

**206. Oblique projection of circles.*** When the plane of a circle is parallel to the plane of projection, it is drawn with a compass in the ordinary way, because the projection is equal to the circle itself (202). When the plane of the circle is perpendicular to the plane of projection, however, it is shown as an ellipse. Both cases will be illustrated by Fig. 7, which shows a cube in oblique projection. In the face **abcd**, the circle is shown as such, because the plane of the circle is parallel to the plane of projection, which, in this case, is the plane of the paper. It will be noticed that the circle in **abcd** is tangent at points midway between the extremities of the lines. If similar points of tangency are laid off in the faces **aefb** and **fbcg** and a smooth curve be drawn through these points, the result will be an ellipse; this ellipse is, therefore, the oblique projection of a circle, whose plane is perpendicular to the plane of projection. The additional lines in Fig. 7 show how four additional points may be located on the required ellipse.

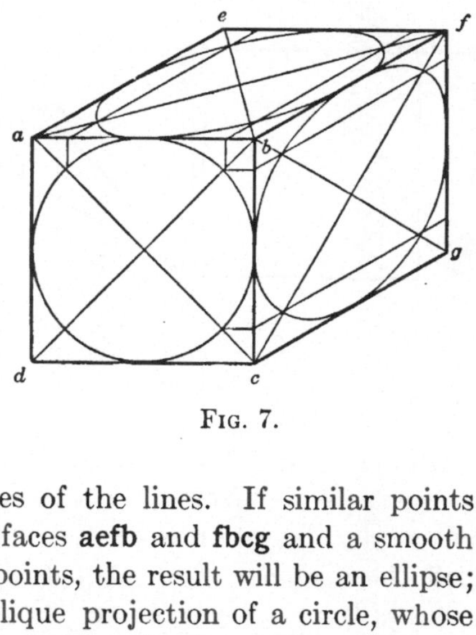


FIG. 7.

It may be shown that a circle is projected as an ellipse in all cases except when its plane is parallel to the plane of projection, or, when its plane is chosen parallel to the projecting lines. In the latter case, it is a line of a length equal to the diameter of the

* When projecting circles in perpendicular planes, the 30° slope offers an advantage because the ellipse is easily approximated. See Art. 405.

circle. The reason for this will become evident later in the subject. (It is of insufficient import at present to dwell on it at length.)

**207. Oblique projection of inclined lines and angles.** At times, lines must be drawn that are neither parallel nor perpendicular to the plane of projection. A reference to Fig. 8 will show how this is done. It is desired to locate a hole in a cube whose edge measures 12″. The hole is to be placed in the side **bfgc**, 8″ back from the point c and then 4″ up to the point **h**. To bring this about, lay off **ck**=8″ and **kh** (vertically) =4″ and, then **h** is the required point. Also, **hkc** is the oblique projection of a right angled triangle, whose plane is perpendicular to the plane of projection. Suppose, further, it is desired to locate the point **m** on the face **abfe**, 7″ to the right of the point a and 5″ back. The dimensions show how this is done. Again, **man** is the oblique projection of a right angled triangle, whose legs are 5″ and 7″. This method of laying off points is virtually a method of **offsets.*** The point **m** is offset a distance of 5″ from ab; likewise **h** is offset 4″ from **cg**. If it be required to lay off the diagonal of a cube, it is accomplished by making three offsets from a given point. For instance, consider the diagonal **ce**. If c is the starting point, draw **cg** perpendicular to the plane (shown as an inclined line), then **fg**, vertically upward, and finally **fe**, horizontally to the left; therefore, **ce** is the diagonal of the cube, if **eg**=**gf**=**fe**.†

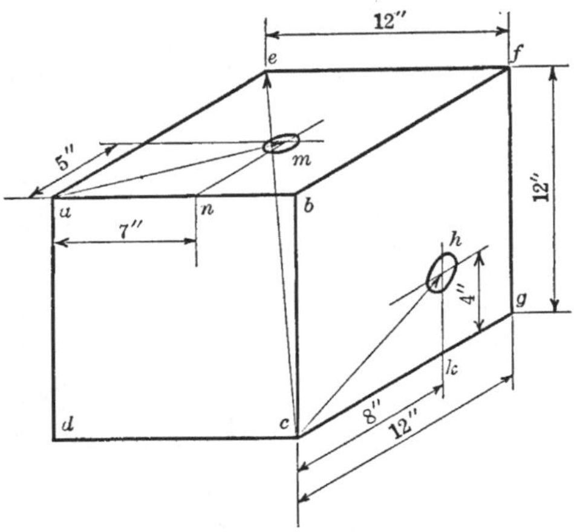

FIG. 8.

* This method is of importance in that branch of mathematics known as Vector Analysis. Vectors are best drawn in space by means of oblique projection.

† If two given lines are parallel in space, their oblique projections are parallel under any conditions. The projecting lines from the extremities of

A word may be said in reference to round holes appearing in the oblique faces of a cube. As has been shown, circles are here represented as ellipses (206), but if it were desired to cut an elliptical hole at either **h** or **m**, then their projections would **not** give a clear idea of the fact. Such cases, when they occur, must be covered by a note to that effect; an arrow from the note pointing to the hole would then indicate, unmistakably, that the hole is to be drilled (for a round hole), otherwise its shape should be called for in any way that is definite. It seems, therefore, that oblique projection cannot fulfill the needs of commercial drawing in every respect; and, indeed, this is true. Other methods also have certain advantages and will be treated subsequently.‡

**208. Representation of visible and invisible lines.** While viewing an object, the observer finds that some lines on the object are visible. These lines are drawn in full on the projection. There are, however, other lines, invisible from the point of view chosen and these, when added, are shown **dotted.** Fig. 9 shows all the visible and invisible lines on a hollow circular cylinder. Dimensions are appended and the cylinder shaded so that no question should arise as to its identity. It can be observed that the drawing is clear in so far as it shows that the hole goes entirely through the cylinder. Were the dotted lines omitted, one could not tell whether the hole went entirely through, or only part way through. Hence, dotted lines may add to the clearness of a drawing; in such cases they should be added. At times, however, their addition may lead to confusion; and, then, only the

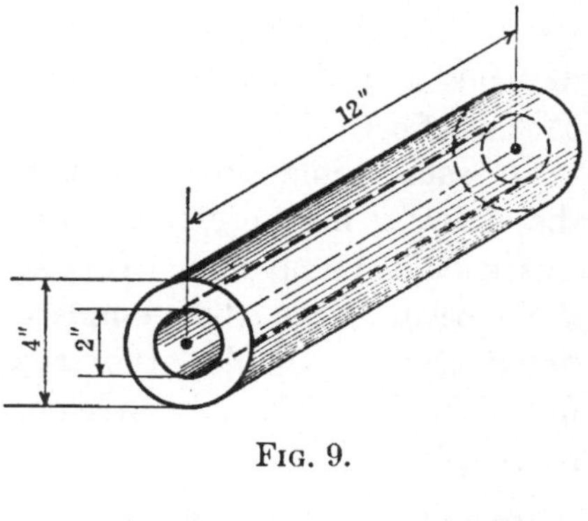


FIG. 9.

the given lines determine planes that cut the plane of projection in lines which are the projections of the given lines. The projecting planes from the given lines are parallel, and, hence, their projections are parallel, since it is the case of two parallel planes cut by a third plane.

‡ The student will obtain many suggestions by copying such simple illustrations as Figs. 1, 2, 7, 8 and 9.

more important dotted lines added, and such others, considered unnecessary, should be omitted. Practice varies in this latter respect and the judgment of the draftsman comes into play at this point; ability to interpret the drawing rapidly and accurately is the point at issue.

**209. Drawings to scale.** Objects of considerable size cannot be conveniently represented in their full size. The shape is maintained, however, by reducing the length of each a definite proportion of its original length, or, in other words, by drawing **to scale.** Thus, if the drawing is one-half the size of the object, the scale is 6″=1 ft. and is so indicated on the drawing by a note to that effect. The scales in common use are 12″=1 ft. or full size; 6″=1 ft. or half-size; 3″=1 ft. or quarter size; $1\frac{1}{2}$″; 1 $\frac{3}{4}$″; $\frac{1}{2}$″; $\frac{3}{8}$″; $\frac{1}{4}$″; $\frac{3}{16}$″; $\frac{1}{8}$″; $\frac{1}{16}$ ; $\frac{1}{32}$″; etc.=1 ft. The smaller sizes are used for very large work and vice versa. In railway work, scales like 100′=1 inch, or 10000′=1 inch are common. In watch mechanism, scales like 48 =1 ft. or "four times actual size" or even larger are used, since, otherwise, the drawings would be too small for the efficient use of the workman. Irrespective of the scale used, the actual dimensions are put on the drawing and the scale is indicated on the drawing by a note to that effect.

If some dimensions are not laid out to the scale adopted, the drawing may create a wrong impression on the reader and this should be avoided if possible. When changes in dimensions occur after the completion of a drawing and it is impracticable to make the change, the dimension may be underlined and marked conveniently near it **N** T **S,** meaning "not to scale."

**210. Examples of oblique projection.** Fig. 10 shows a square block with a hole in its centre. The dimension lines indicate the size and the method of making the drawing when the planes of the circles are chosen parallel to the plane of the paper (plane of projection). The circle in the visible face is drawn with a compass to the desired scale. The circle in the invisible face (invisible from the point of view chosen) is drawn to the same radius, but, its centre is laid off on an inclined line, a distance back of the visible circle, equal to the thickness of the block. The circle in the front face is evidently not in the same plane as that in the distant face. The line joining their centres is thus perpendicular to the plane of projection, and is, hence, laid off as an inclined line.

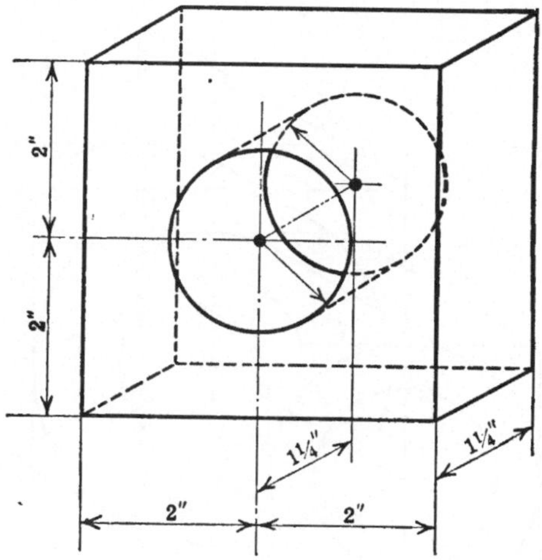


FIG. 10.

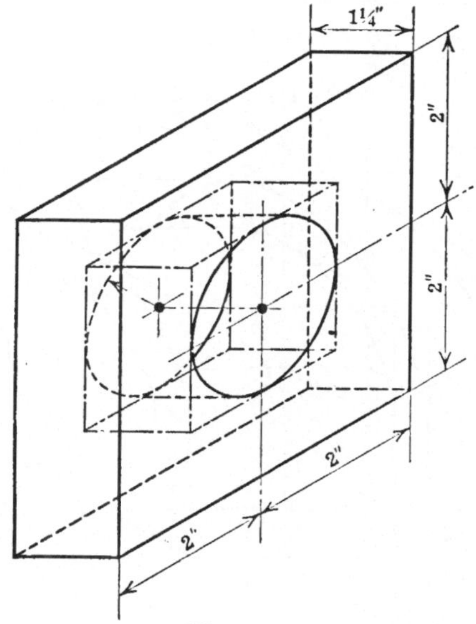


FIG. 11.

When the plane of the circles is made perpendicular to the plane of projection, the circles are projected as ellipses. Fig. 11 shows how the block of Fig. 10 is drawn when such is the case. It is to be observed, that the bounding square is to be drawn first and then the ellipse (projection of the circle) is inscribed. When the circles in both faces are to be shown, the **bounding**

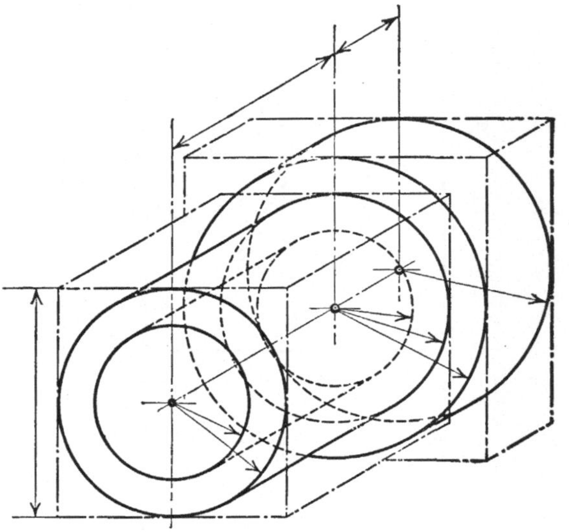

FIG. 12.

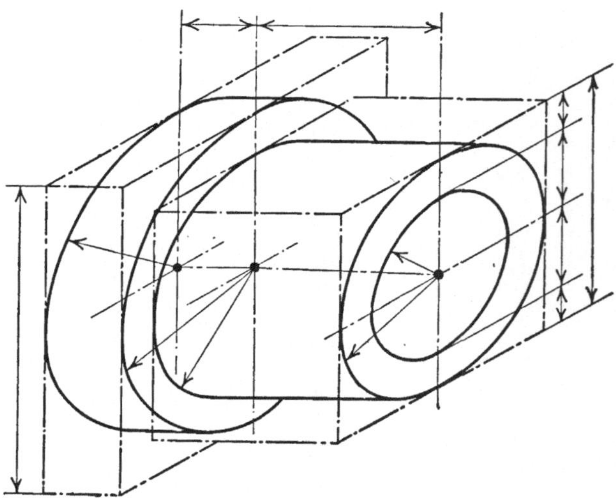

FIG. 13.

square must be replaced by a bounding rectangular prism. This rectangular prism is easily laid out and the ellipses are inserted in the proper faces. The method of using bounding figures of simple shape is of considerable importance when applying the foregoing principles to oblique projection.

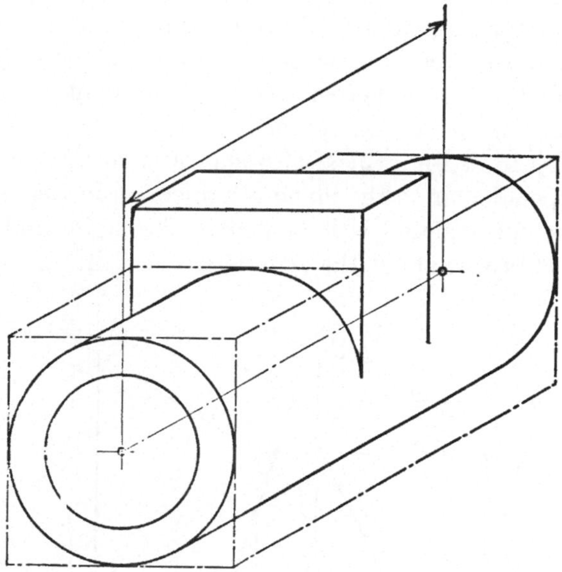

FIG. 14.

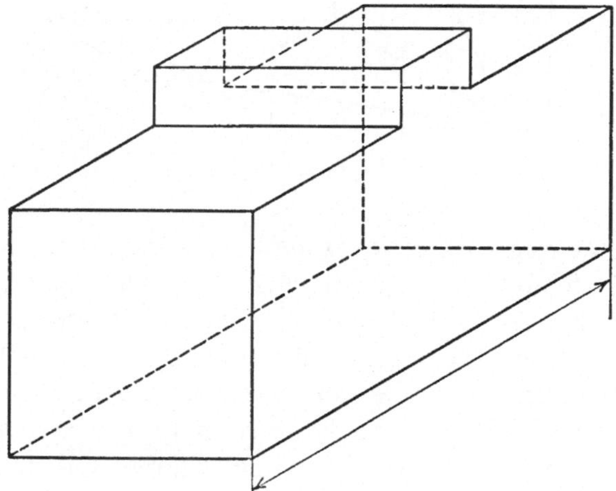

FIG. 15.

Fig. 12 is another illustration of an object, differing from Figs. 10 and 11 in so far as the hole does not go entirely through from face to face. The centres for the different circles are found on the axis. The distances between the centres, measured on the inclined line, is equal to the distances between the planes of the corresponding circles. Since the circles are drawn as such, the planes must, therefore, be parallel to the plane of projection. The axis of the hole is perpendicular to the plane of projection, and, hence, is projected as an inclined line.

The object in Fig. 12 is also shown with the planes of the circles perpendicular to the plane of projection in Fig. 13. Every step of the construction is indicated in the figure and the series of bounding prisms about the cylinders is also shown.

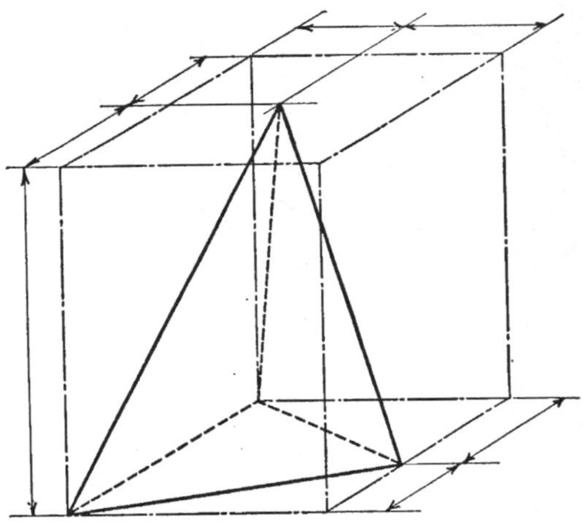

FIG. 16.

A somewhat different example, showing the necessity of bounding figures, is given in Fig. 14. The bounding figure, shown in Fig. 15, is laid out as given and it becomes a simple matter to insert the object subsequently. It should be noted how the rectangular projection becomes tangent to the cylinder and that the only way to be certain of the accuracy of the drawing, is to use these bounding figures and make mental record of the relative location of the lines that make up the drawing.

If objects are to be drawn whose lines are inclined to each other, the principles so far developed offer simple methods for their presentation. Fig. 16 shows a tetrahedron with a bounding rectangular prism. The apex is located on the top face and its position is determined from the geometric principles imposed. Solids, as represented in the text-books on geometry, are drawn in this way. Some confusion may be avoided by observing that angles are only preserved in their true relation in the planes parallel to the plane of projection (207).

The concluding example of this series is given in Fig. 17. It is known as a bell-crank and has circles shown in two planes at right angles to each other. The example furnishes the clue

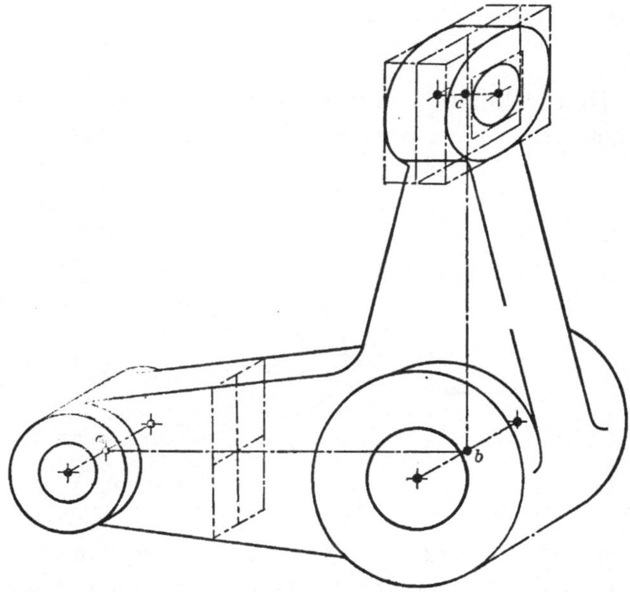


FIG. 17.

to constructing any object, however complicated it may be. Base lines **ab** and **bc** are first laid out to the required dimensions and to the desired scale. In this example, the base lines are chosen parallel to the plane of projection, and hence are projected as a right angle, true to dimensions. The thickness of the two lower cylinders is laid off as an inclined line from each side of the base line and the circles are then drawn. The upper circles (shown as ellipses) may need some mention. A bounding rectangular prism is first drawn, half of which is laid off on each side of the base line (true in this case but it may vary in others).

The circles and inclined lines are filled in after the guiding details are correctly located. This drawing may present some difficulty at first, but a trial at its reproduction will reveal no new principles, only an extreme application.

On completion of the drawing, the bounding figure may be removed if its usefulness is at an end. When inclined lines appear frequently on the drawing, the bounding figures can be made to serve as dimension lines, and so help in the interpretation. The draftsman must determine what is best in each case, remembering, always, that the drawing must be clear not only to himself, but to others who may have occasion to read it.

**211. Distortion of oblique projection.** A view of a completed machine suffers considerable distortion when drawn in

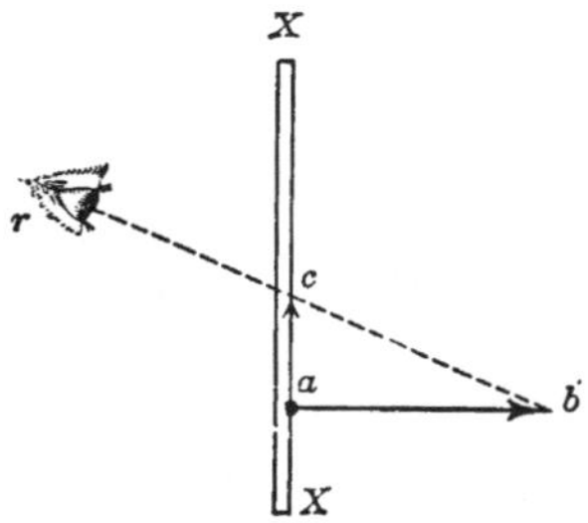


FIG. 18.

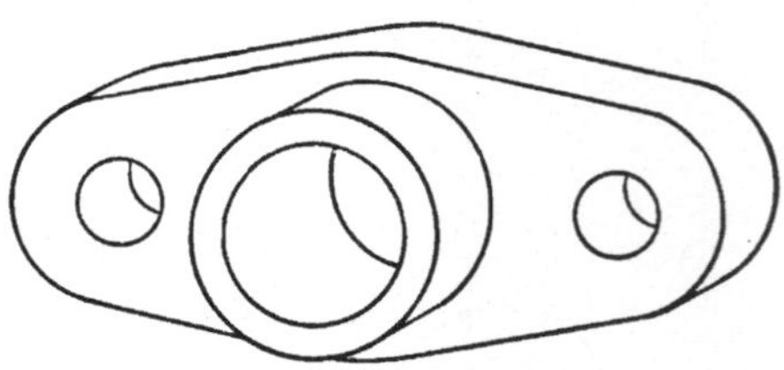

FIG. 19.

oblique projection because the eye cannot be placed in any one position, whereby it can view the drawing in the manner the projection was made.* To overcome this difficulty to some extent and to avoid bringing the distortion forcibly to the attention of the observer, the projecting lines can be so chosen that the perpendicular to the plane of projection is projected as a shorter line than the perpendicular itself. Fig. 18 shows this in construction. **XX** is a vertical transparent plate, similar to that shown in Fig. 4. The ray **rb** makes an angle with **XX** greater than 45°, and, by inspection, it is seen that the projection of ab on **XX** is ac, which is shorter than ab, the perpendicular.

The application of the foregoing reduces simply to this: All lines and curves parallel to the plane of projection are shown

* This condition is satisfied in Perspective Projections.

exactly the same as in oblique projection with 45° ray inclination. The lines that are perpendicular to the plane of projection are reduced to $\frac{1}{2}$, $\frac{1}{4}$, $\frac{1}{8}$, etc. of their original length and reduced or increased to the scale adopted in making the drawing. This mode of representation* is suitable for making catalogue cuts and the like. It gives a sense of depth without very noticeable distortion, due to two causes: the impossible location of the eye while viewing the drawing, and, the knowledge of the apparent decrease in size of objects as they recede from the eye. A single illustration is shown in Fig. 19.

**212. Commercial application of oblique projection.** Oblique projection is useful in so far as it presents the three dimensions in a single view. When curves are a part of the outline of the object, it is desirable to make the plane of the curve parallel to the plane of projection, thereby making the projection equal to the actual curve and also economizing time in making the drawing. Sometimes it is not possible to carry this out completely. Fig. 17, already quoted, shows an example of this kind. It is quite natural to make the drawing as shown, because the planes of most of the circles are parallel to the plane of projection, leaving, thereby, only one end of the bell-crank to be projected with ellipses.

Oblique projections, in general, are perhaps the simplest types of drawings that can be made, if the objects are of comparatively simple shape. They carry with them the further advantage that even the uninitiated are able to read them, when the objects are not unusually intricate. The making of oblique projections is simple, but, at the same time, they call on the imagination to some extent for their interpretation. This is largely due to the fact that the eye changes its position for each point projected, and that no one position of the eye will properly place the observer with respect to the object.

The application of oblique projection to the making of drawings for solid geometry is already known to the student and the resulting clarity has been noticed. Other types of projections have certain advantages which will be considered in due order.

* This type of projection has been called Pseudo Perspective by Dr. MacCord in his Descriptive Geometry.

The convenience of oblique projection to the laying out of piping diagrams is worthy of mention. Steam and water pipes, plumbing, etc., when laid out this way, result in an exceedingly readable drawing.

## QUESTIONS ON CHAPTER II

1. What is an oblique projection?
2. What is a plane of projection?
3. What is a projecting line?
4. Prove that when a rectangle is parallel to the plane of projection the projection of the rectangle is equal to the rectangle itself.
5. Does the distance of the object from the plane have any influence on the size of the projection? Why?
6. Prove that any line, whether straight or curved, is projected in its true form when it is parallel to the plane of projection.
7. Show under what conditions a projection may be considered as a shadow.
8. Prove that when a line is perpendicular to the plane of projection, it is projected as a line of equal length, when the projecting rays make an angle of 45° with the plane of projection. Use a diagram.
9. Prove that any limited portion of a line is projected as a line of equal length, when the line is perpendicular to the plane of projection and the projecting lines make an angle of 45° with the plane of projection.
10. Show how a perpendicular may be projected as a longer or a shorter line, if the angle of the projecting lines differs from 45°.
11. Why can not the projecting lines be selected parallel to the plane of projection?
12. Show that when a line is parallel to the plane of projection, it is projected as a line of equal length, irrespective of the angle of the projecting lines, provided the projecting lines are inclined to the plane of projection.
13. Why may the slope of the projection of a line perpendicular to the plane of projection be drawn at any angle?
14. Prove that when two lines are parallel to each other and also to the plane of projection, their projections are parallel.
15. Prove that when two lines are perpendicular to the plane of projection, their projections are parallel to each other.
16. Draw two rectangular planes at right angles to each other so that the edges of the planes are parallel or perpendicular to the plane of the paper (or projection).
17. Draw a cube in oblique projection and show which lines are assumed parallel to the plane of projection and which lines are perpendicular to the plane of projection.
18. Draw a cube in oblique projection and show how the circles are inserted in each of the visible faces.

19. Show how angles are laid off on the face of a cube in oblique projection.
20. Under what conditions is the angular relation between lines preserved?
21. Draw a line that is neither parallel nor perpendicular to the plane of projection. (Use the cube, in projection, as a bounding figure.)
22. Prove that any two lines in space are projected as parallels when they themselves are parallel.
23. Under what conditions will the oblique projection of a line be a point?
24. How are visible and invisible lines represented on a drawing?
25. What is meant by drawing to scale?
26. Why is it desirable to have all parts of the same object drawn to true scale?

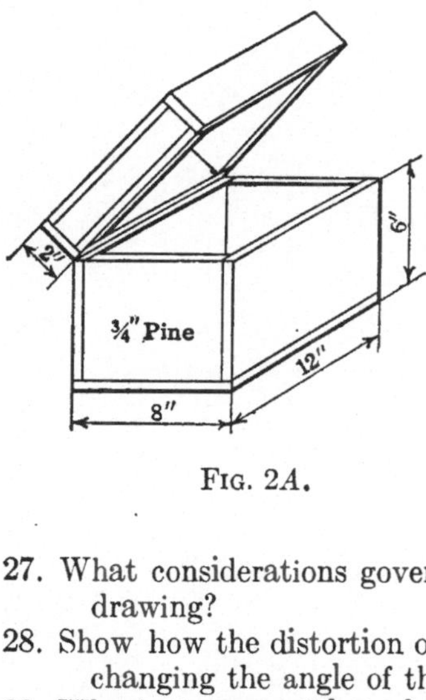


FIG. 2A.

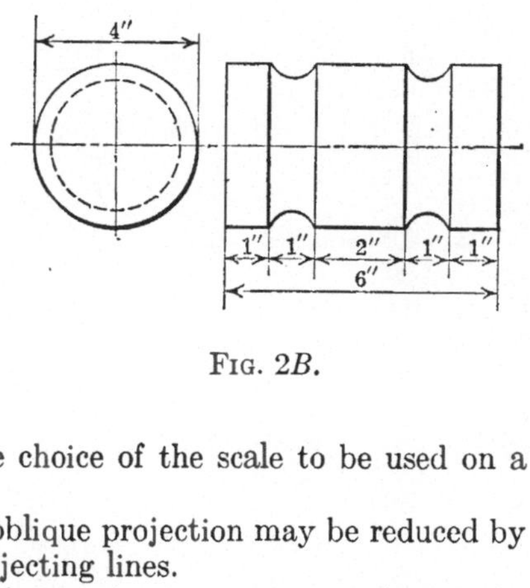


FIG. 2B.

27. What considerations govern the choice of the scale to be used on a drawing?
28. Show how the distortion of an oblique projection may be reduced by changing the angle of the projecting lines.
29. Why is it impossible to locate the eye in one position and view the projection in the manner in which it was made?
30. Draw a rectangular box with a hinged cover, in oblique projection, and show the cover partly raised.
31. Draw a lever, having a round hole on one end so as to fit over a shaft. Have the plane of the circles parallel to the plane of projection.
32. Draw an oblong block, 2″×3″×6″ long, in oblique projection, having a 1″ hole in its centre, 4″ deep.
33. Draw a cylindrical shaft, 6″ in diameter and 18″ long, in oblique projection, having a rectangular hole, 2″×3″×5″ deep, from each end. Lay out to a scale of 3″=1 ft. and affix all dimensions.

34. Draw a triangular prism, in oblique projection, showing how the bounding figure is used.
35. Draw a hexagonal prism, in oblique projection, and show all the invisible (dotted) lines on it.
36. Draw a hexagonal pyramid in oblique projection.
37. Make a material list for the box shown in Fig. 2*A*.
38. Draw the circular cylinder, 4″ diameter and 6″ long, shown in Fig. 2*B*. On the surface of this cylinder, two semi-circular grooves are cut, as shown by the dimensions. Make two drawings in oblique projection, one showing the plane of the circles parallel to the plane of projection and the other, with the plane of the circles perpendicular to the plane of projection.

NOTE.—For additional drawing exercises see examples in Chapters III and IV.

# CHAPTER III

## ORTHOGRAPHIC PROJECTION

**301. Nature of orthographic projection.** Take, for example, a box 6″×12″×4″ high, made of wood, ½″ thick. This box is shown orthographically in Fig. 20, and requires two distinct views to illustrate it properly. The upper view, or **elevation,** shows the side of the box whose outside dimensions are 4″×12″, while the thickness of the wood is indicated by the

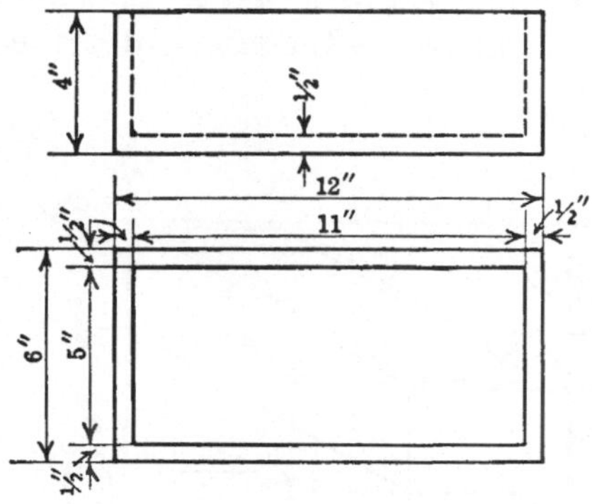


FIG. 20.

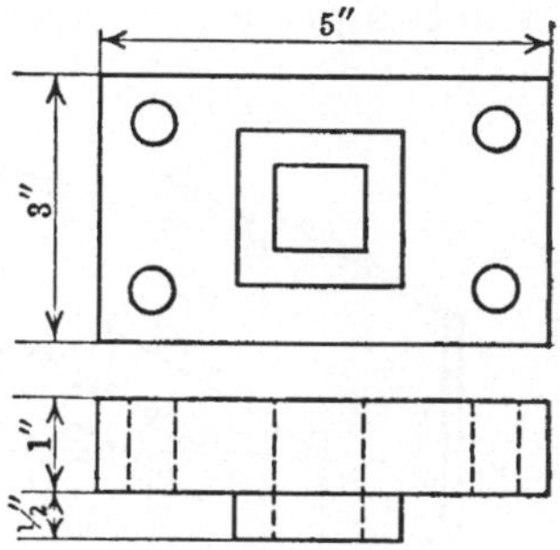


FIG. 21.

dotted lines. The lower view is called the **plan,** and is obtained by looking down into the inside of the box. It is thus to be remembered that the **two views** are due to **two** distinct **directions of vision** on the part of the observer.

As another example of this mode of representation, consider the object shown in Fig. 21. It is here a rectangular plate, 5″×3″ and 1″ thick, with a square hole in its centre. The metal around the square hole projects ½″ above the surface of the plate. In addition, there are four bolt holes which enable the part to be secured to a machine with bolts. As before, two views are shown with the necessary dimensions for construction.

**302. Theory of orthographic projection.** Let Fig. 22 represent an oblique projection of two plane surfaces **HH** and **VV**, at right angles to each other. For mechanical operations to be performed later, it is assumed that they are hinged at their intersection so that both planes may be made to lie as one flat surface, instead of two separate surfaces at right angles to each other. The plane **HH**, shown horizontally, is the **horizontal plane of projection**; that shown vertically, is the **vertical plane of projection**; their intersection is called the **ground line.** The two planes, taken together, are known as the **principal planes**

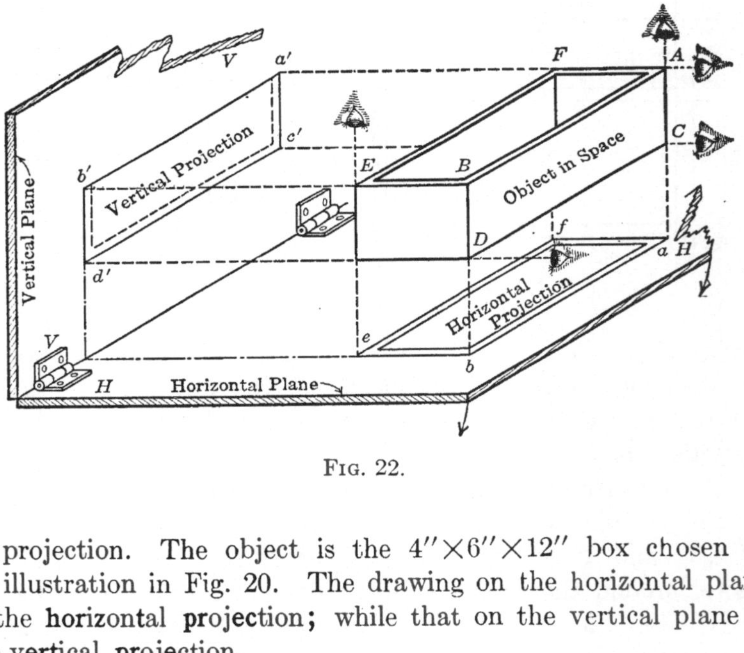


Fig. 22.

of projection. The object is the 4″×6″×12″ box chosen as an illustration in Fig. 20. The drawing on the horizontal plane is the **horizontal projection**; while that on the vertical plane is the **vertical projection.**

The method of constructing the projection consists of dropping perpendiculars from the object upon the planes of projection. Thus, in other words, the **projecting lines** are **perpendicular** to the plane of projection. To illustrate: The box is so located in space that the bcttom of it is parallel to the horizontal plane (Fig. 22) and the 4″×12″ side is parallel to the vertical plane. From the points **A, B, C,** and **D**, perpendiculars are drawn to the vertical plane and the points, where these perpendiculars **pierce** or **impinge** on the plane, are marked **a′, b′, c′,** and **d′**, to correspond with the similarly lettered points on the object. By joining these points with straight lines, to correspond with the lines on the object, the vertical projection is completed, when the dotted lines showing the inside of the box are added.

Turning to the projection on the horizontal plane, it is seen that **A**, **B**, **E**, and F are the corners of the box in space, and that perpendiculars from these points to the horizontal plane determine **a**, b, **e**, and **f** as the horizontal projection. It is assumed that the observer is looking down on the horizontal plane and therefore sees the inside of the box; these lines are hence shown in full, although the projecting perpendiculars are omitted so as to avoid too many lines in the construction.

**303. Revolution of the horizontal plane.** It is manifestly impracticable to carry two planes at right angles to each other, each containing one projection of an object. A more convenient way is to represent both projections on a single plane surface, so that such drawings can be represented on a flat sheet of paper. The evident expedient, in this case, is to **revolve** the horizontal plane about the ground line as an axis, until it coincides with the plane of the vertical plane. The conventional direction of rotation is shown by the arrow in Fig. 22, and to accomplish this coincidence, a 90° revolution is required. In passing, it may be well to note that it makes no difference whether the horizontal plane is revolved as suggested, or whether the vertical plane is revolved in the opposite direction into coincidence with the horizontal plane. **Both** accomplish the same purpose, and hence either method will answer the requirements.

**304. Position of the eye.** The perpendicular projecting lines drawn to the planes of projection correspond with a line of sight that coincides with these perpendiculars. Each point found on the projection, corresponds to a new position of the eye. All projecting lines to one plane are then evidently parallel because they are all perpendicular to the same plane. As two projections are required, two general directions of vision are necessary. That for the horizontal projection requires the eye above that plane, continually directed perpendicularly against it; thus the eye is continually shifting in position, although the direction of vision is fixed. Also, the vertical projection requires that the eye be directed perpendicularly against it, but in this case, the line of sight is perpendicular to that required for the horizontal projection.

**305. Relation of size of object to size of projection.** The object is projected on the planes by lines perpendicular to it. If the plane of the object is parallel to the plane of projection, then the projection is equal to the object in magnitude. This is true because the projecting lines form a right prism and

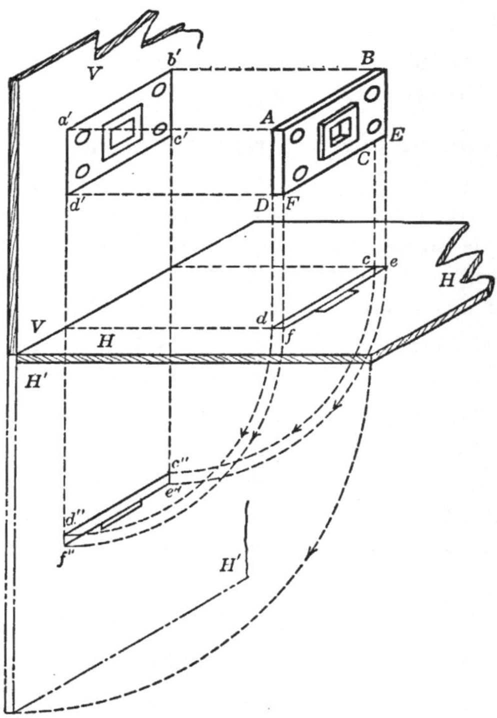


FIG. 23.

all the parallel plane sections are the same (compare with 202). Fig. 23 gives the construction of the projection in Fig. 21. **ABCDa′b′c′d′** is such a right prism because the plane of the object is parallel to the plane of projection and the projecting lines are perpendicular to the plane of projection.

**306. Location of object with respect to the planes of projection.** For purposes of drawing, the location of the object to the planes of projection is absolutely immaterial. In fact, the draftsman intuitively makes the projections and puts corresponding projections as close as is necessary to economize room on the sheet.

**307. Location of projections with respect to each other.** In Figs. 20 and 21, the vertical projection is placed directly above the horizontal projection. Reference to Fig. 23 will show why such is the case. When the horizontal plane is revolved into coincidence with the vertical plane, the point **d** will describe the arc of a circle **dd″** * which is a quadrant; **d″** is the ultimate position of the point **d** after revolution, and must be on a line **d′d″** which is perpendicular to the original position of the horizontal plane. So, too, every point of the horizontal projection is located directly under the corresponding point in the vertical projection, and the scheme for finding its position is identical to that for finding **d** at **d″**.

**308. Dimensions on a projection.** When the principal planes of the object are turned so that they are parallel to the planes of projection, then the edges will, in the main, be perpendicular to the planes of projection. In Fig. 23, **DF** is one edge of the object and it is perpendicular to the vertical plane of projection **VV**. The projection of this line is **d′**, because the projecting perpendicular from any point on **DF** will coincide with **DF** itself. The result of this is that the thickness of the object is not shown when the length and breadth are shown, or, in other words, only two of the three principal dimensions are shown in a single view. Thus, another view is required to show the thickness. If **DC** be considered a length, and **DF** a thickness, the horizontal projection shows both as dc and **df**. The vertical projection does not show the thickness **DF** as it is perpendicular to the vertical plane of projection. Hence, in reading orthographic projections, both views must be **interpreted simultaneously**, as each shows but **two** of the **three principal dimensions** and only one of the three is common to both projections.

**309. Comparison between oblique and orthographic projections.** It is of interest here to show wherein the orthographic projection differs from the oblique. When the plane

* d′ is read d prime; d″ is read d second; d‴ is read d third; and so on.

of the object is parallel to the plane of projection, the projection on that plane is equal to the object, whether it is projected orthographically or obliquely. When a line is perpendicular to the plane of projection its extremities have **two** distinct **projections** in **oblique** projection, but only **one** in **orthographic** projection. This latter statement means simply that if the projecting lines instead of being oblique to the plane of projection, gradually assume the perpendicular position, the two projections of the extremities of any line approach each other until they coincide when the projecting lines are perpendicular. Therefore, in orthographic projection, the third dimension vanishes and a new view must be made in addition to the other, in order to represent a solid.

**310. Orthographic projection considered a shadow.** The horizontal and the vertical projections may be considered as shadows on their respective planes. The source of light must be such that the rays emanate in parallel lines, and are directed perpendicularly to the planes of projection. Evidently, the two views are due to two distinct positions of the source of light, one whose rays are perpendicular to the horizontal plane while casting the horizontal shadow, and the other, whose rays are perpendicular to the vertical plane while casting the vertical shadow.

**311. Profile plane.** Let **A**, in Fig. 24, be the horizontal projection and **B**, the vertical projection of an object. The two views are identical, and to one unfamiliar with the object, they are indefinite, as it is impossible to tell whether they are projections of a cylinder or of a prism. By the addition of either view **C** or **D**, it is at once apparent that the object in question is a circular cylinder, a hole running part way through it and with one end square.

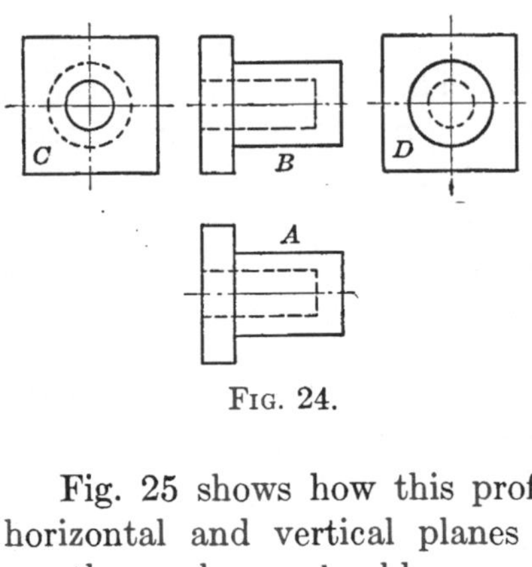

FIG. 24.

Fig. 25 shows how this profile is made. As customary, the horizontal and vertical planes are present and the projection on these planes should now require no further mention. A

**profile plane** (or end plane as it may be called) is shown on the far side of the object and is a plane that is perpendicular to **both** the horizontal and vertical planes (like the two adjacent

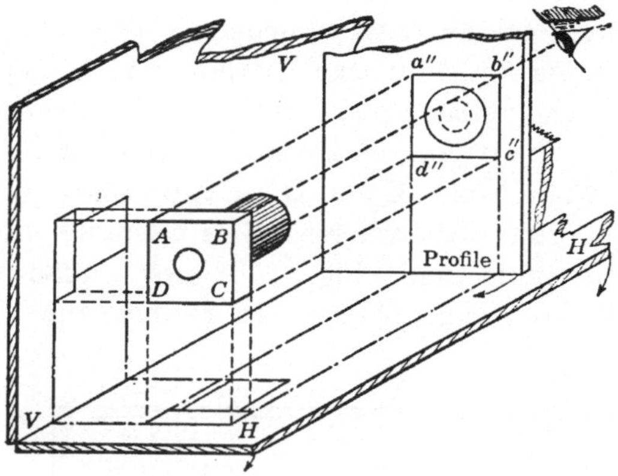


FIG. 25.

walls and the floor of a room meeting in one corner). A series of perpendiculars is dropped from the object upon this profile

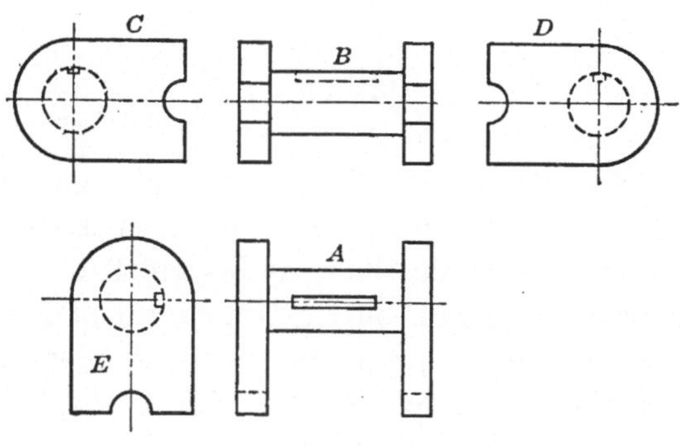


FIG. 26.

plane, as shown by the dotted lines, and thus the side view is determined.

**312. Location of profiles.** If the profile view is to show the object as seen from the left side, it is put on the left side of the drawing, and vice versa. Fig. 24 shows two profile views located in accordance with this direction. Either views **B** and **C**

or **B** and **D** completely represent the object. In this case, although this is not always so, the horizontal projection is not essential.

Fig. 26 gives still another illustration of an object that is not as symmetrical as that immediately preceding. The illustration is chosen to show exactly how the profile planes are revolved into the vertical plane, if the vertical plane be assumed as the plane of the paper. **A** is the horizontal and **B** the vertical projection of the object. **C** and **D** are two profiles, drawn against the vertical projection, whereas **E** is a profile drawn against the horizontal projection. Fig. 27 shows a plan view of the vertical and two profile planes. In reading this drawing, the

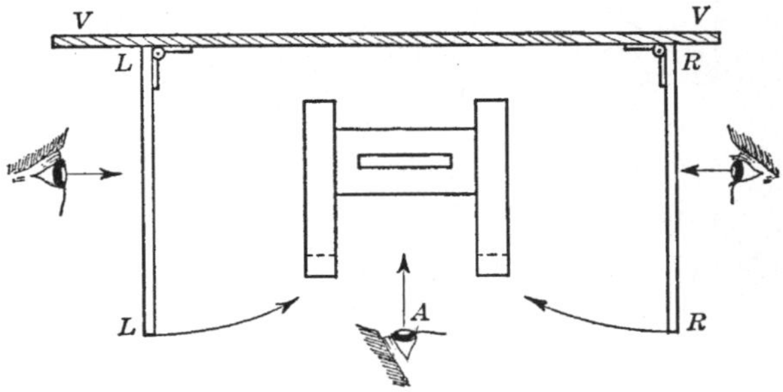


FIG. 27.

horizontal plane is the plane of the paper, while the vertical plane is seen on edge and is shown as **VV**, as are also the left and right profile planes indicated respectively as **LL** and **RR**.

In making the projection on the horizontal plane, the object is above the plane and the projecting perpendiculars are dropped from points on the object to the horizontal plane, which in this case is the plane of the paper. The construction of the vertical projection (that on **VV**) is indicated by the arrow **A**. The arrangement here shown corresponds to the views **A** and **B** in Fig. 26.

When making the profile projections, the planes are assumed as transparent, and are located between the object and the observer. As the observer traces the outline on these profile planes, point by point, each ray being perpendicular to the plane, the resultant picture so drawn becomes the required projection. If, then, the planes **LL** and **RR** be revolved in the direction of the arrows until they coincide with the vertical plane, and then the vertical plane be further revolved into the plane of the paper, the final result will be that of Fig. 26 with view **E** omitted.

View **E** is a profile drawn against the horizontal projection and is shown on the left because it is the projection on the profile plane **LL**. It has been revolved into the horizontal plane, by revolving the profile plane so that the upper part of the plane moves toward the object into coincidence with the horizontal plane.

Fig. 26 has more views than are necessary to illustrate the object completely. In practice, all would not be drawn, their presence here is necessary only to show the method.

**313. Section plane.** The addition of dotted lines to the drawing of complicated objects is unsatisfactory at times on account of the resultant confusion of lines. This difficulty can be overcome by cutting the object by planes, known as **section planes.** The solid material when so exposed is **sectioned** or cross-**hatched** by drawing a series of equidistant lines over the exposed area. A convenient mnemonic in this connection is to assume that the cut is made by a saw and that the resultant tooth marks represent the section lines. Fig. 28 shows what is known as a stuffing box on a steam engine. This is a special case where but one projection is shown in **section** and one profile. The left-hand view might have been shown as an outside view, but the interior lines would then have been shown dotted. As it is, the object is cut by the plane ab and this half portion is shown to the left, sectioned of course, because the cut is not actual.

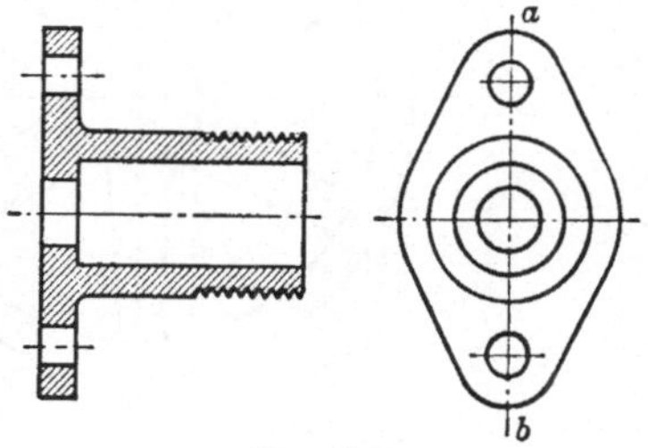

FIG. 28.

Another example is seen in Fig. 29, where a fly-wheel is represented in much the same way as in the illustration in Fig. 28. It differs somewhat from that immediately preceding in so far as the two views do not have the theoretical relation. Were the wheel actually cut by the plane **ab** then the arms (spokes) shown in the profile would have to be sectioned. As shown, however, the arms appear in full as though the section plane passed through the wheel a short distance ahead of the spokes. The convention is introduced for a double purpose: In the first place it avoids peculiar projections as that for the plane **cd** for instance, where the spokes would be foreshortened because they incline to the plane of projection. In the second place, the sectioning of the spokes is the conventional method of showing a band wheel,* that is, a wheel with a solid web, or, in other words, without spokes. Hence, it appears that although it may not seem like a rational method of drawing, still the attending advantages are such as make it a general custom. The mechanics who use the drawings understand this, and therefore it becomes common practice.

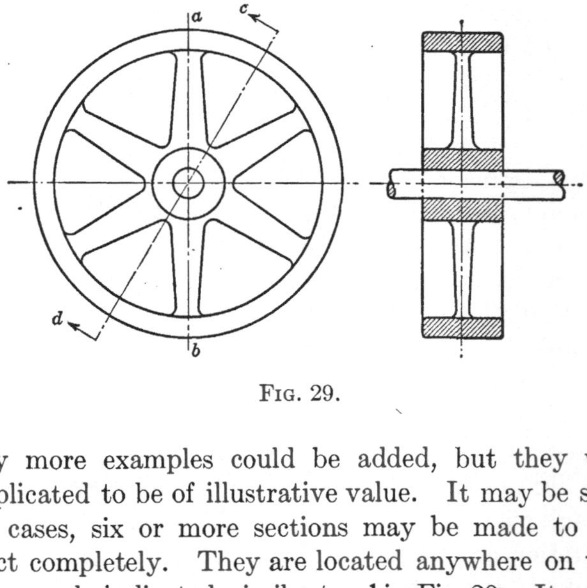


FIG. 29.

Many more examples could be added, but they would be too complicated to be of illustrative value. It may be said, that, in some cases, six or more sections may be made to illustrate the object completely. They are located anywhere on the drawing and properly indicated, similar to **cd** in Fig. 29. It may also be mentioned, that in cases like that of the fly-wheel, the shaft is not cut by the section plane but is shown in full as it appears in Fig. 29.

**314. Supplementary plane.** Fig. 30 shows a **Y** fitting used in pipe work for conveying steam, water, etc., and consists of a hollow cylindrical shell terminating in two flanges, one at

* Fig. 43 is an example of a band wheel.

each end. From this shell there emerges another shell (in this case, smaller in diameter), also terminating in a flange. **A** is the **Y** fitting proper; **B** is the end view of one flange, showing the bolt holes for fastening to a mating flange on the next piece of pipe, not shown. The view **B** shows only the one flange that is represented by a circle, because the profile plane is chosen so as to be parallel to that flange. If the flange at **C** be projected on this same profile plane, it would appear as an ellipse, and, as such, could not be drawn with the same facility as a circle. Here, then, is an opportunity to locate another plane,

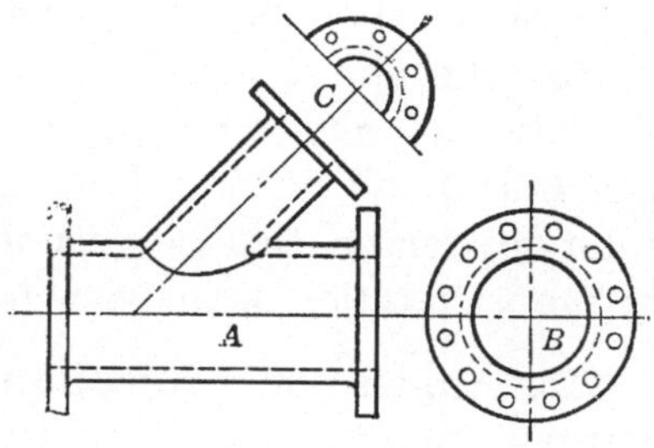


FIG. 30.

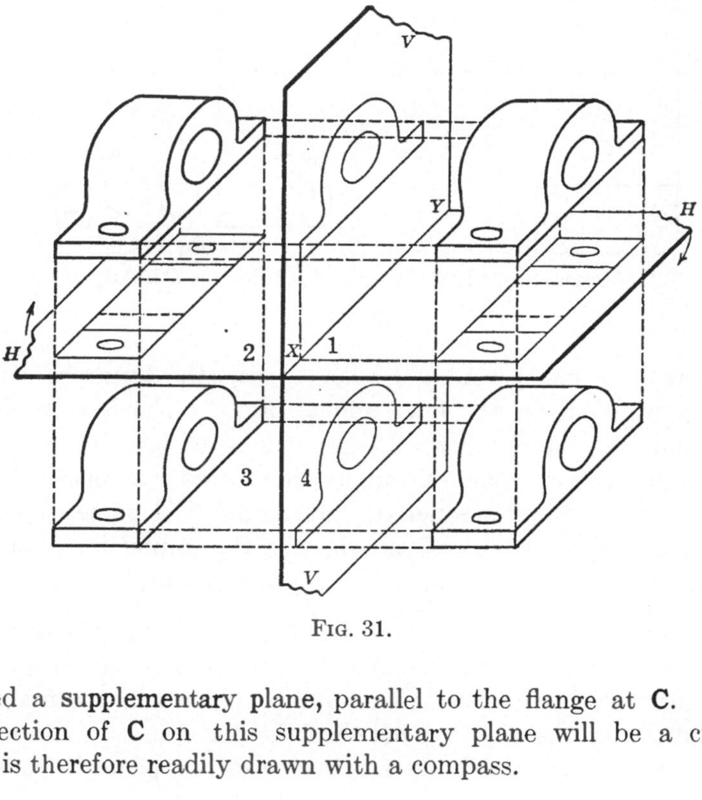


FIG. 31.

called a **supplementary plane,** parallel to the flange at **C**. The projection of **C** on this supplementary plane will be a circle and is therefore readily drawn with a compass.

Only one-half of the actual circle may be shown if desired so as to save time, space, or both time and space. The bolt holes are shown in the supplementary view at **C** just the same as in view **B**. Either plane may be considered supplementary to the other; on neither plane is the entire projection made, because the object is of so simple a character. To avoid the possibility of any error arising, the supplementary projection is, if it is at all possible, located near the part to be illustrated. If, for any reason, this view cannot be so located, a note indicating the proper position of the view is added to the drawing.

**315. Angles of projection.** Up to the present point, no attention has been devoted to the angles in which the pro-

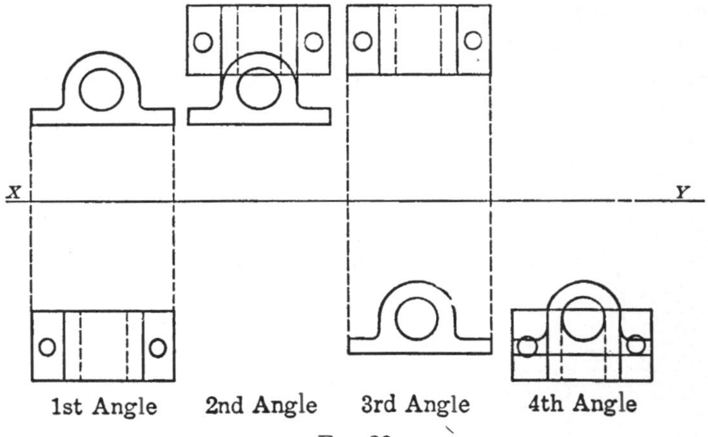


FIG. 32.

jections were made. As will soon appear, the examples so far chosen were all in the first angle. Fig. 31 shows two planes **HH** and **VV**, intersecting at right angles to each other. The planes form four dihedral angles, numbered consecutively in a counter-clockwise manner as indicated. The same object is shown in all four angles, as are also the projections on the planes of projection, thus making four distinct projections.

**316. Location of observer in constructing projections.** The eye is always located above the horizontal plane in making any horizontal projection. That is, for objects in the **first** and **second** angles, the **object** is **between** the **plane** and the **observer;** for objects in the **third** and **fourth** angles the **plane** is between the **object** and the **observer.** While constructing the vertical projections the eye is always located in front of the vertical plane. That is, for objects in the **first** or **fourth** angles, the **object** is **between** the **plane** and the **observer;** but in the **second** and **third** angles, the **plane** is **between** the **object** and the **observer.** This latter means simply that the observer stands to the right of this vertical plane **VV** and views it so that the line of sight is always perpendicular to the plane of projection.

**317. Application of angles of projection to drawing.** If the horizontal plane be revolved about the ground line **XY** as indicated by the arrows, until it coincides with the vertical plane of projection, it will be seen that that portion of the horizontal plane in front of the vertical plane will fall below the ground line, whereas that portion of the horizontal plane behind the vertical plane will rise above the ground line.

Supposing that in each position of the object in all four angles, the projections were made by dropping the customary perpendiculars to the plane of projection, and in addition, that the revolution of the horizontal plane is accomplished, then the resultant state of affairs will be as shown in Fig. 32. For purposes of illustration, the ground line **XY** is drawn although it is never used in the actual drawing of objects.* Also, the object has been purposely so located with respect to the planes that the second and fourth angle projections overlap. Manifestly the second and fourth angles cannot be used in drawing if we wish to be technically correct. It may be possible so to locate the object in the second and fourth angles, by simply changing the distance from one plane or the other, that the two projections do not conflict, but a little study will show that the case falls either under first or third angle projection, depending upon whether the vertical projection is above the horizontal projection, or, below it.

It will be seen that in the first angle of projection, the plan is below and the elevation is above; whereas in the third angle of projection the condition is reversed, that is, the plan is above and the elevation is below. Strictly speaking, the profile, section and supplementary planes, have nothing to do with the angle

* When lines, points, and planes are to be represented orthographically, the ground line becomes a necessary adjunct.

of projection, but it is quite possible to take a single projection with its profile, and locate it so that it corresponds to a third angle projection. Thus, there appears a certain looseness in the application of these principles. In general, **the third angle of projection is used more than any other** * as the larger number

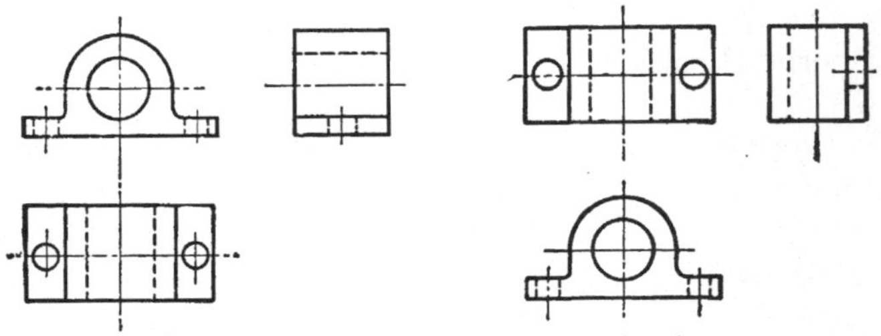

1st Angle 3rd Angle

FIG. 33.

of mechanics are familiar with the reading of drawings in this angle. Fig. 33 shows the same object in the first and third angles of projection. A profile, or end view, is also attached to each, thus making a complete, though simple illustration.

**318. Commercial application of orthographic projection.** Orthographic projection is by far the most important method of making drawings for engineering purposes. Other types of drawing have certain advantages, but, in general, they are limited to showing simple objects, made up principally of straight lines.

Some experience is required in reading orthographic projections because two or more views must be interpreted simultaneously. This experience is readily acquired by practice, both in making drawings and in reading the drawings of others.

To compensate for the more difficult interpretation of this type of drawing, there are inherent advantages, which permit the representation of any object, if it has some well defined shape. By the aid of sections, profiles, and supplementary planes, any side of a regular body can be illustrated at will, and further than this, the curves are shown with such peculiarity as characterizes them. Bodies, such as a lump of coal, or a spade

* The third angle of projection should be used in preference to the first because the profile, section, and supplementary planes conform to third angle projection.

ull of earth, are considered shapeless, and are never used in ngineering construction. Even these can be represented ortho-›raphically, however, although it is quite difficult to draw on he imagination in such cases.

## QUESTIONS ON CHAPTER III

1. What are the principal planes of projection? Name them.
2. What is the ground line?
3. What angles do the orthographic projecting lines make with the plane of projection?

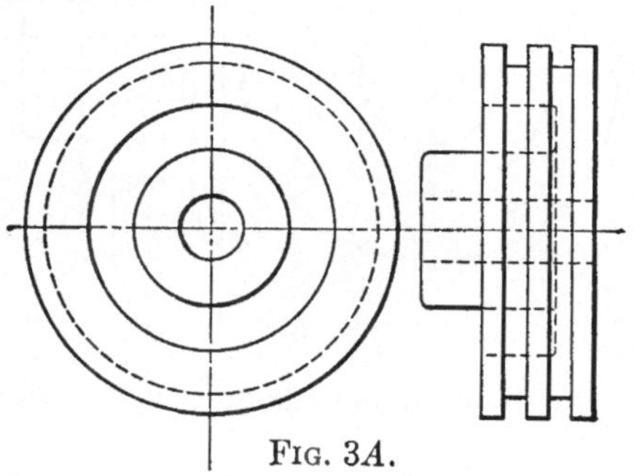

FIG. 3A.

4. What is the horizontal projection?
5. What is the vertical projection?
6. Why is the horizontal plane revolved 90° after making the projections?

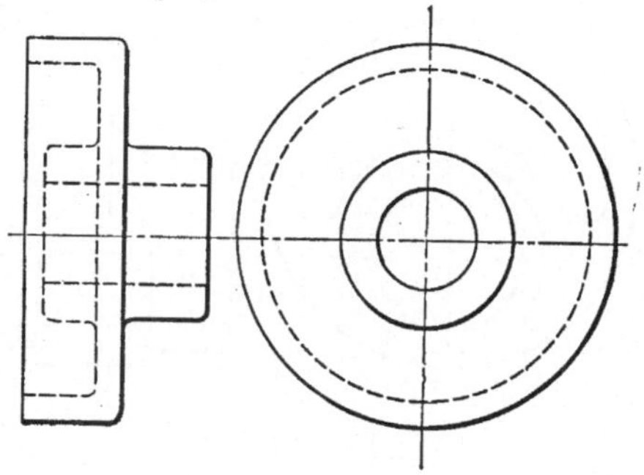

FIG. 3B.

7. Could the vertical plane be revolved instead of the horizontal plane?
8. Make a sketch of the planes of projection and show by arrow how the revolution of the planes is accomplished.
9. How is the eye of the observer directed in making an orthographic projection?

10. What is the general angular relation between the projecting lines to the horizontal plane and the vertical plane of projection?
11. Why is the projection of the same size as the object?
12. Why is the ground line omitted in making orthographic projections?
13. Why are corresponding projections located directly over each other? Show by diagram.
14. Why does an orthographic projection show only two of the three principal dimensions of the object?

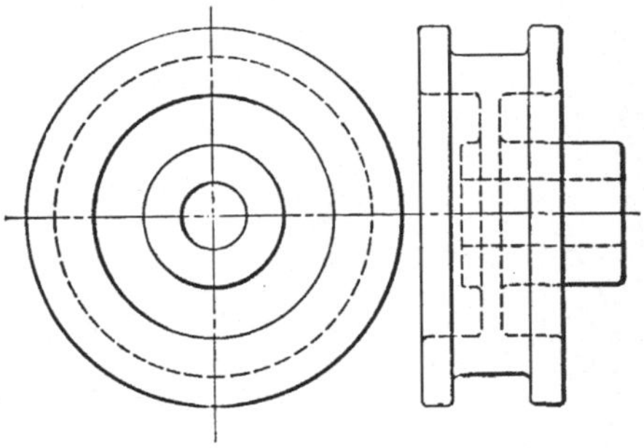

FIG. 3*C*.

15. Why must the two views of an orthographic projection be interpreted simultaneously?
16. Compare the direction of the projecting lines of oblique projection with those of orthographic projection.
17. Show how the source of light must be located in order that the shadow should correspond to a true projection.

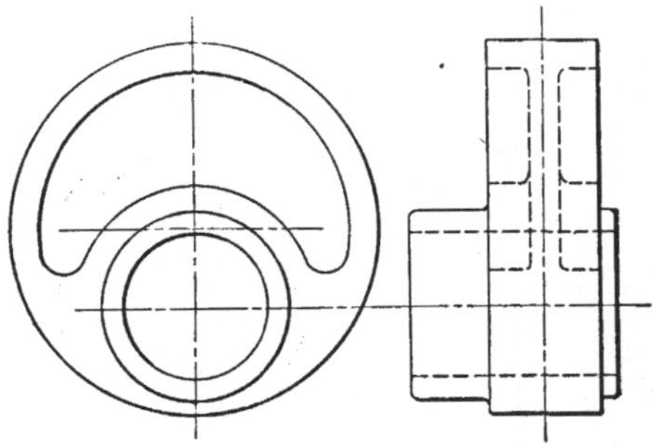

FIG. 3*D*.

18. To cast the horizontal and vertical shadows, is it necessary to have two distinct positions for the source of light?
19. What is a profile plane?
20. How is the profile plane located with respect to the principal planes of projection?
21. How is the profile plane revolved into the plane of the drawing? Show by diagram.

22. How are the profiles located with respect to the main projection? Show by some simple sketch.
23. What is a section plane?.
24. When is a section plane desirable?
25. How is the section constructed?

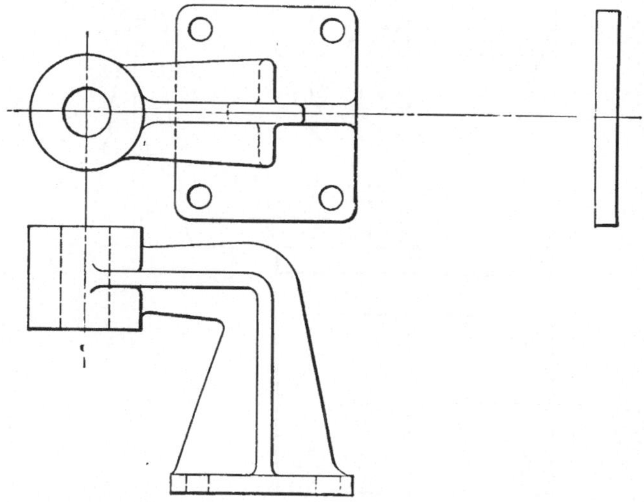

FIG. 3E.

26. How is the section located with respect to the main projection?
27. Show a simple case where only one projection and one section completely determine an object.

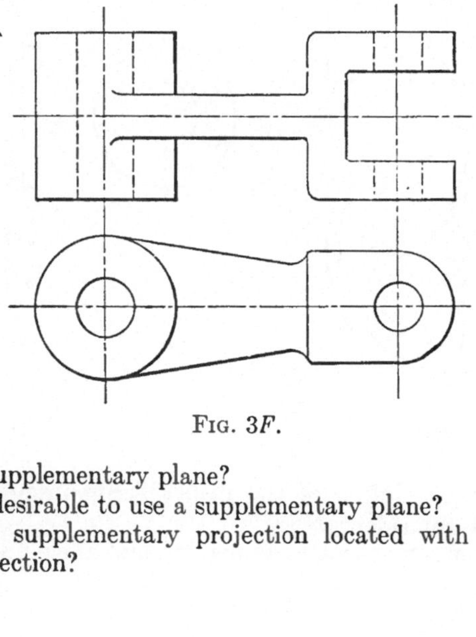

FIG. 3F.

28. What is a supplementary plane?
29. When is it desirable to use a supplementary plane?
30. How is the supplementary projection located with respect to the main projection?

31. Show why the profile plane is a special case of the supplementary plane.
32. Make a diagram showing the four angles of projection and show how they are numbered.

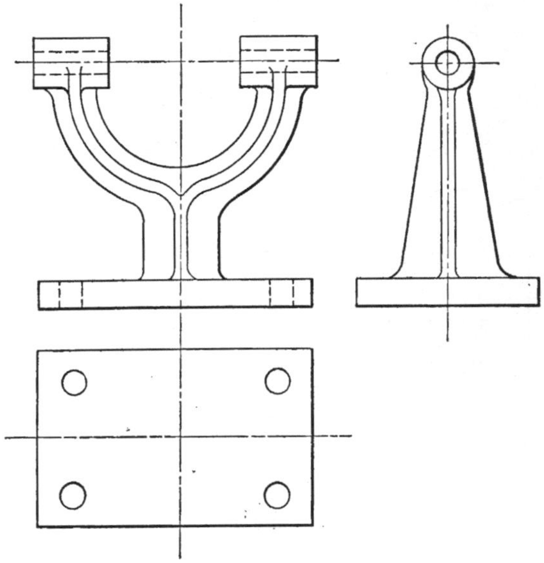

FIG. 3G.

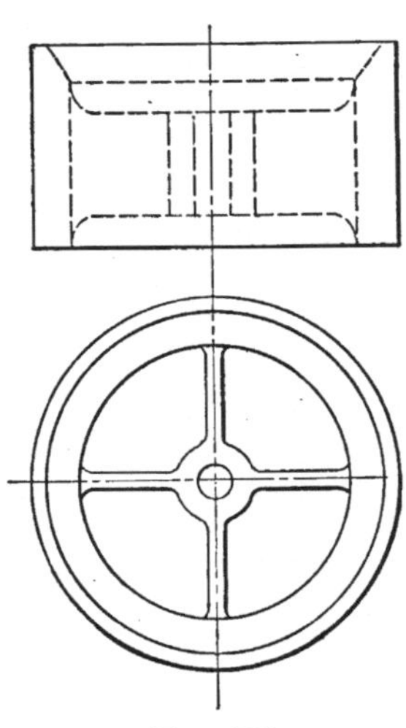

FIG. 3H.

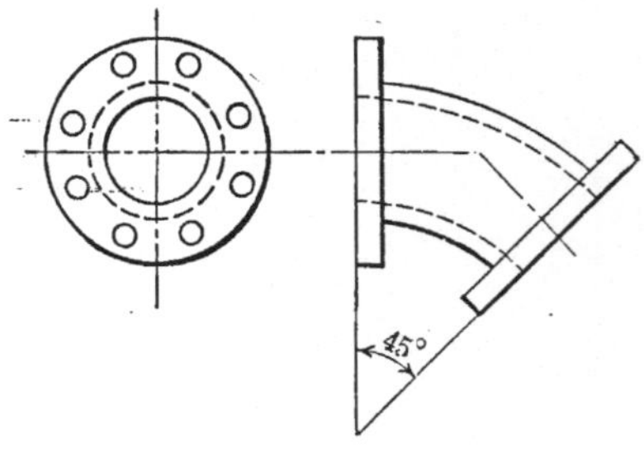


FIG. 3I.

33. How is the revolution of the planes accomplished so as to bring them into coincidence?
34. How is the observer located in making first angle projections?

35. How is the observer located in making second angle projections?
36. How is the observer located in making third angle projections?
37. How is the observer located in making fourth angle projections?
38. Why are only the first and third angles of projection used in drawing?
39. How does the third angle differ from the first angle projection? Show by sketch.
40. Why is the third angle to be preferred?

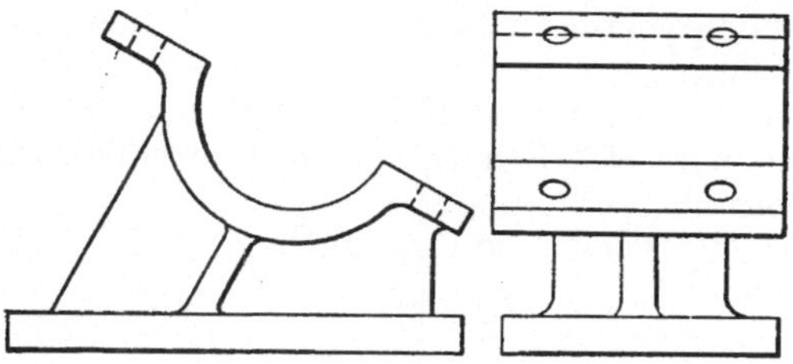

FIG. 3*J*.

41. Why is it more difficult to read orthographic projections than oblique projections?
42. What distinct advantages has orthographic projection over oblique projection?

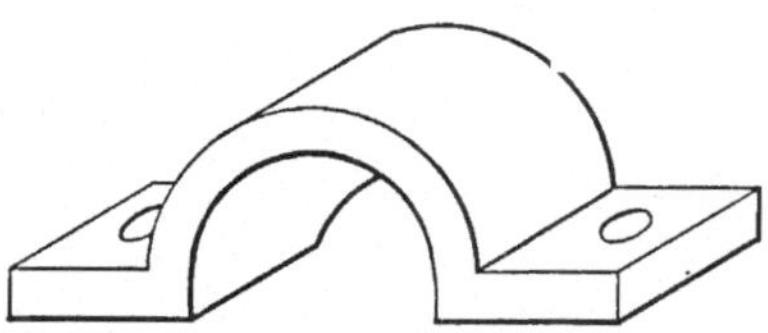

FIG. 3*K*.

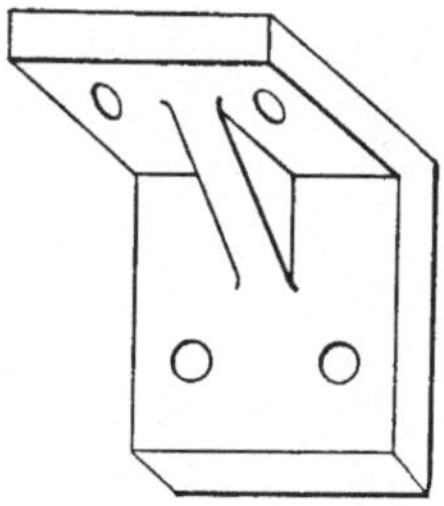

FIG. 3*L*.

43. Make a complete working drawing of 3–A and show one view in section. Assume suitable dimensions.

NOTE: A working drawing is a drawing, completely dimensioned, with all necessary views for construction purposes.

44. Make a complete working drawing of 3–B and show one view in section. Assume suitable dimensions.
45. Make a complete working drawing of 3–C and show one view in section. Assume suitable dimensions.
46. Make a complete working drawing of 3–D and show one view in section. Assume suitable dimensions.

47. Make a complete working drawing of 3–E and show the profile on the left, to the top view. Assume suitable dimensions.
48. Make a complete working drawing of 3–F and show the profile on the left, to the top view. Assume suitable dimensions.
49. Make a complete working drawing of 3–G and show the lower view as a first angle projection. Assume suitable dimensions.
50. Rearrange 3–G and show three views in third angle projection.
51. Make a section of 3–H through the web and observe that the web is not sectioned. Assume suitable dimensions.
52. Make a supplementary view of the 45° ell shown in 3–I. Assume suitable dimensions.
53. Make a supplementary view of 3–J. Assume suitable dimensions.
54. Make three views of 3–K in third angle projection. Assume suitable dimensions.
55. Make three views of 3–L in third angle projection. Assume suitable dimensions.

# CHAPTER IV

## AXONOMETRIC PROJECTION

**401. Nature of isometric projections.** Consider three lines intersecting at a point and make the angles between each pair of lines equal to 120°; the three angles will then total 360° which is the total angle about a point. If on one of these lines, or lines parallel thereto, lengths are laid off, on the other line, or lines parallel thereto, breadths are laid off, and on the remaining line, or lines parallel thereto, thicknesses are laid off, it seems quite reasonable that a method may be devised whereby the three principal dimensions can be plotted so as to represent objects in a single view. This method when carried out to completion results in an **isometric projection.**

Let, in Fig. 34, **OA**, **OB**, and **OC** be the three lines, drawn as directed, so that the angles between them are 120°. Suppose it is desired to draw a box 4″×6″×12″, made of wood ½″ thick. Lay off 12″ on **OB** (to any convenient scale), 6″ on **OA** and 4″ on **OC**. From **A**, draw a line **AD** parallel to **OB** and **AE** parallel to **OC**; also, from **C** draw **CE**, parallel to **OA** and **CF**, parallel to **OB**. The thickness of the wood is to be added and the direction in which this is laid off is indicated by the direction of the corresponding dimension line. In the drawing, the line **OC** was purposely chosen vertical so that **OA** and **OB** may be readily drawn with a 60° triangle. The other lines, added to indicate the construction, are self-explanatory.

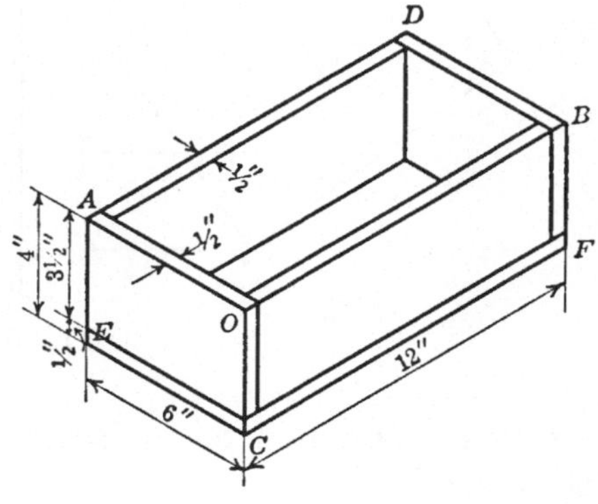


Fig. 34.

This, then, is an isometric projection, and, as may be noted, is a rapid method of representing objects in a single view. Comparison may be made with Figs. 1 and 20, which show the same box in oblique and orthographic projection, respectively.

**402. Theory of isometric projection.** Let Fig. 35, represent a cube shown on the left side of a transparent plane **VV**. If the observer, located on the right, projects this cube orthographically (projecting lines perpendicular to the plane) on the plane **VV**, and at the same time has the cube turned so that each of the three visible faces is projected equally on the plane, the

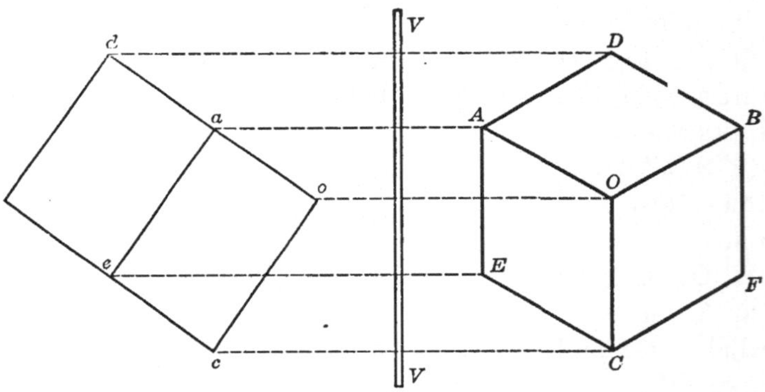


FIG. 35

resultant projection is an **isometric projection** of the cube on the plane **VV**.

The illustration on the right of Fig. 35 shows how this cube appears when orthographically projected. **OA**, **OB**, and **OC** are called the **isometric axes.** As each face of the cube is initially equal to the other faces, and as each edge is also equal, then, with equal inclination of the three faces, their projections are equal. Hence, the three angles are each equal to 120° and the three isometric axes are equal in length. To use these axes for drawing purposes merely requires that all dimensions of one kind (lengths, for instance) be laid off on any one line, or lines parallel thereto, and that this process be observed for the three principal dimensions.

Isometric projection, is, therefore, a special case of orthographic projection; because, in its conception, the principal planes of the object are inclined to the plane of projection. As solids are thereby represented in a single view, only one projection is necessary.

**403. Isometric projection and isometric drawing.** When a line is inclined to the plane of projection, the orthographic projection of the line is shorter than that of the line itself, for, if the degree of inclination continue, the line will eventually become perpendicular to the plane and will then be projected as a point. Thus, in Fig. 35, **OA**, **OB**, and **OC** are drawn shorter than the actual edges of the cube, and the projection on the right is a true isometric projection. In the application of this mode of pro-

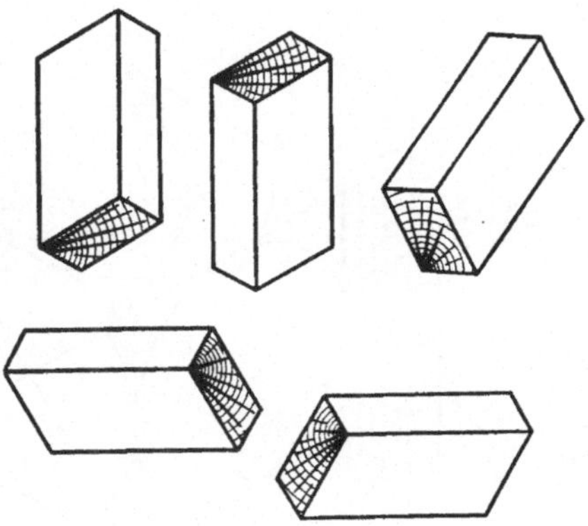

FIG. 36

jection, however, it is easier to lay off the actual distance (or any proportion of it) rather than this foreshortened distance. If commercial scales are used in laying out the drawing instead of the true isometric projections, then it is called an **Isometric Drawing.**

The distinction between the two is a very fine one, since, if the ratio of foreshortening * be used as a scale to which the drawing is made, then it is possible by a simple statement, to change from isometric drawing to isometric projection. The commercial name will be followed and they will be called isometric drawings, always bearing in mind that the distinction means little.

* This ratio of the actual dimension to the true projected dimension is 100 : 83 and may be computed by trigonometry.

**404. Direction of axes.** It is usual to assume one of the axes as either horizontal, or vertical, as under these circumstances, the other two can be drawn with the 60° triangles which are standard appliances in the drawing room. Fig. 36 shows a wood block in several positions, each of which is an isometric drawing; here, the location of the observer with respect to the block is at once apparent.

**405. Isometric projection of circles.** As no line is shown in its true length when it lies in the faces of the cube and is projected isometrically, then, also, no curve that lies in these faces can be shown in its true length and, therefore, in its true shape. This is due to the foreshortening caused by the inclination of the plane of the three principal dimensions to the plane of projection.

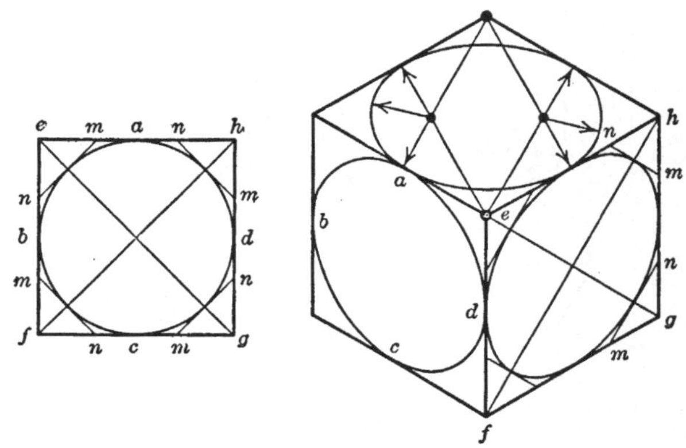


FIG. 37

Fig. 37 shows two cubes, the one on the left appears as a single square because it is an orthographic projection and this plane was parallel to the plane of projection. On the right, an isometric drawing is shown. In the orthographic projection on the left, a circle is inscribed in the face of the cube. The circle, so drawn, is tangent to the sides of the square at points midway between the extremities of the lines. When this square and its inscribed circle is shown isometrically, the points of tangency do not change, but, as the square is projected as a rhombus, the circle is projected as an ellipse, and is a smooth curve that is tangent at mid-points of the sides of the rhombus. A rapid, though approximate method of drawing an ellipse * is shown in the upper face of the isometric cube. The major and the minor axes of the ellipse can be laid off accurately by drawing the diagonals **eg** and **fh** (the notation being alike in both views); a tangent to the circle is perpendicular to the radius, and, for points on the diagonals, this tangent is shown as **mn** (all four are alike because they are equal). Showing **mn** isometrically means that the **gm**=**gn** in one view is equal to the **gm**=**gn** in the other view; the **hm**=**hn** in one view is equal to the **hm**=**hn** in the other view, and so on, for the four possible tangents at the diagonals.

**406. Isometric projection of inclined lines and angles.** Suppose it is desired to locate the centre of a hole in one of the faces of a cube as at **h** (Fig. 38). The hole is 12″ back from the point f, on the line **fm**, and 6″ up from the point **m**; **hfm** is the isometric representation of a right triangle whose legs are 6″ and 12″. It will be observed that none of the right angles of the cube are shown as such, therefore, the angle **hfm** is not the true angle corresponding to these dimensions; and, hence, it cannot be measured with a protractor in the ordinary way.

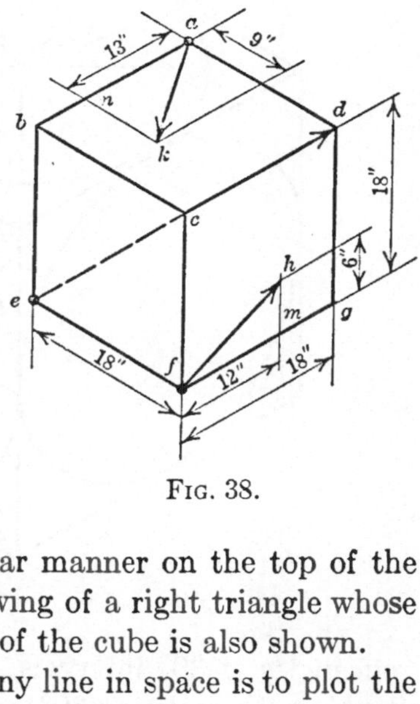

FIG. 38.

The point **k** is located in a similar manner on the top of the cube, while **ank** is the isometric drawing of a right triangle whose legs are 9″ and 13″. A diagonal **ed** of the cube is also shown.

The general method of drawing any line in space is to plot the three components of the line. For instance, the point **d** is located with respect to the point **e**, by first laying off **ef**, then **fg**, and finally **gd**.

**407. Isometric graduation of a circle.**† If the plane of a circle is parallel to the plane of projection, the projection is

* The exact method of constructing an ellipse will be found in any text-book on geometry.

† This method is also applicable to oblique projection.

equal to the circle itself and, hence, it can be drawn with a compass to the required radius. Any angle is then shown in its true size and thus the protractor can be applied in its graduation.

When circles are shown isometrically, however, their projections are ellipses, and the protractor graduation is applicable no longer. In the upper face of the cube, shown isometrically in Fig. 39, the circle is shown as an ellipse whose major and minor axes are respectively horizontal and vertical. If, on the major axis **ab**, a semicircle is drawn, and graduated by laying

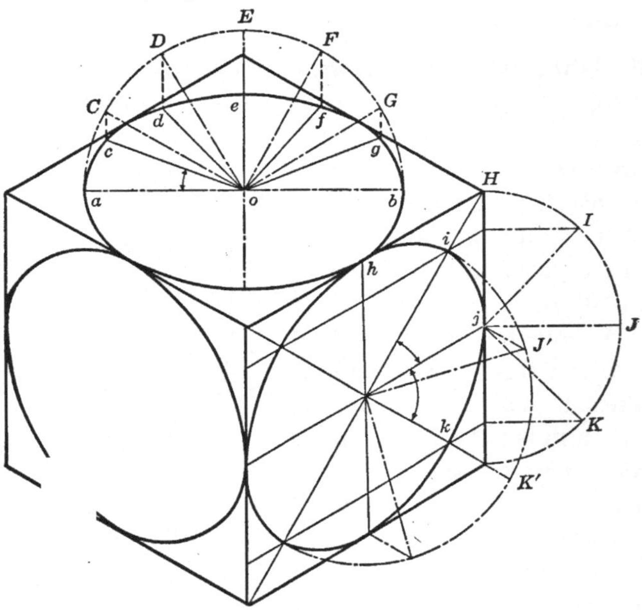


FIG. 39.

off angles at 30° intervals, the points **CDEF** and **G** are obtained making six angles at 30°, or a total of 180°, the angular measure of a semicircle. If, then, the plane of the circle is rotated about **ab** as an axis, until the point **E** coincides with **e**, each point of division on the semicircle will find itself on the similarly lettered point of the ellipse; because, then, the plane of the semicircle coincides with the plane of the upper face of the cube. Therefore, **aoc, cod, doe,** etc., are 30° angles, shown isometrically.

In the side face of the same cube are shown two methods of laying off 45° angles. The fact that both methods locate the same points tends to show that either method, alone, is applicable. The lettering is such that the construction should be clear without further explanation.

**408. Examples of isometric drawing.** As an example, the steps in the drawing of a wooden horse, shown in Fig. 40 and used in the building trades for supporting platforms and the like, will be followed. The making and the subsequent interpre-

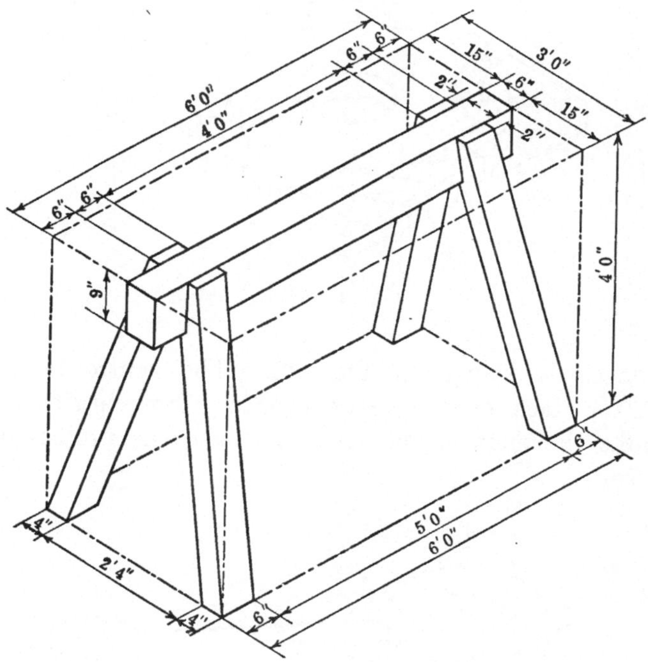


FIG. 40.

tation of drawings of this kind is facilitated by the introduction of bounding figures of simple shape. In the example chosen, the horse is bounded by a rectangular prism. The attached dimensions show the necessary slopes and may be introduced so as to replace the bounding figure. There is nothing new in this drawing and therefore the description will not be needlessly exhaustive. The bounding figure, when appended to a drawing like that of **Fig. 40**, helps to emphasize the slopes of the various lines. In general, the bounding figure should be removed on completion of the drawing.

Fig. 41 shows a toothed wheel. The plane of the circles corresponds to the plane of the top face of a cube. To construct it, it is necessary to lay out the prism first and then to insert the ellipses. The graduation of the circle is similar to that indicated in Art. 407.

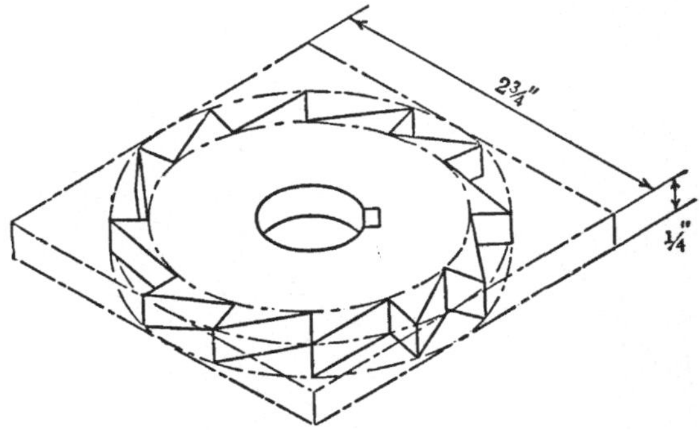


Fig. 41.

A lever is shown in Fig. 42. The centre line **ab** lies in the top face of the lever proper. Circumscribing prisms determine the ends of the lever and also the projecting cylindrical ends.

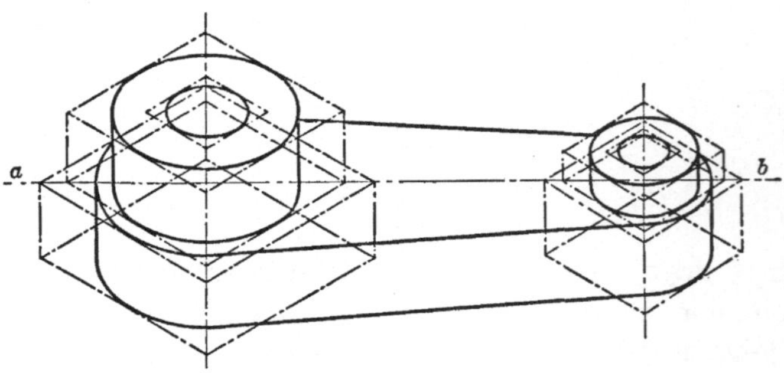


Fig. 42.

A gas-engine fly-wheel is illustrated in Fig. 43. Here the fly-wheel is shown so that the planes of the circles correspond to one of the side faces of a cube. The wheel has a solid web (without spokes) and a quarter of it is removed and shown in section.

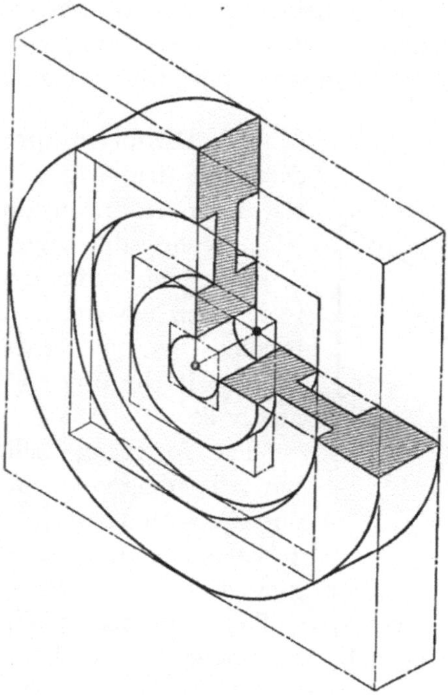

Fig. 43.

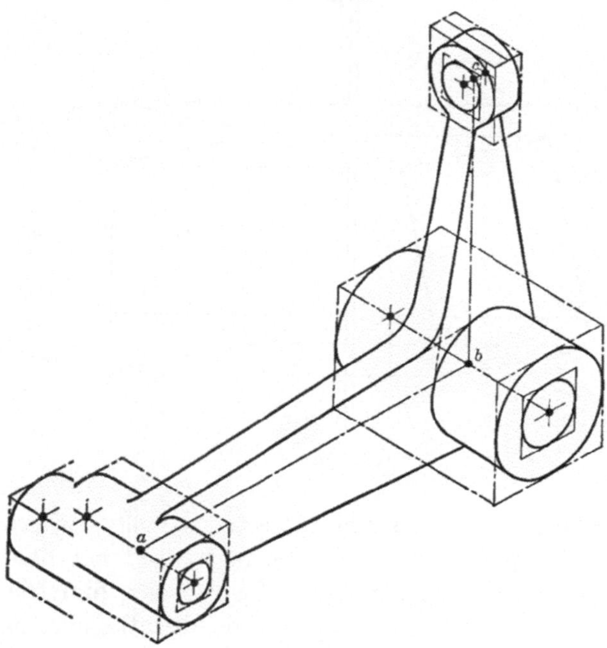


Fig. 44.

Fig. 44 represents a bell-crank. Again the scheme of using base-lines in connection with circumscribing prisms is shown. This view should be compared with that given in Fig. 17.

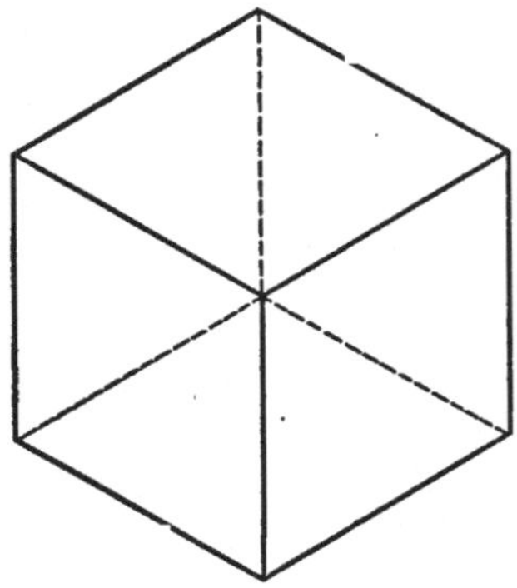

FIG. 45.

**409. Dimetric projection and dimetric drawing.** Let Fig. 45 be the isometric projection of a cube, with the invisible edges shown dotted. A disturbing symmetry of the lines is at once apparent. This objection becomes serious when applied to drawing if the objects are cubical, or nearly so.

The foregoing difficulty may be partially overcome by turning the cube so that only two faces are projected equally and the remaining face may be larger or smaller at pleasure. Fig. 46 shows this condition represented. The angle **aoc** is larger than either the angles **aob** or **cob**, the latter two (**aob** and **cob**) being

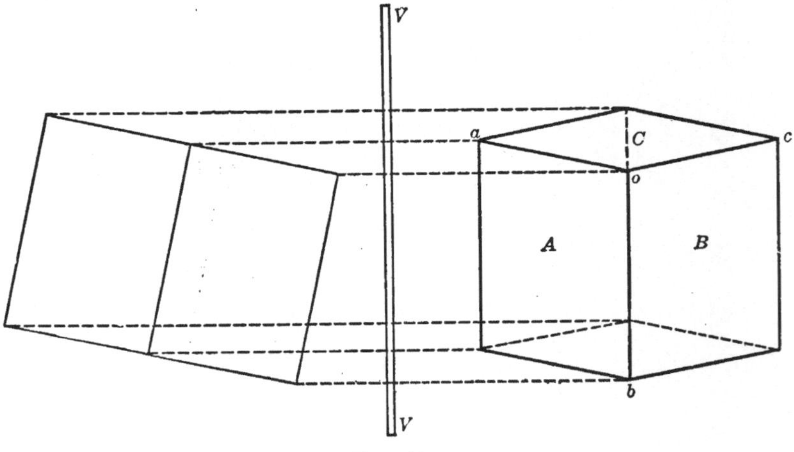


FIG. 46.

equal. The faces **A** and **B** are projected equally, whereas **C** is smaller in this particular case, though it need not be. The illustration as shown on the right of Fig. 46 is a **dimetric projection** and, as such, the same scale is applied to the axes **oa** and

**oc** because they are projected equally. The axis **ob** is longer, since the corresponding edge is more nearly parallel to the plane of projection **VV** than either **oa** or **oc**. Hence, to be theoretically correct, a different scale must be used on the axis **ob**.

When dimetric projection is to be commercially applied, confusion may result from the use of two distinct scales. If one scale is used on all three axes the combination becomes a **dimetric drawing.** Hence, a dimetric drawing differs from an isometric drawing, in so far, as two of three angles are equal to each other for the dimetric drawing; whereas, in isometric drawing, all three are equal, that is, the axes are 120° apart.

What is true of the direction of the axes in isometric drawing is equally true here, that is, the angular relation between the axes, alone, determines the type of projection, the direction of any one is entirely arbitrary.

Dimetric drawings do not entirely remove the objectionable symmetry, yet they find some use in practice, although they present no distinct advantage over any other type.

**410. Trimetric projection and trimetric drawing.** Fig. 47 shows a cube which is held in such a position that the orthographic projection of it will result in the unequal projection of the three visible faces. This, then, becomes a **trimetric projection.**

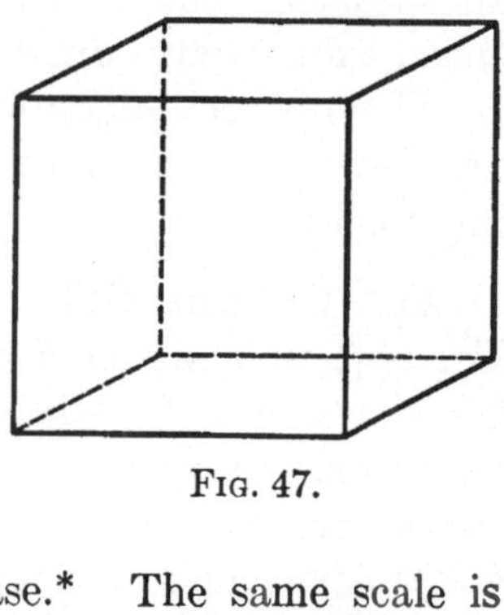

FIG. 47.

To make true projections, three different scales must be used. This, of course, is objectionable and, hence, recourse is had to a **trimetric drawing.** A trimetric drawing, therefore, requires three axes. The angles between the axes differ, but no one angle can be a right angle in any case.* The same scale is applied to all three. Also, the axes may have any direction,

* This evidently makes it an oblique projection. It is impossible to project a cube orthographically to produce this; since, if two axes are parallel to the plane of projection, the third axis must be perpendicular and is hence projected as a point. The oblique projection of a cube, which is turned as it would be in isometric drawing, presents no new feature since it results, generally speaking, in a trimetric projection.

so long as attention is paid to the angular relation between them.

If isometric drawings introduce the disturbing symmetry, then the trimetric is to be recommended, unless one of the other types of drawing is found to be more suitable. No examples are given in this connection, because the application of dimetric and trimetric drawings involve no new features. It is only to be remembered, that artistic taste may dictate the direction of the axes, so as to present the best view of the object to be illustrated.

**411. Axonometric projection and axonometric drawing.** Isometric, dimetric, and trimetric projection form a group which may be conveniently styled as **axonometric projections.** All three are the result of the orthographic projection of a cube, so that the three principal axes are projected in a manner as already indicated. Axonometric projections are therefore a special case of orthographic projection, but their advantages are sufficiently prominent to warrant separate classification.

For isometric projection, one scale is used throughout; for dimetric projection, two separate scales are used; and for trimetric projection, three distinct scales are used. When applying axonometric projections to drawing, the same scale is used on all axes, and the group then represents a series which may be called **axonometric drawing.**

The distinction between isometric projection and isometric drawing has been pointed out (Art. 403). It becomes more prominent, however, in dimetric and trimetric projection.

**412. Commercial application of axonometric projection.** For objects of simple shape, with few curves, isometric drawings serve a useful purpose, because they are easily made and are easily read by those unfamiliar with drawing in general. When curves are frequent and it is desirable to picture objects in a single view, oblique projections offer advantages over isometric drawings because it may be possible to make the planes of the curves parallel to the plane of projection. The curves will then be projected as they actually appear. When curves appear in many planes, then orthographic projections will answer requirements best, but, as already mentioned, their reading is more difficult, due to the simultaneous interpretation of two or more views.

Before dismissal of the subject of projections in general, attention is called to Fig. 48 which is a peculiar application of isometric drawing. It is frequently used as an example of an optical illusion. By concentrating the vision at the centre of the picture, there seems to be a sudden change from six to seven cubes, or vice versa, depending upon whether the central corner be regarded as a projecting or a depressed corner. This is due to the fact that all of the cubes are shown of the same size, a condition which is contrary to our everyday experience. As objects recede from the eye, they appear smaller; and in isometric projection there is no correction for this. In fact, all the projections so far considered, draw on the imagination for their interpretation,* and, therefore, they cannot present a perfectly natural appearance.

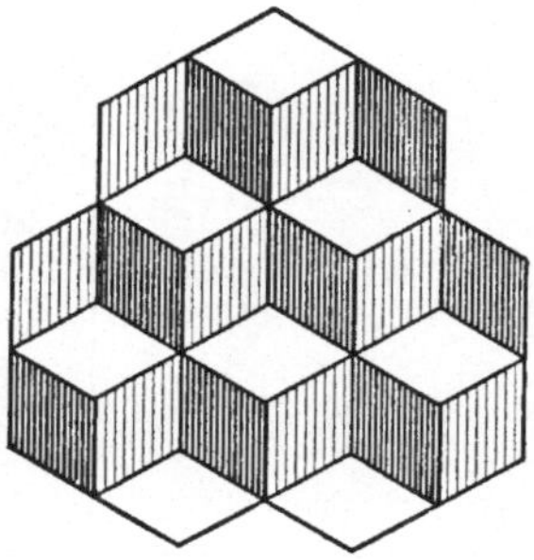

FIG. 48.

**413. Classification of projections.** All projections having parallel projecting lines may be classified according to the method by which they are made. This classification furnishes a useful survey of the entire subject and also serves to emphasize the distinction between the different methods.

It will be found, on analysis, that if the object be conceived in space with its parallel projecting lines, the oblique projections result when the plane of projection cuts the projecting lines obliquely. When the plane of projection cuts the projecting lines at a right angle, then the orthographic series of projections arise. If, still further, the projecting lines, coincide with some of the principal lines on the object, and the plane of projection is at right angles to the projecting lines, then the two-dimension orthographic projections result, and these are commonly called **mechanical drawings.** If the projecting lines do not coincide with some of the principal lines on the object, then the axonometric series of projections follow.

* The projections that overcome these objections are known as Perspective Projections. In these, the projecting lines converge to a point at which the observer is supposed to be located. Photographs are perspectives in a broad sense.

## CLASSIFICATION OF PROJECTIONS HAVING PARALLEL PROJECTING LINES

**PROJECTIONS**

- **On Plane Surfaces:**
  - **Oblique.** Projecting lines inclined to plane of projection but parallel to each other.
    - Inclination of projecting lines 45° with plane of projection.
      - All lines projected equal in length. Hence, same scale used on all.
    - Inclination of projecting lines greater than 45° with plane of projection.
      - Lines parallel to plane of projection drawn to equal length. Lines perpendicular to plane, projected as shorter lines to diminish distortion.
  - **Orthographic.** Projecting lines perpendicular to the plane of projection.
    - **Mechanical Drawing.** showing two principal dimensions on a single view. Hence, at least two views needed
      - Principal lines of object parallel or perpendicular to planes of projection. Sometimes called **Orthographic projection.**
    - **Axonometric.** projection, showing three dimensions in a single view.
      - **Isometric.** All three axes of cube projected equally, hence, axes are 120° apart and equal in length. Applied as **Isometric Drawing.**
      - **Dimetric.** Two of the three axes projected equally, hence, only two angles equal. Applied as **Dimetric Drawing.**
      - **Trimetric.** Axes projected unequally, hence, all three angles differ. Applied as **Trimetric Drawing.**
- **On Curved Surfaces:**
  - Not used in Engineering drawing.

## QUESTIONS ON CHAPTER IV

1. What are the isometric axes?
2. How are they obtained?
3. What is the angular relation between the pairs of axes?
4. Show why the isometric projection is a special case of orthographic.
5. What is the distinction between isometric projection and isometric drawing?
6. What direction do the axes have for their convenient application to drawing?
7. How is a circle projected isometrically?
8. Show the approximate method of drawing the isometric circle.
9. How are inclined lines laid off isometrically?
10. How are angles laid off isometrically?
11. Show that the laying off of an inclined line is accomplished by laying off the components of the line.
12. How is the isometric circle graduated in the top face of the cube?
13. Show how the graduation is accomplished in one of the side faces of the cube.
14. What is a dimetric projection?
15. What is a dimetric drawing?
16. What angular relation exists between the axes of a dimetric projection?
17. What is a trimetric projection?
18. What is a trimetric drawing?
19. What angular relation exists between the axes of a trimetric drawing?
20. Show why the trimetric drawing eliminates the disturbing symmetry of an isometric drawing.
21. Why cannot the angle between one pair of axes be a right angle?
22. What are axonometric projections?
23. Why do projections with parallel projecting lines draw on the imagination for their interpretation?
24. Draw the object of Question 33 in Chapter 2 in isometric drawing. Use bounding figure.
25. Draw a triangular prism in isometric drawing. Use a bounding figure.
26. Make an isometric drawing of a hexagonal prism. Use a bounding figure.
27. Make an isometric drawing of a hexagonal pyramid. Use a bounding figure.
28. Make an isometric drawing of 3–A (Question in Chapter 3).
29. Make an isometric drawing of 3–B.
30. Make an isometric drawing of 3–C.
31. Make an isometric drawing of 3–D.
32. Make an isometric drawing of 3–F.
33. Make an isometric drawing of 3–G.
34. Make an isometric drawing of 3–H.

35. Make an isometric drawing of 3–I.
36. Make an isometric drawing of 3–J.
37. Make an isometric drawing of 3–K.
38. Make an isometric drawing of 3–L.
39. Make a complete classification of all projections having parallel projecting lines.

# PART II

## *GEOMETRICAL PROBLEMS IN ORTHOGRAPHIC PROJECTION*

## CHAPTER V

### REPRESENTATION OF LINES AND POINTS

**501. Introductory.** Material objects are bounded by **surfaces**, which may be **plane** or **curved** in any conceivable way. The surfaces themselves are limited by **lines**, the forms of which may be **straight** or **curved**. Still further, these lines terminate in **points**. Thus, a solid is really made up of surfaces, lines and points, in their infinite number of combinations; and these may be considered as the **mathematical elements** that make up the solid. The mathematical elements must be considered as **concepts** as they have no material existence and, hence, are purely imaginative; that is, a surface has no thickness, therefore, it has no volume. A line or a point is a still further reduction along this line of reasoning. The usefulness of these concepts must be admitted, however, in view of the fact that they play such an important role in the conception of objects.

In general, the outline of any object is found by intuitively locating certain points, and joining the points by proper lines; the lines, when taken in their proper order determine certain surfaces, and the space included between them forms the solid (the material object) in question. Hence, to view material objects analytically, the nature of their mathematical elements must be known.

In Part II of this book, the graphical representation of mathematical concepts engages the attention. Whether the treatment of the subject be from the viewpoint of mathematics or of drawing, entirely depends upon the ultimate use. In the two chapters to be presented (V and VI), the method of representing lines, points and planes, orthographically, will be discussed. So far, attention has been directed to the representation of material objects, as common every day experience renders such objects familiar to us.

Before proceeding with the subject in all its detail, familiarity must be gained with certain fundamental operations on lines, points and planes, as well as with their graphical representation on two assumed planes called the planes of projection. The fundamental operations are grouped and studied without apparent reference to future application. It is desirable to do this so as to avoid frequent interruptions in the chain of reasoning when applying the operations to the solution of problems.

The student will save considerable time if he is well versed in the fundamental operations. In view of this, many questions are given at the end of the chapters so that his grasp of the subject may be tested from time to time. It may be needless to say that the solution of subsequent problems is utterly impossible without this thorough grounding. Frequent sketches should be made, representing lines, points and planes in positions other than shown in this book. These sketches should be made both in orthographic and in oblique projection. By this means, the student will increase his experience in the subject, much more than is possible by all the reading he might do. The proof of one's ability always lies in the correct execution of the ideas presented. The subject under consideration is a graphical one, and, as such, drawing forms the test mentioned. It has been considered necessary to caution the student so as to avoid the complications that will result later, due to insufficient preparation. Only in this way will the subject become of interest, to say nothing of its importance in subsequent commercial applications.

**502. Representation of the line.** Let Fig. 49 be an oblique projection of two planes intersecting at right angles to each other. The plane **VV** is called the vertical **plane of projection** and **HH** is called the **horizontal plane of projection**; these planes intersect in a line **XY** which is termed the **ground line**. The two planes taken as a whole are known as the **principal planes**; and by their intersection, they form four angles, numbered as shown in the figure. In what immediately follows, attention will be concentrated on operations in the first angle of projection, and later, extended to all four angles.

Suppose a cube **ABCDEFGH** is located in the first angle of projection, so that one face lies wholly in the horizontal plane and another face lies wholly in the vertical plane. The two faces then lying in the principal planes, intersect in a line which coincides with the ground line for the conditions assumed. Suppose, further, that it is ultimately desired orthographically to represent the diagonal **AG** of the cube. For the present, the reasoning will be carried out by the aid of the oblique projection.

The construction of the horizontal projection consists in dropping upon the horizontal plane, perpendiculars from points on

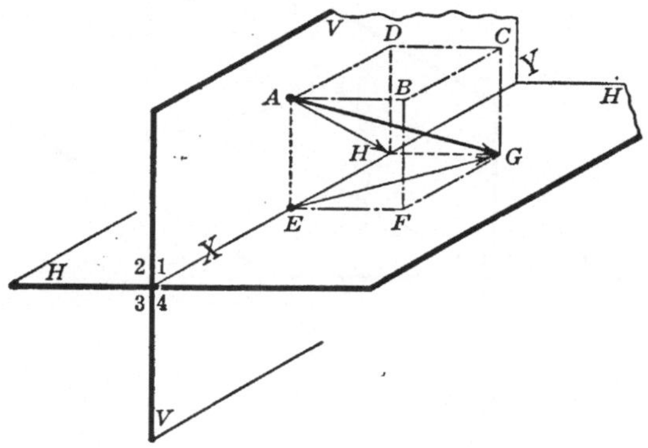


FIG. 49.

the line. For the line **AG**, the projecting perpendicular from the point **A** is **AE**, and **E** is then the horizontal projection of the point **A** in space.* As for the point **G** on the line, that already lies in the horizontal plane and is its own horizontal projection. Thus, two horizontal projections of two points on the line are established, and, hence, the **horizontal projection** of the line is determined by joining these two projections. This is true, because all the perpendiculars from the various points on the line lie in a plane, which is virtually the horizontal **projecting plane** of the line. It cuts the horizontal plane of projection in a line **EG**, which is the horizontal projection of the line **AG** in space.

* It is to be noted that the projection of a point is found at the place where the projecting line pierces the plane of projection.

Putting this in another form, the projection **EG** gives the same mental impression to an absever viewing the horizontal plane from above as does the line **AG** itself; in fact, **EG** is a drawing of the line **AG** in space.

Directing attention for a moment to the vertical plane, it is found that the construction of the vertical projection consists in dropping a series of perpendiculars from the line **AG** to that plane. For point **G**, the perpendicular to the vertical plane is **GH**, and **H** is thus the vertical projection of **G**. The point **A** lies in the vertical plane and, hence, is its own vertical projection. A line joining **A** and **H** is the vertical projection of **AG**. Again, a plane passed through **AG**, perpendicular to the vertical plane,

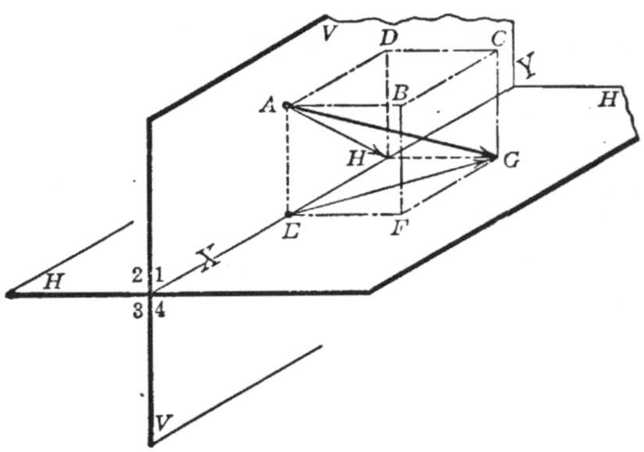


FIG. 49.

will cut from it the line **AH**, which is the vertical projection as has been determined. Thus, **AH** is a drawing of **AG** because it conveys the same mental impression to an observer who views it in the way the projection was made.

**503. Line fixed in space by its projections.** The location of the principal planes is entirely arbitrary, as is also the line in question; but, when both are once assumed, the line is fixed in space by its projections on the principal planes. If a plane be passed through the horizontal projection **EG** (Fig. 49), perpendicular to the horizontal plane, it will contain the line **AG** in space, since the method is just the reverse of that employed in finding the projection. Similarly, a plane through the vertical projection, perpendicular to the vertical plane, will also contain the line **AG**. It naturally follows that the line **AG** is the intersection of the horizontal and vertical projecting planes and, therefore, the line is absolutely fixed, with reference to the principal planes, by its projections on those planes.

**504. Orthographic representation of a line.** The line that has been considered so far is again represented in the left-hand view of Fig. 50, in oblique projection. The edges of the cube have been omitted here in order to concentrate attention to the line in question. **AG** is that line, as before, **EG** is its horizontal projection and **AH** is its vertical projection.*

Suppose that the plane **HH** is revolved in the direction of the arrows, 90° from its present position, until it coincides with the

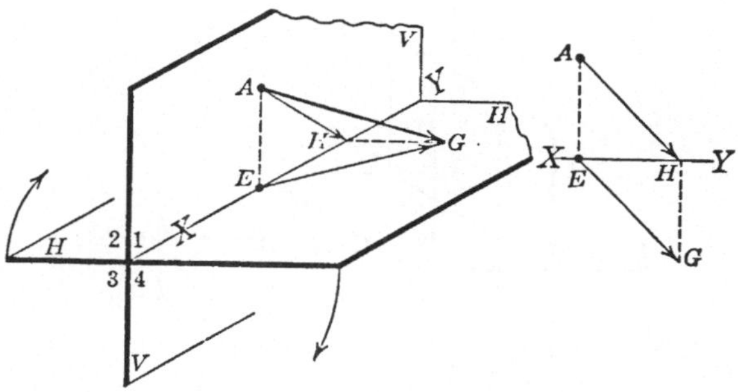


FIG. 50.

vertical plane **VV**. The view on the right of Fig. 50 shows the resultant state of affairs in orthographic projection. **AH** is the vertical projection and **EG** is the horizontal projection. **AE** in one view is the equivalent of **AE** in the other; **HG** and **EH** in one view are the equivalents of **HG** and **EH** in the other. Both views represent the same line **AG** in space. At first sight, it may appear that the oblique projection is sufficiently clear, and such is the case; but, in the solution of problems, the orthographic projection as shown on the right possesses many advantages. In due time, this mode of representation will be considered, alone, without the oblique projection.

* The projections of a line may be considered as shadows on their respective planes. The light comes in parallel rays, perpendicularly directed to the planes of projection. See also Arts. 203 and 310 in this connection.

**505. Transfer of diagrams from orthographic to oblique projection.** It is desirable to know how to transfer diagrams from one kind of projection to the other. If the orthographic projection appears confusing, the transfer to oblique projection may be of service. On the right of Fig. 50, is given the orthographic projection of the line **AG.** To construct the oblique projection from this, draw the principal planes as shown in the left-hand diagram. From any point **E** on the ground line in the oblique projection, lay off **EA**, vertically, equal to **EA** in the orthographic projection. On the sloping line (ground line), lay off **EH** equal to **EH** in the orthographic projection. Then draw **HG** in the horizontal plane, equal to **HG** in the orthographic projection. A line joining **A** and **G** in the oblique projection

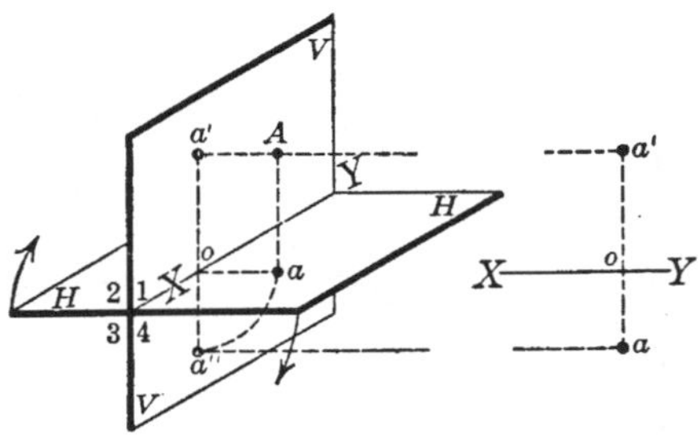


FIG. 50.

gives the actual line in space; hence, in the oblique projection. the actual line and both of its projections are shown. In the orthographic projection, only the projections are given; the line itself must be imagined. Compare the method of constructing the oblique projection with Art. 207 and note the similarity.

**506. Piercing points of lines on the principal planes.** If **AG** (Fig. 50) be considered as a limited portion of line indefinitely extended in both directions, then **A** and **G** are the piercing points on the vertical and horizontal planes respectively. On observation, it will be found that the vertical piercing point lies on the vertical projection of the line, and also on a perpendicular to the ground line **XY** from the point where the horizontal projection intersects the ground line; hence, it is at their intersection.

Likewise, the horizontal piercing point lies on the horizontal projection of the line and also on the perpendicular erected at the intersection of the vertical projection with the ground line; hence, again, it is at the intersection of these two lines.

In Fig. 51 let **ab** be the horizontal projection of a line **AB** in space, and **a′b′** be the corresponding vertical projection. The line, if extended, would pierce the horizontal plane at **c** and the vertical plane at **d′**. This line is shown as an oblique projection in Fig. 52. All the lines that are required in the mental process are shown in this latter view. The actual construction in orthographic projection is given in Fig. 51. To locate the vertical piercing point prolong both projections, and at the point where the horizontal projection intersects the ground line, erect a perpendicular until it intersects the prolongation of the vertical projection. This locates the vertical piercing point. To find the horizontal piercing point, prolong the vertical projection until it intersects the ground line, and at this point, erect a perpendicular to the ground line. Then, the point at which this perpendicular intersects the prolongation of the horizontal projection is the horizontal piercing point.

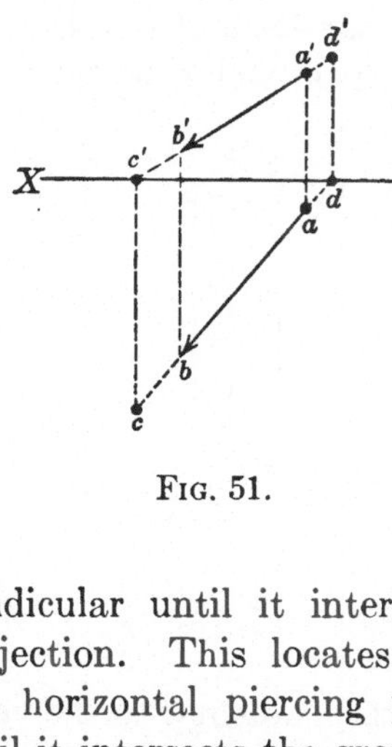


Fig. 51.

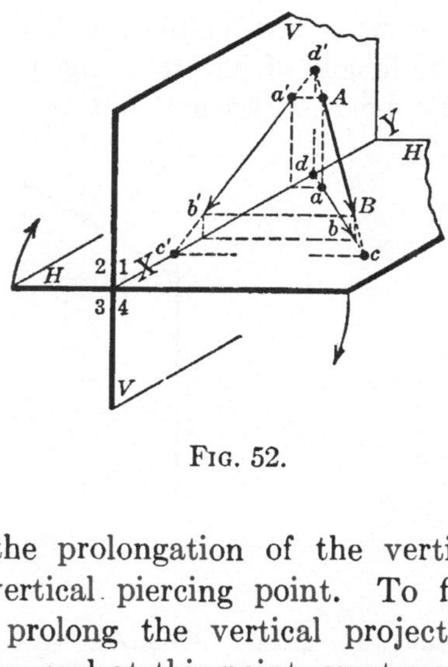


Fig. 52.

A convenient way of looking at cases of this kind is to assume that **XY** is the edge of the horizontal plane while viewing the vertical projection, therefore, **AB** must pierce the horizontal plane somewhere in a line perpendicular to the vertical plane at the point **c′**. In viewing the horizontal plane, **XY** now represents the vertical plane on edge. Here, again, the line **AB** must pierce the vertical plane somewhere in a line perpendicular to the horizontal plane at the point **d**.

**507. Nomenclature of projections.** In what follows, the actual object will be designated by the capital letters, as the line **AB** for instance. The horizontal projections will be indicated by the small letters as the line **ab**, and the vertical projections by the small prime letters as the line **a′b′**. **It should always be remembered that in orthographic projection, the projections alone are given, the actual object is to be imagined.**

**508. Representation of points.** A single point in space is located with respect to the principal planes as shown in Fig. 53. **A** is the actual point while **a** is its horizontal, and **a′** its vertical projection. The distance of **A** above the horizontal plane is equal to the length of its projecting perpendicular **Aa** and this is equal to **a′o** because **Aa** and **a′o** are both perpendicular to the hori-

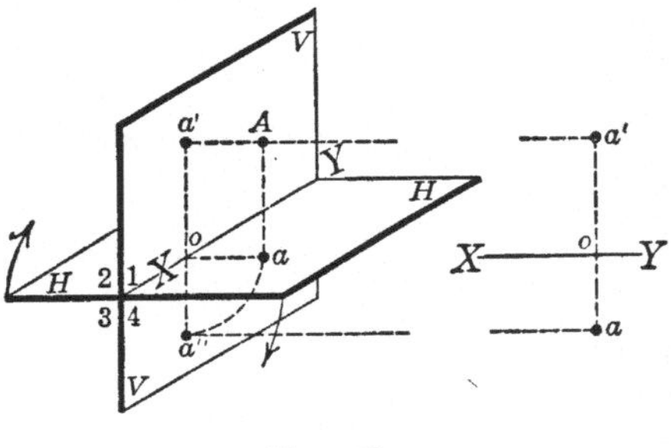


FIG. 53.

zontal plane **HH**. Also, **Aa′** and **ao** are perpendicular to the vertical plane, therefore, the figure **Aaoa′** is a rectangle, whose opposite sides are necessarily equal. Hence, also, the distance of **A** from the vertical plane is equal to the length of its projecting perpendicular **Aa′** which also equals **ao**. Performing the usual revolution of the horizontal plane, **a** will reach **a″** on a line **a′a″** which is perpendicular to the ground line **XY**. It has been shown that **a′**o is perpendicular to **XY** and it only remains to prove that **oa″** is a continuation of **a′o**. This must be so, because **a** revolves about the ground line as an axis, in a plane determined by the two intersecting lines **a′o** and **ao**. This plane cuts from the vertical plane the line **a'a''** which is perpendicular to **XY** because a portion (**a'o**) of it is perpendicular. As the point **a** revolves about **XY** as an axis, it describes a circle, whose radius is **oa**, and hence **oa''** must equal **oa**.

In projection,* this is shown on the right-hand diagram of Fig. 53. Both figures are lettered to correspond as far as consistent. The actual point **A** is omitted, however, in the right-hand diagram because the very object of this scheme of representation is to locate the point from two arbitrary planes (principal planes), solely by their projections on those planes. This latter is an exceedingly important fact and should always be borne in mind.

**509. Points lying in the principal planes.** If a point lies in one of the principal planes, it is its own projection in that plane and its corresponding projection lies in the ground line. Fig. 54 shows such cases in projection. **A** is a point lying in the vertical plane, at a distance **a'a** above the horizontal plane; its vertical projection is **a'** and its corresponding horizontal projection is **a**. **B** is another point, lying in the horizontal plane, at a distance **bb'** from the vertical plane; **b** is its horizontal and **b'** the corresponding vertical projection.

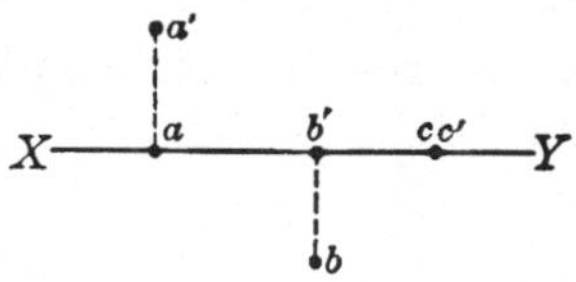

FIG. 54.

If a point lies in both planes, the point coincides with both of its projections and must therefore be in the ground line. **C** is such a point, and its two projections are indicated by **cc'**, both letters being affixed to the one point. The use of these cases will appear as the subject develops.

**510. Mechanical representation of the principal planes.** For the time being, the reader may find it desirable to construct two planes † so that lines and points may be actually represented

* Hereafter, orthographic projection will usually be designated simply as "in projection."

† For classroom work, a more serviceable device can be made of hinged screens, constructed of a fine mesh wire. Wires can be easily inserted to represent lines and the projections drawn with chalk. The revolution of the planes can be accomplished by properly hinging the planes so that they can be made to lie approximately flat.

with reference to them. If two cards be slit as shown in Fig. 55, they can be put together so as to represent two planes at right angles to each other. Lines may be represented by use of match-sticks and points by pin-heads, the pin being so inserted as to represent its projecting perpendicular to one plane. The idea is recommended until the student becomes familiar with the involved operations. As soon as this familiarity is obtained, the cards should be dispensed with, and the operations reasoned out in space, as far as possible, without the use of any diagrams.

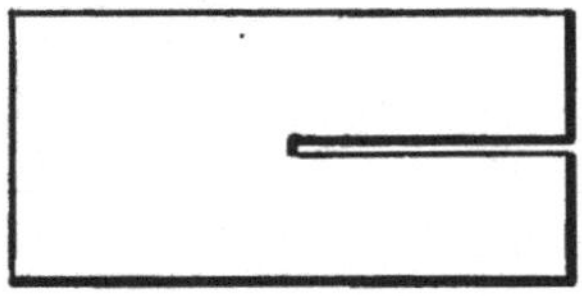

Fig. 55.

**511. Lines parallel to the planes of projection.** Assume a line parallel to the horizontal plane. Evidently this line cannot pierce the horizontal plane on account of the parallelism. It will pierce the vertical plane, however, if it is inclined to that plane.

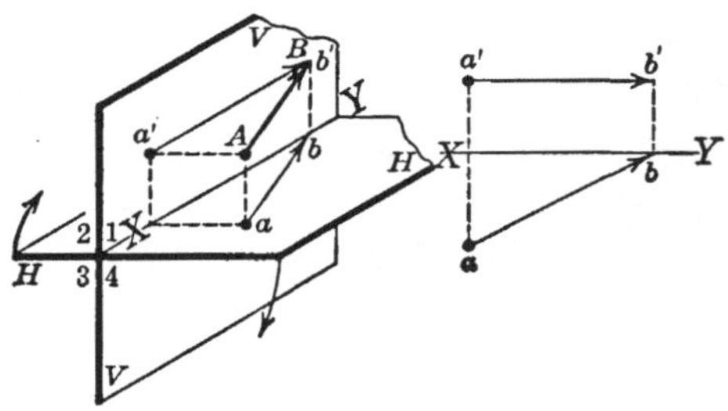


Fig. 56.

In Fig. 56 this line is shown both in oblique and orthographic projection. The piercing point on the vertical plane is found by erecting a perpendicular at the point where the horizontal projection intersects the ground line. It will also lie on the vertical projection of the line. As the line is parallel to the horizontal plane, its vertical projection is parallel to the ground line. The piercing point will therefore lie at the intersection of the two lines; that is, of the perpendicular from the ground line and the vertical projection of the line. In both views of the figure, **AB** is the given line and **b′** is its piercing point.

If, on the other hand, the line is parallel to the vertical plane

(Fig. 57) and inclined to the horizontal plane, it will pierce the horizontal plane at some one point. Its horizontal projection is now parallel to the ground line **XY**. The horizontal piercing

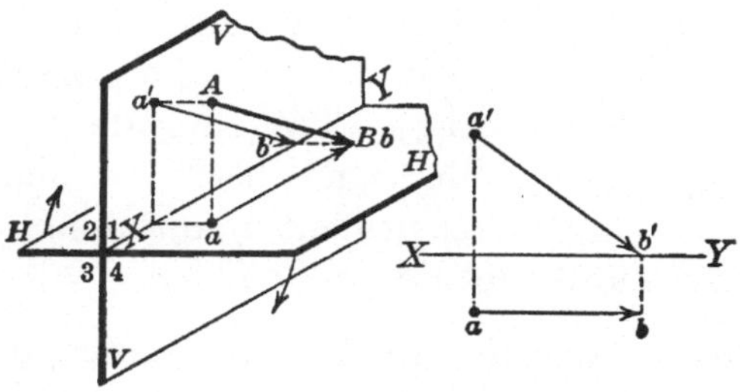


FIG. 57.

point is at **b**, as shown, and is found in much the same way as that in the illustration immediately preceding.

A case where the line is parallel to both planes is shown in

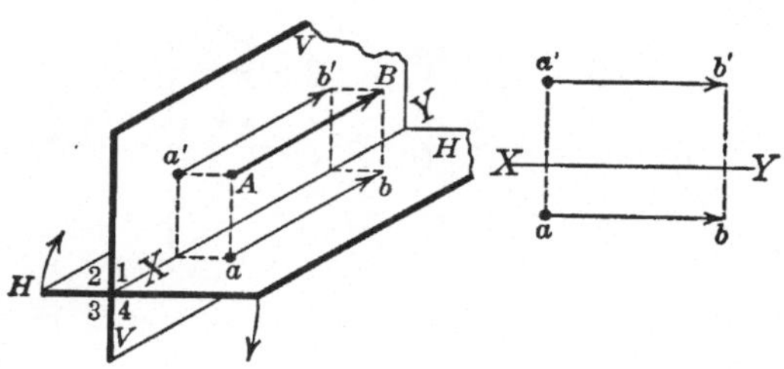


FIG. 58.

Fig. 58. This line cannot pierce either plane and, therefore, both its projections must be parallel to the ground line as depicted.

**512. Lines lying in the planes of projection.** If a line lies in the plane of projection, it is its own projection in that plane, and its corresponding projection lies in the ground line. When the line lies in both planes of projection it must therefore coincide with the ground line. Fig. 59 shows in projection the three cases possible. The first is a line lying in the horizontal plane, ab is its horizontal projection and

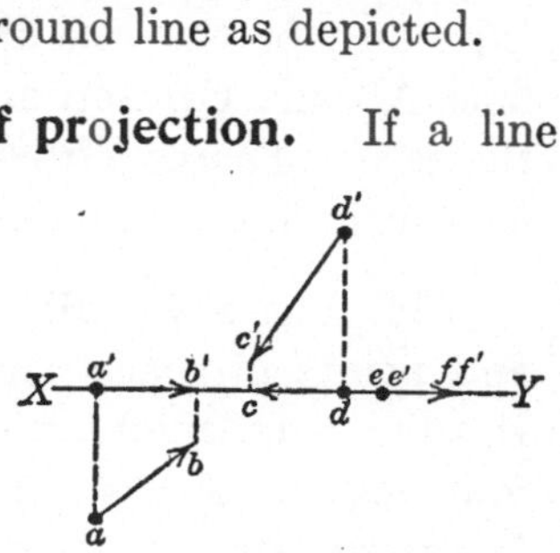


FIG. 59.

**a′b′** is its corresponding vertical projection. The second is a line lying in the vertical plane, **c′d′** is its vertical projection and **cd** is its corresponding horizontal projection. The third case shows a line in both planes and its horizontal and vertical projections coincide with the ground line and also the line itself; the coincident projections are indicated as shown at **ee′** and ff′, read **ef** and **e′f′**.

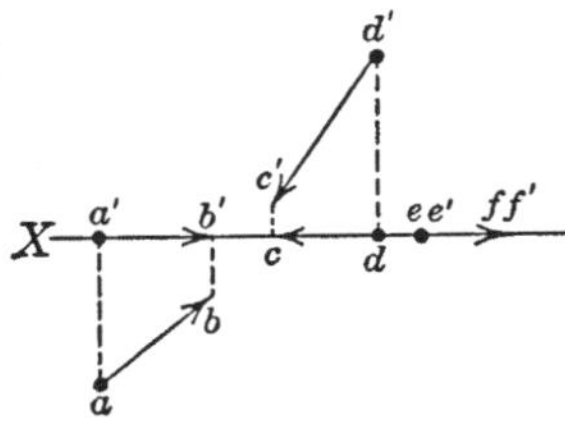


FIG. 59.

**513. Lines perpendicular to the planes of projection.** If a line is perpendicular to the horizontal plane, its projection on that plane is a point, because both projecting perpendiculars from the extremities must coincide with the perpendicular line. The vertical projection, however, shows the line in its true length, perpendicular to the ground line, as such a line is parallel to the vertical plane.

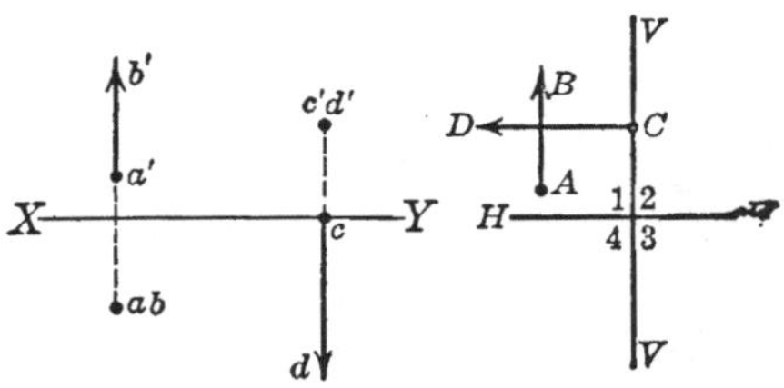


FIG. 60.

Fig. 60 shows this in projection as **AB**, and, in addition a **profile plane** is added which indicates the fact more clearly. **CD** is a line perpendicular to the vertical plane with one extremity of the line in that plane. In the profile plane, the lines **AB** and **CD** appear to intersect, but this is not necessarily the case. The construction of the projections of the line **CD** is identical with that immediately preceding.

**514. Lines in all angles.** So far, the discussion of lines and points in space has been limited entirely to the first angle. If a line is indefinite in extent, it may pass through several of the four angles. A case in each angle will be taken and the salient features of its projections will be pointed out.

Fig. 61 shows a line passing through the first angle. It continues beyond into the second and fourth angles. In projection, the condition is shown on the right. The projections **ab** and **a′b′** show those of the limited position that traverses the first angle.

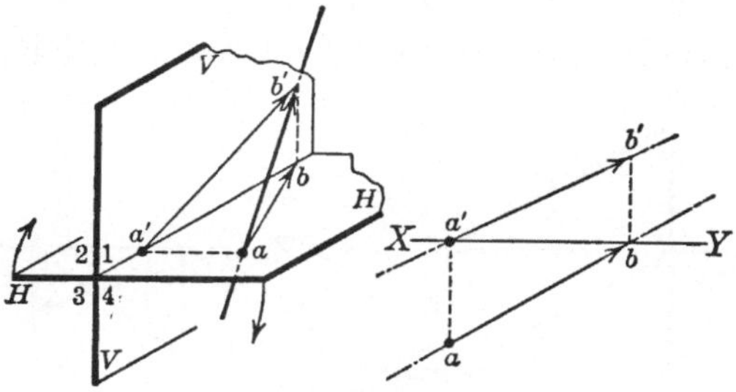

FIG. 61.

The dotted extensions show the projection of the indefinite line, and are continued, at pleasure, to any extent.

A line in the second angle is shown in Fig. 62. The horizontal projection is **ab** and the vertical projection is **a′b′**. If the horizontal plane be revolved into coincidence with the vertical plane, the view in projection will show that, in this particular case, the projections of the lines cross each other. Only the limited portion in the second angle is shown, although the line may be indefinitely extended in both directions.

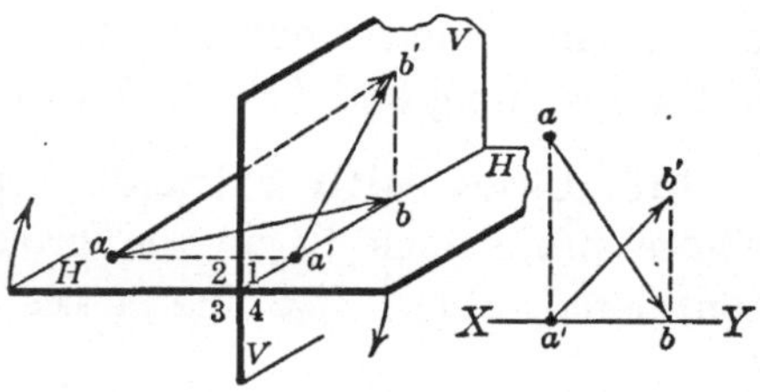

FIG. 62.

A third angle line is illustrated in Fig. 63. It may be observed,

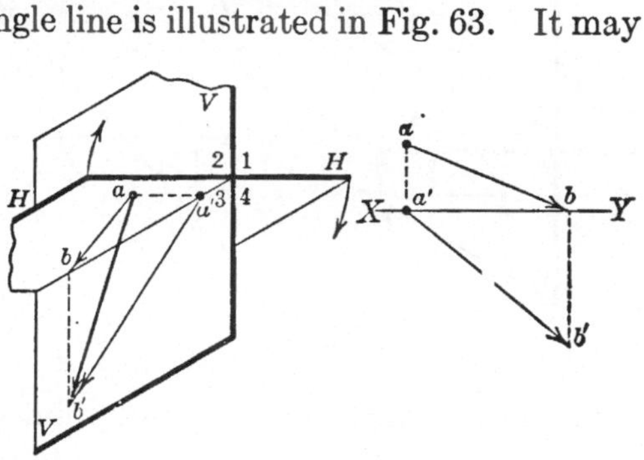

FIG. 63.

in comparison with a line in the first angle, that the horizontal and vertical projections are interchanged for the limited portion of the line shown. In other words the horizontal projection of the line is above the ground line and the vertical projection is below it. The case may be contrasted with Fig. 61.

The last case is shown in the fourth angle and Fig. 64 depicts

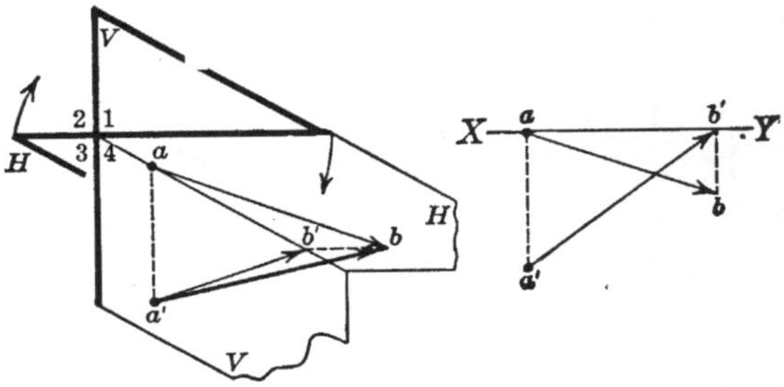


FIG. 64.

this condition. Both projections now cross each other below the ground line. Contrast this with Fig. 62. The similarity of the foregoing and Arts. 315, 316 and 317 may be noted.

**515. Lines with coincident projections.** Lines, both of whose projections lie in the ground line have been previously considered (511). If a line passes through the ground line from

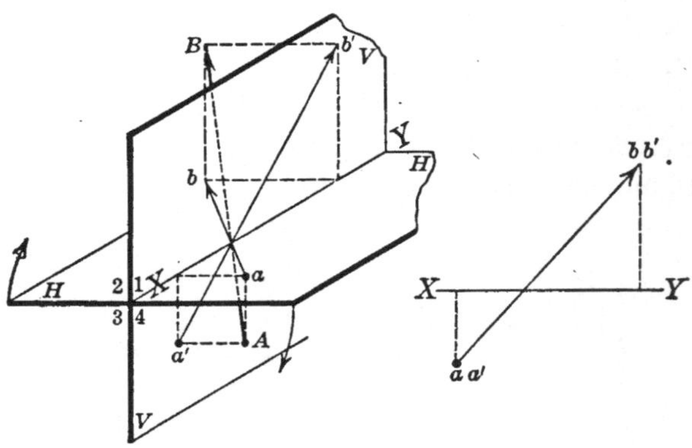


FIG. 65.

the second to the fourth angle, so that any point on the line is equidistant from both planes, then the two projections of the line will be coincident. Fig. 65 illustrates such a condition. The line is not indeterminate by having coincident projections, however, because the oblique projections can be constructed from the orthographic representation. The projection on the profile plane shows that this line bisects the second and fourth angles.

If the line passes through the ground line, from the second to the fourth angles, but is not equidistant from the principal planes, then both projections will pass through the same point on the ground line.

**516. Points in all angles.** Fig. 66 shows four points **A, B, C,** and **D**, lying, one in each angle. The necessary construction lines are shown. On the right, the condition is depicted in projection, the number close to the projection indicating the angle in which the point is located.

Observation will show that the first and third angle projec-

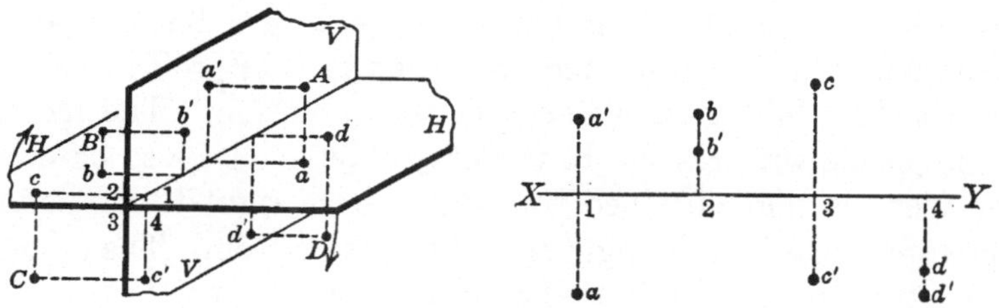

FIG. 66.

tions are similar in general appearance, but with projections interchanged. The same is true of the second and fourth angles; although, in the latter cases, both projections fall to one or the other side of the ground line.

**517. Points with coincident projections.** It may be further observed in Fig. 66 that in the second and fourth angles, the projection **b**, **b′** and **d**, **d′** may be coincident. This simply means that the points are equidistant from the planes of projection.

The case of the point in the ground line has been noted (508), such points lie in no particular angle, unless a new set of principal planes be introduced. It can then be considered under any case at pleasure, depending upon the location of the principal planes.

**518. Lines in profile planes.** A line may be located so that both of its projections are perpendicular to the ground line.

The projections must therefore be coincident,* since they pass through the same point on the ground line. Fig. 67 shows an example of this kind. Although the actual line in space can be determined from its horizontal projection **ab** and its vertical

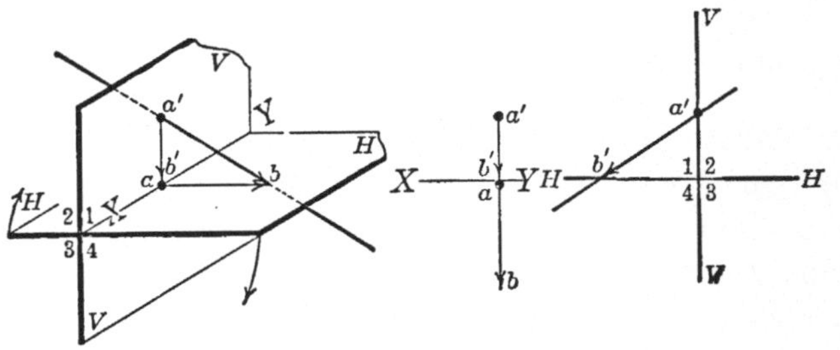


FIG. 67.

projection **a'b'**, still this is only true because a limited portion of the line was chosen for the projections. The profile shown on the extreme right clearly indicates the condition. The location of the profile with respect to the projection should also be noted. The view, is that obtained by looking from right to left, and is therefore located on the right side of the projection. The numbering on the angles should also help the interpretation.

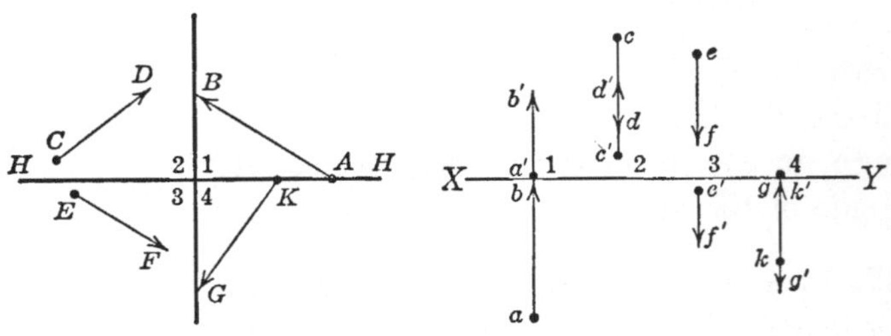


FIG. 68.

Fig. 68 shows a profile (on the left-hand diagram) of one line in each angle. The diagram on the right shows the lines in projection. The numbers indicate the angle in which the line is located.

* Compare the coincident projections in this case with those of Art. 515.

## QUESTIONS ON CHAPTER V

1. Discuss the point, the line, and the surface, and show how the material object is made up of them.
2. What are the mathematical elements of a material object?
3. Why are the mathematical elements considered as concepts?
4. How is the outline of a material object determined?
5. What is meant by the graphical representation of mathematical concepts?
6. What are the principal planes of projection?
7. What is the ground line?
8. How many dihedral angles are formed by the principal planes and how are they numbered? Make a diagram.
9. How is a line orthographically projected on the principal planes?
10. How many projections are required to fix the line with reference to the principal planes? Why?
11. Show how one of the principal planes is revolved so as to represent a line in orthographic projection.
12. Assume a line in the first angle in orthographic projection and show how the transfer is made to an oblique projection.
13. Under what conditions will a line pierce a plane of projection?
14. Assume a line that is inclined to both planes of projection and show how the piercing points are determined orthographically. Give the reasoning of the operation.
15. Do the orthographic projections of a line represent the actual line in space? Why?
16. Show a point in oblique projection and also the projecting lines to the principal planes. Draw the corresponding diagram in orthographic projection showing clearly how one of the principal planes is revolved.
17. Draw, in projection, a point lying in the horizontal plane; a point lying in the vertical plane; a point lying in both planes. Observe nomenclature in indicating the points.
18. Indicate in what angle the points shown in Fig. 5–A are located.
19. Draw a line parallel to the horizontal plane but inclined to the vertical plane in orthographic projection. Transfer diagram to oblique projection.
20. Draw a line parallel to the vertical plane but inclined to the horizontal plane in orthographic projection. Transfer diagram to oblique projection.

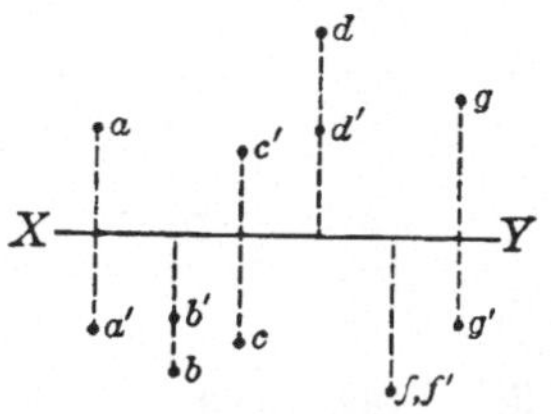

FIG. 5–A.

21. Draw a line parallel to both principal planes in orthographic projection. Transfer diagram to oblique projection.
22. When a line is parallel to both principal planes is it parallel to the ground line? Why?

23. In Fig. 5–B, make the oblique projection of the line represented.
24. Draw the projections of a line lying in the horizontal plane.
25. Draw the projections of a line lying in the vertical plane.
26. Draw the projections of a line lying in the ground line, observing the nomenclature in the representation.

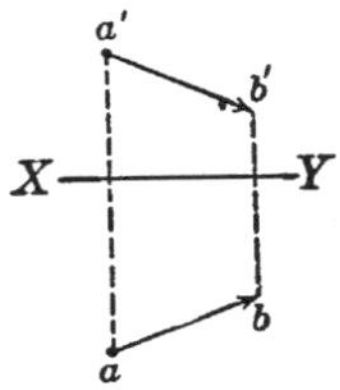


FIG. 5–B.

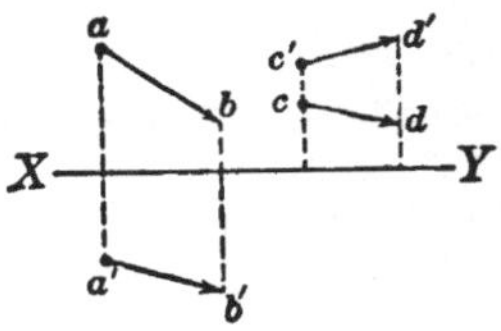


FIG. 5–C.

27. In Fig. 5–C give the location of the lines represented by the orthographic projections. Construct the corresponding oblique projections.
28. Show two lines, one perpendicular to each of the planes and also draw a profile plane for each indicating the advantageous use in such cases.
29. When a line is perpendicular to the horizontal plane, how is it projected on that plane?
30. When a line is perpendicular to the vertical plane, why is the horizontal projection equal to it in length?
31. Draw a line in the second angle, in orthographic projection. Transfer the diagram to oblique projection.
32. Draw a line in the third angle, in orthographic projection. Transfer the diagram to oblique projection.
33. Draw a line in the fourth angle, in orthographic projection. Transfer the diagram to oblique projection.
34. In Fig. 5–D, specify in which angles each of the lines are situated.

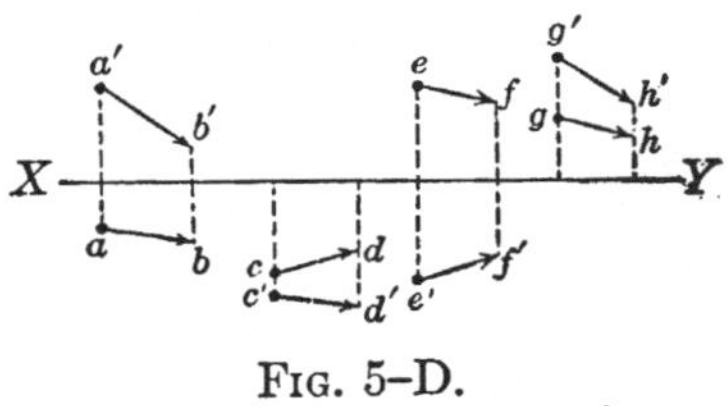


FIG. 5–D.

35. Draw lines similar to 5–D in orthographic projection and transfer the diagrams to oblique projection.
36. Make the orthographic projection of a line with coincident projections and show by a profile plane what it means. Take the case where the line passes through one point on the ground line and is perpendicular to it, and the other case where it is inclined to the ground line through one point.

37. Locate a point in each angle and observe the method of indicating them.
38. Make an oblique projection of the points given in Question 37.
39. Make an orthographic projection of points with coincident projections and show under what conditions they become coincident.
40. In what angles are coincident projections of points possible? Show by profile.
41. Make the oblique projections of the lines shown in Fig. 68 of the text. Use arrows to indicate the lines.
42. Why is it advantageous to use a profile plane, when the lines are indefinite in extent, and lie in the profile plane?

# CHAPTER VI

## REPRESENTATION OF PLANES

**601. Traces of planes parallel to the principal planes.** Let Fig. 69 represent the two principal planes by **HH** and **VV** intersecting in the ground line **XY**. Let, also, **RR** be another plane passing through the first and fourth angles and parallel to **VV**. The plane **RR** intersects the horizontal plane **HH** in a line **tr**, which is called the **trace** of the plane **RR**. As **RR** is parallel

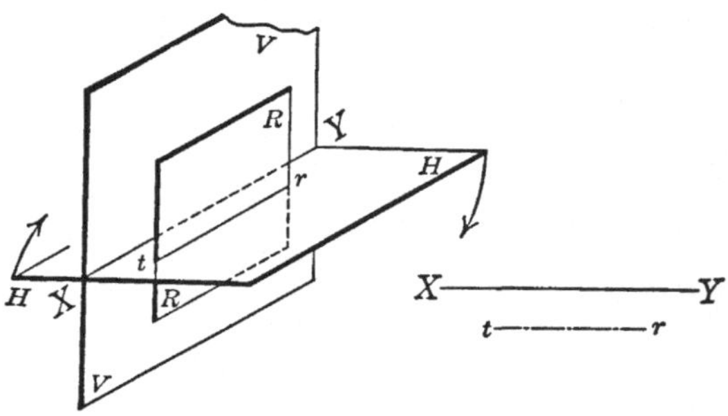


Fig. 69.

to **VV**, the case is that of two parallel planes cut by a third plane, and, from solid geometry, it is known that their intersections are parallel. If the horizontal plane is revolved, by the usual method, into coincidence with the vertical plane, the resulting diagram as shown on the right will be the orthographic representation of the trace of a plane which is parallel to the vertical plane.

If, as in Fig. 70, the plane is parallel to the horizontal plane, the condition of two parallel planes cut by a third plane again presents itself, the vertical plane of projection now being the cutting plane. The trace **t′r′** is then above the ground line, and, as before, parallel to it.

**602. Traces of planes parallel to the ground line.** When a plane is parallel to the ground line, and inclined to both planes of projection, it must intersect the principal planes. The line of intersection on each principal plane will be parallel to the ground

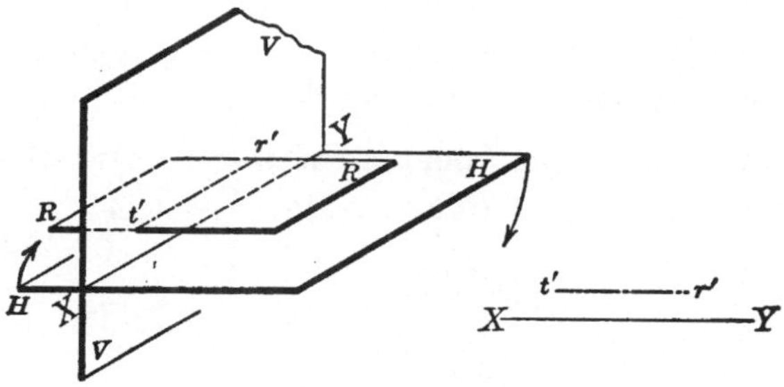


Fig. 70.

line because the given plane is parallel to the ground line and, hence, cannot intersect it. Fig. 71 shows this condition in oblique

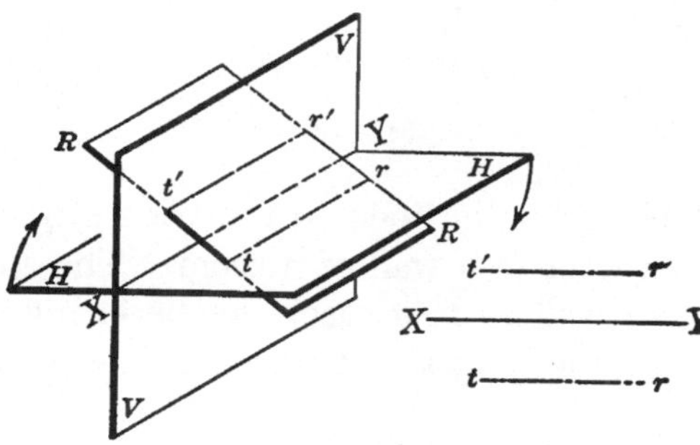


Fig. 71.

and orthographic projection, in which **tr** is the **horizontal trace** and **t′r′** is the **vertical trace.**

A special case of this occurs if the plane passes through the ground line. Both traces then coincide with the ground line and the orthographic representation becomes indeterminate unless the profile plane is attached.

Fig. 72 is a profile and shows several planes passing through the ground line, each of which is now determined. It may be possible, however, to introduce a new horizontal plane **H′H′**, parallel to the principal horizontal plane. Such an artifice will bring the case into that immediately preceding. It may then be shown as an ordinary

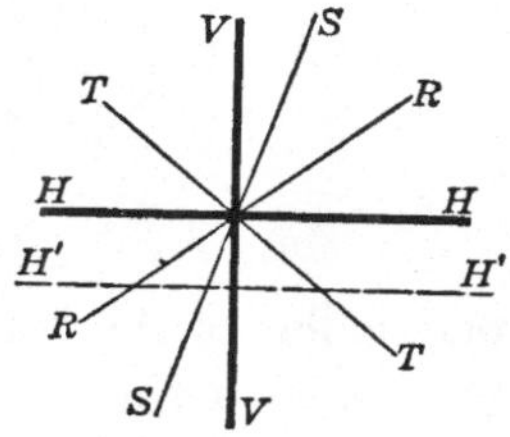


Fig. 72.

orthographic projection, just as though the original horizontal plane were absent. The same would still be true if a new vertical plane were added instead of the horizontal plane, or, if an entirely new set of principal planes were chosen so that the new principal planes would be parallel to the old ones.

**603. Traces of planes perpendicular to one of the principal planes.** Fig. 73 shows a plane that is perpendicular to

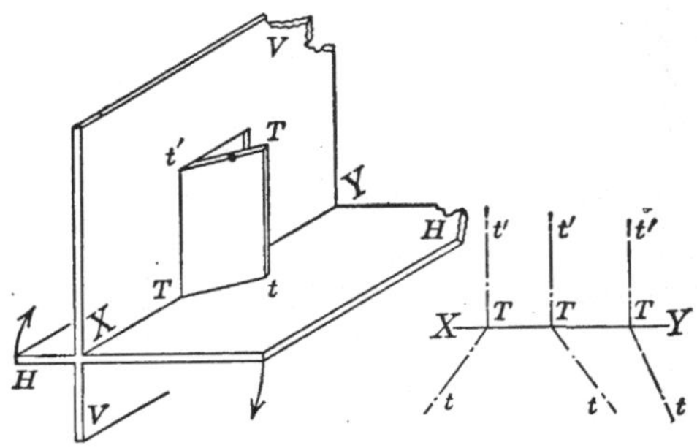

FIG. 73.

the horizontal plane but inclined to the vertical plane. It may be imagined as a door in a wall of a room. The angle with the vertical plane (or wall in this case) can be changed at will by swinging it about the hinges, yet its plane always remains per-

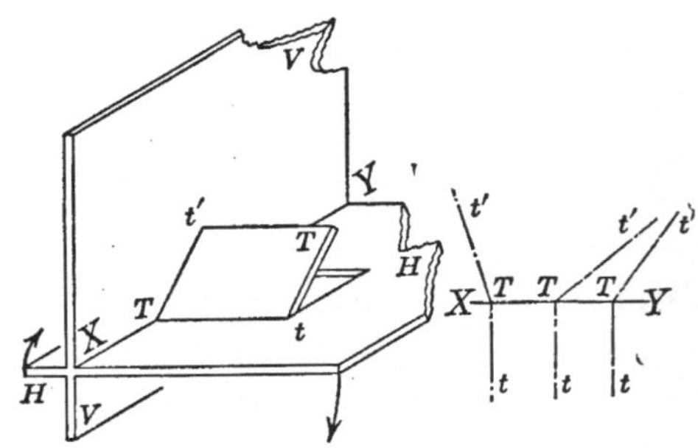

FIG. 74.

pendicular to the horizontal plane (floor of the room). The intersection with the vertical plane is perpendicular to the horizontal plane because it is the intersection of two planes (the given plane and the vertical plane), each of which is perpendicular to the horizontal. As a consequence the vertical trace is perpendicular to the ground line, because, when a line is perpendicular to a plane it is perpendicular to every line through its foot (from geometry). The orthographic representation of three distinct planes is shown on the right; the cases selected all show **Tt′** perpendicular to the ground line.

What is true regarding planes perpendicular to the horizontal plane is equally true for planes similarly related with respect to the vertical plane. Fig. 74 gives an illustration of such a case. Here, the horizontal trace is perpendicular to the ground line but the vertical trace may make any angle, at will, with the ground line.

**604. Traces of planes perpendicular to both principal planes.** When a plane is perpendicular to both principal planes,

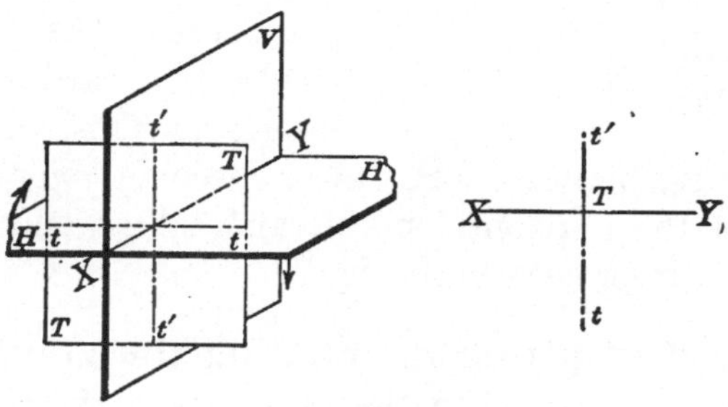


FIG. 75.

its two traces are perpendicular to the ground line. Such a plane is a **profile plane** and is shown in Fig. 75.

**605. Traces of planes inclined to both principal planes.** It may be inferred from the preceding, that, if the plane is

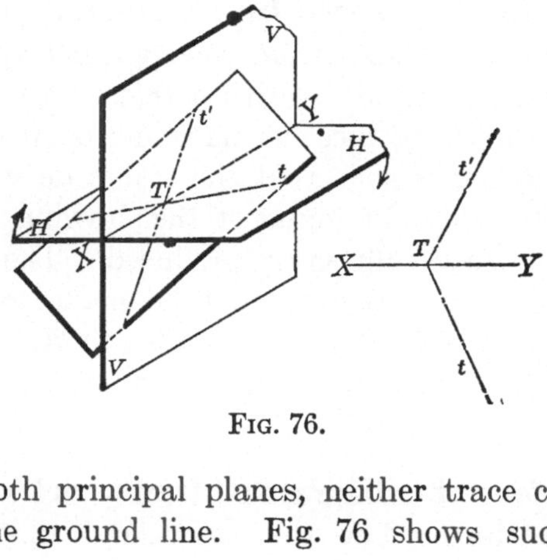


FIG. 76.

inclined to both principal planes, neither trace can be perpendicular to the ground line. Fig. 76 shows such a case, the orthographic representation of which in projection is shown on the right.

Fig. 77 shows two cards, each slit half way, as indicated. These can be fitted together to represent the principal planes. If at any point, a and a′, on **XY** slits **tt** and **t′t′** be made, it will be found on assembling the cards that a third card can be inserted.

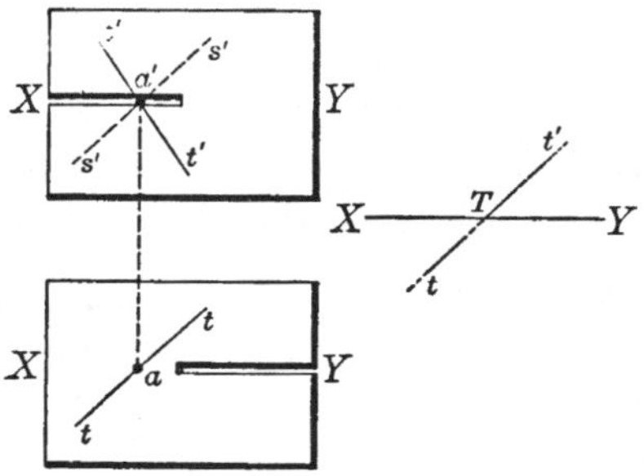


FIG. 77.

In the upper card, another slit **s′s′** may be made, through the point a′, with its direction parallel to **tt**. As in the previous instance, a card can again be inserted. This case is of interest, however, because both traces become coincident on the revolution of the horizontal plane, and fall as one straight line **tTt′**, as shown in projection in Fig. 77.

**606. Traces of planes intersecting the ground line.** It must have been observed in the cases where the given plane is inclined to the ground line that both traces pass through the same point on the ground line. This becomes further evident when it is considered that the ground line can intersect a plane at but one point, if at all. This one point lies in the ground line, and, hence, it has coincident projections (509).

**607. Plane fixed in space by its traces.** Two intersecting lines determine a plane (from solid geometry). Hence, the two traces of a plane fix a plane with reference to the principal planes because the traces meet at the same point on the ground line. If the diagram is such that the traces do not intersect in the ground line within the limits of the drawing, it is assumed that they will do so if sufficiently produced. The limiting position of a plane whose traces cannot be made to intersect the ground line is evidently a plane parallel to it. This plane is then parallel to the ground line and its traces must also be parallel to it (602).

**608. Transfer of diagrams from orthographic to oblique projection.** Let the right-hand diagram of Fig.

78 represent a plane in orthographic projection. Through any point **S**, on the ground line, pass a profile plane **sSs′**, intersecting the two traces **tT** and **Tt′** at points **o** and **p**. To transfer the orthographic to the oblique projection, lay off the principal planes **HH** and **VV** as shown, intersecting in the ground line

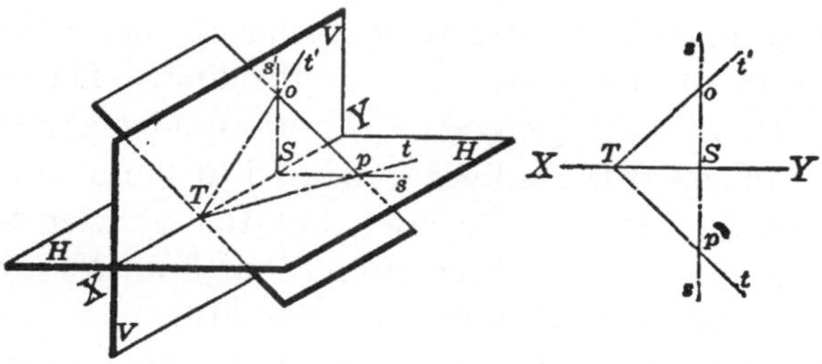


FIG. 78.

**XY**. Lay off any point **S** on the ground line in the oblique projection and then make **So** and **Sp** of the orthographic equal to the similarly lettered lines in the oblique projection. The profile plane **sSs′** is therefore determined in the oblique projection. Make **TS** of one diagram equal to the **TS** of the other, and com-

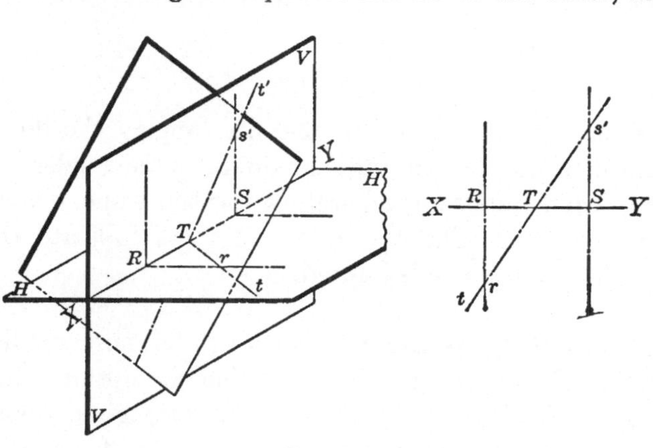


FIG. 79.

plete by drawing the traces through **T**, o and **T, p**. To increase the clarity of the diagram, a rectangular plane may be shown as though it passes through the principal planes. Fig. 78 has this plane added.

A case where the two traces are coincident is shown in Fig. 79. Two profile planes are required, but only one trace of each is needed. All the necessary construction lines are shown in this diagram.

**609. Traces of planes in all angles.** As planes are indefinite in extent, so are their traces; and, therefore, the traces are not limited to any one angle. In the discussion of most problems, it may be possible to choose the principal planes so as to limit the discussion to one angle—usually the first. The advantage to be gained thereby is the greater clarity of the diagram, as then the number of construction lines is reduced to a minimum. Third angle projection may also be used, but the transfer to oblique projection is undesirable. Second and fourth angles are avoided because the projections overlap (317, 514, 516).

Fig. 80 shows the complete traces of a given plane T. The

Fig. 80.

Fig. 81.

full lines indicate the traces in the first angle; the dotted lines show the continuation in the remaining three angles. Fig. 81 represents each quadrant separately for the same plane that is shown in Fig. 80. The appended numbers indicate the angle to which the given plane is limited.

**610. Projecting plane of lines.** It is now evident that the finding of the projection of a line is nothing more nor less than the finding of the trace of its projecting plane. The two perpendiculars from a line to the plane of projection are necessarily parallel and therefore determine a plane. This plane is the projecting plane of the line and its intersection (or trace) with the plane of projection contains the projection of the line.

Manifestly, any number of lines contained in this projecting plane would have the same projection on any one of the principal planes, and that projection therefore does not fix the line in space.

If the projection on the corresponding plane of projection be taken **into** consideration, the projecting planes will intersect, and this

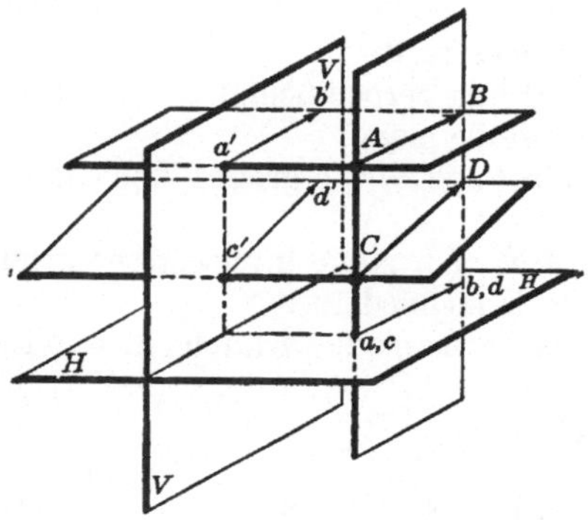


FIG. 82.

intersection will be the given line in space. Fig. 82 illustrates the point in question.

## QUESTIONS ON CHAPTER VI

1. What is the trace of a plane?
2. Draw a plane parallel to the vertical plane passing through the first and fourth angles, and show the resulting trace. Make diagram in oblique and orthographic projection.
3. Take the same plane of Question 2 and show it passing through the second and third angles.
4. Show how a plane is represented when it is parallel to the horizontal plane and passes through the first and second angles. Make diagram in oblique and orthographic projection.
5. Take the same plane of Question 4 and show the trace of the plane when it passes through the third and fourth angles.
6. Show how a plane is represented when it is parallel to the ground line and passes through the first angle.
7. How is a plane represented when it is parallel to the ground line and passes through the second angle? Third angle? Fourth Angle?
8. Show how a plane passing through the ground line is indeterminate in orthographic projection.
9. When a plane passes through the ground line show how the profile plane might be used to advantage in representing the plane.
10. When a plane passes through the ground line, show how an auxiliary principal plane may be used to obtain determinate traces.
11. When a plane is perpendicular to the horizontal plane and inclined to the vertical plane, show how this is represented orthographically. Make, also, the oblique projection of it.

12. When a plane is perpendicular to the vertical plane and inclined to the horizontal plane show how this is represented orthographically. Make, also, the oblique projection of it.
13. When a plane is perpendicular to both principal planes draw the orthographic traces of it.
14. Why is the ground line perpendicular to both traces in Question 13? Is this plane a profile plane?
15. When a plane is inclined to the ground line show how the traces are represented.
16. Why do both traces of a plane intersect the ground line at a point when the plane is inclined to it?
17. Why do the traces fix the plane with reference to the principal planes?

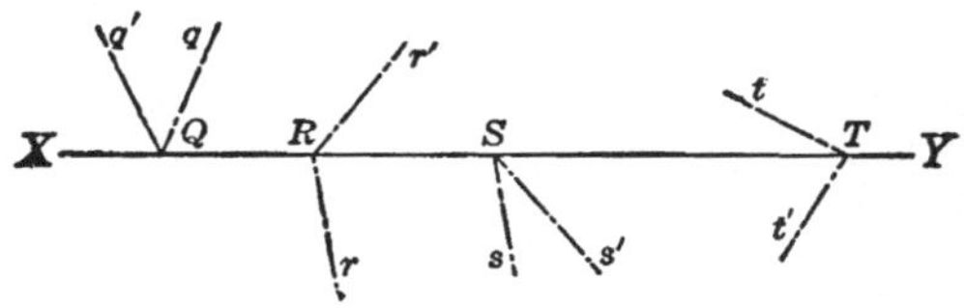


FIG. 6–A.

18. When a plane is parallel to the ground line, why are the traces of the plane parallel to it?
19. Show an oblique plane in all four angles of projection (use only the limited portion in one angle and use the same plane as in the illustration).
20. In what angles are the planes whose traces are shown in Fig. 6–A?

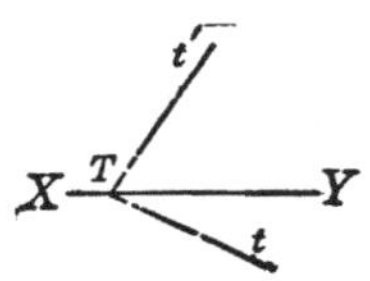


FIG. 6–B.

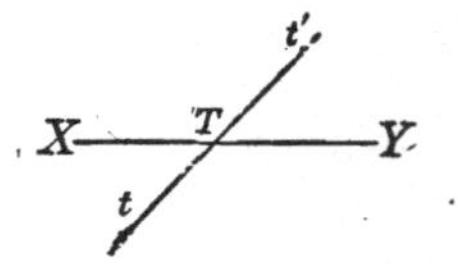


FIG. 6–C.

21. Show how a line in space and its projecting perpendiculars determine a plane which is the projecting plane of the line. Is the projection of the line the trace of the projecting plane of the line?
22. Is it possible to have two separate hnes whose projections are coincident on one plane? How are such lines determined?
23. Given the traces of a plane in orthographic projection as shown in Fig. 6–B construct the oblique projection of it.
24. Construct the oblique projection of a plane having coincident projections (Fig. 6–C).

# CHAPTER VII

## ELEMENTARY CONSIDERATIONS OF LINES AND PLANES

**701. Projection of lines parallel in space.** When two lines in space are parallel, their projecting planes are parallel, and their intersection with any third plane will result in parallel lines. If this third plane be a plane of projection, then the traces of the two projecting planes will result in parallel projections.

Fig. 83 shows two lines, **AB** and **CD** in space. The lines are

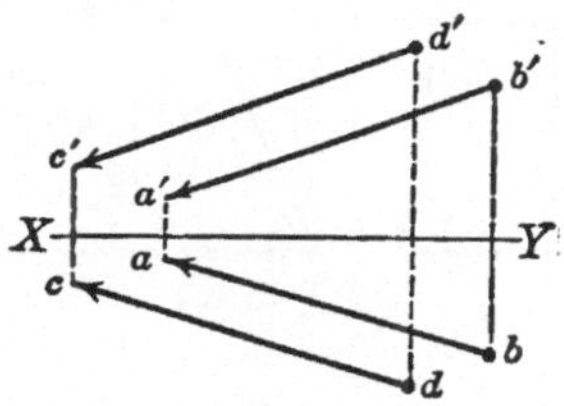


FIG. 83.

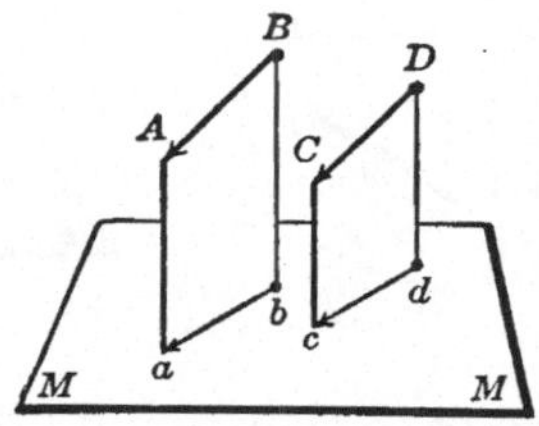


FIG. 84.

shown by their horizontal projections **ab** and **cd**, which are parallel to each other, and by their vertical projections **a′b′** and **c′d′**, which are also parallel to each other. A perfectly general case is represented pictorially on a single plane of projection in Fig. 84.

**702. Projection of lines intersecting in space.** If two lines in space intersect, their projections intersect, because the two lines in space must meet in a point. Further, the projection of this point must be common to the projections of the lines.

In Fig. 85 two such lines, **AB** and **CB** are shown, represented, as usual, by their projections. **O** is the intersection in space, indicated by its horizontal and vertical projections o and **o′**,

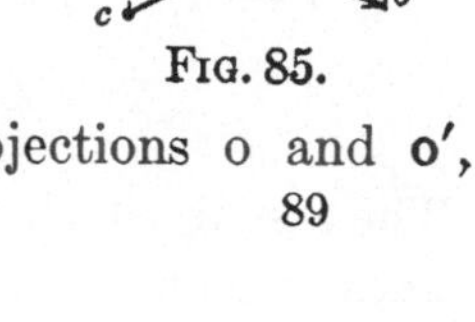


FIG. 85.

respectively. **EF** and **GH** (Fig. 86) are two other lines, chosen to show how in the horizontal plane of projection, the two projections may coincide, because the plane of the two lines happens also to be the horizontal projecting plane. The case is not indeterminate, however, as the vertical projection locates the point **M** in space. The reverse of this is also true, that is, the vertical

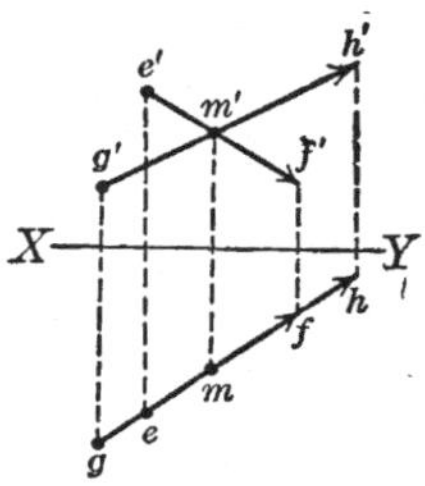


FIG. 86.

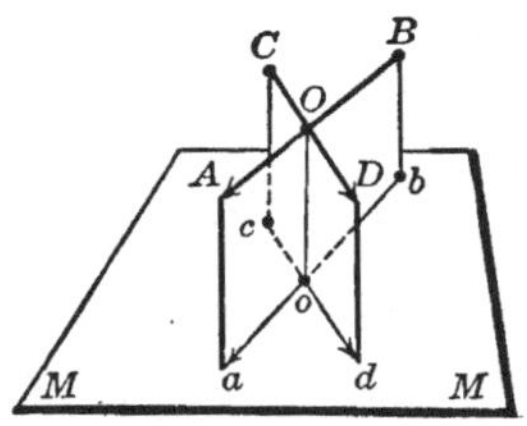


FIG. 87.

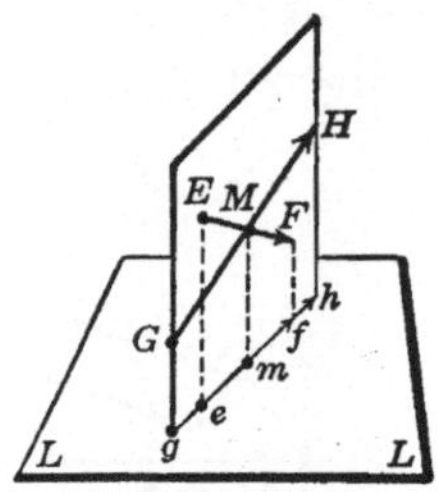


FIG. 88.

instead of the horizontal projections may be coincident. General cases of the above are represented pictorially in Figs. 87 and 88.

Should the horizontal and the vertical projections be coincident, the lines do not intersect but are themselves coincident in space and thus form only one line.

**703. Projection of lines not intersecting in space.*** There are two possible cases of lines that do not intersect in space.

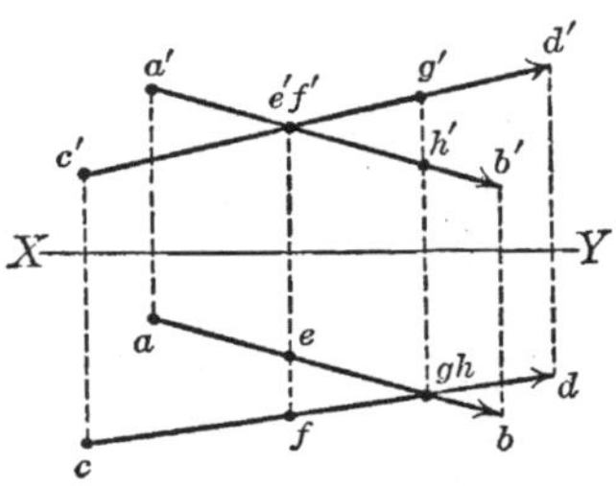


FIG. 89.

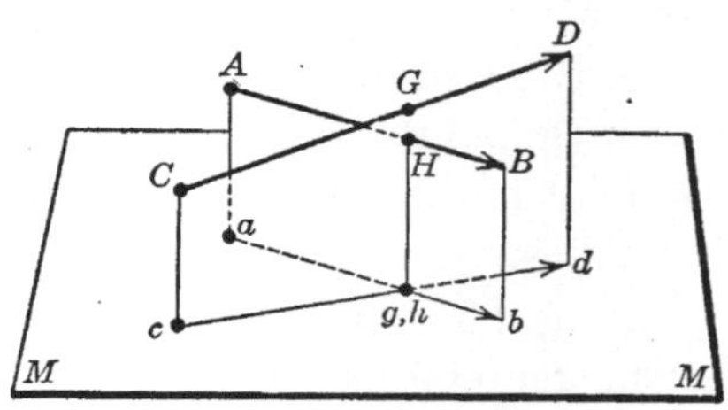


FIG. 90.

The case in which the lines are parallel to each other has previously been discussed (701). If the two lines cannot be made to lie in the same plane, they will pass each other without intersecting. Hence, if in one plane of projection, the projections intersect, they cannot do so in the corresponding projection.

This fact is depicted in Fig. 89. **AB** and **CD** are the two

* Called skew lines.

lines in space. Two distinct points **E** and F, on the lines are shown in the horizontal projection as **e** and f; their vertical projections are, however, coincident. Similarly, **G** and **H** are also two distinct points on the lines, shown as **g′** and **h′** in the vertical projection, and coincident, as **g** and **h** in the horizontal projection. The pictorial representation is given in Fig. 90.

**704. Projection of lines in oblique planes.** When a third plane is inclined to the principal planes, it cuts them in lines of intersection, known as traces (601). Any line, when inclined to the principal planes will pierce them in a point. Hence, if a plane is to contain a given line, the piercing points of the line must lie in the traces of the plane. Viewing this in another way, a plane may be passed through two parallel or two intersecting lines. On the resulting plane, any number of lines may be drawn, intersecting the given pair. Hence, an inclined line must pass through the trace, if it is contained in the plane.*

Fig. 91 shows a plane **tTt′** indicated by its horizontal trace **tT** and its vertical trace **Tt′**. It is required to draw a line **AB** in this plane. Suppose the horizontal piercing point is assumed at **b**, its corresponding vertical projection will lie in the ground line (509). Also, if its vertical piercing point is assumed at **a′**, its corresponding horizontal projection will be **a**. With two horizontal projections of given points on a line and two vertical projections, the direction of the line is determined, for, if the horizontal and vertical projecting planes be erected, their intersection determines the given line (610).†

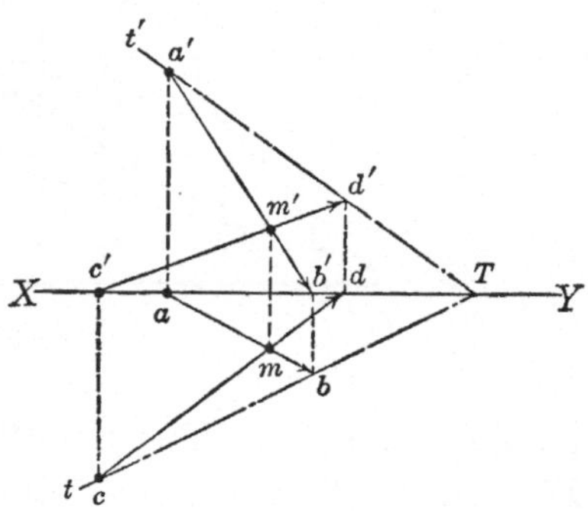

FIG. 91.

As a check on the correctness of the above, another line **CD** may be assumed. If the two lines lie in the same plane and are not parallel, they must intersect. This point of intersection

* When the plane is parallel to the ground line, a line in this plane parallel to the principal planes cannot pierce in the traces of the plane. See Art. 602.

† It must be remembered that the principal planes must be at right angles to each other to determine this intersection. In the revolved position, the planes would not intersect in the required line.

is **M** shown horizontally projected at **m** and vertically, at **m′**. The line joining the two is perpendicular to the ground line (508). This is illustrated in oblique projection in Fig. 92.

It should be here noted that if the line is to be contained by the plane, only the direction of one projection can be assumed, and that the corresponding projection must be found by the principles so far developed.

A converse of this problem is to draw a plane so that it shall contain a given line. As an unlimited number of planes can be passed through any given line, the direction of the traces is not fixed. Suppose **AB** (Fig. 91) is the given line, then through the horizontal piercing point **b** draw any trace **tT**, and from **T** where this line intersects the ground line, draw **Tt′**, through the vertical

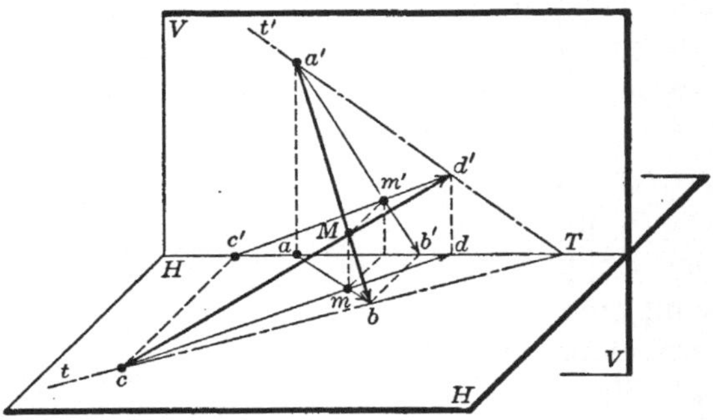


FIG. 92.

piercing point a′. The point T may be located anywhere along **XY**. All of these planes will contain the line **AB**, if their traces pass through the piercing points of the line.

Still another feature of Fig. 91 is the fact that from it can be proved that two intersecting lines determine a plane. If **AB** and **CD** be the two lines intersecting at **M**, their horizontal piercing points are **b** and **c** and their vertical piercing points are **a′** and **d′** respectively. Two points fix the direction of a line, and, hence, the direction of the traces is fixed; **tT** is drawn through **cb** and **Tt′** is drawn through **a′d′**. The check lies in the fact that both traces intersect at one point **T** on the ground line (606).

**705. Projection of lines parallel to the principal planes and lying in an oblique plane.** If a line is horizontal, it is parallel to the horizontal plane, and its vertical projection must be parallel to the ground line (511). If this line lies in an oblique plane, it can have only one piercing point and that with the vertical plane, since it is parallel to the horizontal. Thus, in Fig. 93, let **tTt′** be the given oblique plane, represented, of course, by its traces. The given line is **AB** and **a′b′** is its vertical projection, the piercing point being at a′. The corresponding horizontal projection of **a′** is **a**. When a line is horizontal, as in this case, it may be considered as being cut from the plane **tTt** by a horizontal plane, and, as such, must be parallel to the principal horizontal plane. These two parallel horizontal planes are cut by the given oblique plane **tTt′** and, from geometry, their lines of intersection are parallel. Hence, the horizontal projection

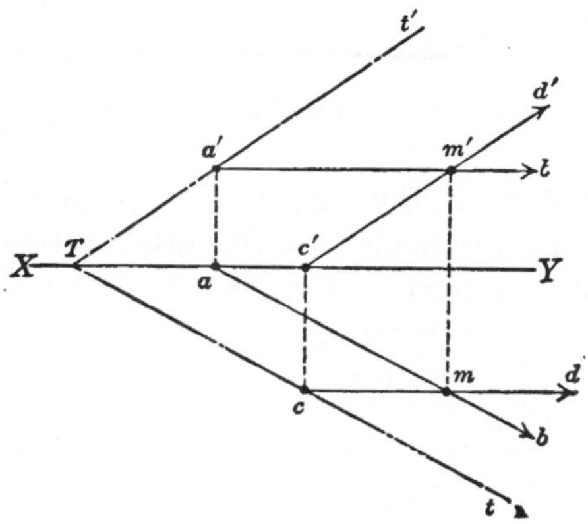


FIG. 93.

of the horizontal line must be parallel to the horizontal trace, of the given plane because parallel lines in space have parallel projections. Accordingly, from **a**, draw **ab**, parallel to **Tt**, and the horizontal line **AB** is thus shown by its projections.

A line, parallel to the vertical plane, drawn in an oblique plane follows the same analysis, and differs only in an interchange of the operation. That is to say, the horizontal projection is then parallel to the ground line and pierces in a point on the horizontal trace of the given plane; its vertical projection must be parallel to the vertical trace of the given plane. In Fig. 93, **CD** is a line parallel to the vertical plane and **cd** is the horizontal projection, piercing the horizontal plane at c vertically projected at **c′**; **c′d′** is, therefore, the required vertical projection.

A check on the problem lies in the fact that these two lines must intersect because they lie in the same plane by hypothesis. The point of intersection **M** is shown as **m** in the horizontal

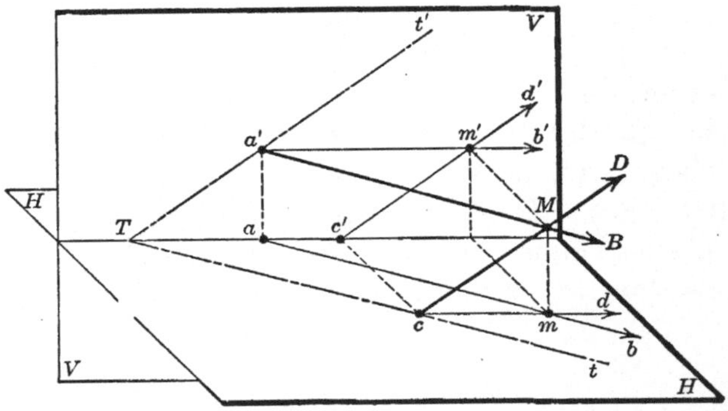


FIG. 94.

projection, and as **m′** in the vertical projection. The line joining these points is perpendicular to the ground line. The oblique projection of this is shown in Fig. 94.

Fig. 95 is a still further step in this problem. Three lines

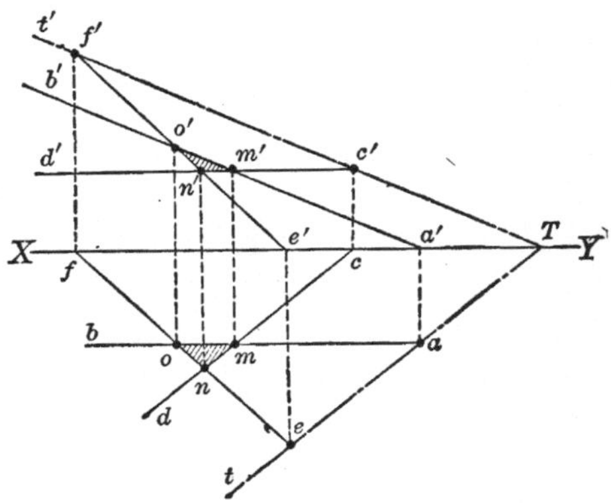


FIG. 95.

**AB, CD,** and **EF** are shown, all being in the plane **tTt′**. **AB** is parallel to the vertical plane, **CD** is parallel to the horizontal plane and **EF** is any other line. It will be observed that the three lines intersect so as to form a triangle **MNO** shown by having the area shaded in both its projections.

**706. Projections of lines perpendicular to given planes.** If a line is perpendicular to a given plane, the projections of the line are perpendicular to the corresponding traces of the plane.

Let, in Fig. 96, **LL** be any plane and **MM** any other plane intersecting it in the trace **tr.** Also, let **AB** be any line, perpendicular to **MM**, and **ab** be the projection of **AB** on **LL.** It is desired to show that the projection **ab** is perpendicular to the trace **tr.** Any plane through **AB** is perpendicular to the plane **MM**, because it contains a line perpendicular to the plane by hypothesis. Also, any plane through **Bb**, a perpendicular to the plane **LL**, is perpendicular to **LL.** Hence, any plane containing both lines (it can do so because they intersect at **B**) will be perpendicular both to **LL** and **MM.** As the plane through **ABb** is perpendicular to the two planes **LL** and **MM**, it is also perpendicular to a line common to the two planes, such as **tr.** Thus, **ab** is perpendicular to **tr.** In fact, any line perpendicular to a plane will have its projection on any other plane perpendicular to the trace of the plane, because, instead of **LL** being assumed as the plane of projection and **BA** a perpendicular to another plane **MM**, the conditions may be reversed and **MM** be assumed as the plane of projection and **Bb** the perpendicular.

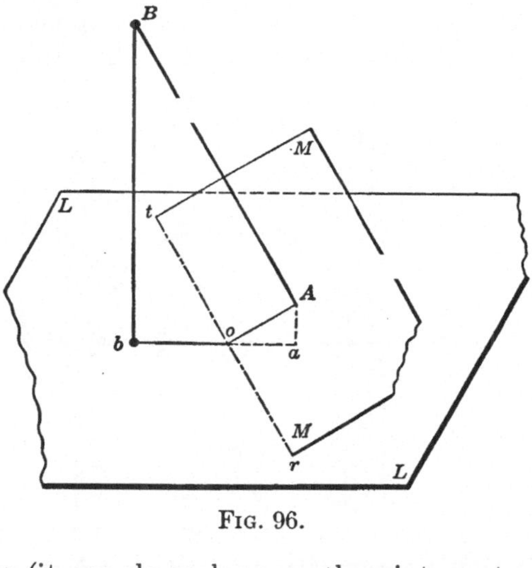


FIG. 96.

The converse of this is also true. If **Ao** be assumed the projection of **Bb** on **MM**, a plane passed through the line **Ao** perpendicular to the trace **tr** will contain the lines **AB** and **Bb**, where

**Bb** is the given line and **AB** then the projecting perpendicular to the plane **MM.**

**707. Revolution of a point about a line.** Frequently it is desirable to know the relation of a point with respect to a line, for, if the line and point are given by their projections, the true relation may not be apparent. To do this, revolve the point about the line so that a plane through the point and the line will either coincide or be parallel to the plane of projection, then they will be projected in their true relation to each other. The actual distance between the point and the line is then shown as the perpendicular distance from the point to the line.

Consider the diagram in Fig. 97* and assume that the point **A** is to be revolved about the point **B.** The projection of **A** on

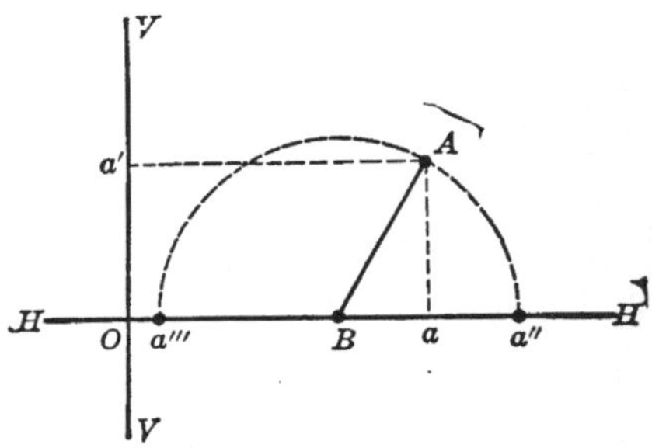


FIG. 97.

the line **Oa″** is **a** and, to an observer looking down from above the line **Oa″**, the apparent distance between **A** and **B** is **aB. Oa′** is the apparent distance of **A** from **B** to an observer, looking orthographically, from the right at a plane perpendicular to the plane of the paper through **Oa′.** Neither projection gives the true relation between **A** and **B** from a single projection. If the point **A** is revolved about **B** as an axis, with **BA** as a radius, until it coincides with the line **Oa″**, **A** will either be found at **a″** or at **a‴**, depending upon the direction of rotation. During the revolution, **A** always remains in the plane of the paper and describes a circle, the plane of which is perpendicular to the axis, through **B**, the centre of the circle.

* This diagram is a profile plane of the given point and of the principal planes.

A more general case is shown in Fig. 98 where **BB** is an axis lying in a plane, and **A** is any point in space not in the plane containing **BB.** If **A** be revolved about **BB** as an axis, it will describe a circle, the plane of which will be perpendicular to the axis. In other words, **A** will fall somewhere on a line Ba″ perpendicular to **BB.** The line **Ba″** must be perpendicular to **BB** because it is the trace of a perpendicular plane (706). This point is **a″** and **Ba″** is equal to the radius **BA.** Contrast this

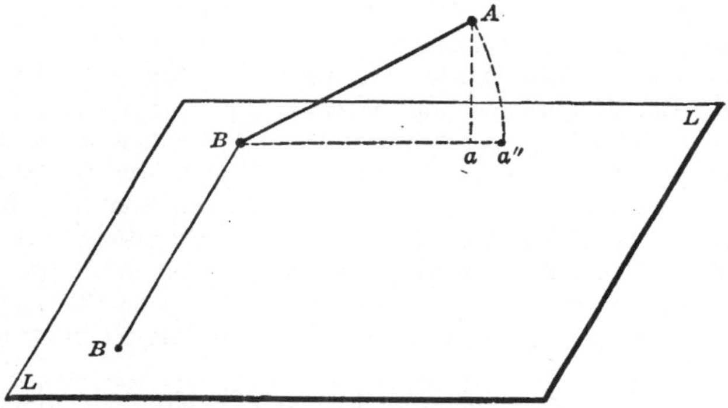


FIG. 98.

with **a,** the orthographic projection of **A** on the plane containing **BB.** Evidently, then, **a** is at a lesser distance from **BB** than **a″.** Indeed, **BA** equals **Ba″** and is equal to the hypothenuse of a right triangle, whose base is the perpendicular distance of the projection of the point from the axis, and whose altitude is the distance of the point above the plane containing the line. The angle **AaB** is a right angle, because **a** is the orthographic projection of **A.**

## QUESTIONS ON CHAPTER VII

1. If two lines in space are parallel, prove that their projections on any plane are parallel.
2. When two lines in space intersect, prove that their projections, on any plane, intersect.
3. Draw two lines in space that are not parallel and still do not intersect.
4. Show a case of two non-intersecting lines whose horizontal projections are parallel to each other and whose vertical projections intersect. Show also, that the horizontal projecting planes of these lines are parallel.

5. Make an oblique projection of the lines considered in Question 4.
6. Prove that when a line lies in a plane it must pass through the traces of the plane.
7. Given one projection of a line in a plane, find the corresponding projection.
8. Given a plane, draw intersecting lines in the plane and show by the construction that the point of intersection satisfies the orthographic representation of a point.
9. Show how two intersecting lines determine a plane by aid of an oblique projection.
10. In a given oblique plane, draw a line parallel to the horizontal plane and show by the construction that this line pierces the vertical plane only. Give reasons for the construction.
11. In Question 9, draw another line parallel to the vertical plane and show that this second line intersects the first in a point.
12. Given an oblique plane, draw three lines; one parallel to the horizontal plane, one parallel to the vertical plane and the last inclined to both planes. Show, by the construction, that the three lines form a triangle (or meet in a point in an exceptional case).
13. Prove that when a line is perpendicular to a plane the projection of this line on any other plane is perpendicular to the trace of the plane. Show the general case and also an example in orthographic projection.
14. A line lies in a given plane and a point is situated outside of the plane. Show how the point is revolved about the line until it is contained in the plane.
15. Prove that the point, while revolving about the line, describes a circle the plane of which is perpendicular to the axis (the line about which it revolves).

# CHAPTER VIII

## PROBLEMS INVOLVING THE POINT, THE LINE, AND THE PLANE

**801. Introductory.** A thorough knowledge of the preceding three chapters is necessary in order to apply the principles, there developed, in the solution of certain problems. The commercial application of these problems frequently calls for extended knowledge in special fields of engineering, and for this reason, the application, in general, has been avoided.

Countless problems of a commercial nature may be used as illustrations. All of these indicate, in various ways, the importance of the subject. In general, the commercial problem may always be reduced to one containing the mathematical essentials (reduced to points, lines and planes). The solution, then, may be accomplished by the methods to be shown subsequently.

**802. Solution of problems.** In the solution of the following problems, three distinct steps may be noted: the **statement,** the **analysis,** and the **construction.**

The **statement** of the problem gives a clear account of what is to be done and includes the necessary data.

The **analysis** entails a review of the principles involved, and proceeds, logically, from the given data to the required conclusion. On completion of the analysis, the problem is solved to all intents and purposes.

The **construction** is the graphical presentation of the analysis. It is by means of a drawing and its description that the given data is associated with its solution. It may be emphasized again that the drawings are made **orthographically,** and that the actual points, lines and planes are to be imagined.

By a slight change in the assumed data, the resultant construction may appear widely different from the diagrams in the book. Here, then, is an opportunity to make several constructions for the several assumptions, and to prove that all follow the general analysis. The simpler constructions might be taken and transformed from orthographic to oblique projection; this will show the projections as well as the actual points, lines and planes in space. By performing this transformation (from orthographic to oblique projection), the student will soon be able to picture the entire problem in space, without recourse to any diagrams.

To bring forcibly to the student's attention the difference between the analysis and the construction, it may be well to note that the analysis gives the reasoning in its most general terms, while the construction is specific, in so far as it takes the assumed data and gives the solution for that particular case only.

**803. Problem 1. To draw a line through a given point, parallel to a given line.**

**Analysis.** If two lines in space are parallel, their projecting planes are parallel and their intersection with the principal planes are parallel (701). Hence, through the projections of the given point, draw lines parallel to the projections of the given lines.

**Construction.** Let **AB,** Fig. 99, be the given line in space, represented by its horizontal projection **ab** and its vertical projection **a′b′.** Further, let **G** be the given point, similarly represented by its horizontal projection **g** and its vertical projection **g′.** Through the horizontal projection **g,** draw **cd** parallel to **ab** and through **g′,** draw **c′d′** parallel to **a′b′.**

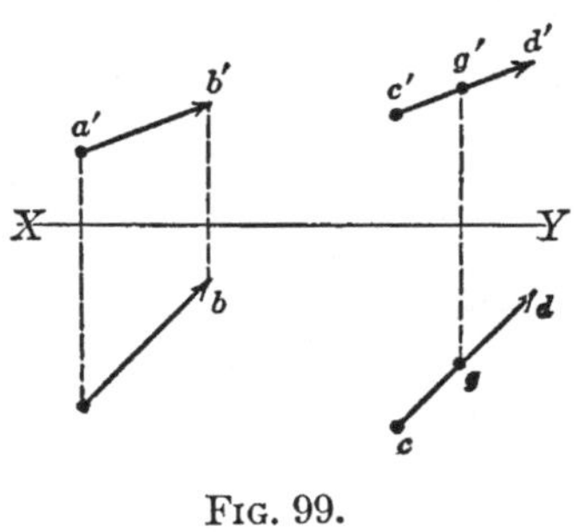


Fig. 99.

As the length of the line is not specified, any line that satisfies the condition of parallelism is permissible. Therefore, **CD** is the line in space that is parallel to **AB** through the point **G.** A pictorial representation of this is shown in Fig. 84.

**804. Problem 2. To draw a line intersecting a given line at a given point.**

**Analysis.** If two lines in space intersect, they intersect in a point that is common to the two lines. Therefore, their projecting planes will intersect in a line which is the projecting line of the given point (702). Hence, through the projections of the given point, draw any lines, intersecting the projections of the given lines.

**Construction.** Let **AB,** Fig. 100, be the given line, shown horizontally projected as **ab** and vertically projected as **a′b′**. Let, also, G be the given point, situated on the line **AB.** As no direction is specified for the intersecting line, draw any line **cd** through the horizontal projection **g** and this will be the horizontal projection of the required line. Similarly, any other line **c′d′** through **g′** will be the vertical projection of the required line. Hence, **CD** and **AB** are two lines in space, intersecting at the point **G.** The pictorial representation of this case is depicted in Figs. 87 and 88.

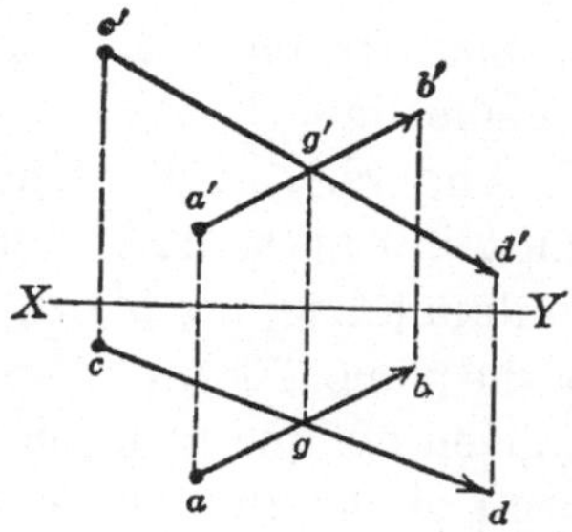


Fig. 100.

**805. Problem 3. To find where a given line pierces the principal planes.**

**Analysis.** If a line is oblique to the principal planes, it will pierce each of these in a point, the corresponding projection of which will be in the ground line. Hence, a piercing point in any principal plane must be on the projection of the line in that plane. It must also be on a perpendicular erected at the point where the corresponding projection crosses the ground line. Therefore, the required piercing point is at their intersection.

**Construction.** Let **AB,** Fig. 101, be a limited portion of an indefinite line, shown by its horizontal projection **ab** and its vertical projection **a′b′**. The portion chosen **AB** will not pierce the principal planes, but its continuation, in both directions, will. Prolong the vertical projection **a′b′** to **c′** and at c′, erect a perpendicular to **XY,** the ground line, and continue it, until it intersects the prolongation of ab at c. This will be the horizontal piercing point. In the same way, prolong **ab** to **d,** at **d,** erect a perpendicular to the ground line as **dd′,** the intersection of which with the prolongation of **a′b′,** at **d′** will give the vertical piercing point. Hence,

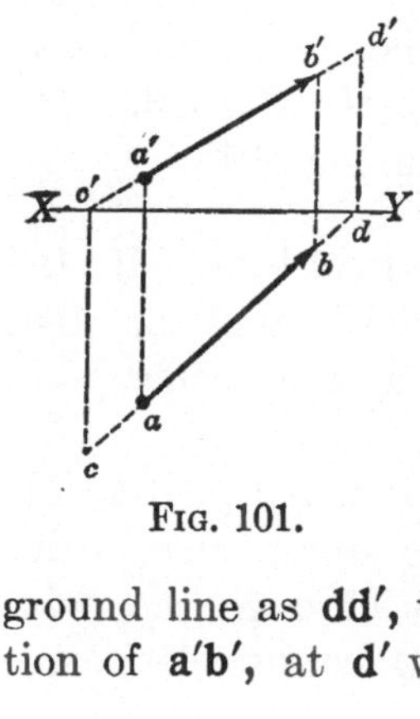


Fig. 101.

if **CD** be considered as the line, it will pierce the horizontal plane of projection at c and the vertical plane of projection at **d′**. A pictorial representation in oblique projection is shown in Fig. 52.

**806. Problem 4.** To **pass an** oblique **plane, through a given** oblique line.

**Analysis.** If a plane is oblique to the principal planes, it must intersect the ground line at a point (606); and if it is to contain a line, the piercing points of the line must lie in the traces of the plane (704). Therefore, to draw an oblique plane containing a given oblique line, join the piercing points of the line with any point of the ground line and the resulting lines will be the traces of the required plane.

**Construction.** Let **AB,** Fig. 102, be the given line. This

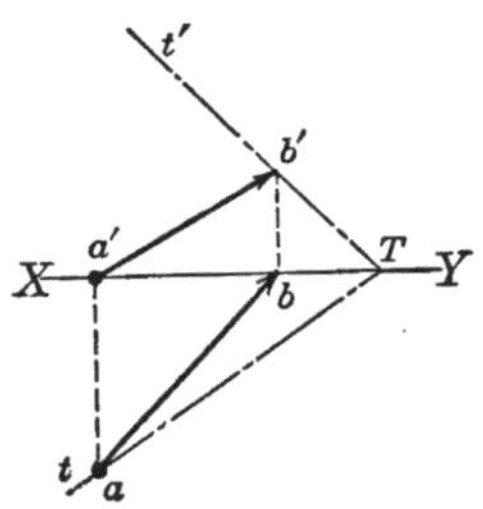


FIG. 102.

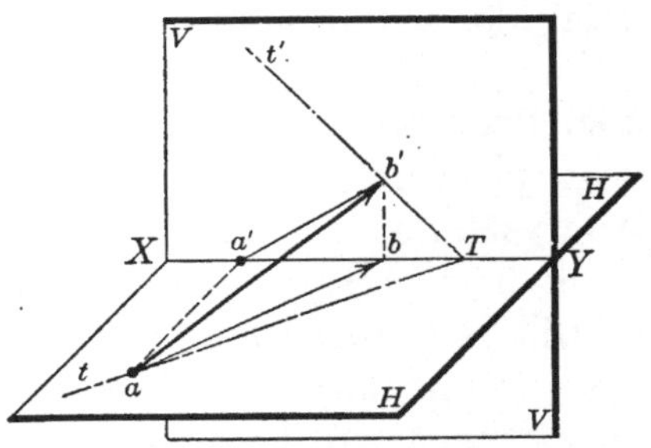


FIG. 103.

line pierces the horizontal plane at **a** and the vertical plane at **b′**. Assume any point T on the ground line **XY,** and join T with a and also with b′. **Ta** and Tb′ are the required traces, indicated, as usual, by **tTt′**. Thus, the plane T contains the line **AB.** The construction in oblique projection is given in Fig. 103.

**807. Special cases of the preceding problem.** If the line is parallel to both planes of projection, the traces of the plane will be parallel to the ground line (602), and the profile plane may be advantageously used in the drawing.

If the line is parallel to only one of the principal planes, join the one piercing point with any point on the ground line, which results in one trace of the required plane. Through the point on the ground line, draw the corresponding trace, parallel to the projection of the line in the plane containing this trace. The case is evidently that considered in Art. 705.

**808. Problem 5.** To **pass an oblique plane, through a given point.**

**Analysis.** If the oblique plane is to contain a given point, it will also contain a line through the point. Hence, through the given point, draw an oblique line and find the piercing points of this line on the principal planes. Join these piercing points with the ground line and the result will be the required traces of the plane.

**Construction.** Let **C,** Fig. 104, be the required point, and let **AB** be a line drawn through this point. **AB** pierces the hori-

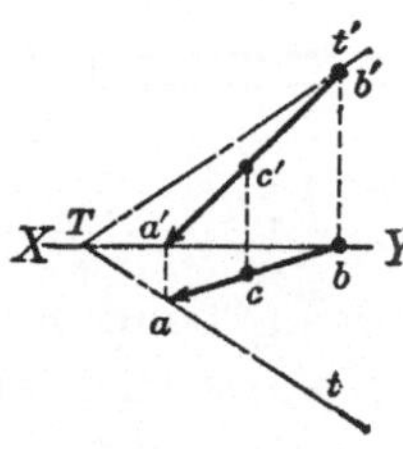


FIG. 104.

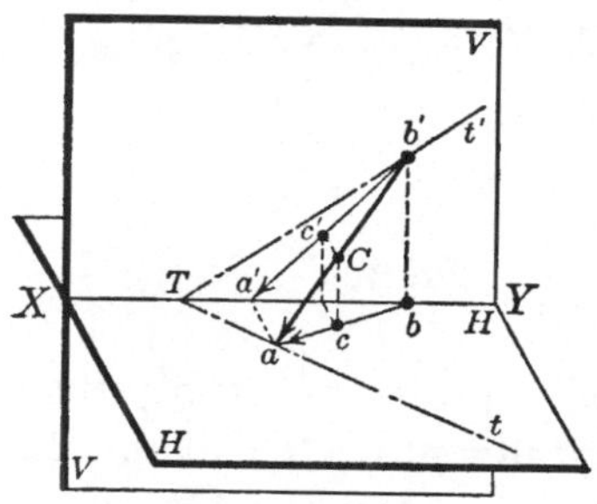


FIG. 105.

zontal plane at **a** and the vertical plane at **b′**. Join **a** and **b′** with any assumed point T and **tTt′** will be the required traces. The plane T, contains the point **C,** because it contains a line **AB** through the point **C.** Fig. 105 shows this pictorially.

NOTE. An infinite number of planes may be passed through the point, hence the point T was **assumed.** It might have been assumed on the opposite side of the point and would still have contained the given point, or the auxiliary line through the point.

Also, it is possible to draw a line through the given point parallel to the ground line. A profile construction will then be of service (602).

Again, a perpendicular line may be drawn through the given point and a plane be passed so that it is perpendicular to one or both planes of projection (603, 604).

**809. Problem 6. To find the intersection of two planes, oblique to each other and to the principal planes.**

**Analysis.** If two planes are oblique to each other, they intersect in a line. Any line in a plane must pass through the traces of the plane. As the line of intersection is common to the two planes, it must pass through the traces of both planes and hence it passes through the intersection of these traces.

**Construction.** Let T and S, Fig. 106, be the given planes. The horizontal piercing point of their line of intersection is at **b**, vertically projected at **b′**; the vertical piercing point is at a′, horizontally projected at **a.** Join ab and **a′b′**, as they are the projections of the line **AB**, which is the intersection of the planes T and **S.** In oblique projection, this appears as shown in Fig. 107.

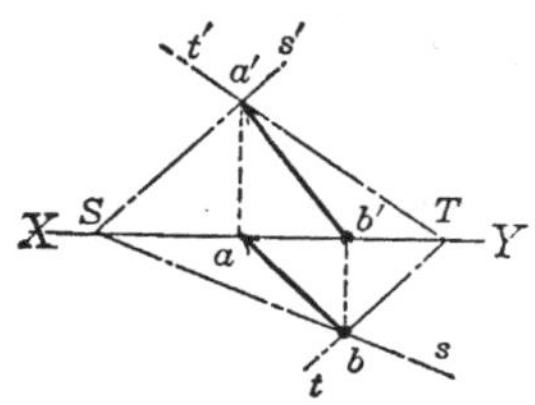


Fig. 106.

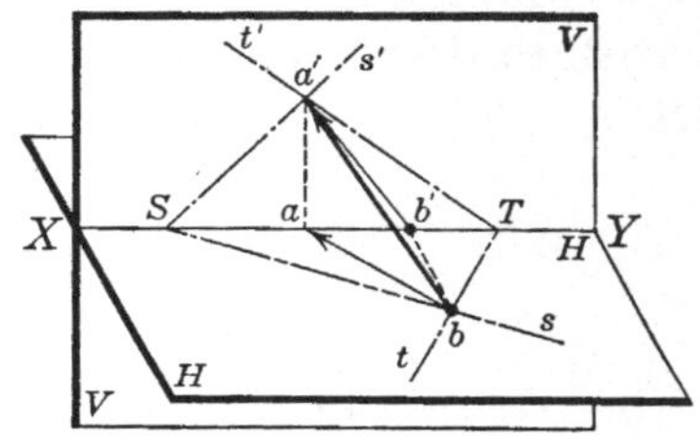


Fig. 107.

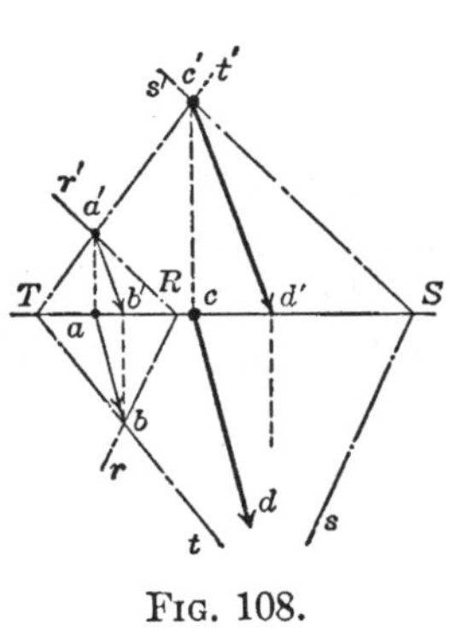


Fig. 108.

**810. Special case of the preceding problem.** If the two planes are chosen so that the traces in one plane do not intersect within the limits of the drawing, then draw an auxiliary plane **R** (Fig. 108) and find the intersection, **AB** as shown. From **c′** draw **c′d′**, parallel to **a′b′** and from c, draw **cd,** parallel to ab. The line of intersection of the given planes is thus determined.

**811. Problem 7. To find the corresponding projection of a given point lying in a given oblique plane, when one of its projections is given.**

**Analysis.** If a line lies in a given plane and also contains a given point, the projections of this line will also contain the projections of the given point. Hence, through the projection of the given point, draw the projection of a line lying in the given plane. Then find the corresponding projection of the line. The required projection of the given point will lie on the intersection of a perpendicular to the ground line, through the given projection of the point with the corresponding projection of the line.

**Construction.** Let **tTt′**, Fig. 109, be the traces of the given plane and c the horizontal projection of the given point. Draw **ab,** the horizontal projection of a line in the plane, through **c** the horizontal projection of the given point. The horizontal

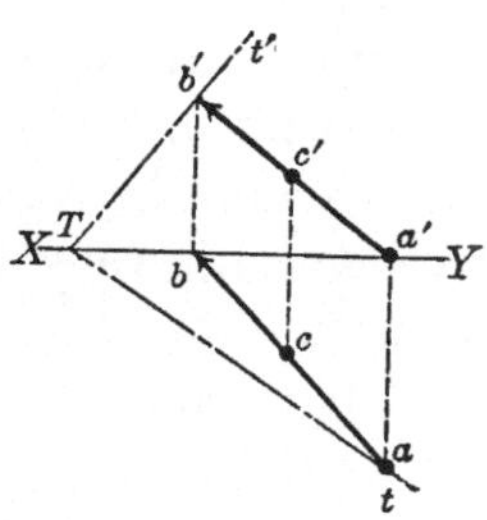

FIG. 109.

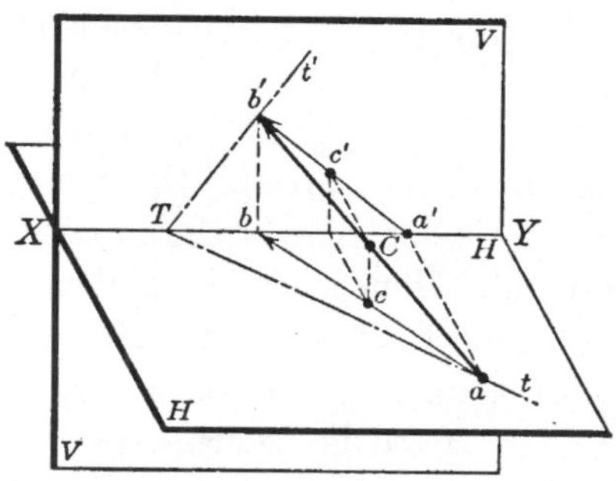

FIG. 110.

piercing point of the line **AB** is in the trace **Tt** at **a,** and its corresponding projection lies in the ground line at **a′**. Further, the vertical piercing point lies on a perpendicular to the ground line from the point b and also in the trace **Tt′**, hence, it is at **b′** and **a′b′** is thus the corresponding projection of the line **ab**. The required projection of the given point lies on a line through c, perpendicular to the ground line, and also on **a′b′**; hence, it is at their intersection c′. The point **C,** in space, is contained in the plane T, and c and c′, are corresponding projections. The oblique projection of this problem is given in Fig. 110.

**812. Special case of the preceding problem.** The point in the above problem was purposely chosen in the first angle, in order to obtain a simple case. It may be located anywhere, however, because the planes are indefinite in extent. For instance, in Fig. 111 the vertical projection is selected below the ground line. However, a single projection does not locate a point in space. It may be assumed as lying either in the third or fourth angles (515). Subsequent operations are dependent upon the angle in which the point is chosen. Assume, for instance, that the point is in the fourth angle; the traces of the given plane must then also be assumed as being in the fourth angle. Thus, with the given plane T, **Tt** is the horizontal trace, and **Tt‴** is the vertical trace (609). In completing the construction by the usual method, let **c′** be the assumed vertical projection, and through it, draw **a′b′** as the vertical projection of the assumed line through the given point and lying in the given plane. This line pierces the horizontal plane at **b** and the vertical plane at **a′**. Hence, **ab** and **a′b′** are the corresponding projections of the line **AB** in space which is situated in the fourth angle. The corresponding horizontal projection of c′ is c, and thus the point **C** in space is determined.

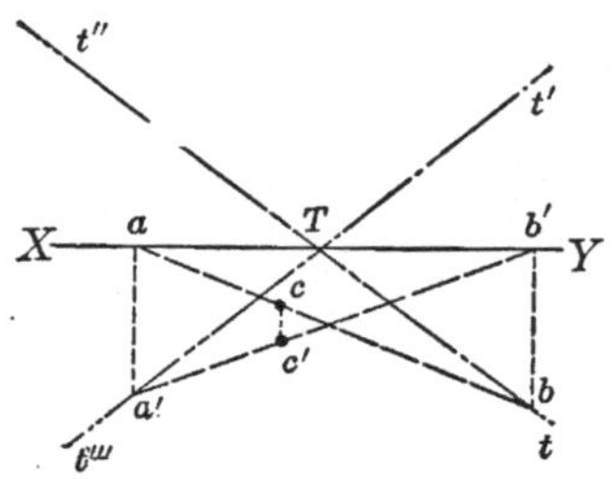


Fig. 111.

Had the point been assumed in the third angle, then the traces **Tt″** and **Tt‴** would have been the ones to use, **Tt″** being the horizontal, and **Tt‴** the vertical trace. The construction would then, in general, be the same as the previous.

**813. Problem 8.** To **draw a plane which contains a given point and is parallel to a given plane.**

**Analysis.** The traces of the required plane must be parallel to the traces of the given plane. A line may be drawn through the given point parallel to an assumed line in the given plane. This line will then pierce the principal planes in the traces of the required plane. Hence, in the given plane, draw any line. Through the given point, draw a line parallel to it, and find the piercing points of this line on the principal planes. Through these piercing points draw the traces of the required plane parallel to the corresponding traces of the given plane. The plane so drawn is parallel to the given plane.

**Construction.** Let T, Fig. 112 be the given plane, and **G**

the given point. In the plane T, draw any line **CD** as shown by **cd** and **c′d′** its horizontal and vertical projections respectively. Through **G**, draw **AB**, parallel to **CD** and **ab** and **a′b′** will be the projections of this line. The piercing points are **a** and **b′** on the horizontal and vertical planes respectively. Draw **b′S** parallel to **t′T** and **aS** parallel to **tT**, then **sSs′** will be the traces

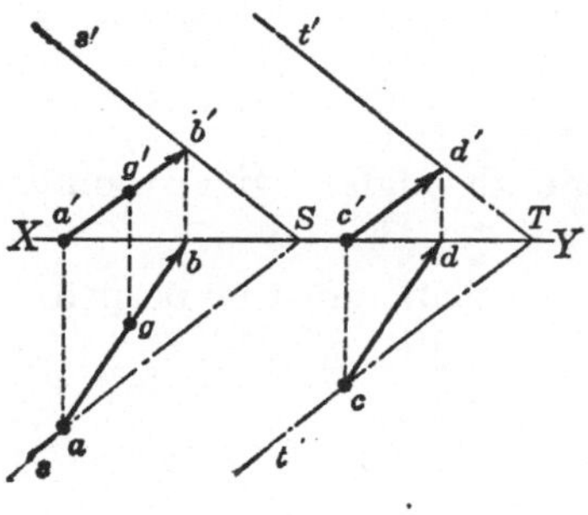


FIG. 112.

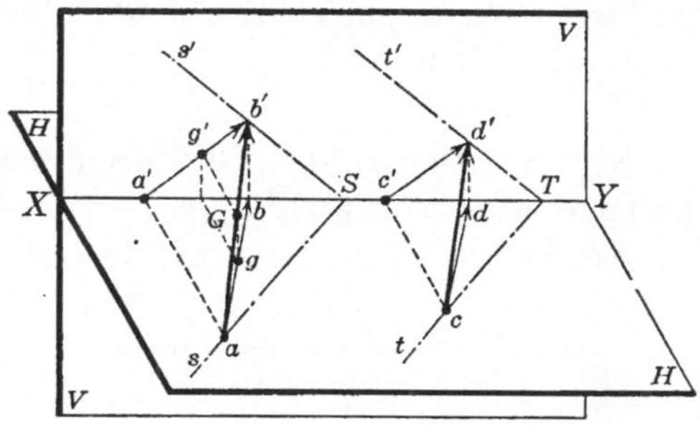


FIG. 113.

of the required plane, parallel to the plane T and containing a given point **G**. A check on the accuracy of the construction is furnished by having the two traces meet at **S**. Also, only one plane will satisfy these conditions because the point **S** cannot be selected at random. This construction is represented pictorially in Fig. 113.

**814. Problem 9.** To **draw a line perpendicular to a given plane through a given point.**

**Analysis.** If a line is perpendicular to a given plane the projections of the line are perpendicular to the corresponding traces of the plane. Hence, draw through each projection of the given point, a line perpendicular to the corresponding trace (706).

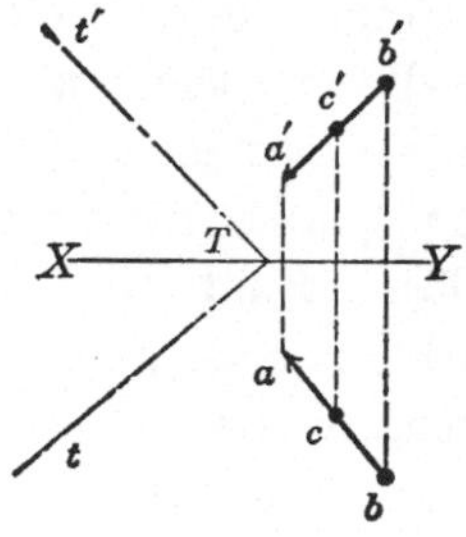


FIG. 114.

**Construction.** Let T, Fig. 114, be the given plane, and **C**, the given point. Through **c**, the horizontal projection of the given point, draw **ab**, perpendicular to **Tt**; and through **c′**, the vertical projection of the given point, draw **a′b′**, perpendicular to **Tt′**.

Thus, **AB** is perpendicular to the plane T. An oblique projection of this problem is given in Fig. 115.

**815. Special case of the preceding problem.** If the point is chosen in the third angle, then it must be observed that **Tt″** is the horizontal trace (Fig. 116) and **Tt‴** is the vertical trace. Again, the line **AB** is drawn perpendicular to T, by making **a′b′**, through c′, perpendicular to **Tt‴**, and **ab**, through c, perpendicular to **Tt″**.

**816. Problem 10.** To **draw a plane through a given point perpendicular to a given line.**

**Analysis.** The traces of the required plane must be perpen-

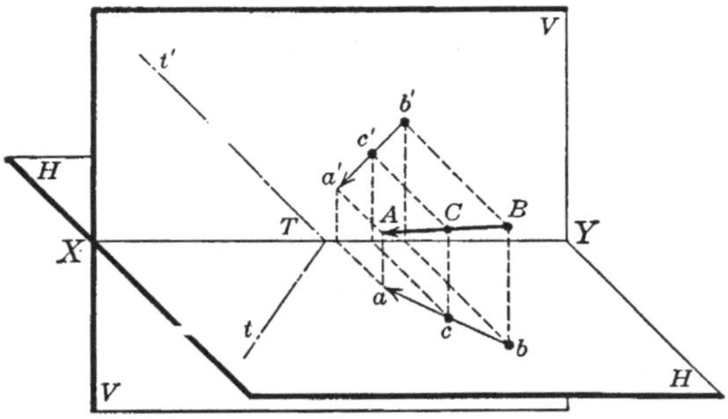


FIG. 115.

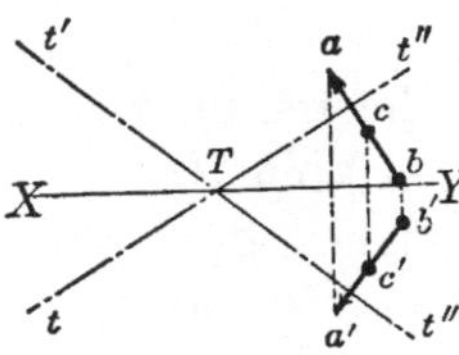


FIG. 116.

dicular to the corresponding projections of the given line (706). Through one projection of the given point, draw an auxiliary line parallel to the trace; the corresponding projection of this line will be parallel to the ground line, because it is a line parallel to that plane in which its projection is parallel to the trace (705). Find the piercing point of this auxiliary line, and through this point, draw a line perpendicular to the corresponding projection of the given line. Where this intersects the ground line, draw another line, perpendicular to the corresponding projection of the given line. The traces are thus determined.

**Construction.** Let, in Fig. 117, **AB** be the given line, and **C** the given point. For convenience, assume a horizontal line in the plane as the auxiliary line. Then, through c, draw **cd,**

perpendicular to ab, and through c′, draw **c′d′**, parallel to the ground line. The piercing point of this auxiliary line is d′, and only one point on either trace is required. Hence, through **d′**, draw **Tt′**, perpendicular to **a′b′**, and from T, draw **Tt**, perpendicular to **ab.** T is, therefore, the required plane, and **Tt** must be parallel to **cd** because both must be perpendicular to **ab.** Fig. 118 shows a pictorial representation of the same problem.

Note. Instead of having assumed a line parallel to the horizontal plane, a line parallel to the vertical plane might have been assumed. In the latter case, the vertical projection would have been perpendicular to the vertical projection of the line,

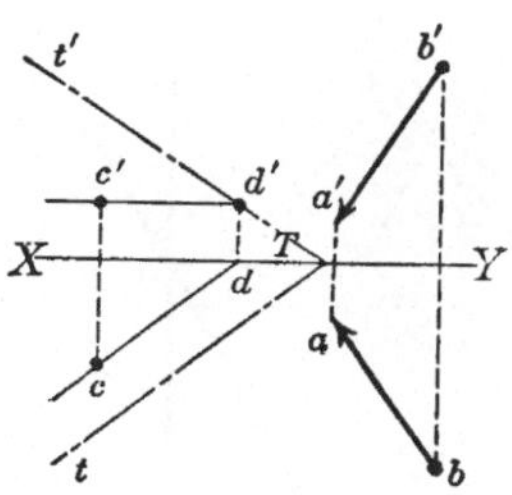


Fig. 117.

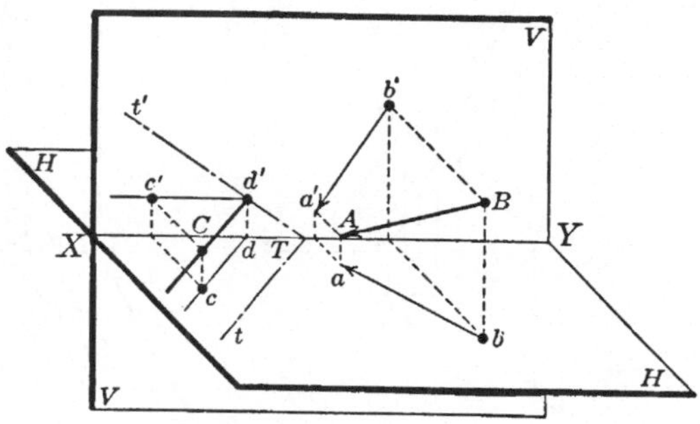


Fig. 118.

and the horizontal projection would therefore have been parallel to the ground line. Also, a point in the horizontal plane would have fixed the traces, instead of a point in the vertical plane as shown in the problem.

**817. Problem 11. To pass a plane through three given points not in the same straight line.**

**Analysis.** If two of the points be joined by a line, a plane may be passed through this line and revolved so that it contains the third point. In this position, the plane will contain a line joining the third point with any point on the first line. Hence, join two points by a line, and from any point on this line, draw another line, through the remaining point. Find the piercing points of these two lines, and thus establish the traces of the required plane.

**Construction.** Let **AB** and **C,** in Fig. 119, be the three given points. Join **A** and **B** and find where this line pierces the principal planes at **d** and **e′**. Assume any point H, on the line **AB,** and join H and **C;** this line pierces the principal planes at **g** and **f′**. Join **dg** and **f′e′** and the traces obtained are those of the required plane. A check on the accuracy of the work is furnished by the fact that both traces must meet at one point on the ground line, as shown at T. Hence, the plane T contains the points **A, B** and **C.** Fig. 120 is an oblique projection of this problem.

NOTE. In the construction of this and other problems, it may be desirable to work the problem backwards in order to

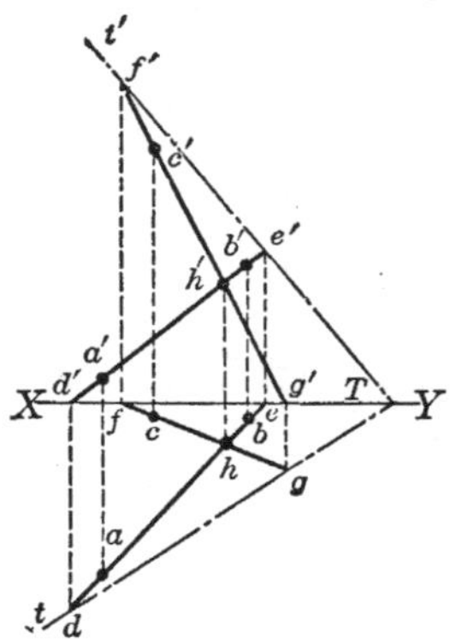

FIG. 119.

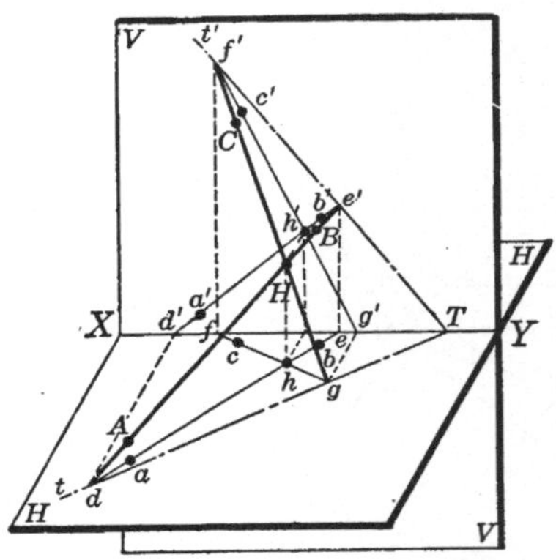

FIG. 120.

obtain a simpler drawing. It is quite difficult to select three points of a plane, at random, so that the traces of the plane shall meet the ground line within the limits of the drawing. In working the problem backwards, the traces are first assumed, then, any two distinct lines are drawn in the plane, and, finally, three points are selected on the two assumed lines of the plane. It is good practice, however, to assume three random points and proceed with the problem in the regular way. Under these conditions, the piercing points are liable to be in any angle, and, as such, furnish practice in angles other than the first.

**818. Problem 12.** To **revolve a given point, not in the principal planes, about a line** lying **in one** of **the principal planes.**

**Analysis.** If a point revolves about a line, it describes a circle, the plane of which is perpendicular to the axis of revolution. As the given line is the axis, the point will fall somewhere in the trace of a plane, through the point, perpendicular to the axis. The radius of the circle is the perpendicular distance from the point to the line; and is equal to the hypothenuse of a triangle, whose base is the distance from the projection of the point to line in the plane, and whose altitude is the distance of the corresponding projection of the point from the plane containing the line (707).

**Construction.** Assume that the given line **AB**, Fig. 121, lies in the horizontal plane and therefore is its own projection, **ab**, in that plane; its corresponding projection is **a′b′** and lies in the ground line. Also, let **C** be the given point, shown by its projections **c** and **c′**. Through c, draw **cp**, perpendicular to the line **ab**; **cp** is then the trace of the plane of the revolving point and the revolved position of the point will fall somewhere along this line. The radius of the circle is found by making an auxiliary view, in which **c′o** is the distance of the point above the horizontal plane, and **oq**=**cp** is the distance of the horizontal projection of the given point from the axis. Hence, **c′q** is the radius of the circle, and, therefore, lay off **pc″**=**c′q**. The revolved position of the point **C** in space is, therefore, **c″**. The distance **pc″** might have been revolved in the opposite direction and thus would have fallen on the opposite side of the axis. This is immaterial, however, as the point is always revolved so as to make a clear diagram.

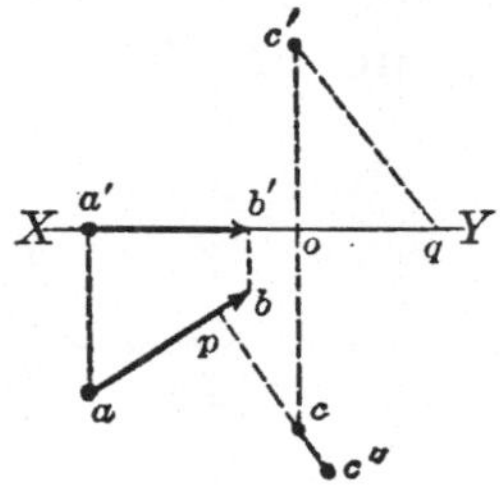

FIG. 121.

NOTE. In the construction of this problem, the line was assumed as lying in the horizontal plane. It might have been assumed as lying in the vertical plane, and, in this case, the operations would have been identical, the only difference being that the trace of the plane containing the path of the point would then lie in the vertical plane. The auxiliary diagram for determining the radius of the circle may be constructed below the ground line, or, if desirable, in an entirely separate diagram.

**819. Problem 13. To find the true distance between two points in space as given by their projections. First method.**

**Analysis.** The true distance is equal to the length of the line joining the two points. If, then, one projecting plane of the line be revolved until it is parallel to the corresponding plane of projection, the line will be shown in its true length on the plane to which it is parallel.

**Construction. Case 1.** When both points are above the plane of projection.—Let **AB,** in Fig. 122, be the given line. For convenience, revolve the horizontal projecting plane about the projecting perpendicular from the point **A** on the line. The point **B** will describe a circle, the plane of which is perpendicular to the axis about which it revolves. As the plane of the circle (or arc) is parallel to the horizontal plane, it is projected as the arc **bc.** The corresponding projection is **b′c′,** because its

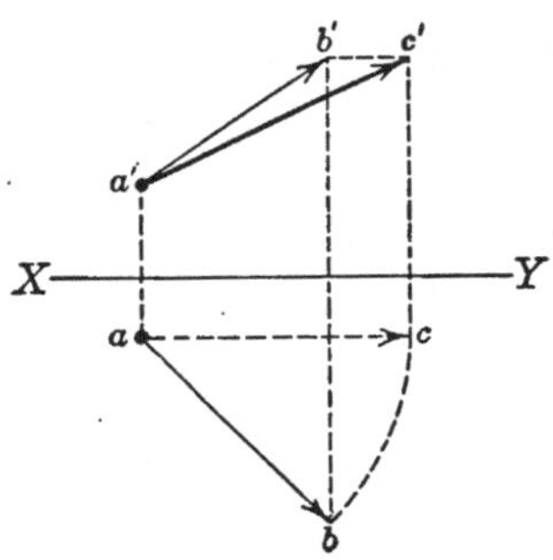


FIG. 122.

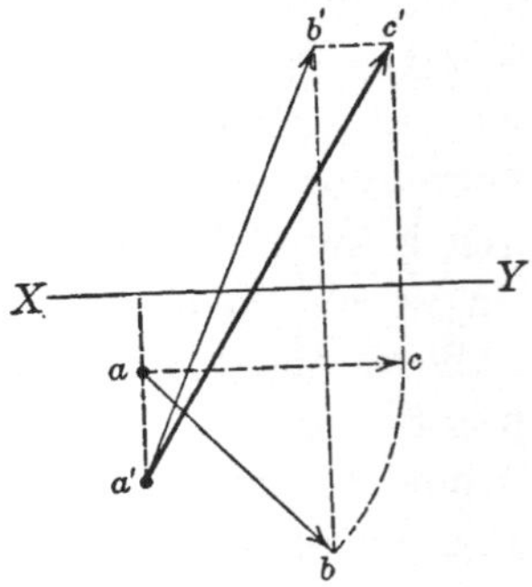


FIG. 123.

plane is perpendicular to the vertical plane. In the position **ac,** the projecting plane of **AB** is parallel to the vertical plane, and **c′** is the vertical projection of the point **b,** when so revolved. Hence, **a′c′** is the true length of the line **AB** in space.

**820. Case 2.** When the points are situated on opposite sides of the principal plane.—Let **AB,** in Fig. 123, be the given line. Revolve the horizontal projecting plane of the line about the horizontal projecting perpendicular from the point **A** on the line. The point **B** will describe an arc which is horizontally projected as **bc** and vertically projected as **b′c′.** The ultimate position of **b′** after revolution is at **c′,** whereas **a′** remains fixed. Hence, **a′c′** is the true length of the line **AB.**

**821. Problem 13. To find the true distance between two points in space as given by their projections. Second method.**

**Analysis.** The true distance is equal to the length of a line joining the two points. If a plane be passed through the line and revolved about the trace into one of the principal planes, the distance between the points will remain unchanged, and in its revolved position, the line will be shown in its true length.

**Construction. Case 1.** When both points are above the plane of projection.—Let **A** and **B** Fig. 124 be the two points in question. For convenience, use the horizontal projecting plane of the line as the revolving plane; its trace on the horizontal plane is **ab,** which is also the projection of the line. The points **A** and **B,** while revolving about the line **ab,** will describe circles, the planes of which are perpendicular to the axis, and, hence, in their revolved position, will lie along lines **aa″** and **bb″.** In this case, the distance of the projections of the points from the axis is zero, because the projecting plane of the line joining the points was used. The altitudes of the triangles are the distances of the points above the horizontal plane, and, hence, they are also the hypothenuses of the triangles which are the radii of the circles.* Therefore, lay off **aa″ = a′o** and **bb″ = b′p** along lines **aa″** and **bb″,** which are perpendicular to **ab.** Hence, **a″b″** is the true distance between the points **A** and **B** in space.

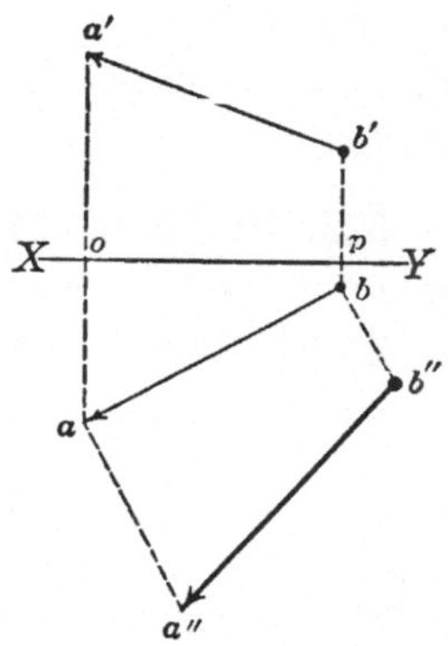

FIG. 124.

**822. Case 2.** When the points are situated on opposite sides of the principal plane.—Let **AB,** Fig. 125, be the two points. From the projections it will be seen that **A** is in the first angle and **B** is in the fourth angle. If, as in the previous case, the horizontal projecting plane is used as the revolving plane then the horizontal projection **ab** is the trace of the revolving plane as before. The point **A** falls to **a″** where **aa″ = a′o.** Similarly, **B** falls to **b″** where **bb″ = b′p,**

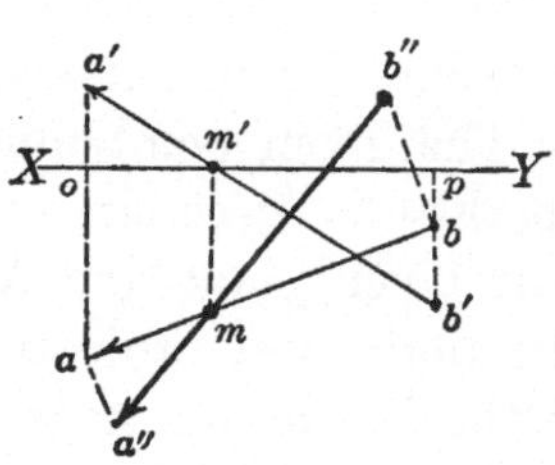

FIG. 125.

* See the somewhat similar case in Problem 12.

but, as must be noticed, this point falls on that side of **ab**, opposite to the point **a″**. A little reflection will show that such must be the case, but it may be brought out by what follows: The line **AB** pierces the horizontal plane at **m** and this point must remain fixed during the revolution. That it does, is shown by the fact that the revolved position of the line **a″b″** passes through this point.

NOTE. In both cases, the vertical projecting plane might have been used as the revolving plane and after the operation is performed, the true length of the line is again obtained. It must of necessity be equal to that given by the method here indicated.

**823. Problem 14. To find where a given line pierces a given plane.**

**Analysis.** If an auxiliary plane be passed through the

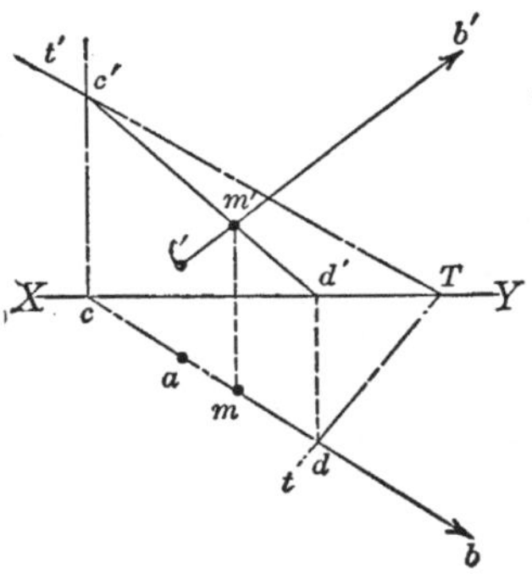

FIG. 126.

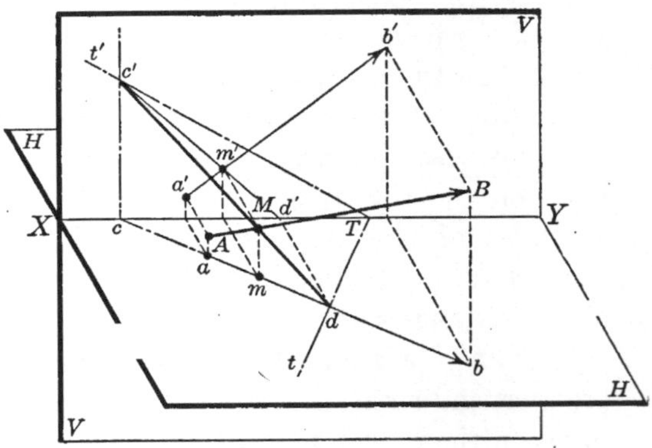

FIG. 127.

given line, so that it intersects the given plane, it will cut from it a line that contains the given point. The given point must also lie on the given line, hence it lies on their intersection.

**Construction.** Let T, Fig. 126, be the given plane and **AB** the given line. For convenience, use the horizontal projecting plane of the line as the auxiliary plane; the horizontal trace is **cb** and the vertical trace is **cc′**. The auxiliary plane cuts from the plane T the line **CD**. The vertical projection is shown as **c′d′** and the horizontal projection **cd** is contained in the trace of the horizontal projecting plane, because that plane was purposely taken as the cutting plane through the line. It is only in the vertical projection that the intersection **m′** is determined; its horizontal projection **m** is indeterminate in that plane (except from the fact that it is a corresponding projection) since the given line and the line of intersection have the same horizontal projecting plane. An oblique projection of this problem is given in Fig. 127.

**824. Problem 15. To find the distance of a given point from a given plane.**

**Analysis.** The perpendicular distance from the given point to the given plane is the required distance. Hence, draw a perpendicular from the given point to the given plane, and find where this perpendicular pierces the given plane. If the line joining the given point and the piercing point be revolved into one of the planes of projection, the line will be shown in its true length.

**Construction.** Let T, Fig. 128, be the given plane, and **A,** the given point. From **A,** draw **AB,** perpendicular to the plane T; the projections of **AB** are therefore perpendicular to the traces of the plane. If the horizontal projecting plane of the line **AB** be used as the auxiliary plane, it cuts the given plane in the line **CD,** and pierces it at the point **B**. Revolve the projecting plane of **AB** about its horizontal trace **ab** into the horizontal plane of projection. **A** will fall to **a″,** where **aa″ = a′o,** and **B** will fall to **b″,** where **bb″ = b′p.** Therefore, **a″b″** is the distance from the point **A** to the plane T.

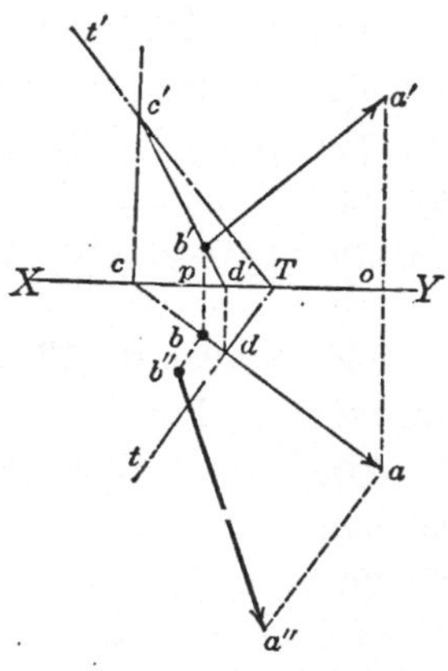

FIG. 128.

**825. Problem 16. To find the distance from a given point to a given line.**

**Analysis.** Through the given point pass a plane perpendicular to the given line. The distance between the piercing point of the given line on this plane and the given point is the required distance. Join these two points by a line and revolve this line into one of the planes of projection; the line will then be seen in its true length.

**Construction.** Let **AB,** Fig. 129, be the given line, and **G,** the given point. Through **G,** draw a plane perpendicular to **AB** (816), by drawing **gc** perpendicular to **ab,** and **g′c′,** parallel to the ground line; the piercing point of this line on the vertical plane is c′. Hence, the traces **Tt′** and **Tt,** perpendicular to **a′b′** and **ab,** respectively, through the point **c′,** will be the traces of the required plane. **AB** pierces this plane at **B,** found by using the horizontal projecting plane of **AB** as a cutting plane, this cutting plane intersecting in a line **DE.** The point **B** must be on both **AB** and **DE.** The projected distance, then, is the distance between the points **B** and **G**; the true distance is found by revolving **BG** into the horizontal plane. The latter operation is accomplished by using the horizontal projecting plane of **BG** and revolving it about its trace **bg; G** falls to **g″,** where **gg″ = g′p,** and **B** falls to **b″,** where **bb″=b′o.** Thus, **g″b″** is the true distance between the point **G** and the line **AB.**

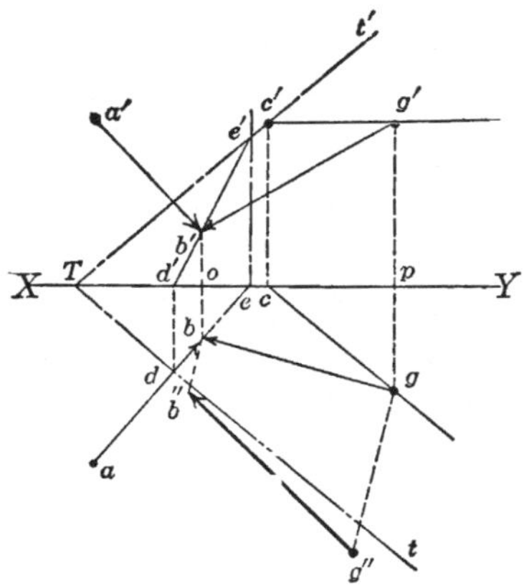

FIG. 129.

**826. Problem 17. To find the angle between two given intersecting lines.**

**Analysis.** If a plane be passed through these lines and revolved into one of the planes of projection, the angle will be shown in its true size. Hence, find the piercing points of the given lines on one of the planes of projection; the line joining these piercing points will be the trace of the plane containing the lines. Revolve into that plane and the revolved position of the two lines shows the true angle.

**Construction.** Let **AB** and **AC,** Fig. 130, be the two given lines intersecting at **A.** These lines pierce the horizontal plane of projection at **b** and **c** and **bc** is the trace of a plane containing the two lines. If **A** be considered as a point revolving about the line **bc,** it then describes a circle, the plane of which is perpendicular to **bc** and the point **A** will coincide with the horizontal plane somewhere along the line **oa″.** The radius of the circle described by **A** is equal to the hypothenuse of a right triangle, where the distance ao, the projection of **a** from the axis, is the base, and **a′p**, the distance of the point above the plane, is the altitude. This is shown in the triangle **a′pq**, where **pq** is equal to **ao** and therefore **a′q** is the required radius. Hence, make **oa″ = a′q**, and **a″** is the revolved position of the point **A** in space. The piercing points **b** and **c** of the given lines do not change their relative positions. Thus **a″b** and **a″c** are the revolved position of the given lines, and the angle **ba″c** is the true angle.

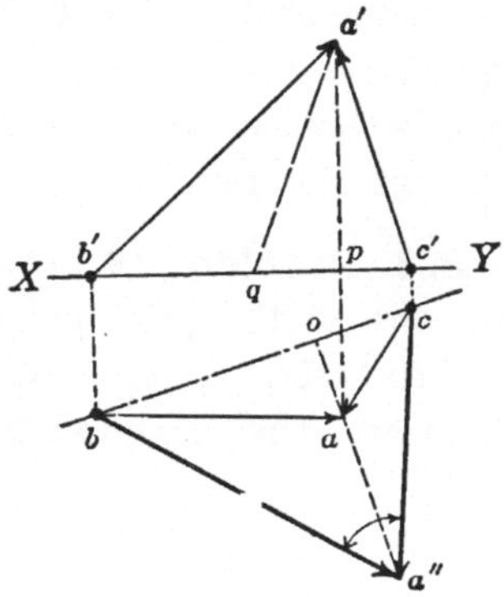

FIG. 130.

**827. Problem 18.** To **find the angle between two given planes.**

**Analysis.** If a plane be passed perpendicular to the line of intersection of the two given planes, it will cut a line from each plane, the included angle of which will be the true angle. Revolve this plane, containing the lines, about its trace on the principal plane, until it coincides with that plane, and the angle will be shown in its true size.

**Construction.** Let T and **S**, Fig. 131, be the two given planes, intersecting, as shown, in the line **AB**. Construct a supplementary plane to the right of the main diagram. **H′H′** is the new horizontal plane, shown as a line parallel to **ab.** The line **AB** pierces the vertical plane at a distance **a′a** above the horizontal plane. Accordingly, **a′a** is laid off on **V′V′**, perpendicular to **H′H′**; it also pierces the horizontal plane at **b** shown in both views. The supplementary view shows **ba′** in its true relation to the horizontal plane, and is nothing more or less than a side view of the horizontal projecting plane of the line **AB.** If, in this supplementary view, a perpendicular plane **cd** be drawn, it will intersect the line **AB** in **c**, and the horizontal plane in the trace **dfe** shown on end. The lettering in both views is such that similar letters indicate similar points. Hence, **dfe** is the trace of the plane as shown in the main diagram, and **ec** and **dc** are the two lines cut from the planes T and **S** by the plane

**cde.** When the plane **cde** is revolved into coincidence with the horizontal plane, **c** falls to **c″** in the supplementary view and is projected back to the main diagram as **c″**. Therefore, **ec″d** is the true angle between the planes, because **e** and **d** remain fixed in the revolution.

**828. Problem 19. To find the angle between a given plane and one of the principal planes.**

**Analysis.** If an auxiliary plane be passed through the given plane and the principal plane so that the auxiliary plane is per-

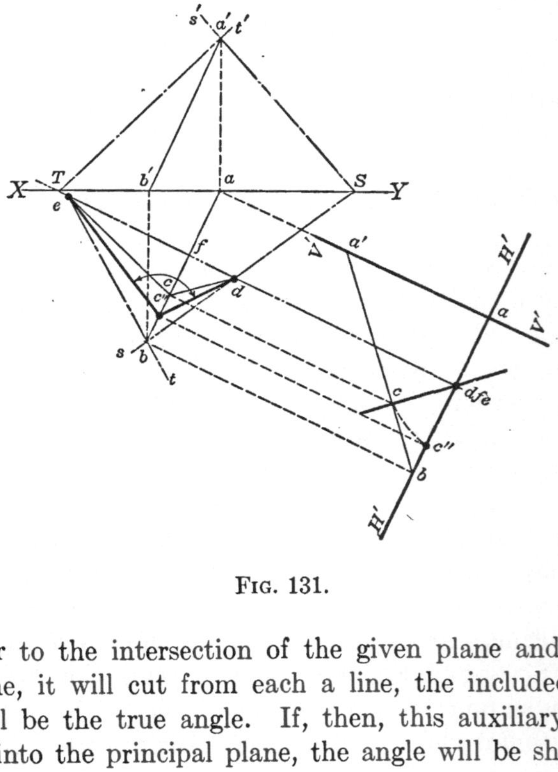


FIG. 131.

pendicular to the intersection of the given plane and the principal plane, it will cut from each a line, the included angle of which will be the true angle. If, then, this auxiliary plane be revolved into the principal plane, the angle will be shown in its true size.

**Construction.** Let T, Fig. 132, be the given plane. The angle that this plane makes with the horizontal plane is to be determined. Draw the auxiliary plane **R,** so that its horizontal trace is perpendicular to the horizontal trace of the given plane; the vertical trace of the auxiliary plane must as a consequence be perpendicular to the ground line as **Rr′**. A triangle **rRr′** is cut by the auxiliary plane from the given plane and the two principal planes. If this triangle be revolved into the horizontal plane, about **rR** as an axis, the point **r′** will fall to **r″** with **Rr′** as a radius. Also, the angle **rRr″** must be a right angle, because it is cut from the principal planes, which are at right angles to each other. Hence, **Rrr″** is the angle which the plane T makes with the horizontal plane of projection.

The construction for obtaining the angle with the vertical plane is identical, and is shown on the right-hand side, with plane **S** as the given plane. All construction lines are added and no comment should be necessary.

NOTE. The similarity of Probs. 18 and 19 should be noted. In Prob. 19 the horizontal trace is the intersection of the given

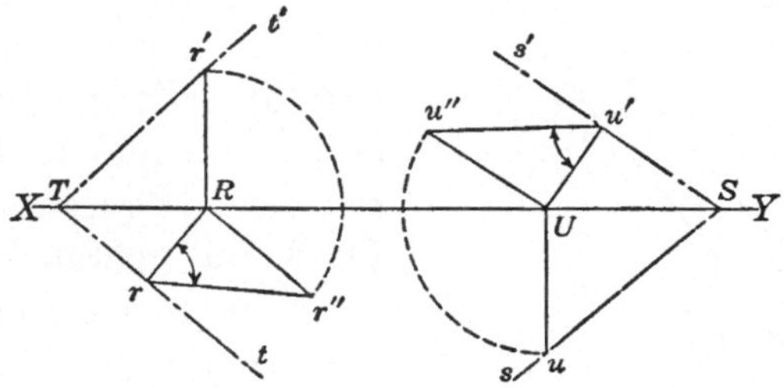


FIG. 132.

plane and the horizontal plane; hence, the auxiliary plane is passed perpendicular to the trace. A similar reasoning applies to the vertical trace.

**829. Problem 20. To draw a plane parallel to a given plane, at a given distance from it.**

**Analysis.** The required distance between the two planes is the perpendicular distance, and the resulting traces must be parallel to the traces of the given plane. If a plane be passed perpendicular to either trace, it will cut from the principal planes and the given plane a right angled triangle, the hypothenuse of which will be the line cut from the given plane. If, further, the triangle be revolved into the plane containing the trace and the required distance between the planes be laid off perpendicular to the hypothenuse cut from the given plane, it will establish a point on the hypothenuse of the required plane. A line parallel to the hypothenuse through the established point will give the revolved position of a triangle cut from the required plane. On the counter revolution, this triangle will determine a point in each plane, through which the required traces must pass. Hence, if lines be drawn through the points so found, parallel to the traces of the given plane, the traces of the required plane are established.

**Construction.** Let T, Fig. 133, be the given plane, and **r″g** the required distance between the parallel planes. Pass a plane **rOr′**, perpendicular to the horizontal trace **Tt**; its vertical trace **Or** is, therefore, perpendicular to the ground line. The revolved position of the triangle cut from the two principal planes and the given plane is **rOr″**. Lay off **r″g**, perpendicular to **rr″**, and equal to the required distance between the planes. Draw **uu″** parallel to **rr″** and the triangle cut from the principal planes and the required plane is obtained. On counter revolution, **u″** becomes **u′** and **u** remains fixed; **Su′** and **Su,** parallel respectively to **Tr′** and **Tr,** are the required traces. Therefore, the distance between the planes T and **S** is equal to **r″g.**

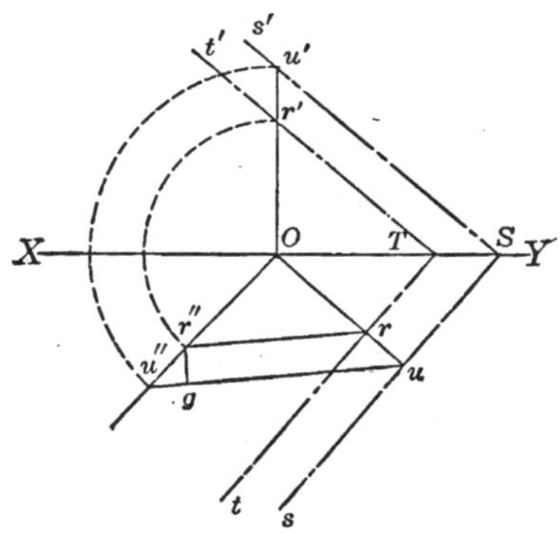

FIG. 133.

**830. Problem 21. To project a given line on a given plane.**

**Analysis.** If perpendiculars be dropped from the given line upon the given plane, the points, so found, are the projections of the corresponding points on the line. Hence, a line joining the projections on the given plane is the required projection of the line on that plane.

**Construction.** Let T, Fig. 134, be the given plane, and **AB** the given line. From **A,** draw a perpendicular to the plane T; its horizontal projection is **ac** and its vertical projection is **a′c′.** To find where **AC** pierces the given plane, use the horizontal projecting plane of **AC** as the cutting plane; **FE** is the line so cut, and **C** is the resultant piercing point. Thus, **C** is the projection of **A** on the plane T. A construction, similar in detail, will show that **D** is the projection of **B** on the plane T. Hence, **CD** is the projection of **AB** on the plane T.

**831. Problem 22.** To **find the angle between a given line and a given plane.**

**Analysis.** The angle made by a given line and a given plane is the same as the angle made by the given line and its projection

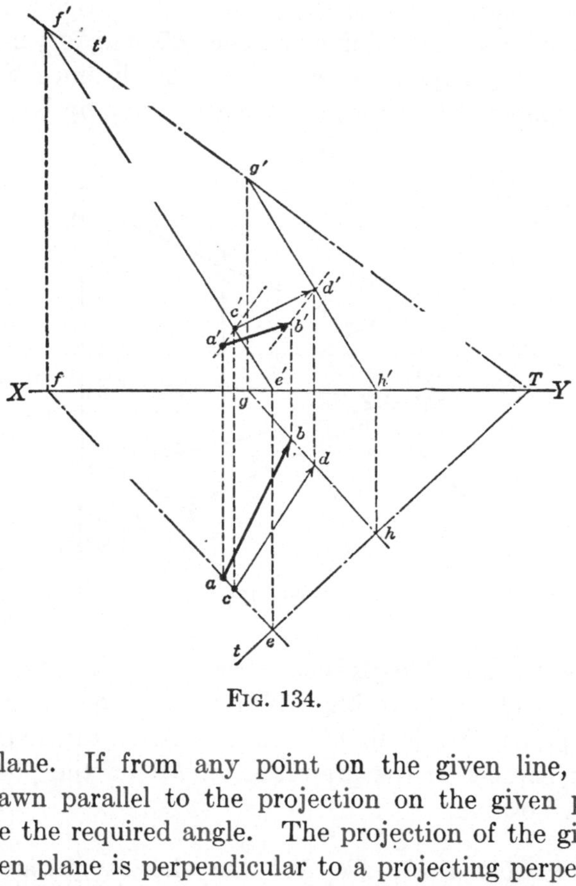


Fig. 134.

on that plane. If from any point on the given line, another line be drawn parallel to the projection on the given plane, it will also be the required angle. The projection of the given line on the given plane is perpendicular to a projecting perpendicular from the given line to the given plane. Hence, any line, parallel to the projection and lying in the projecting plane of the given line to the given plane is also perpendicular to this projecting perpendicular. Therefore, pass a plane through the given line and the projecting perpendicular from the given line to the given plane. Revolve this plane into one of the planes of projection, and, from any point on the line, draw a perpendicular to the projecting perpendicular. The angle between this line and the given line is the required angle.

**Construction.** Let T, Fig. 135, be the given plane, and **AB** the given line. From **B,** draw a perpendicular to the plane T, by making the projections respectively perpendicular to the traces of the given plane. Find the piercing points **e** and **f,** on the horizontal plane, of the given line and this perpendicular. Revolve the plane containing the lines **BE** and **BF; B** falls to **b″,** on a line **b″p,** perpendicular to **ef.** The distance **b″p** is equal to the hypothenuse of a right triangle, where **bp** is the base and

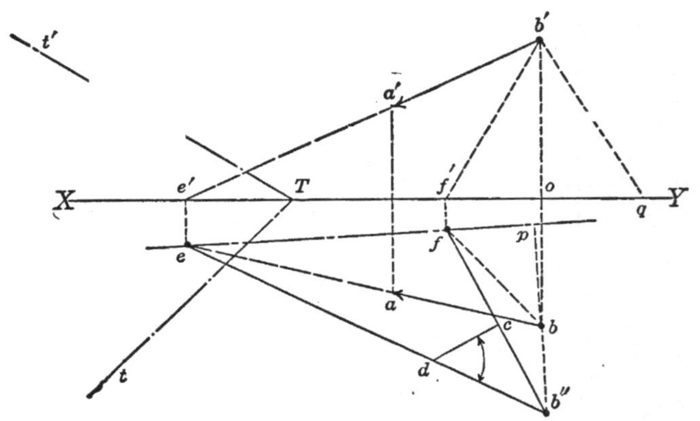


FIG. 135.

**b′o** is the altitude; **b′oq** is such a triangle, where **oq** = **bp.** Hence, **b″p** is laid off equal to **b′q.** If from any point **d,** a line **dc** be drawn, perpendicualr to **b″f,** then **b″dc** is the required angle, as **dc** is parallel to the projection of **AB** on the plane **T** in its revolved position.

**832. Problem 23.** To **find the shortest distance between a pair of skew * lines.**

**Analysis.** The required line is the perpendicular distance between the two lines. If through one of the given lines, another line be drawn parallel to the other given line, the intersecting lines will establish a plane which is parallel to one of the given lines.

* Skew lines are lines which are not parallel and which do not intersect.

The length of a perpendicular from any point on the one given line to the plane containing the other given line, is the required distance.

**Construction.** Let **AB** and **CD**, Fig. 136, be the two given

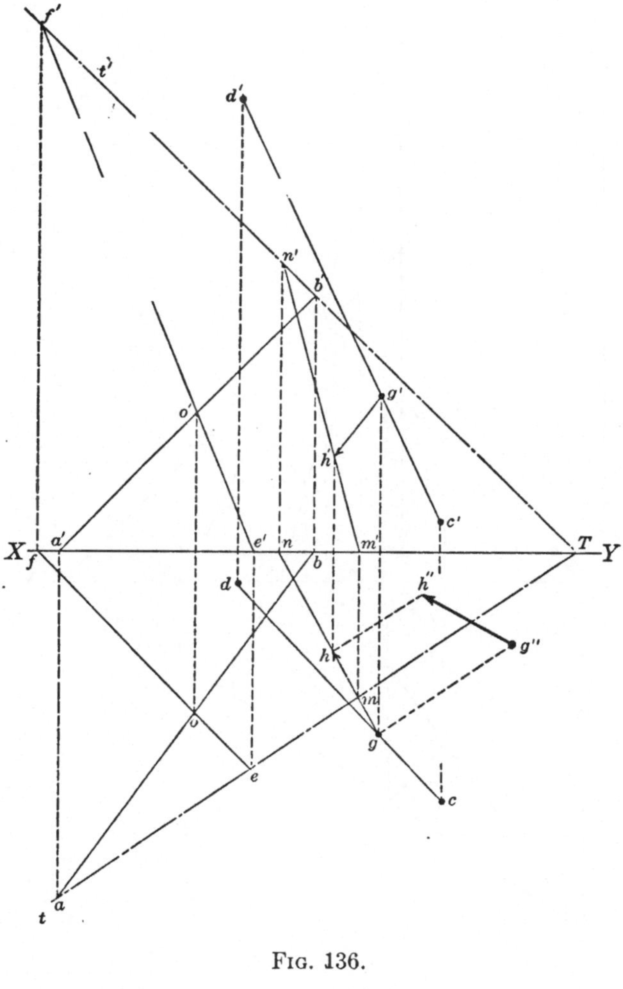


Fig. 136.

lines. Through any point **O,** on **AB,** draw **FE,** parallel to **CD,** and determine the piercing points of the lines **AB** and **FE; a, e** and **f′, b′** are these piercing points, and, as such, determine the plane T. **CD** is then parallel to the plane T. From any point **G,** on **CD,** draw **GH,** perpendicular to the plane T, and find its piercing point on that plane. This point is H, found by drawing **gh** perpendicular to **Tt** and **g′h′** perpendicular to **Tt′**; the horizontal projecting plane cuts from the plane T, a line **MN,** on which is found H, the piercing point. **GH** is therefore the required distance, but to find its true length, revolve

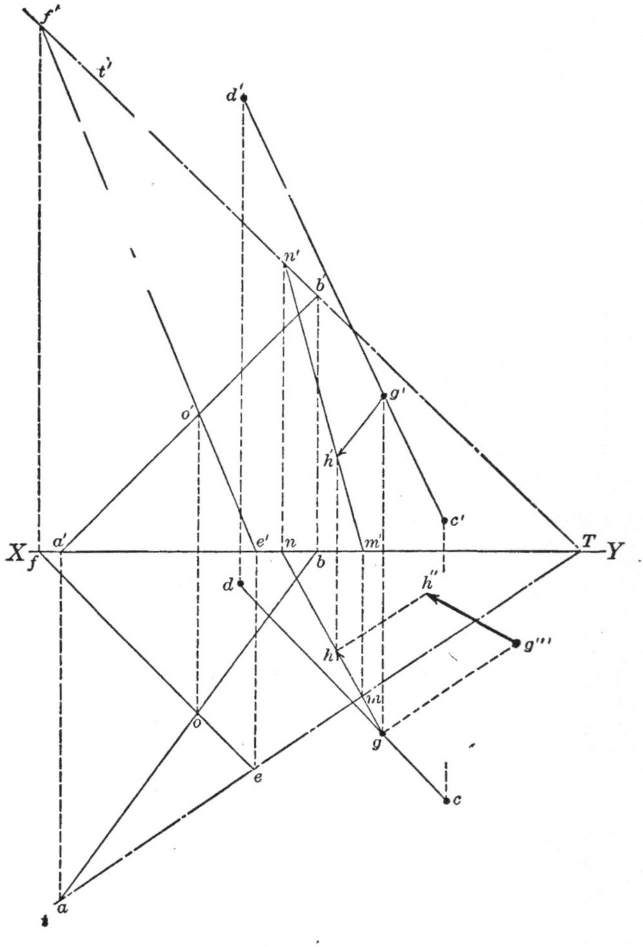


FIG. 136.

the horizontal projecting plane of **GH** into the horizontal plane. On revolution, H falls to **h″,** where **hh″** is equal to the distance **h′** above the ground line; and, similarly, **G** falls to **g″.** Therefore, **h″g″** is the true distance between the lines **AB** and **CD.**

NOTE. In order to find the point on each of the lines at which this perpendicular may be drawn, project the one given line on the plane containing the other. Where the projections cross, the point will be found.

### ADDITIONAL CONSTRUCTIONS

**833. Application to other problems.** The foregoing problems may be combined so as to form additional ones. In such cases, the analysis is apt to be rather long, and in the remaining few problems it has been omitted. The construction of the

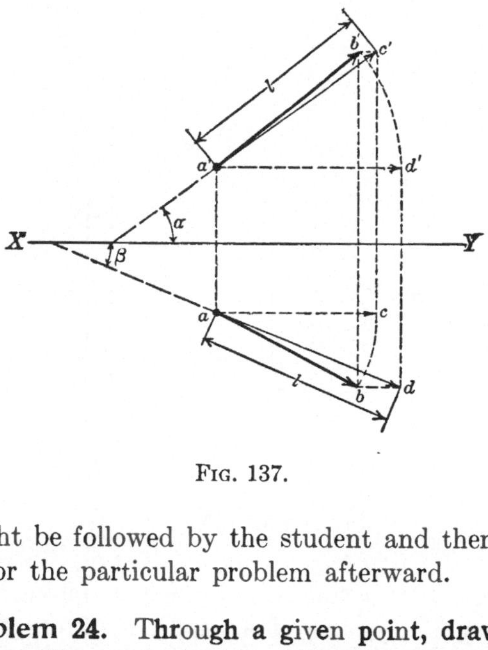


FIG. 137.

problem might be followed by the student and then an analysis worked up for the particular problem afterward.

**834. Problem 24. Through a given point, draw a line of a given length, making given angles with the planes of projection.**

**Construction.** Consider the problem solved, and let **AB**, Fig. 137, be the required line, through the point **A.** The construction will first be shown and then the final position of the line **AB** will be analytically considered. From **a′**, draw **a′c′** of a length **l**, making the angle $\alpha$ with the ground line, and draw **ac**, parallel to the ground line. The horizontal projecting plane of **AB** has been revolved about the horizontal projecting perpendicular, until it is parallel to the vertical plane, and, therefore

**a′c′** is shown in its true length and inclination to the horizontal plane. On the counter-revolution of the projecting plane of **AB,** it will be observed that the point **A** remains fixed, because it lies in the axis; **B** describes a circle, however, whose plane is parallel to the horizontal plane, and is, therefore, projected as the arc **cb,** while its vertical projection (or trace, if it be considered as a plane instead of the moving point) is **b′c′,** a line parallel to the ground line. The angle that the line **AB** makes with the horizontal plane is now fixed, but the point **B** is not finally located as the remaining condition of making the angle β with the horizontal plane is yet conditional.

In order to lay off the angle that the line makes with the

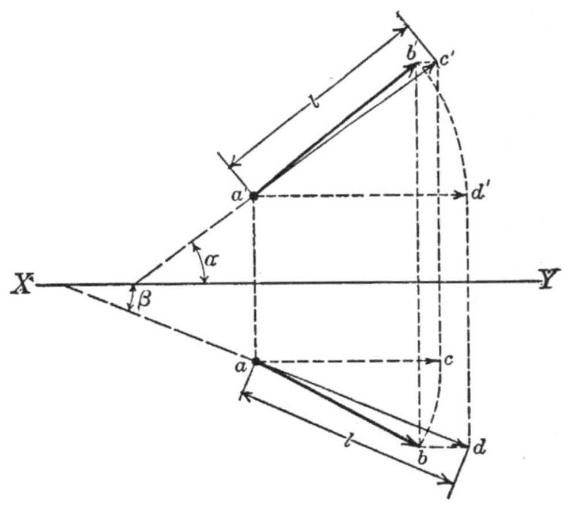


FIG. 137.

vertical plane, draw a line **ad,** through **a,** making the angle β with the ground line, and of a length **l.** From **a′**, draw **a′d′**, so that **d′** is located from its corresponding projection **d.** Draw **bd,** through **d,** parallel to the ground line, and where its intersection with the arc **cb,** locates **b,** the final position of the horizontal projection of the actual line. The corresponding projection **b′**, may be located by drawing the arc **d′b′**, and finding where it intersects the line **b′c′**, through c′, parallel to the ground line. The points **b** and **b′** should be corresponding projections, if the construction has been carried out accurately. In reviewing the latter process, it is found that the vertical projecting plane of the line has been revolved about the vertical projecting perpendicular through **A,** until it was parallel to the horizontal plane. The horizontal projection is then **ad,** and this is shown in its true length and inclination to the vertical plane.

It may also be noted that the process of finding the ultimate position of the line is simply to note the projections of the path of the moving point, when the projecting planes of the line are revolved. That is, when the horizontal projecting plane of the line is revolved, the line makes a constant angle with the horizontal plane; and the path of the moving point is indicated by its projections. Similarly, when the vertical projecting plane of the line is revolved, the line makes a constant angle with the vertical plane; and the path of the moving point is again given

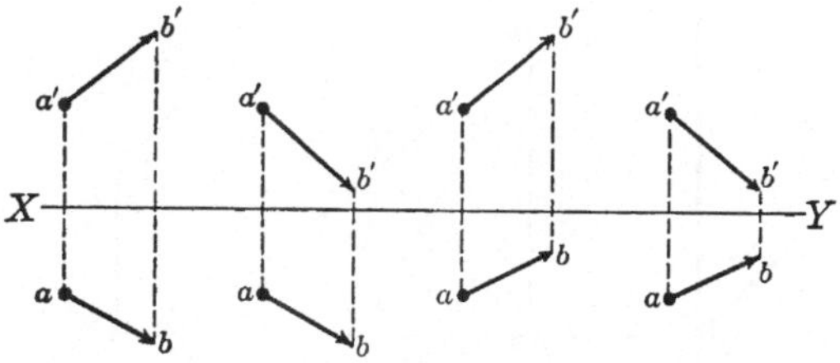


FIG. 138.

by its projections. Where the paths intersect, on the proper planes, it is evidently the condition that satisfies the problem.

There are four possible solutions for any single point in space, and they are shown in Fig. 138. Each is of the required length, and makes the required angles with the planes of projection. The student may try to work out the construction in each case and show that it is true.

**835. Problem 25. Through a given point, draw a plane, making given angles with the principal planes.**

**Construction.** Prior to the solution of this problem, it is desirable to investigate the property of a line from any point on the ground line, perpendicular to the plane. If the angles that this line makes with the principal planes can be determined, the actual construction of it, in projection, is then similar to the preceding problem. To draw the required plane, hence, resolves itself simply into passing a plane through a given point, perpendicular to a given line (816).

Let, in Fig. 139, T be the required plane, making the required angles $\alpha$ with the horizontal plane, and $\beta$ with the vertical plane. To find the angle made with the horizontal plane, pass a plane perpendicular to the horizontal trace as **AOB**, through any assumed point **O** on the ground line; **OA** is thus perpendicular to **Tt** and **OB** is perpendicular to the ground line. This plane cuts from the plane T, a line **AB**, and the angle **BAO** is the required angle $\alpha$. Similarly, pass a plane **COD**, through **O** perpendicular to the vertical trace, then **CO** is perpendicular to **Tt** and **OD** is perpendicular to the ground line; **DCO** is the required angle $\beta$, which the plane T makes with the vertical plane. The planes **AOB** and **COD** intersect in a line **OP**. **OP** is perpendicular

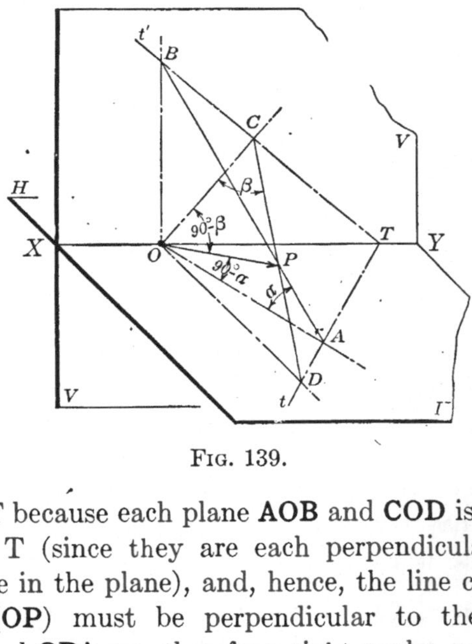


Fig. 139.

to the plane T because each plane **AOB** and **COD** is perpendicular to the plane T (since they are each perpendicular to a trace, which is a line in the plane), and, hence, the line common to the two planes (**OP**) must be perpendicular to the plane. The angles **OPC** and **OPA** are, therefore, right angles, and, as a result, angle **POA**$=90°-\alpha$, and angle **POC**$=90°-\beta$. Hence, to draw a perpendicular to the required plane, draw a line making angles with the principal planes equal to the **complements** (90° minus the angle) of the corresponding angles. It is evident that any line will do, as all such lines, when measured in the same way, will be parallel, hence, it is not necessary, although convenient, that this line should pass through the ground line.

To complete the problem, let **AB**, Fig. 140, be a line making angles $90°-\alpha$ with the horizontal plane, and $90°-\beta$ with the vertical plane. Through **G,** the given point, draw a perpendicular plane to **AB,** and the resultant plane T is the required plane

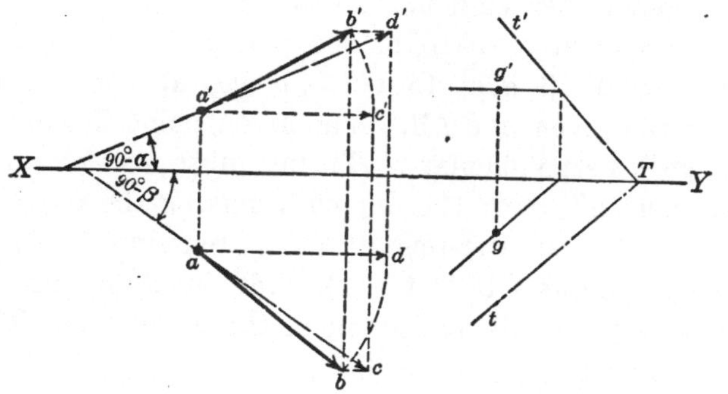

FIG. 140.

making an angle $\alpha$, with the horizontal plane, and an angle $\beta$, with the vertical plane.

NOTE. As there are four solutions to the problem of drawing a line making given angles with the principal planes, there are also four solutions to this problem. The student may show these cases and check the accuracy by finding the angle between a given plane and the principal planes (828).

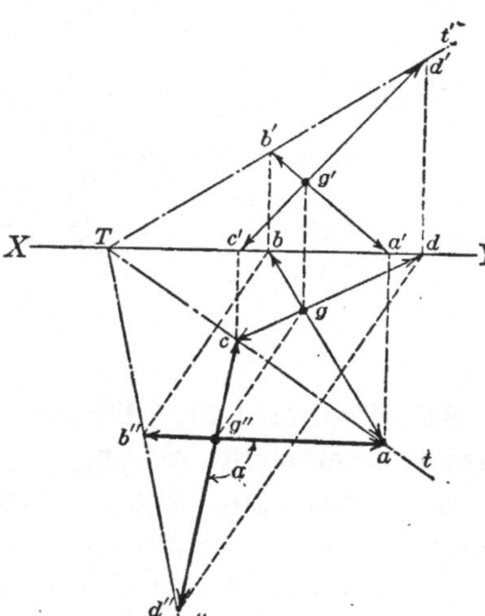

FIG. 141.

**836. Problem 26. Through a given line, in a given plane, draw another line, intersecting it at a given point, and at a given angle.**

**Construction.** Let **AB,** Fig. 141, be the given line, T the given plane and **G** the given point. Revolve the limited portion of the plane **tTt′** into coincidence with the horizontal plane. **Tt** remains fixed but **Tt′** revolves to **Tt″.** To find the direction of **Tt″**, consider any point **b′** on the original position of the trace **Tt′**. The distance **Tb′** must equal **Tb″** as this length does not change on revolution; since **Tt** is the axis of revolution, the point **B** describes a circle, the plane of which is perpendicular to the axis, and, therefore, **b″** must also lie on a line **bb″**, from **b**, perpendicular to the trace **Tt.**

In the revolved position of the plane, the point **a** remains unchanged, while **B** goes to **b″**. Hence, **ab″** is the revolved position of the given line **AB.** The given point **G** moves to **g″**, on a line **gg″**, perpendicular to **Tt** and must also be on the line **ab″**. Through **g″**, draw the line **cd″**, making the required angle $\alpha$ with it. On counter-revolution, **c** remains fixed, and **d″** moves to **d′**. Thus **CD** is the required line, making an angle $\alpha$ with another line **AB**, and lying in the given plane **T.**

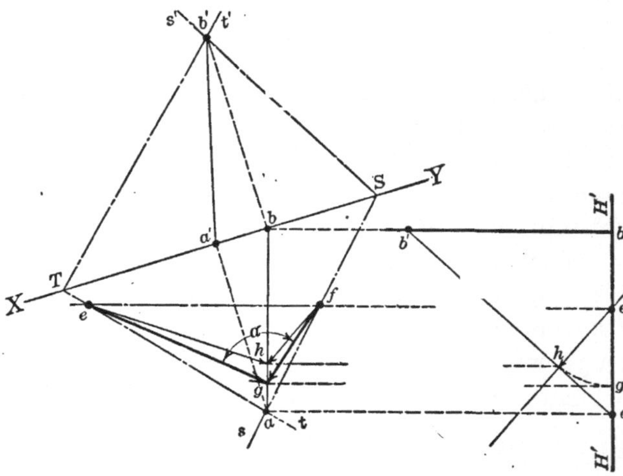


FIG. 142.

**837. Problem 27. Through a given line in a given plane, pass another plane, making a given angle with the given plane.**

**Construction.** Let T, Fig. 142, be the given plane, **AB** the given line in that plane, and $\alpha$ the required angle between the planes. Construct a supplementary view of the line **AB**; **H′H′** is the new horizontal plane, the inclination of **ab′** is shown by the similar letters on both diagrams. The distance of b′ above the horizontal plane must also equal the distance **b′** above **H′H′** and so on. Through **h,** in the supplementary view, draw a plane **hf** perpendicular to ab′. Revolve h about **f** to **g** and locate **g** as shown on the horizontal projection **ab,** of the main diagram. The line **eg** is cut from the plane T, by the auxiliary plane **egf,** hence, lay off the angle $\alpha$ as shown. This gives the direction **gf** of the line cut from the required plane. The point **f** lies on **gf** and also on **ef** which is perpendicular to **ab.** Hence, join **af** and produce to **S**; join **S** and **b′** and thus estab-

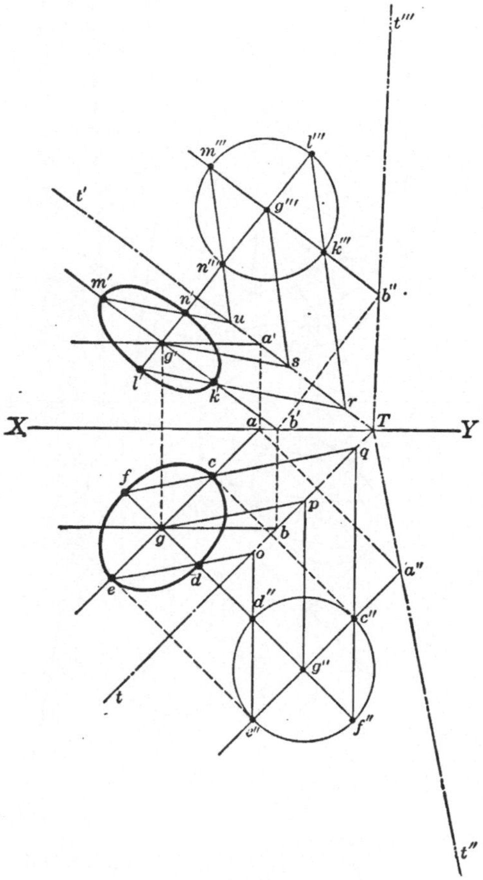


FIG. 143.

lish the plane **S.** The plane **S** passes through the given line **AB** and makes an angle $\alpha$ with the given plane T (827).

**838. Problem 28.** To construct the projections of a circle lying in a given oblique plane, of a given diameter, its centre in the given plane being known.

**Construction.** Let T, Fig. 143, be the given plane, and **G**

the given point lying in the plane T. When **g′**, is assumed, for instance, **g** is found by drawing a horizontal line **g′a′** and then **ga** is its corresponding projection; **g** can therefore be determined as shown. When the plane of a circle is inclined to a plane of

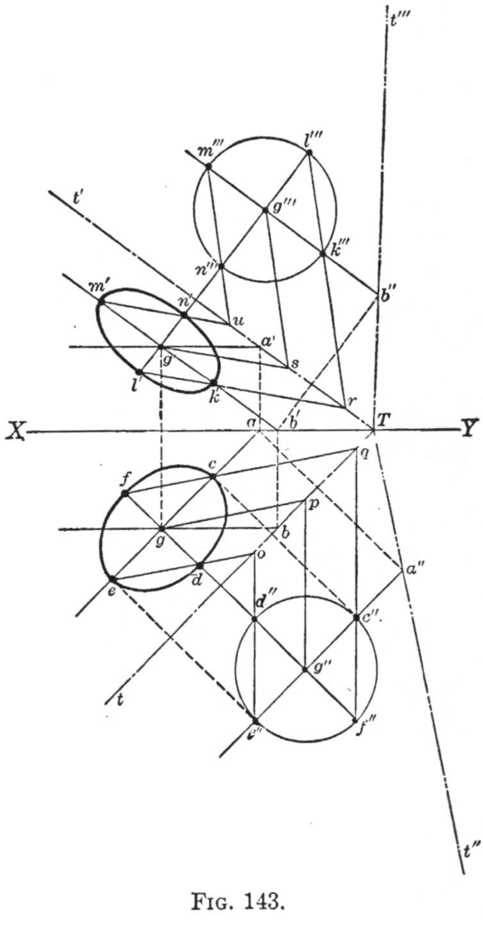


FIG. 143.

projection, it is projected as an ellipse. An ellipse is determined, and can be constructed, when its major and minor axes are given.*

To construct the horizontal projection, revolve the plane T about **Tt,** until it coincides with the horizontal plane as **Tt″.** The direction of **Tt″** is found by drawing **aa″** perpendicular to **Tt** and laying off **Ta′=Ta″** (836). The centre of the circle in

* For methods of constructing the ellipse see Art. 906.

its revolved position is found by drawing **a″g″** parallel to **Tt** and **gg″** perpendicular to **Tt**; **g″** is this revolved position. With the given radius, draw **c″d″e″f″**, the circle of the given diameter. Join **e″d″** and **f″c″**; prolong these lines to **o** and **q**, and also draw **g″p** parallel to these. Thus, three parallel lines in the revolved position of the plane T, are established and on counter revolution, they will remain parallel. The direction **gp**, of one of them is known, hence, make **fq** and **eo** parallel to **gp**. The points **cdef** are the corresponding positions of **c″d″e″f″** and determine the horizontal projection of the circle. The line **ec** remains equal to **e″c″** but **fd** is shorter than **f″d″**, hence, the major and minor axes of an ellipse (projection of the circle) are determined. The ellipse may now be drawn by any convenient method and the horizontal projection of the circle in the plane T will be complete.

By revolving the plane T into coincidence with the vertical plane, **Tt‴** is found to be the revolved position of the trace **Tt** and **g‴**, the revolved position of the centre. The construction is identical with the construction of the horizontal projection and will become apparent, on inspection, as the necessary lines are shown indicating the mode of procedure. As a result, **k′l′m′n′** determine the major and minor axes of the ellipse, which is the vertical projection of the circle in the plane T.

NOTE. As a check on the accuracy of the work, tangents may be drawn in one projection and the corresponding projection must be tangent at the corresponding point of tangency.

## QUESTIONS ON CHAPTER VIII

1. Mention the three distinct steps into which the solution of a problem may be divided.
2. What is the statement of a problem?
3. What is the analysis of a problem?
4. What is the construction of a problem?
5. What type of projection is generally used in the construction of a problem?

**Note.** In the following problems, the construction, except in a few isolated cases, is to be entirely limited to the first angle of projection.

6. Draw a line through a given point, parallel to a given line. Cive analysis and construction.

7. Draw a line intersecting a given line at a given point. Give analysis and construction.
8. Find where a given oblique line pierces the planes of projection. Give analysis and construction.
9. Transfer the diagram of Question 8 to oblique projection.
10. Pass an oblique plane through a given oblique line. Give analysis and construction.
11. Make an oblique projection of the diagram in Question 10.
12. Pass a plane obliquely through the principal planes and through a line parallel to the ground line. Give analysis and construction. Hint: Use a profile plane in the construction.
13. Transfer the diagram of Question 12 to an oblique projection.
14. Pass an oblique plane through a line which is parallel to the horizontal plane but inclined to the vertical plane. Give analysis and construction.
15. Transfer the diagram of Question 14 to an oblique projection.
16. Pass an oblique plane through a line which is parallel to the vertical plane but inclined to the horizontal plane. Give analysis and construction.
17. Transfer the diagram of Question 16 to an oblique projection.
18. Pass an oblique plane through a given point. Give analysis and construction.
19. Make an oblique projection of the diagram in Question 18.
20. Find the intersection of two planes, oblique to each other and to the principal planes. Give analysis and construction.
21. Transfer the diagram of Question 20 to an oblique projection.
22. Find the intersection of two planes, oblique to each other and to the principal planes. Take the case where the traces do not intersect on one of the principal planes. Give analysis and construction.
23. Find the corresponding projection of a given point lying in a given oblique plane, when one projection is given. Give analysis and construction.
24. Transfer the diagram of Question 23 to an oblique projection.
25. Draw a plane which contains a given point and is parallel to a given plane. Give analysis and construction.
26. Transfer the diagram of Question 25 to an oblique projection.
27. Draw a line through a given point, perpendicular to a given plane. Give analysis and construction.
28. Transfer the diagram of Question 27 to an oblique projection.
29. Draw a plane through a given point, perpendicular to a given line. Give analysis and construction.
30. Transfer the diagram of Question 29 to an oblique projection.
31. Pass a plane through three given points, not in the same straight line. Give analysis and construction.
32. Transfer the diagram of Question 31 to an oblique projection.
33. Revolve a given point, not in the principal planes, about a line lying in one of the principal planes. Give analysis and construction.

34. Transfer the diagram of Question 33 to an oblique projection and show also the plane of the revolving point.
35. Find the true distance between two points in space, when both points are in the first angle of projection. Use the method of revolving the projecting plane of the line until it is parallel to one plane of projection. Give analysis and construction.
36. Make an oblique projection of the diagram in Question 35 and show the projecting plane of the line.
37. Find the true distance between two points in space, when one point is in the first angle and the other is in the fourth angle. Use the method of revolving the projecting plane of the line until it is parallel to one plane of projection. Give analysis and construction.
38. Make an oblique projection of the diagram in Question 37 and show the projecting plane of the line.
39. Find the true distance between two points in space, when both points are in the first angle of projection. Use the method of revolving the projecting plane of the line into one of the planes of projection. Give analysis and construction.
40. Transfer the diagram of Question 39 to an oblique projection and show the projecting plane of the line and the path described by the revolving points.
41. Find the true distance between two points in space, when one point is in the first angle and the other is in the fourth angle of projection. Use the method of revolving the projecting plane of the line into one of the planes of projection. Give analysis and construction.
42. Transfer the diagram of Question 39 to an oblique projection and show the projecting plane of the line and the path described by the revolving points.
43. Find where a given line pierces a given plane. Give analysis and construction.
44. Transfer the diagram of Question 43 to an oblique projection.
45. Find the distance of a given point from a given plane. Give analysis and construction.
46. Transfer the diagram of Question 45 to an oblique projection. Omit the portion of the construction requiring the revolution of the points.
47. Find the distance from a given point to a given line. Give analysis and construction.
48. Transfer the diagram of Question 47 to an oblique projection. Omit the portion of the construction requiring the revolution of the points.
49. Find the angle between two given intersecting lines. Give analysis and construction.
50. Make an oblique projection of the diagram in Question 49.
51. Find the angle between two given planes. Give analysis and construction.
52. Make an oblique projection of the diagram in Question 51.

53. Find the angle between a given plane and the horizontal plane of projection. Give analysis and construction.
54. Transfer the diagram of Question 53 to an oblique projection.
55. Find the angle between a given plane and the vertical plane of projection. Give analysis and construction.
56. Transfer the diagram of Question 55 to an oblique projection.
57. Draw a plane parallel to a given plane at a given distance from it. Give analysis and construction.
58. Project a given line on a given plane. Give analysis and construction.
59. Make an oblique projection of the diagram in Question 58.
60. Find the angle between a given line and a given plane. Give analysis and construction.
61. Make an oblique projection of the diagram in Question 60.
62. Find the shortest distance between a pair of skew lines. Give analysis and construction.
63. Make an oblique projection of the diagram in Question 62.
64. Through a given point, draw a line of a given length, making given angles with the planes of projection.
65. Show the construction for the three remaining cases of the problem in Question 64.
66. Through a given point, draw a plane, making given angles with the principal planes.
67. Prove that the construction in Question 66 is correct by finding the angles that the given plane makes with the principal planes. (Note that there are four possible cases of this problem.)
68. Show the construction for the three remaining cases of the problem in Question 66.
69. Prove that the constructions in Question 68 are correct by finding the angles that the given plane makes with the principal planes.
70. Through a given line, in a given plane, draw another line intersecting it at a given point, and at a given angle.
71. Transfer the diagram of Question 70 to an oblique projection.
72. Through a given line in a given plane, pass another plane, making given angles with the given plane.
73. Make an oblique projection of the diagram in Question 72.
74. Construct the projections of a circle lying in a given oblique plane, the diameter and its centre in the given plane being known.

**Note.** The following exercises embrace operations in all four angles.

75. Given a line the first angle and a point in the second angle, draw a line through the given point, parallel to the given line.
76. Given a line in the first angle and a point in the third angle, draw a line through the given point, parallel to the given line.
77. Given a line in the first angle and a point in the fourth angle, draw a line through the given point, parallel to the given line.
78. Given a line in the second angle and a point in the third angle, draw a line through the given point, parallel to the given line.

79. Given a line in the third angle and a point in the fourth angle, draw a line through the given point, parallel to the given line.
80. Given a line in the fourth angle and a point in the second angle, draw a line through the given point, parallel to the given line.
81. Draw two intersecting lines in the second angle .
82. Draw two intersecting lines in the third angle.
83. Draw two intersecting lines in the fourth angle.
84. Find where a given line pierces the principal planes when the limited portion of the line is in the second angle.
85. Find where a given line pierces the principal planes when the limited portion of the line is in the third angle.
86. Find where a given line pierces the principal planes when the limited portion of the line is in the fourth angle.
87. Show the second angle traces of a plane passed through a second angle oblique line.
88. Show the third angle traces of a plane passed through a third angle oblique line.
89. Show the fourth angle traces of a plane passed through a fourth angle oblique line.
90. Given a line in the second angle and parallel to the ground line, pass an oblique plane through it. Use a profile plane as part of the construction.
91. Given a line in the third angle and parallel to the ground line, pass an oblique plane through it. Use a profile plane as a part of the construction.
92. Given a line in the fourth angle and parallel to the ground line, pass an oblique plane through it. Use a profile plane as a part of the construction.
93. Given a point in the second angle, pass an oblique plane through it. Show only second angle traces.
94. Given a point in the third angle, pass an oblique plane through it. Show only third angle traces.
95. Given a point in the fourth angle, pass an oblique plane through it. Show only fourth angle traces.
96. Given the second angle traces of two oblique planes, find their intersection in the second angle.
97. Given the third angle traces of two oblique planes, find their intersection in the third angle.
98. Given the fourth angle traces of two oblique planes, find their intersection in the fourth angle.
99. Given the first angle traces of an oblique plane and one projection of a second angle point, find the corresponding projection.
100. Given the first angle traces of an oblique plane, and one projection of a third angle point, find the corresponding projection.
101. Given the first angle traces of an oblique plane, and one projection of a fourth angle point, find the corresponding projection.
102. Given the second angle traces of an oblique plane, and one projection of a third angle point, find the corresponding projection.

103. Given the third angle traces of an oblique plane, and one projection of a fourth angle point, find the corresponding projection.
104. Given the first angle traces of an oblique plane, and a point in the second angle, pass a plane through the given point and parallel to the given plane.
105. Given the first angle traces of an oblique plane, and a point in the third angle, pass a plane through the given point and parallel to the given plane.
106. Given the first angle traces of an oblique plane, and a point in the fourth angle, pass a plane through the given point and parallel to the given plane.
107. Given the second angle traces of an oblique plane, and a point in the third angle, pass a plane through the given point and parallel to the given plane.
108. Given the third angle traces of an oblique plane, and a point in the fourth angle, pass a plane through the given point and parallel to the given plane.
109. Given the first angle traces of an oblique plane and a point in the second angle, draw a line through the given point perpendicular to the given plane.
110. Given the first angle traces of an oblique plane and a point in the third angle, draw a line through the given point perpendicular to the given plane.
111. Given the first angle traces of an oblique plane and a point in the fourth angle, draw a line through the given point perpendicular to the given plane.
112. Given the second angle traces of an oblique plane and a point in the fourth angle, draw a line through the given point perpendicular to the given plane.
113. Given the first angle traces of a plane perpendicular to the horizontal plane but inclined to the vertical plane, and a point in the third angle, draw a line through the given point perpendicular to the given plane.
114. Given the third angle traces of a plane perpendicular to the vertical plane but inclined to the horizontal plane, and a point in the fourth angle, draw a line through the given point, perpendicular to the given plane.
115. Given the first angle traces of a plane parallel to the ground line and a point in the third angle, draw a line through the given point perpendicular to the given plane.
116. Draw a profile plane of the diagram in Question 115.
117. Make an oblique projection of the diagram in Question 115.
118. Given the fourth angle traces of a plane parallel to the ground line and a point in the second angle, draw a line through the given point perpendicular to the given plane.
119. Draw a profile plane of the diagram in Question 118.
120. Make an oblique projection of the diagram in Question 118.

121. Given a line in the first angle and a point in the second angle, pass a plane through the given point perpendicular to the given line.
122. Given a line in the first angle and a point in the third angle, pass a plane through the given point perpendicular to the given line.
123. Given a line in the first angle and a point in the fourth angle, pass a plane through the given point perpendicular to the given line.
124. Given a line in the second angle and a point in the third angle, pass a plane through the given point perpendicular to the given line.
125. Given a line in the third angle and a point in the fourth angle, pass a plane through the given point perpendicular to the given line.
126. Given three points in the second angle, pass a plane through them.
127. Given three points in the third angle, pass a plane through them.
128. Given three points in the fourth angle, pass a plane through them.
129. Given two points in the first angle and one point in the second angle, pass a plane through them.
130. Given a point in the first angle, one in the second angle, and one in the third angle, pass a plane through them.
131. Given a point in the second angle, one in the third angle, and one in the fourth angle, pass a plane through them.
132. Given a line in the horizontal plane and a point in the second angle, revolve the point about the line until it coincides with the horizontal plane.
133. Given a line in the horizontal plane and a point in the third angle, revolve the point about the line until it coincides with the horizontal plane.
134. Given a line in the horizontal plane and a point in the fourth angle revolve the point about the line until it coincides with the horizontal plane.
135. Given a line in the vertical plane and a point in the second angle, revolve the point about the line until it coincides with the vertical plane.
136. Given a line in the vertical plane and a point in the fourth angle, revolve the point about the line until it coincides with the vertical plane.
137. Given two points in the second angle, find the true distance between them.
138. Given two points in the third angle, find the true distance between them.
139. Given two points in the fourth angle, find the true distance between them.
140. Given one point in the first angle and one point in the second angle, find the true distance between them.
141. Given one point in the first angle and one point in the third angle, find the true distance between them.
142. Given one point in the second angle and one point in the third angle, find the true distance between them.

143. Given one point in the second angle and one point in the fourth angle, find the true distance between them.
144. Given the first angle traces of a plane and a line in the second angle, find where the given line pierces the given plane.
145. Given the first angle traces of a plane and a line in the third angle, find where the given line pierces the given plane.
146. Given the first angle traces of a plane and a line in the fourth angle, find where the given line pierces the given plane.
147. Given the second angle traces of a plane and a line in the third angle, find where the given line pierces the given plane.
148. Given the second angle traces of a plane and a line in the fourth angle, find where the given line pierces the given plane.
149. Given the third angle traces of a plane and a line in the fourth angle, find where the given line pierces the given plane.
150. Given the first angle traces of a plane and a point in the second angle, find the distance from the point to the plane.
151. Given the first angle traces of a plane and a point in the third angle, find the distance from the point to the plane.
152. Given the first angle traces of a plane and a point in the fourth angle, find the distance from the point to the plane.
153. Given the second angle traces of a plane and a point in the third angle, find the distance from the point to the plane.
154. Given the second angle traces of a plane and a point in the fourth angle, find the distance form the point to the plane.
155. Given the third angle traces of a plane and a point in the fourth angle, find the distance from the point to the plane.
156. Given a line in the first angle and a point in the second angle, find the distance from the point to the line.
157. Given a line in the first angle and a point in the third angle, find the distance from the point to the line.
158. Given a line in the first angle and a point in the fourth angle, find the distance from the point to the line.
159. Given a line in the second angle and a point in the third angle, find the distance from the point to the line.
160. Given a line in the second angle and a point in the fourth angle, find the distance from the point to the line.
161. Given a line in the third angle and a point in the fourth angle, find the distance from the point to the line.
162. Given two intersecting lines in the second angle, find the angle between them.
163. Given two intersecting lines in the third angle, find the angle between them.
164. Given two intersecting lines in the fourth angle, find the angle between them.
165. Given two intersecting lines, one in the first and one in the second angle, find the angle between them.
166. Given two intersecting lines, one in the first and one in the third angle, find the angle between them.

167. Given two intersecting lines, one in the first and one in the fourth angle, find the angle between them.
168. Given two intersecting lines, one in the second and one in the third angle, find the angle between them.
169. Given two intersecting lines, one in the second and one in the fourth angle, find the angle between them.
170. Given two intersecting lines, one in the third and one in the fourth angle, find the angle between them.
171. Given the second angle traces of two intersecting planes, find the angle between them.
172. Given the third angle traces of two intersecting planes, find the angle between them.
173. Given the fourth angle traces of two intersecting planes, find the angle between them.
174. Given the first angle traces of one plane and the second angle traces of another plane, find the angle between them.
175. Given the first angle traces of one plane and the third angle traces of another plane, find the angle between them.
176. Given the first angle traces of one plane and the fourth angle traces of another plane, find the angle between them.
177. Given the second angle traces of one plane and the third angle traces of another plane, find the angle between them.
178. Given the second angle traces of one plane and the fourth angle traces of another plane, find the angle between them.
179. Given the third angle traces of one plane and the fourth angle traces of another plane, find the angle between them.
180. Given a plane in the second angle, find the angle between the given plane and the horizontal plane.
181. Given a plane in the second angle, find the angle between the given plane and the vertical plane.
182. Given a plane in the third angle, find the angle between the given plane and the horizontal plane.
183. Given a plane in the third angle, find the angle between the given plane and the vertical plane.
184. Given a plane in the fourth angle, find the angle between the given plane and the horizontal plane.
185. Given a plane in the fourth angle, find the angle between the given plane and the vertical plane.
186. Given the second angle traces of a plane, draw another parallel plane at a given distance from it.
187. Given the third angle traces of a plane, draw another parallel plane at a given distance from it.
188. Given the fourth angle traces of a plane, draw another parallel plane at a given distance from it.
189. Given the first angle traces of a plane and a line in the second angle, project the given line on the given plane.
190. Given the first angle traces of a plane and a line in the third angle, project the given line on the given plane.

191. Given the first angle traces of a plane and a line in the fourth angle, project the given line on the given plane.
192. Given the second angle traces of a plane and a line in the third angle, project the given line on the given plane.
193. Given the second angle traces of a plane and a line in the fourth angle, project the given line on the given plane.
194. Given the third angle traces of a plane and a line in the fourth angle, project the given line on the given plane.
195. Given the fourth angle traces of a plane and a line in the second angle, project the given line on the given plane.
196. Given the first angle traces of a plane and a line in the second angle, find the angle between the given line and the given plane.
197. Given the first angle traces of a plane and a line in the third angle, find the angle between the given line and the given plane.
198. Given the first angle traces of a plane and a line in the fourth angle, find the angle between the given line and the given plane.
199. Given the second angle traces of a plane and a line in the third angle, find the angle between the given line and the given plane.
200. Given the second angle traces of a plane and a line in the fourth angle, find the angle between the given line and the given plane
201. Given the third angle traces of a plane and a line in the fourth angle, find the angle between the given line and the given plane.
202. Given the fourth angle traces of a plane and a line in the second angle, find the angle between the given line and the given plane.
203. Given the fourth angle traces of a plane and a line in the third angle, find the angle between the given line and the given plane.
204. Given a line in the first angle and another line in the second angle (skew lines). find the shortest distance between them.
205. Given a line in the first angle and another line in the third angle (skew lines), find the shortest distance between them.
206. Given a line in the first angle and another line in the fourth angle (skew lines), find the shortest distance between them.
207. Given a line in the second angle and another line in the third angle (skew lines), find the shortest ditstance between them.
208. Given a line in the second angle and another line in the fourth angle (skew lines); find the shortest distance between them.
209. Given a line in the third angle and another line in the fourth angle (skew lines), find the shortest distance between them.
210. Through a given point in the second angle, draw a line of a given length, making given angles with the planes of projection.
211. Through a given point in the third angle, draw a line of a given length, making given angles with the planes of projection.
212. Through a given point in the fourth angle, draw a line of a given length, making given angles with the planes of projection.
213. Through a given point in the second angle, draw a plane making given angles with the principal planes.
214. Through a given point in the third angle, draw a plane making given angles with the principal planes.

**215.** Through a given point in the fourth angle, draw a plane making given angles with the principal planes.

**216.** Given the second angle traces of a plane, a line, and a point in the plane, draw another line through the given point, making a given angle with the given line.

**217.** Given the third angle traces of a plane, a line. and a point in the plane, draw another line through the given point, making a given angle with the given line.

**218.** Given the fourth angle traces of a plane, a line and a point in the plane, draw another line through the given point, making a given angle with'the given line.

**219.** Given the second angle traces of a plane, and a line in the plane, draw through the line another plane making a given angle with the given plane.

**220.** Given the third angle traces of a plane, and a line in the plane, draw through the line another plane making a given angle with the given plane.

**221.** Given the fourth angle traces of a plane, and a line in the plane, draw through the line another plane making a given angle with the given plane.

**222.** Given the second angle traces of a plane, the diameter and the centre of a circle, construct the projections of the circle.

**223.** Given the third angle traces of a plane, the diameter and the centre of a circle, construct the projections of the circle.

**224.** Given the fourth angie traces of a plane, the diameter, and the centre of a circle, construct the projections of the circle.

# CHAPTER IX

## CLASSIFICATION OF LINES

**901. Introductory.** Lines are of an infinite variety of forms. The frequent occurrence in engineering of certain varieties makes it desirable to know their properties as well as their method of construction. It must be remembered that lines and points are **mathematical concepts** and that they have no material existence. That is to say, a line may have so many feet of length but as it has no width or thickness, its volume, therefore, is zero. Hence, it cannot exist except in the imagination. Likewise, a point is a still further reduction and has position only; it has no dimensions at all. Of course, the material representation of lines and points requires finite dimensions, but when speaking of them, or representing them, it is the **associated idea,** rather than the representation, which is desired.

**902. Straight line. A straight line** may be defined as the **shortest distance** between **two points.*** It may also be described as the locus (or path) of a **generating point** which moves in the **same direction.** Hence, a straight line is fixed in space by two points, or, by a point and a direction.

**903. Singly curved line. A singly curved line** is the locus (plural:–loci) of a **generating point** which moves in a **varying direction** but remains in a single plane. Sometimes the singly curved line is called a **plane curve** because all points on the curve must lie in the same plane.

**904. Representation of straight and singly curved lines.** Straight and singly curved lines are represented by their **projections.** When singly curved lines are parallel to the plane

* Frequently, this is called a right line. There seems no reason, however, why this new nomenclature should be used; hence, it is here avoided.

of projection, they are projected in their true form and require only one plane of projection for their complete representation. If the plane of the curve is perpendicular to the principal planes, a **profile** will suffice. If the plane of the curve is inclined to the planes of projection, both horizontal and vertical projections may be necessary, unless a **supplementary** plane be used, which is parallel to the plane of the curve.* This latter condition is then similar to that obtained when the plane of the curve is parallel to one of the principal planes.

**905. Circle.** The circle is a **plane curve,** every point of which is **equidistant** from a fixed point called the **centre.** The path described by the moving point (or locus) is frequently designated as the "circumference of the circle."† To define such curves consistently, it is necessary to limit the definition to the **nature** of the line forming the curve. Therefore, what is usually known as the circumference of the circle should simply be known as the **circle** and then subsequent definitions of other curves become consistently alike.

In Fig. 144 a **circle** is shown; **abedc** is the curve or circle proper. The fixed point **o** is called the **centre** and every point on the circle is equidistant from it. This fixed distance is called the **radius; oa, oc,** and **ob** are all radii of the circle; **bc** is a **diameter** and is a straight line through the centre and equal to two radii in length. The straight line, **de,** limited by the circle is a **chord** and when it passes through the centre it becomes a diameter; when the same line is extended like **gh** it is a **secant.** A limited portion of the circle like ac is an **arc;** when equal to one-quarter of the whole circle it is a **quadrant;** when equal to one-half of the whole circle it is a **semicircle** as **cab** or **bfc.** The area included between two radii and the circle is a **sector** as **aoc;** that between any line like **de** and the circle is

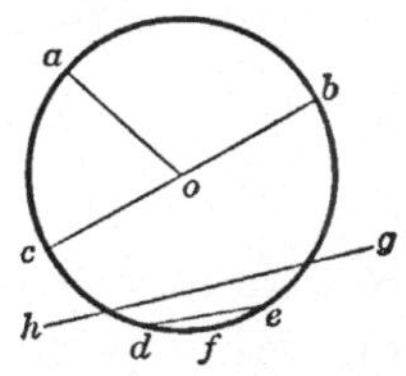

FIG. 144.

* In all these cases, the plane of the curve may be made to coincide with the plane of projection. This, of course, is a special case.

† The introduction of this term makes it necessary to define the circle as the enclosed area. This condition is unfortunate, as in the case of the parabola, hyperbola, and numerous other curves, the curves are open and do not enclose an area.

a **segment.** If any other circle is drawn with the same centre of the circles are **concentric,** otherwise **eccentric;** the distance between the centres in the latter case is the **eccentricity.**

**906. Ellipse.** The **ellipse** is a **plane curve,** in which the **sum** of the distances of any point on the curve from two fixed points is constant. Fig. 145 shows this curve as **adbc;** The **major axis** is ab, and its length is the constant distance of the definition; cd is the **minor axis** and is perpendicular to ab through its middle point **o.** The fixed points or foci (either one is a focus) are **e** and f and are located on the major axis.

If ab be assumed as the constant distance, and **e** and f be assumed as the foci, the minor axis is determined by drawing arcs from **e** and f with **oa,** equal to one-half of the major axis,

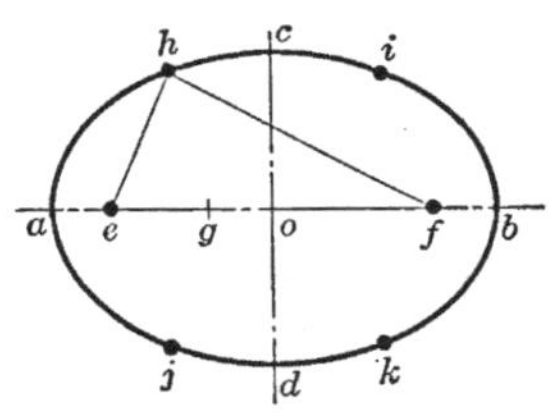

FIG. 145.

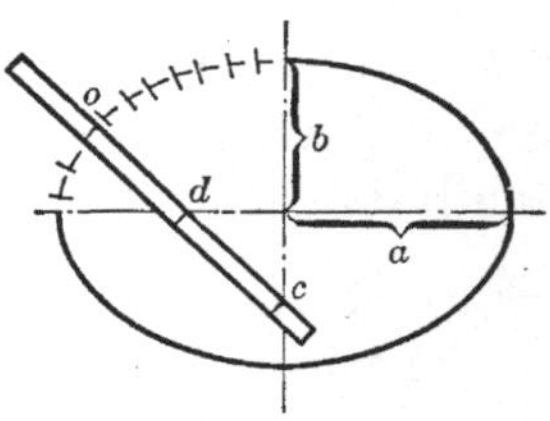

FIG. 146.

as a radius. Thus **ec+cf=ab** and also **ed+df=ab.** To find any other point on the curve, assume any distance as **bg,** and with **bg** as a radius and f as a centre, draw an arc fh. With the balance of the major axis **ag** as a radius, draw an arc **eh** from the focus **e** as a centre. These intersecting arcs locate **h,** a point on the curve. Thus **eh+hf=ab** and therefore satisfies the definition of the curve. With the same radii just used, the three other points i, j and **k** are located. In general, four points are determined for any assumption except for the points a, **c,** b or d. It can be shown that a and **b** are points on the curve, because **oa=ob** and **oe=of.** Hence **ae=fb,** therefore, fa+**ea=** ab and also **eb+fb=ab.**

In the construction of this, or any other curve, the student should avoid trying to save time by locating only a few points. This is a mistaken idea, as, within reasonable limits, time is saved by drawing numerous points on the curve, particularly where the curve changes its direction rapidly. The direction of the curve at any point should be known with a reasonable degree of accuracy.

Another method of drawing an ellipse is shown in Fig. 146. It is known as the **trammel** method. Take any straight ruler and make **oc = a** and **od = b.** By locating c on the minor axis and d on the major axis, a point is located at o, as shown. This method is a very rapid one, and is the one generally used when a true ellipse is to be plotted, on account of the very few lines required in the construction. Both methods mentioned are theoretically accurate, but the latter method is perhaps used oftener than the former.

In practice, ellipses are usually approximated by employing four circular arcs, of two different radii as indicated in Art. 405. The major and minor axes are laid off and a smooth looking curve drawn between these limits. Of course, the circular arcs do not produce a true ellipse, but as a rule, this method is a rapid one and answers the purpose in conveying the idea.

**907. Parabola.** The **parabola** is a **plane curve,** which is the locus of a point, moving so that the **distance** from a **fixed point** is always equal to the **distance** from a **fixed** line. The fixed point is the **focus** and the fixed line is the **directrix.** A line through the focus and perpendicular to the directrix as **cg,** Fig. 147, is the axis with respect to which the curve is symmetrical. The intersection of the axis and the curve is the **vertex** shown at f.

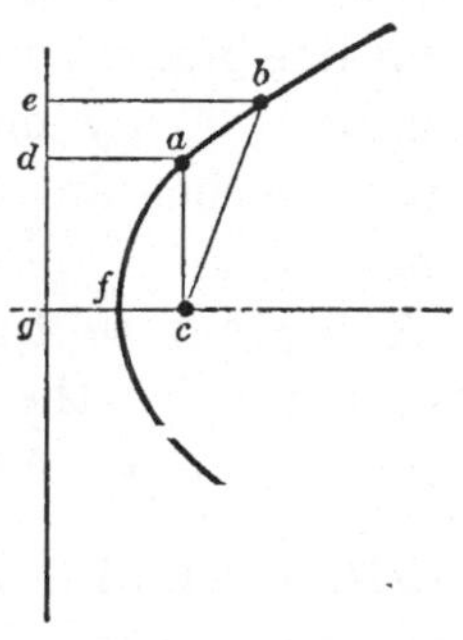

FIG. 147.

The point **a** on the curve is so situated that **ac = ad;** also **b** is so situated that **bc = be.** Points beyond **b** become more and more remote, from both the axis and directrix. Hence, it is an open curve, extending to infinity. Discussions are usually limited to some finite portion of the curve.

**908. Hyperbola.** The hyperbola is a **plane curve,** traced by a point, which moves so that the **difference** of its **distances** from **two fixed** points is **constant.** The fixed points **a** and b,

Fig. 148, are the **foci.** The line **ab,** passing through them, is the **transverse** * **axis;** the point at which either curve crosses the axis as **e** or **f** is the **vertex** (plural:—vertices), and the line **kl,** perpendicular to **ab** at its middle point, is the **conjugate axis.**

To draw the curve, lay off the foci a and **b;** also lay off **ef,** the constant distance, so that **eo = of** and **o** is the middle of ab. It must be observed that **ef** is always smaller than **ab** otherwise the curve cannot be constructed. Take any radius **bc,** greater than bf, and draw an indefinite arc; from **a,** draw **ac,** so that ac − **bc = ef,** hence, **ac = bc + ef.** The point **c** is thus on the curve. Similarly, draw an arc **ad,** from **a,** and another arc **bd = ad + ef.** This locates **d,** which, in this case, is on another curve. In spection will show that there are two **branches** of this curve. The point **c** has been selected so as to be on one branch, and **d,** on the other. To construct the curve, accurately, many more points must be located than shown. Both branches are open and symmetrical with respect to both axes.

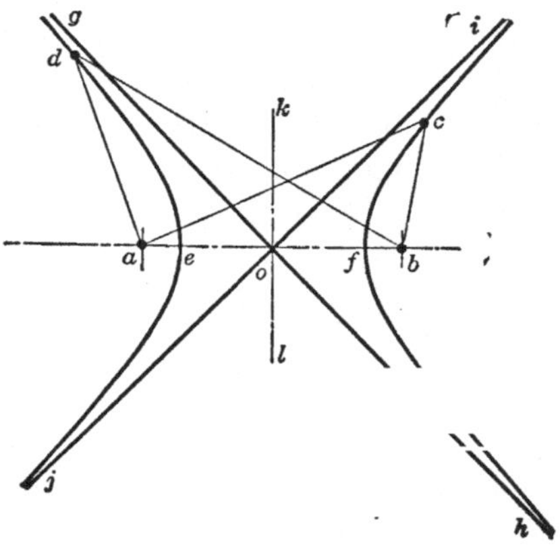


Fig. 148.

A tangent to the curve through **o** is called an **asymptote** when it touches the hyperbola in two points, each at an infinite distance from **o.** As will be observed, there are two asymptotes.

**909. Cycloid.** The **cycloid** is a **plane curve,** traced by a **point** on a circle which **rolls** over a **straight line.** The straight line over which the circle rolls is the **directrix;** the point on the circle may be considered as the **generating point.**

The curve is shown as **abc . . . i** in Fig. 149. To construct it, lay out the directrix **ai,** and to one side, draw an auxiliary circle equal in diameter to the rolling circle as shown at **1′ 2′,** etc. On a line through the centre of the auxiliary circle, draw the line **3′–9** parallel to the directrix **ai.** Lay off the distance

* Sometimes known as the "principal axis."

**1–9** on this line, equal to the length of the circle (3.14×diameter). Assume that when the centre of the rolling circle is at **1**, **a** is the position of the generating point. After one-eighth of a revolution the centre has moved to **2**, where the distance **1–2** is one-eighth of the distance **1–9**. The corresponding position of the generating point is shown at **2′** in the auxiliary circle at the left. Hence, for one-eighth of a revolution the centre of the rolling circle has moved from **1** to **2** and the generating point has moved a distance vertically upward equal to the distance of **2′** above the line **ai**. Therefore, draw a line through **2′**, parallel to **ai**; and then from **2** as a centre, draw an arc with the radius of the rolling circle intersecting this line in the point **b**, a point on the required curve. After a quarter of a revolution, the generating point is above the directrix, at a height equal to the

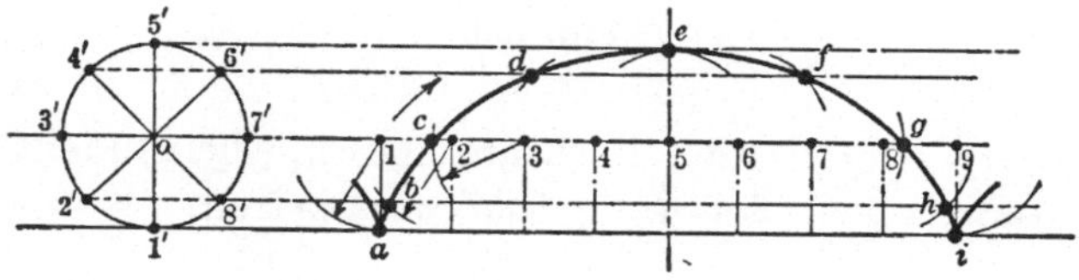


FIG. 149.

distance of **3′** above **ai**. It is also on an arc from **3**, with a radius equal again to the radius of the rolling circle; hence, **c** is the point. This process is continued until the generating point reaches its maximum height **e** after one-half of a revolution, when it begins to descend, to i, as shown, after completing one revolution. Further rolling of the circle causes the generating point to duplicate its former steps, as it continues along the directrix to infinity if desired.

The cycloid is the same curve that is produced by a mark on the rim of a car-wheel, while rolling along the track, only, here, no slipping is permitted. The cycloid is, thus, continuous, each **arch** being an exact duplicate of the preceding.

**910. Epicycloid.** The **epicyloid** is a **plane curve,** which is generated by a point on a circle which **rolls** on the out**side** of another **circle.** The **directrix** is here an arc of a circle. instead of a straight line.

The construction is indicated in Fig. 150. The centre of the rolling circle assumes successive positions as **1, 2, 3,** etc. The length of the arc **ai** is equal to the length of the rolling circle. The points are located much the same as in the cycloid, and, as

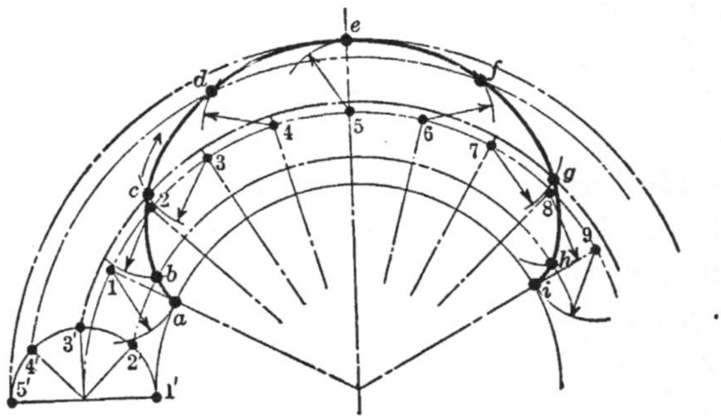

FIG. 150.

the necessary construction lines are shown, the student should have no difficulty in following the construction.

**911. Hypocycloid.** The **hypocycloid** is a **plane curve** generated by a point on a **circle** which **rolls** on the inside o

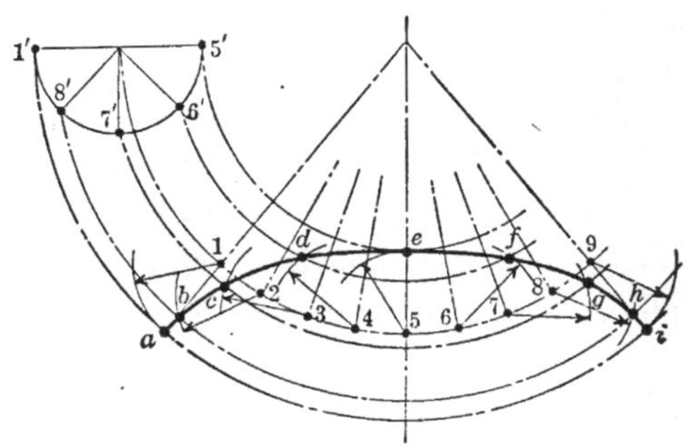

FIG. 151.

another **circle**. The directrix of the epicycloid and the hypocycloid may be the same, the epicycloid is described on the outside of the arc while the hypocycloid is described on the inside.

All the necessary construction lines required to draw the hypocycloid have been added in Fig. 151 and the method is perhaps evident. No confusion should arise even though the curves are drawn in positions other than those shown. For instance, the cycloids (this includes the cycloids, epicycloid and hypocycloid) could be shown upside-down; the curves are generated in much the same way and their properties, therefore, do not change.

**912. Spiral.** The **spiral** is a **plane curve,** generated by a point moving **along** a given line while the given line is **revolving** about some point on the line. An infinite number of spirals may exist, because the point may have a variable velocity along the line, while again the line may have a variable angular velocity about the point. The one having uniform motion of the point along the line, and uniform angular velocity about the point is called the **Spiral of Archimedes.**

Fig. 152 shows the **Archimedian** spiral which is perhaps the simplest type of spiral. If ox be assumed as the primitive position of a line revolving at o, and the point also starts at **o,** then **o** is the starting point of the curve. Suppose that after one-eighth of a revolution the generating point has moved a distance **oa,** then, after one-quarter of a revolution, the point will be at **b,** where **ob** $=2\times$**oa,** and so on. The spiral becomes larger and larger as the revolution continues. Had the line revolved in the other direction, the curve would have been the reverse of the one shown.

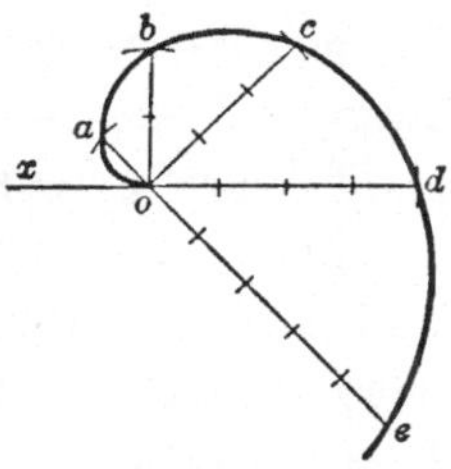

FIG. 152.

**913. Doubly curved line.** A doubly curved line is one whose direction is continually changing and whose points do not lie in one plane. A piece of wire may be twisted so as to furnish a good example of a doubly curved line.

**914. Representation of doubly curved lines.** As no single plane can contain a doubly curved line, it becomes necessary to use two planes and project, orthographically, the line on them. Familiarity is had with the representation of points in space on the principal planes. The line may be conceived as being made up of an infinite number of points and each point can be located in space by its projections.

Fig. 153 represents a curve **ABCD**, shown by its horizontal projection **abcd** and its vertical projection **a′b′c′d′**. Any point on the curve, such as **B**, is found by erecting perpendiculars from **b** and **b′** and extending them to their intersection; this will be the point sought. The principal planes must be at right angles to each other if it is desired to locate a point by erecting these perpendiculars; otherwise, the curve must be imagined from its projections when the planes are revolved into coincidence, as is customary in orthographic projection.

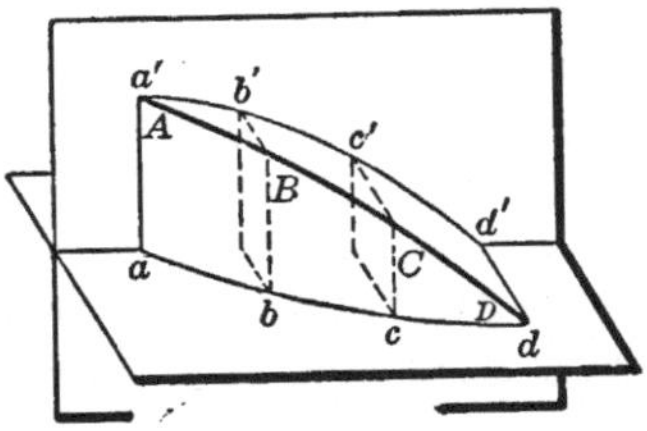


FIG. 153.

**915. Helix.** The helix is a doubly curved line described by a point having motion around a line called the **axis,** and in addition, a motion along it. Unless it is noted otherwise, the helix will be considered as having a uniform circular motion around the axis and also a uniform motion along it. The curve finds its most extensive application on that type of screw known as a machine screw. This is then a **uniform** cylindrical **helix.** Wood screws furnish examples of conical helices.* The helix is also frequently used in making springs of a type known as helical springs.†

Fig. 154 shows the construction of the helix. Assume that the drawing is made in the third angle of projection; the plan is therefore on top. The ground line is omitted because the distance of the points from the principal planes is not required, but only their relative location to each other. To return, **1′**, **2′**, . . . **8′** is the plan (horizontal projection) of the helix, showing the circular motion of the point around the axis **ab.** In the elevation (vertical projection), the starting point of the curve is shown at **1.** If the point revolves in the direction of the arrow, it will, on making one-eighth of a revolution, be at **2′** in plan

* The distinction might be made between cylindrical and conical helices by considering the curve as being drawn on the surface of a cylinder or a cone as the case may be.

† Helical springs are frequently although incorrectly called spiral springs. The spiral has been previously defined; and a spring of that shape is a spiral spring.

and at **2** in elevation. After a quarter of a revolution, the point is at **3′** in plan, and at **3** in elevation. The position **3** is its extreme movement to the right, for at **4,** the point has moved to the left, although continually upward as shown in the elevation. On completion of one revolution, the point is at **9,** ready to proceed with an identical curve beyond it.

The distance between any point and the position of the point after one complete revolution is known as the **pitch.** The distance **p** is that pitch, and may be given from any point on the curve to the succeeding position of that point after one

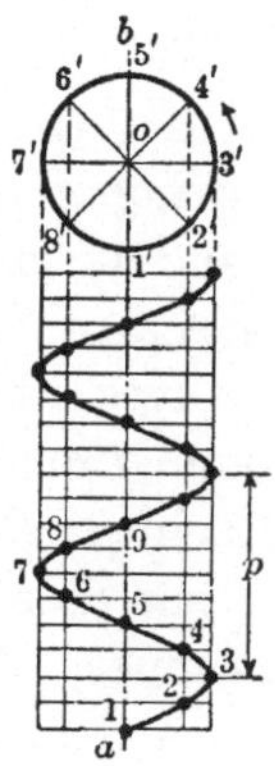


FIG. 154.

FIG. 155.

revolution. The distance **01′, 02′,** etc. is the **radius** of the helix.

Fig. 155 is a double helix and consists simply of two distinct helices, generated so that the starting point of one helix is just one-half of a revolution ahead or behind the other helix. The portion of the helix that is in front of the axis is shown in full; that behind the axis is shown dotted to give the effect of a helix drawn on a cylinder. The pitch again is measured on any **one** curve and requires a complete revolution. It must not be measured from one curve to a similar position on the next curve as the two helices are entirely distinct. **Fig. 155** will show this correctly. Double, and even triple and quadruple helices are used on screws; they are simply interwoven so as to be equal distances apart.

## 916. Classification of lines.

- **Lines**
  - **Straight Lines:** Unidirectional.
  - **Curved Lines:**
    - **Singly Curved Lines:** Direction continually changing, but always in a single plane.
      - circle
      - ellipse
      - parabola
      - hyperbola
      - cycloid
      - epicycloid
      - hypocycloid
      - spiral
      - etc.
    - **Doubly Curved Lines:** Direction continually changing, but not in any one plane.
      - helix
      - etc.

**917. Tangent.** A tangent is the limiting position of a secant as the points of secancy approach and ultimately reach coincidence. Suppose, in Fig. 156, **pq** is a secant to the curve and that it revolves about **p** as a centre. At some time, the secant **pq** will assume some such position as **pr**; the point **q** has then moved to **r** and if it continues, it will pass through **p** and reach **s.** The secant then intersects on the opposite side of **p.** If the rotation be such that **q** passes through **r** and ultimately coincides with **p,** then this limiting position of the secant, shown as **pt,** is the tangent to the curve and **p** is the point of tangency. It will be observed that the tangent is fixed by the point **p,** and the **direction** of the limiting position of the secant.

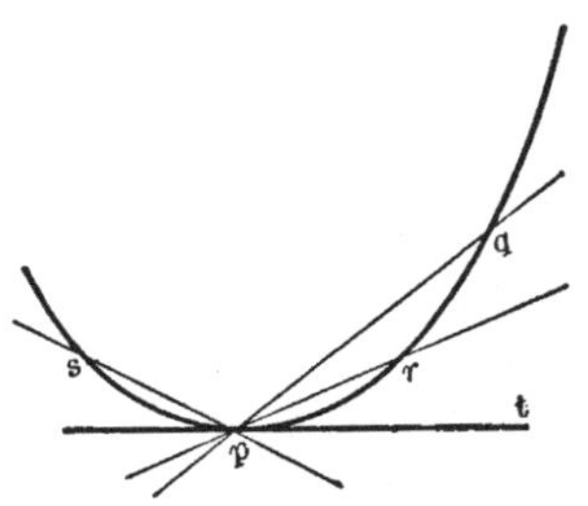

FIG. 156.

The condition of tangency is a mutual relation. That is, the curve is tangent to the line or the line is tangent to the curve. Also, two or more curves may be tangent to each other because the tangent line may be considered (at the point of tangency) as the direction of the curve (see Art. 920).

**918. Construction of a tangent.** If a tangent is to be drawn to a curve from an outside point, the drafting room method is to use a ruler of some sort and place it a slight distance away from the point and then revolve it until it nearly touches the curve; a straight line then drawn through the point and touching the curve will be the required tangent.

If the problem is to draw a tangent at a given point on a curve, however, the quick method would be to estimate the direction so that the tangent appears to coincide with as much of the curve on one side as it does on the other.

A more accurate method of constructing the tangent at a given point on a curve is shown in Fig. 157. Let a be the desired point of tangency. Draw through a, the secants **ab, ac, ad,** the number depending upon the degree of accuracy, but always more than here shown. With a as a centre, draw any indefinite arc **eh,** cutting the prolongations of the secants. Lay off the chord **ab** = **ei, ac** = **fj,** and **ad** = **hk,** but this `etter chord is laid

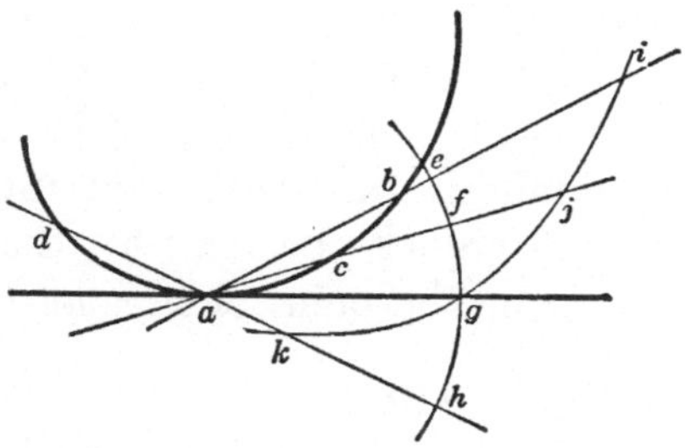


FIG. 157.

off to the left of the arc, because its secant cuts the curve to the left of the desired point of tangency. A smooth curve may now be drawn through i, j, and **k,** and where this curve intersects the indefinite arc at **g,** draw **ga,** the required tangent. The proof of this is quite simple. If **ab,** **ac** and **ad** be considered as **displacements** of the points b, **c** and **d** from the positions that they should occupy when the secant becomes a tangent, then, when these points approach **a,** so as ultimately to coincide with it, the displacement is zero. The secant then becomes a tangent. The curve **ijk** is a curve of displacements from **efh,** the indefinite arc. Hence, the desired tangent must pass through **g,** as it lies on the curve **efh** and its displacement from that curve is therefore zero.

**919.** To **find the point of tangency.** On the other hand, if the tangent is drawn, and it is desired to find the point of tangency, the problem becomes slightly different. Suppose **TT**, Fig. 158, is the given tangent, and **atb** is the given curve. It is desired to find the point of tangency t. Draw **ab, cd** and **ef**, any chords parallel to **TT**. Lay off **hg**, through a, perpendicular to **TT**, and **br**, through **b**, perpendicular also to **TT**. Make **gh = qr = ab**. In the other cases, make **ij = op = cd**, and **kl = mn = ef**. Now draw a smooth curve through **hjlnpr**. Where this curve intersects **TT** at t, the desired point of tangency is found. Again, the proof is quite simple. The lengths of the vertical lines above and below **TT** are equal to the lengths of the corresponding chords. As the chords approach the tangent, they diminish in length and ultimately become zero. Where the curve crosses the tangent, the chord length is zero, and, hence, must be the point of tangency.

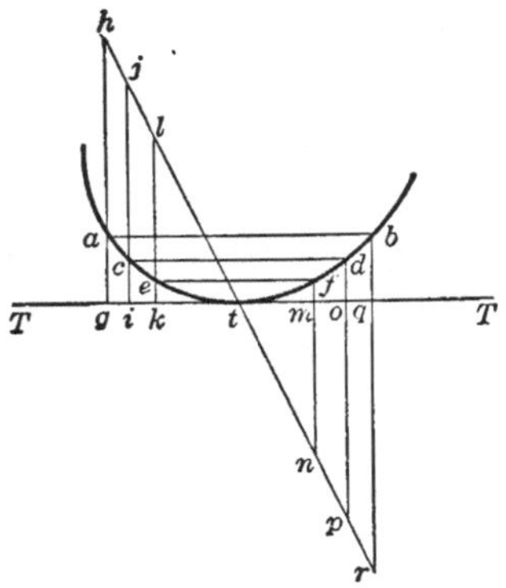


FIG. 158.

**920. Direction of a curve.** A curve continually changes its direction, but at any given point its direction is along the tangent to the curve by definition. It is proved in Mechanics, that if forces act on a particle so as to give it a curved motion, the particle will fly off along a tangent when the impressed forces cease to act.*

**921. Angle between curves.** The angle between two intersecting curves is the same as the angles, made by the tangents at the point of intersection, because the tangents determine the direction of the curve at that point. Hence, to draw **smooth curves**, it is necessary that the tangent at the end of one curve should coincide with the tangent at the beginning of the next curve.

**922. Intersection of lines.** Two lines intersect when they have a point in common. When the term intersection is used in connection with a pair of straight lines, it necessarily implies that the lines make an angle with each other greater than zero;

* See Newton's laws of motion in a text-book on Physics.

since, otherwise, if there is a zero angular relation, the lines become coincident and have all points in common.

When a line meets a curve, the angle between the line and the curve at the point of intersection is the same as the angle between the line and the tangent to the curve at that point. When this angle of intersection becomes zero, however, by having the line coincide with the tangent, then it is the special case of intersection known as tangency.

Similarly when two curves intersect their angle of intersection is the same as the angle between their tangents at the point of intersection. Also, when this angle becomes zero then the curves are tangent to each other.

Thus, in order to differentiate between the two types of intersection, **angular intersection** means intersection at an angle greater than zero; and, as a consequence, the intersection at a zero angle is known as **tangential intersection**. When intersection is unmodified, then angular intersection is implied.

**923. Order of contact of tangents.** A tangent has been previously defined as the limiting position of a secant, as the points of secancy approach and ultimately coincide with each other. This contact, for simple tangency, is of the **first order.** Two curves may also be tangent to each other so as to have contact of the first order, as for example, two circles, internally or externally tangent.

Suppose two curves **acb** and **abe**, Fig. 159, have first order contact at a, and cut each other at the point b. If the curve **abe** be made to revolve about the point a as a centre, so as to maintain simple tangency * and also to have the point b approach a, then at some stage of the revolution the point b can be made to coincide with **a.** Under this condition there is tangency of a higher order because three points were made to ultimately coincide with each other; and it is called **second order** of contact. It is possible to have third order of contact with four coincident points; and so on. The

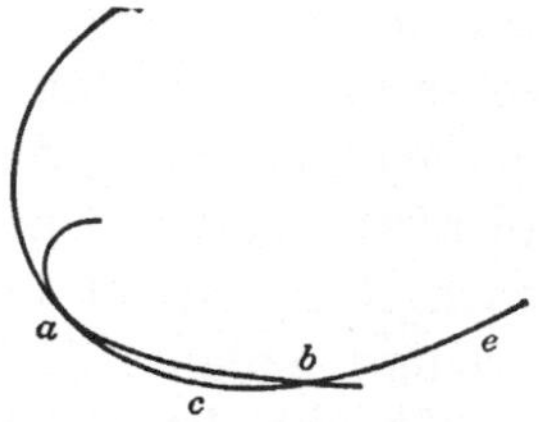

FIG. 159.

* In order to make this a rigid demonstration, the centre of curvature of the two curves, at the point a must not be the same. See Art. 924.

order of contact is always one less than the number of points that approach coincidence.

**924. Osculating circle. Centre of curvature.** Let **abc**, Fig. 160, be a curve and b, a point through which a circle **gdbe** passes, cutting the curve **abc** in three points **d,b** and **e.** If the diameter of the circle is properly chosen, it may be revolved about b as a centre so that the points **d** and **e** will both approach and ultimately coincide with **b** at the same instant. This position of the circle is shown as bf. Hence, the circle **bf** is tangent to the curve abc, and is of the **second order** of contact. This circle is the **osculating circle.** As this osculating circle must more nearly approach the curvature of the curve abc than any other circle, its radius at the point **b** is the **radius of curvature.** At every other point on the curve, there is a new osculating circle, of a new centre, and of a new radius. Thus, the osculating circle is the second order tangent circle at the point; and the **radius of curvature** may be defined as the radius of the osculating circle through the point, the **centre of curvature** being the centre of the osculating circle.

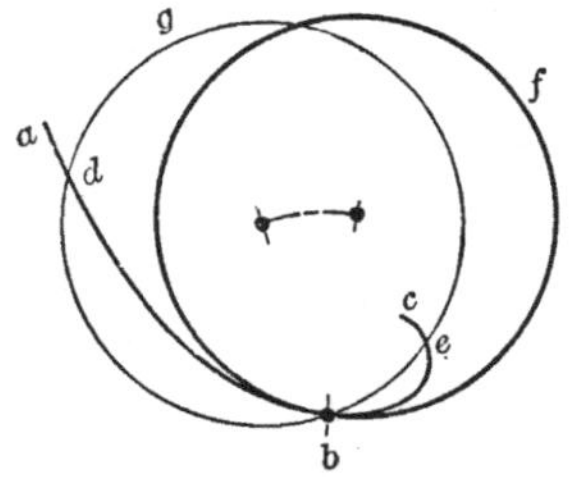

FIG. 160.

**925. Osculating plane.** If a tangent be drawn to any doubly curved line, an infinite number of planes may be passed so as to contain the tangent. If some one position of the plane be selected so as to contain the tangent and a piercing point of the doubly curved line on it, then by proper revolution of the plane the piercing point can be made to approach and ultimately coincide with the point of tangency; in this position, the plane is an **osculating plane.**

To put the matter differently, suppose it is desired to find the osculating plane at some point on a doubly curved line. In this case, draw a pair of secants to the doubly curved line which intersect at the given point. A plane passed through these secants will cut the doubly curved line in three points. As the secants approach tangency, the plane will approach osculation, and this osculating plane is identical with that of the former discussion for the same point on the curve. If the curve under consideration be a plane curve, then the secants will lie in the plane of the curve, and, hence, the osculating plane of the curve will be the plane of the curve.

**926. Point of inflexion. Inflexional tangent.** Assume a curve **dae**, Fig. 161, and through some one point a draw the secant **bc**. If the secant be revolved about the point **a** so that the points of intersection **b** and **c** approach a, at some stage of the revolution they will coincide with it at the same instant if the point **a** is properly chosen. The point **a** must be such that three points on the curve ultimately coincide at the same instant. Further than this, the radius of curvature (centre of the osculating circle) must make an abrupt change from one side of the curve to the other at this point. The **point** of **inflexion** therefore is a point at which the radius of curvature changes from one side of the curve to the other. The **inflexional tangent** is the tangent at the point of inflexion. It may also be noted that the inflexional tangent has a **second order** of contact (three coincident points) and therefore is the **osculating line** to the curve at the point of inflexion.

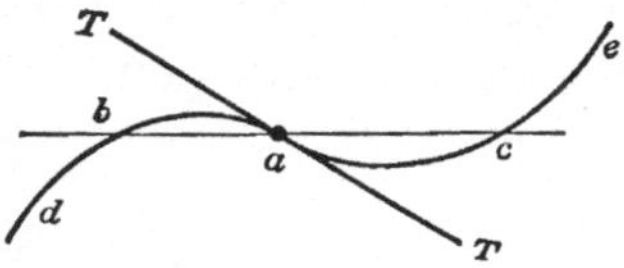


FIG. 161.

**927. Normal.** A normal to a curve is a perpendicular to the tangent at the point of tangency. The **principal normal** lies in the osculating plane. As an infinite number of normals may be drawn to the tangent at the point of tangency, the normal may revolve about the tangent so as to generate a plane which will be perpendicular to the tangent and thus establishes a **normal plane**. In the case of a circle, the radius at the point of tangency is normal to the tangent; in such cases, the tangent is easily drawn, as it must be perpendicular to the radius at the point of contact.

**928. Rectification.** When a curve is made to roll on a straight line, so that no slip occurs between the curve and the line, the distance measured on the line is equal to the corresponding length of the curve. This process of finding the length of the curve is called rectification. Commercially applied, the curve is measured by taking a divider and stepping off very small distances; the number of steps multiplied by the distance between points will give approximately the length of the curve. It must be noticed that the divider measures the chord distance, instead of the arc distance and is therefore always less than the actual length of the curve, but when the distance is taken small enough, the accuracy of the final result is proportional to the care taken in making the measurement.

**929. Involute and evolute.** When a tangent rolls about a fixed curve, any point, on the tangent describes a second curve which is the involute of the first curve. Fig. 162 shows this in construction. Let **aceg** be the fixed curve, and ab, be the position of a taut string that is wound on the curve **aceg.** If a pencil point be attached to the string and unwound, the pencil point will describe the curve **bdfh** which is the involute of the curve **aceg.** The process is the same as though the tangent revolved about the curve **aecg** and some point on the tangent acted as the generating point. At **a**, the radius is ab; at c, the radius is **cd,** which is equal to ab plus the rectified arc **ac** (length of string). It may be observed that the curve **aceg** is the curve of centres for the curve **bdfh.**

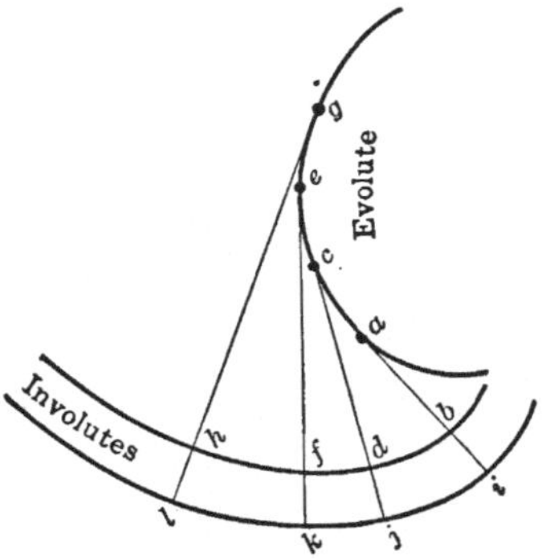

FIG. 162.

If the string be lengthened so that **ai** is the starting position, it will describe the curve **ijkl** which again is an involute. This second involute is parallel to the first, because the distance between the two curves measured along the rolling tangent (or radius of curvature) is constant between the two curves.

The primitive curve **aceg** is the **evolute.** The tangent rolls on the evolute and any point on it describes an involute. As any point on the tangent will answer as the tracing point, it follows that every evolute has an infinite number of involutes, all of which are parallel curves.

Reversing the process of the construction of the involute, the method of drawing the primitive curve or evolute is obtained. If normals are drawn to the involute, consecutive positions of the normals will intersect. The locus of these successive intersections will regenerate the primitive curve from which they have been evolved.*

Again, the length of the tangent to the evolute is the radius of curvature for the involute. As the radius of any circle is perpendicular to the tangent at that point, it follows that the involute is always normal, point for point, to the evolute, since the rolling tangent is the direction of the evolute at the point of contact and that again is normal to the involute.

**930. Involute of the circle.** The involute of the circle is a plane curve, described by a point on a tangent, while the tangent revolves about the circle.

Let **o**, Fig. 163, be the centre of a circle whose radius is **oa.** Let, also, a be the starting point of the involute. Divide the circle in any number of parts, always, however, more than are shown in the illustration. Draw tangents to the various radii. On them, lay off the rectified arc of the circle between the point of tangency and the starting point. For instance, **eb** equals the rectified length of the arc **ea;** also **fc** equals the rectified semicircle **fea; gd** equals the rectified length of the arc **gfea.** The involute may be continued indefinitely for an infinite number of revolutions, but, discussion is usually centred on some limited portion.

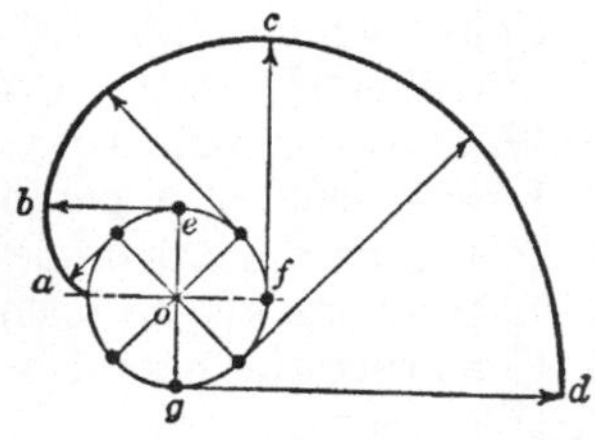

FIG. 163.

The curve here shown is approximately the same as that described by the end of the thread, when a spool is unwound.

## QUESTIONS ON CHAPTER IX

1. Why are lines and points considered as mathematical concepts?
2. How is a straight line defined?
3. By what two means may a straight line be fixed in space?
4. What is a generating point?
5. What is a locus?
6. What is a singly curved line?
7. What is a plane curve?
8. How are plane curves represented?

* The evolute of a circle, therefore, is its centre.

9. Show the mode of representing curves when their planes are parallel to the plane of projection? When perpendicular? When inclined?
10. Is it desirable to use the plane of the curve as the plane of projection?
11. Define the circle.
12. What is the radius? Diameter? Sector? Segment?
13. When the chord passes through the centre of the circle, what does it become?
14. What is a secant? Quadrant? Semicircle?
15. Define concentric circles; eccentric circles; eccentricity.
16. What is an ellipse?
17. Define major axis of an ellipse; minor axis; foci.
18. Describe the accurate method of drawing an ellipse by the intersection of circular arcs.
19. Describe the trammel method of drawing an ellipse.
20. Draw an ellipse whose major axis is 3″ long and whose minor axis is 2″ long. Use the accurate method of intersecting circular arcs.
21. Construct an ellipse whose major axis is 3″ long and whose minor axis is $1\frac{1}{2}$″ long. Use the trammel method.
22. What is a parabola?
23. Define focus of a parabola; directrix; axis; vertex.
24. Is the parabola symmetrical about the axis?
25. Is the parabola an open or a closed curve?
26. Construct the parabola whose focus is 2″ from the directrix.
27. What is a hyperbola?
28. Define foci of hyperbola; transverse axis; conjugate axis; vertex; asymptote.
29. How many branches has a hyperbola? Are they symmetrical about the transverse and conjugate axes?
30. How many asymptotes may be drawn to a hyperbola?
31. Is the hyperbola an open or a closed curve?
32. Construct a hyperbola whose distance between foci is 2″ and whose constant difference is $\frac{1}{2}$″.
33. What is a cycloid?
34. Define rolling circle of a cycloid; directrix.
35. Construct a cycloid whose diameter of rolling circle is $1\frac{1}{2}$″. Draw the curve for one revolution only.
36. What is an epicycloid?
37. What form of directrix has the epycycloid?
38. Construct the epicycloid, whose diameter of rolling circle is $1\frac{1}{2}$″ and whose diameter of directrix is 8″. Draw the curve for one revolution only.
39. What is a hypocycloid?
40. What is the form of the directrix of the hypocycloid?
41. Construct a hypocycloid whose diameter of rolling circle is 2″ and whose diameter of directrix is 9″. Draw the curve for one revolution only.
42. What is a spiral?

43. Construct an Archimedian spiral which expands $1\frac{1}{2}''$ in a complete revolution. Draw the spiral for two revolutions.
44. What is a doubly curved line?
45. Draw a doubly curved line with the principal planes in oblique projection.
46. Construct the orthographic projection from Question 45.
47. What is a helix?
48. Define uniform cylindrical helix; conical helix; diameter of helix; pitch.
49. Construct a helix whose diameter is $2''$, and whose pitch is $1''$. Draw for two revolutions.
50. Construct a triple helix whose diameter is $2''$ and whose pitch is $3''$. The helices are spaced equally and are to be drawn for $1\frac{1}{2}$ revolutions.
51. Make a classification of lines.
52. What is a tangent?
53. Is the tangent fixed in space by a point and a direction?
54. Show that the tangent is the limiting position of a secant.
55. How is a tangent drawn to a curve from a point outside?
56. Given a curve and a point on it, draw a tangent by the accurate method. Prove that the chord length is zero for the tangent position.
57. Given a curve and a tangent, determine the point of tangency. Prove.
58. What is the direction of a curve?
59. What is the angle between two intersecting curves?
60. When several curves are to be joined, show what must be done to make them smooth curves.
61. Define intersection of lines.
62. Show that the tangent intersects the curve at a zero angle.
63. Define order of contact of tangents.
64. If three points become coincident on tangency, what order of contact does the tangent have?
65. Define osculating circle.
66. Define centre of curvature.
67. Is the radius of the osculating circle to a curve the radius of curvature at that point?
68. Show how an osculating circle may have second order contact with a plane curve.
69. What is an osculating plane?
70. When is the osculating plane the plane of the curve?
71. Define point of inflexion.
72. What is an inflexional tangent?
73. Does the radius of curvature change from one side of the curve to the other at a point of inflexion?
74. Define principal normal.
75. Show that the centres of curvature at a point of inflexion lie on opposite sides of the normal to the curve through the point of inflexion.

76. When a normal is drawn to a curve is the one in the osculating plane the one generally understood?
77. How many normals may be drawn to a doubly curved line at a given point?
78. What is meant by rectification?
79. Rectify a 2″ diameter circle. Compute the length of the rectified circle (=2x3.1416) and express the ratio of rectified to computed length as a percentage.
80. Define involute and evolute.
81. Show that all involutes to a curve are parallel curves.
82. Show that the involute is always normal to the evolute at the point for which it corresponds.
83. Show that the drawing of the evolute is the reverse process of drawing the involute.
84. Draw the involute of a circle.
85. Draw the involute to an ellipse.
86. Draw the evolute to an ellipse.
87. Draw the involute to a parabola.
88. Draw the evolute to a parabola.
89. Draw the involute to one branch of a hyperbola.
90. Draw the evolute to one branch of a hyperbola.
91. Draw the involute to a cycloid.
92. Draw the evolute to a cycloid.
93. Draw the involute to an epicycloid.
94. Draw the evolute to an epicycloid.
95. Draw the involute to a hypocycloid.
96. Draw the evolute to a hypocycloid.
97. Draw the involute to an Archimedian spiral.
98. Draw the evolute to an Archimedian spiral.

# CHAPTER X

## CLASSIFICATION OF SURFACES

**1001. Introductory.** A surface may be generated by the successive positions of a line which moves so as to generate an area. As there are infinite varieties of lines and as their motion may again be in an infinite variety of ways, therefore, an infinite variety of possible surfaces result. In engineering it is usual to limit the choice of surfaces to such as may be easily reproduced and easily represented. Surfaces, like lines and points, are **mathematical concepts** because they have no material existence.

When curved surfaces, of a more or less complex nature, are to be represented, they may be shown to advantage, by the effects of light on them. Examples of this kind are treated in Chapters XIV and XV.

**1002. Plane Surface.** A plane surface is a surface such that when any two points in it are joined by a straight line, the line lies wholly within the surface. Thus, three points may be selected in a plane and two intersecting lines may be drawn through the three points; the intersecting lines lie in the plane and, therefore, may be used to determine it. Also, a line and an external point may determine a plane.

The plane surface may also be conceived as being generated by a straight line, moving so as to touch another line, and continually remaining parallel to its original position. Hence, also, two parallel lines determine a plane.

In the latter case, the moving straight line may be considered as a **rectilinear generatrix,** touching a rectilinear **directrix,** and occupying **consecutive positions** in its motion. Any one position of the generatrix may be used as an **element** of the surface.

Fig. 164 shows a plane surface **ABCD** on which straight lines **ab, cd, ef** and **gh** are drawn, all of which must lie wholly within the plane, irrespective of the direction in which they are drawn. Any curve drawn on this surface is a plane curve.

**1003. Conical surface.** If a straight line passes through a given point in space and moves so as to touch a given fixed curve, the surface so generated is a **conical surface.** The straight line is the **rectilinear generatrix,** the fixed point is the **vertex** and the given fixed curve is the **directrix,** which need not be a closed curve. The generatrix in any one position is an **element** of the surface.

Fig. 165 shows a conical surface, generated in the manner

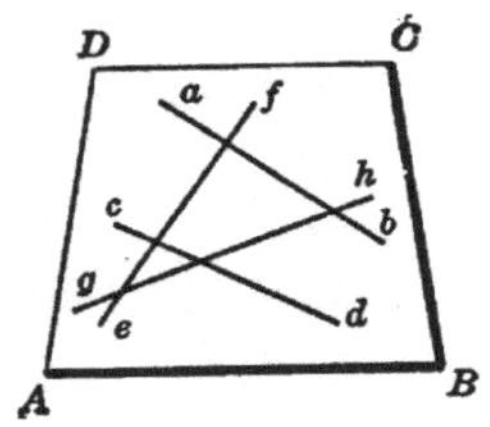

FIG. 164.

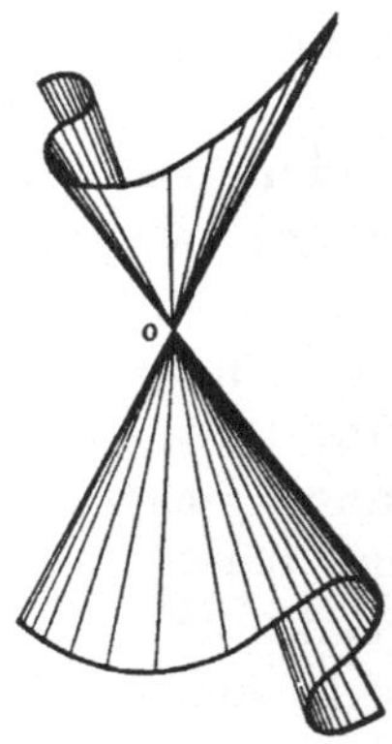

FIG. 165.

indicated. Either the upper or the lower curve may be considered as the directrix. In fact, any number of lines may be drawn on the resulting surface, whether the lines be singly or doubly curved, and any of which will fill the office of directrix. A plane curve is generally used as the directrix.

With a generatrix line of indefinite extent, the conical surface generated is a single surface (not too surfaces as might appear); the vertex **o** is a point of union and not of separation. The portion of the surface from the vertex to either side is called a **nappe**;* hence, there are two nappes to a conical surface.

**1004. Cone.** The cone is a solid, bounded by a closed conical surface of one nappe and a plane cutting all the elements. The

* Pronounced "nap."

curve of intersection of the rectilinear elements and the plane cutting all the elements is the **base.** A **circular** cone has a circle for its base and the line joining the vertex with the centre of the base is the **axis** of the cone. If the axis is perpendicular to the plane of the base the cone is a **right cone.** When the base is a circle, and the axis is perpendicular to the plane of the base, the cone is a **right circular cone** or a **cone of revolution.*** A cone of revolution may be generated by revolving a right triangle about one of its legs as an axis. The hypothenuse is then the **slant height** of the cone. The perpendicular distance from the vertex to the plane of the base is the **altitude** of the cone. The foot of the perpendicular may fall outside of the centre of the base and in such a case, the cone is an **oblique cone.**

The **frustum** (plural:—frusta) of a cone is the limited portion of the solid bounded by a closed conical surface and two parallel planes, each cutting all the elements, and giving rise to the **upper base** and the **lower base** of the frustum of a cone. The terms upper and lower base are relative; it is usual to consider the larger as the lower base and to represent the figure as resting on it. When the cutting planes are not parallel, then the solid is a **truncated** cone.

**1005. Representation of the cone.** A cone, like any other object, is represented by its projections on the principal planes. For convenience in illustrating a cone, the plane of the base is assumed perpendicular to one of the principal planes, as then its projection on that plane is a line. Fig. 166 shows a cone in orthographic projection. The vertex **O** is shown by its projections o and o′; **d′**c′ is the vertical projection of the base since the plane of the base is assumed perpendicular to the vertical plane. The extreme limiting elements **o′c′** and **o′d′** are also shown, thus completing the vertical projection. In the horizontal projection, any curve **acbd** is assumed as the projection of the base so

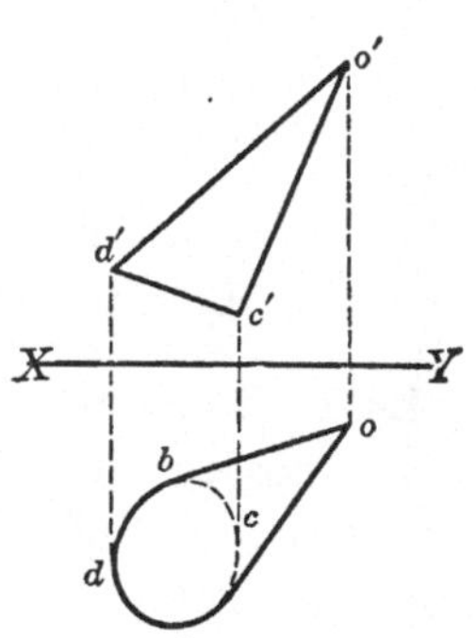


FIG. 166.

* This distinction is made because a cone with an elliptical base may also be a right cone when the vertex is chosen so that it is on a perpendicular to the plane of the base, at the intersection of the major and minor axes.

that **d** and c are corresponding projections of **d′** and c′. From **o,** the lines **ob** and **oa** are drawn, tangent to **acbd,** thus completing the horizontal projection.

It must here be emphasized, that **acbd** is **not** the actual base of the cone, but only its projection. It is impossible to assume two curves, one in each plane of projection, and call them corresponding projections of the same base. The corresponding points must be selected, so that they will lie in one plane, and that plane must be the plane of the base. If it be desired to show the base in both projections, when the plane of the base is inclined to the principal planes, it is necessary to assume one projection of the base. Lines are then drawn in that plane, through the projection of the base and the corresponding projections

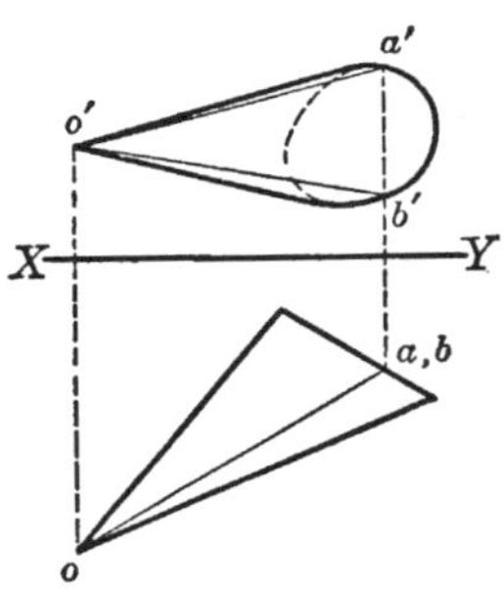


FIG. 167.

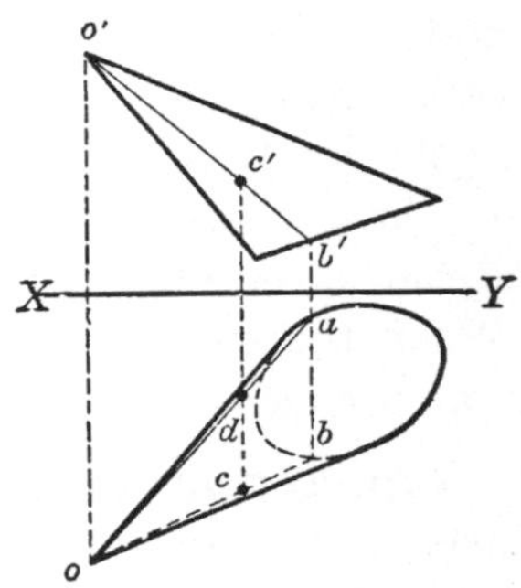


FIG. 168.

of the lines are found. The points can then be determined as they must be situated on these lines. (Arts. 704 and 811.)

**1006. To assume an element on the surface of a cone.** To assume an element of a cone, assume the horizontal projection **oa** in Fig. 167. There are two elements on the cone which have the same horizontal projection and they are shown as **o′a′** and **o′b′** in the vertical projection. If **oa** be considered visible, while viewing the horizontal plane, then **o′a′** is its corresponding projection. If **o′b′** be the one assumed projection then **oa** is on the far side and should in this case be drawn dotted.

**1007. To assume a point on the surface of a cone.** To assume a point on the surface of a cone, assume **c′** in Fig. 168 as the vertical projection, somewhere within the projected area.

Draw the element **o′b′** through **c′** and find the corresponding projection of the element. If **o′b′** is visible to the observer, then **ob** is the corresponding projection, and c on it is the required projection. If **o′b′** is on the far side, then **d** is the desired projection.

A slightly different case is shown in Fig. 169. If c is assumed on the visible element **oa** then **c′** is the corresponding projection on **o′a′**. Otherwise, if ob is dotted (invisible) then **o′b′** is the corresponding element and **d** and **d′** are corresponding projections.

**1008. Cylindrical surface.** When a straight line moves so that it remains continually parallel to itself and touches a given fixed curve, the surface generated is a cylindrical surface.

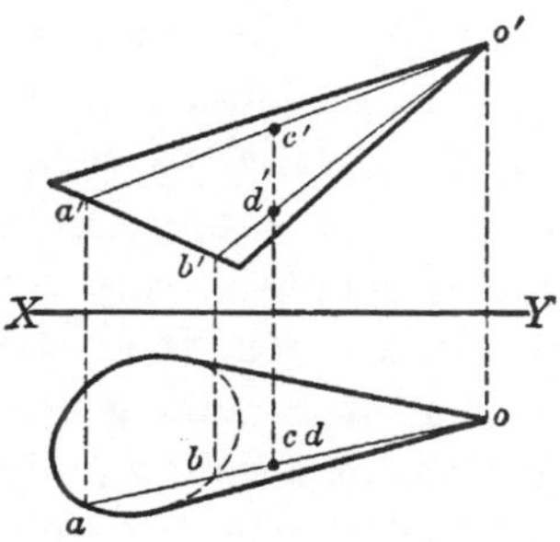


FIG. 169.

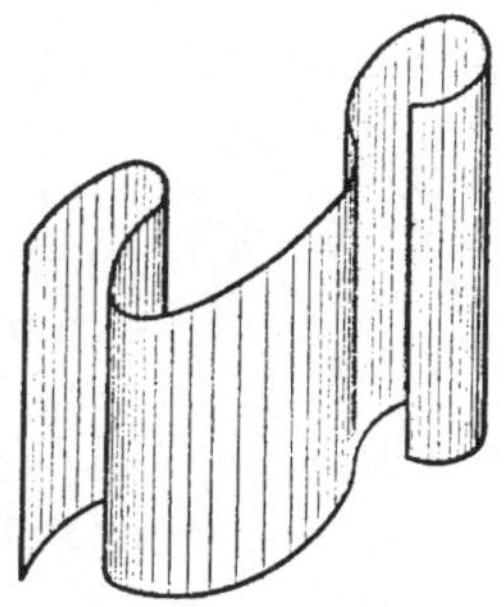

FIG. 170.

The straight line is the **rectilinear generatrix**, the fixed curve is the **directrix** and need not be a closed curve. The generatrix in any one position is an **element** of the surface.

Fig. 170 shows a cylindrical surface, generated in the manner indicated. Any curve, drawn on the resultant surface, whether singly or doubly curved, may be considered as the directrix. The limiting curves that are shown in the figure may also be used as directrices. A plane curve is generally used as a directrix.

**1009. Cylinder.** A cylinder is a solid bounded by a closed cylindrical surface and two parallel planes cutting all the elements. The planes cut curves from cylindrical surface which form the bases of the cylinder and may be termed **upper and lower bases** if the cylinder is so situated that the nomenclature fits. When the planes of the bases are not parallel then it is called a **truncated** cylinder.

Should the bases have a centre, a figure such as a circle for instance, then a line joining these centres is the axis of the cylinder. The axis must be parallel to the elements of the cylinder. If the axis is inclined to the base, the cylinder is an **oblique cylinder.** On the other hand, of the axis is perpendicular to the plane of the base, it is a **right cylinder** and when the base is a circle, it is a **right circular cylinder,** or, a **cylinder of revolution.** The cylinder of revolution may be generated by revolving a rectangle about one of its sides as an axis. A right cylinder need not have a circular base, but the elements must be perpendicular to the plane of the base.

**1010. Representation of the cylinder.** A cylinder, represented orthographically is shown in Fig. 171. Suppose the base is assumed in the horizontal plane, then **e′g′** may be taken as the vertical projection of the base. Also **e′f′** and **g′h′**, parallel to each other, may be taken as the projections of the extreme limiting elements. Any curve, as **aecg**, may be drawn for the horizontal projection so long as **e** and **g** are corresponding projections of **e′** and **g′**. In addition, draw **ab** and **cd** parallel to each other and tangent to the curve **aecg**. The horizontal projection is thus completed. It is to be noted that **aecg** is the true base because it lies in the horizontal plane. If the plane of the base does not coincide with the horizontal plane, then, as in Art. 1005, what applies to the selection of the projection of the base of the cone applies here.

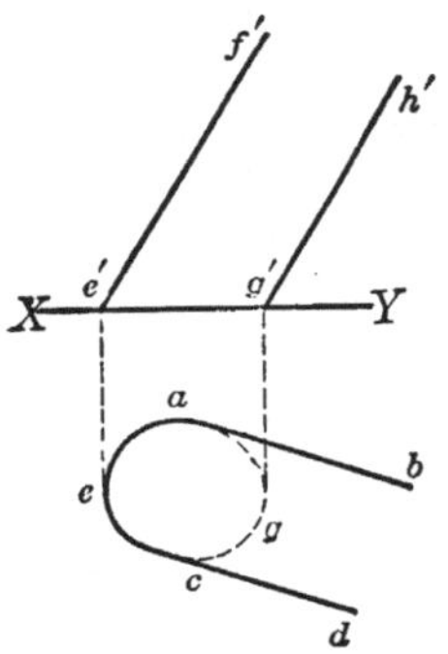

FIG. 171.

**1011.** To **assume an element on the surface of a cylinder.** To assume an element on the surface of a cylinder, select any line, **ab**, Fig. 172, as the horizontal projection. As all parallel lines have parallel projections, then **ab** must be parallel to the extreme elements of the cylinder. If **ab** is assumed as a visible element, then **a′b′** is its corresponding projection, and is shown dotted, because hidden from view on the vertical projection. If **c′d′** is a visible element, then **cd** should be dotted in the horizontal projection.

**1012.** To **assume a point on the surface** of **a cylinder.** To assume a point on the surface of a cylinder, select any point c, Fig. 173, in the horizontal projection, and draw the element ab through it. Find the corresponding projection **a′b′** and on it, locate c′, the required projection. What has been said before (Art. 1005) about the two possible cases of an assumed projection, applies equally well here and should require no further mention.

**1013. Convolute surface.** A convolute surface is a surface generated by a line which moves so as to be continually tangent * to a line of double curvature. For purposes of illustration, the uniform cylindrical helix will be assumed as the line of double

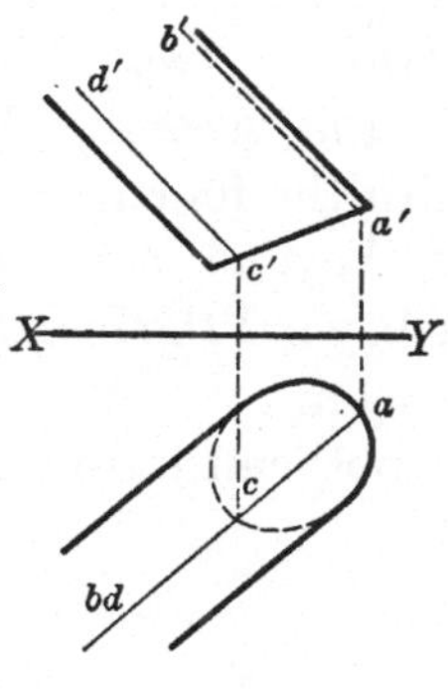


Fig. 172.

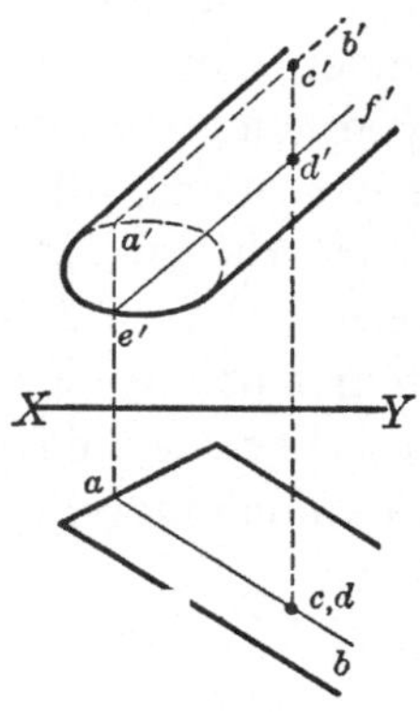


Fig. 173.

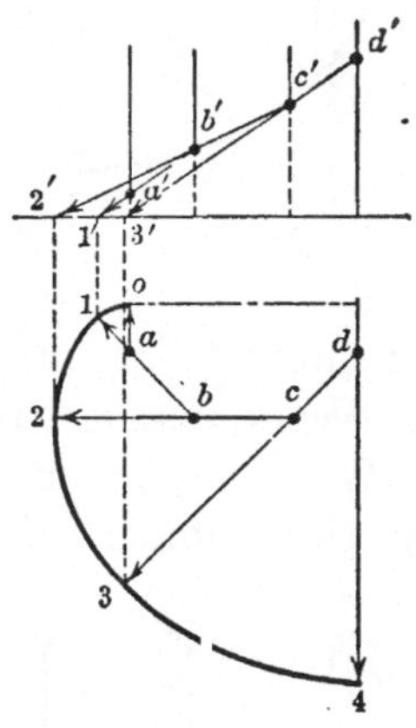


Fig. 174.

curvature, remembering, in all cases, that the helix may be variable in radius and in motion along the axis, so that its characteristics may be imparted to the resulting convolute.

The manner in which this surface is generated may be gained from what follows. Let **abcd**, Fig. 174, be the horizontal projection of a half portion octagonal prism on which is a piece of paper in the form of a right triangle is wound. The base of the triangle is therefore the perimeter of the prism and the hypothenuse will appear as a broken line on the sides of the prism. If the triangle be unwound from the prism and the starting point of the curve described by the hypothenuse on the horizontal

* It may be observed that the tangent to a line of double curvature must ile in the osculating plane (Art. 925).

plane be at **o**, then the portion of the triangle whose base is **oa** will revolve about the edge **a** so as to describe the arc **o1**. At the point **1** the triangle is free along the face **ab** and now swings about **b** as a centre and describes the arc **1–2**. As the process goes on to the point **2**, the triangle is free on the face **bc** and then swings about **c** as a centre and describes the arc **2–3**; and so on. In the vertical projection, the successive positions of the hypothenuse are shown by **a′1′**, **b′2′**, **c′3′** etc. It will be noted that **a′1′** intersects **b′2′** at b′, and **b′2′** intersects **c′3′** at **c′**, etc.; but, **a′1′** does not intersect **c′3′** nor does **b′2′** intersect **d′4′**. Hence, the **elements** of the surface generated by the hypothenuse **intersect two** and **two**. The first element intersects the second; the second the third; the third the fourth, etc.; but the first does not intersect the third, or any beyond, nor does the second intersect the fourth or any elements beyond the fourth.

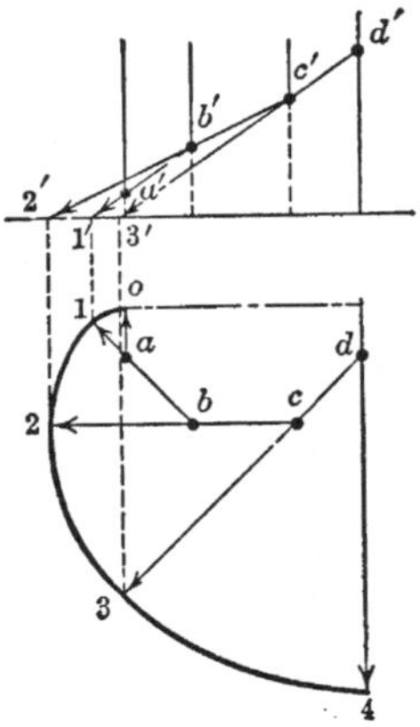


FIG. 174.

When the prism approaches a cylinder as a limit by increasing the number of sides indefinitely, the hypothenuse wound

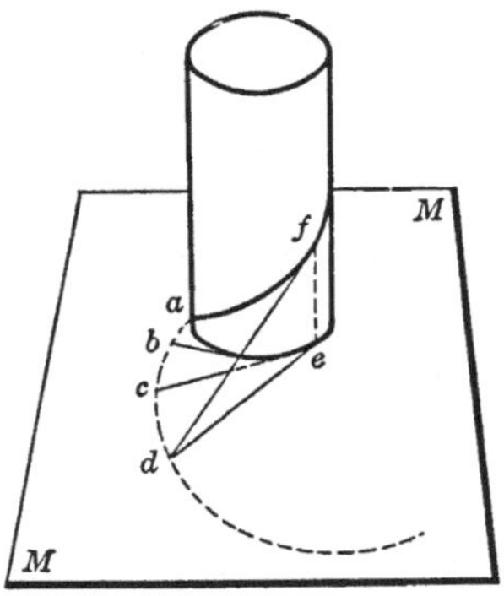


FIG. 175.

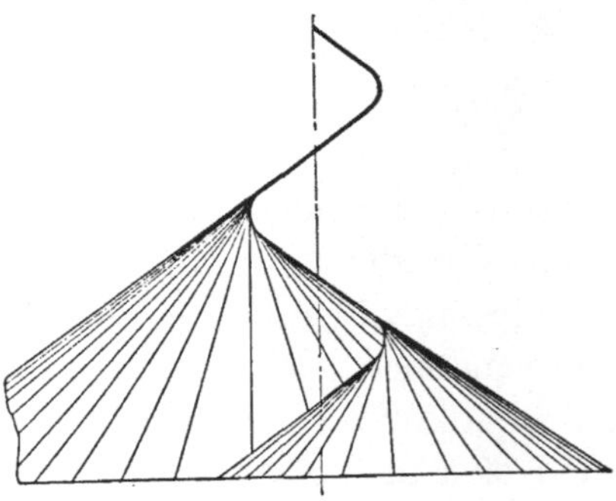

FIG. 176.

around the cylinder approaches a helix as a limit; the unwinding hypothenuse will become the generatrix, tangent to the helix, and will approach the desired convolute surface. The ultimate operation is a continuous one and may be seen in Fig. 175. The curve **abcd** described by the hypothenuse **fd** on the plane **MM** is the involute of a circle, if the cylinder is a right circular cylinder.

Fig. 176 may indicate the nature of the surface more clearly. Examples of this surface may be obtained in the machine shop on observing the spring-like chips, that issue on taking a heavy cut from steel or brass. The surfaces are perhaps not exact convolutes, but they resemble them enough to give the idea.

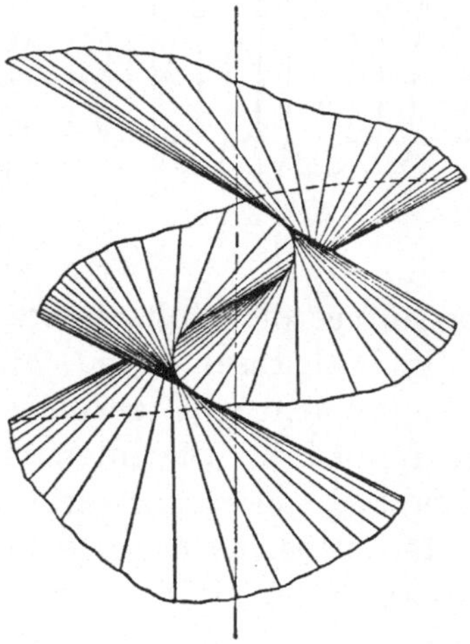

FIG. 177.

It is not necessary to have the tangent stop abruptly at the helix, the tangent may be a line of indefinite extent, and, hence, the convolute surface extends both sides of the helical directrix. No portion of this surface intersects any other portion of the surface, but all the convolutions are distinct from each other. Fig. 177 will perhaps convey the final idea.

**1014. Oblique helicoidal screw surface.*** When the helical directrix of a convolute surface decreases in diameter, it will ultimately coincide with the axis and the helix will become a line. The **oblique helicoidal screw surface,** therefore, resolves itself into the surface generated by a rectilinear generatrix revolving about another line which it intersects, at a constant angle, the intersection moving along the axis at a uniform rate. The application of this surface is shown in the construction of the **V** thread screw which in order to become the United States Standard screw, must make an angle of 60° at the **V** as shown in Fig. 178.

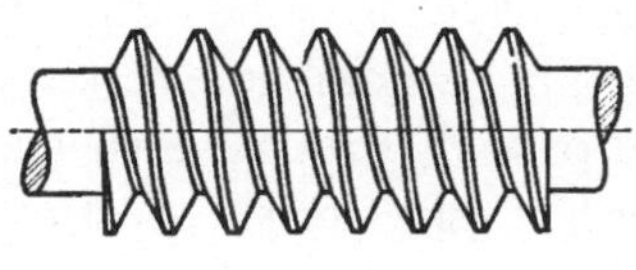

FIG. 178.

* The helicoid proper is a warped surface (1016). If a straight line touches two concentric helices of different diameters and lies in a plane tangent to the inner helix's cylinder, the line will generate a warped surface. When the diameter of the cylinder becomes zero, the helix becomes a line and the helicoidal surface is the same as that here given.

**1015. Right helicoidal screw surface.** If the diameter of the helical directrix still remains zero, and the rectilinear generatrix becomes perpendicular to the axis and revolves so that the intersection of the axis and the generatrix moves along the axis at a constant rate,* a special case of the convolute is obtained. This special case of the convolute is called a **right helicoidal screw surface**, and when applied gives the surface of a square threaded screw as shown in Fig. 179.

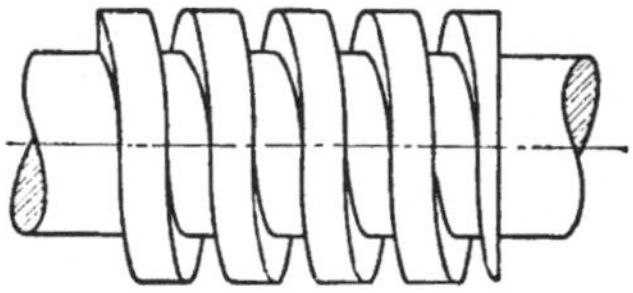

FIG. 179.

In both cases of the oblique and right helicoidal screw surfaces the helices at the outside and root (bottom) of the thread, are formed by the intersection of the screw surface and the outer and inner concentric cylinders. The pitch of both must be the same, as every point on the generatrix advances at a uniform rate. Hence, the angle of the tangent to the helix must vary on the inner and outer cylinders. For this reason, the helices have a different shape notwithstanding their equal pitch.

**1016. Warped surface.** A warped surface is a curved surface, generated by a rectillinear generatrix, moving so that no two successive elements lie in the same plane. Thus, the consecutive elements can neither be parallel nor intersect, hence, they are skew lines. An example of this surface may be obtained by taking a series of straight sticks and drilling a small hole through each end of every stick. If a string be passed through each end and secured so as to keep them together, the series of sticks may be laid on a flat surface and thus represent successive elements of a plane. It may also be curved so as to represent a cylinder. Lastly, it may be given a twist so that no single plane can be passed through the axis of successive sticks; this latter case would then represent a warped surface.

Warped surfaces find comparatively little application in engineering because they are difficult to construct or to duplicate. At times, however, they are met with in the construction of

* If the pitch becomes zero when the diameter of the helix becomes zero, it is the case of a line revolving about another line, through a fixed point; the surface is therefore a cone of revolution, if the generatrix is inclined to the axis. If the generatrix is normal to the axis, the surface is a plane.

" forms " for reinforced concrete work, where changes of shape occur as in tunnels, and similar constructions; in propeller screws for ships; in locomotive " cow-catchers," etc.

**1017. Tangent plane.** If any plane be passed through the vertex of a cone, it may cut the surface in two rectilinear elements under which condition it is a **secant plane.** If this secant plane be revolved about one of the rectilinear elements as an axis, the elements of secancy can be made to approach so as to coincide ultimately. This, then, is a limiting position of the secant plane, in which case it becomes a **tangent plane,** having contact with the cone all along one element.

If through some point on the element of contact, two intersecting curved lines be drawn on the surface of the cone, then, also, two secants may be drawn to these curved lines and intersecting each other at the intersection of the curved lines. The limiting positions of these secants will be tangent lines to the cone, and as these tangents intersect, they determine a tangent plane. The tangent plane thus determined is identical with that obtained from the limiting position of a secant plane.

Instead of drawing two intersecting curves on the surface of the cone, it is possible to select the element of contact and any curve on the cone intersecting it. The tangent plane in this case is determined by the element of contact and the limiting position of one secant to the curve through the intersection of the element and the curve.

As another example, take a spherical surface and on it draw two intersecting lines (necessarily curved). Through the point of intersection, draw two secants, one to each curve and determine the tangent positions. Again, the plane of the two intersecting tangents is the tangent to the sphere. Hence, as a general definition, a tangent plane is the plane established by the limiting position of two intersecting secants as the points of secancy reach coincidence.

**1018. Normal plane.** The normal plane is any plane that is perpendicular to the tangent plane. If a normal plane is to be drawn to a sphere at a given point, for instance, then construct the tangent plane and draw through the point of tangency any plane perpendicular to the tangent plane. An infinite number of normal planes may be drawn, all passing through the given point. The various normal planes will intersect in a common line, which is normal to the tangent plane at the point of tangency.

**1019. Singly curved surface.** A singly curved surface is a surface whose successive rectilinear elements may be made to coincide with a plane. Hence, a tangent plane must be in contact all along some one rectilinear element. As examples, the conical, cylindrical, convolute and the helicoidal screw surfaces may be mentioned.

**1020. Doubly curved surface.** A doubly curved surface is a surface whose tangent plane touches its surface at a point. Evidently, any surface which is not plane or singly curved must be doubly curved. The sphere is a familiar example of a doubly curved surface.

**1021. Singly curved surface of revolution.** A singly curved surface of revolution is a surface generated by a straight line revolving about another straight line in its own plane as an axis, so that every point on the revolving line describes a circle whose plane is perpendicular to the axis, and whose centre is in the axis. Thus, only two cases of singly curved surfaces can obtain, the conical and the cylindrical surfaces of revolution.

**1022. Doubly curved surface of revolution.** A doubly curved surface of revolution is a surface generated by a plane curve revolving about a straight line in its own plane as an axis so that every point on the revolving curve describes a circle whose plane is perpendicular to the axis, and whose centre lies in the axis. Hence, there are infinite varieties of doubly curved surfaces of revolution as the sphere, ellipsoid, hyperboloid, etc., generated by revolving the circle, ellipse, hyperbola, etc., about their axes. In the case of the parabola, the curve may revolve about the axis or the directrix in which cases two distinct types of surfaces are generated. Similarly with the hyperbola, the curve may generate the hyperboloid of one or two nappes depending upon whether the conjugate or transverse axis is the axis of revolution, respectively.

Sometimes, a distinction is made between the outside and inside surfaces of a doubly curved surface. For example, the outside surface of a sphere is called a **doubly convex** surface, whereas, the inside is an illustration of a **doubly concave** surface.

A circular ring made of round wire, and known as a **torus**, is an example of a doubly concavo-convex surface.

**1023. Revolution of a skew line.** An interesting surface is the one generated by a pair of **skew lines** when one is made to revolve about the other as an axis. Fig. 180 gives such a case, and as no plane can be passed through successive elements, it is a warped surface. While revolving about the axis, the line generates the same type of surface as would be generated by a hyperbola when revolved about its conjugate axis. The surface is known as the hyperboloid of revolution of one nappe, and, incidentally, is the only warped surface of revolution.

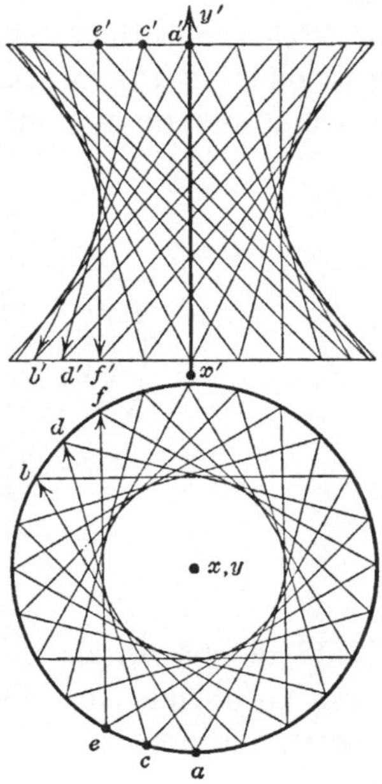

FIG. 180.

**1024. Meridian plane and meridian line.** If a plane be passed through the axis of a doubly curved surface of revolution, it will cut from the surface a line which is the **meridian line.** The plane cutting the meridian line is called the **meridian plane.** Any meridian line can be used as the generatrix of the surface of revolution, because all meridian lines are the same. The circle is the meridian line of a sphere, and for this particular surface, every section is a circle. In general, every plane perpendicular to the axis will cut a circle from any surface of revolution, whether singly or doubly curved.

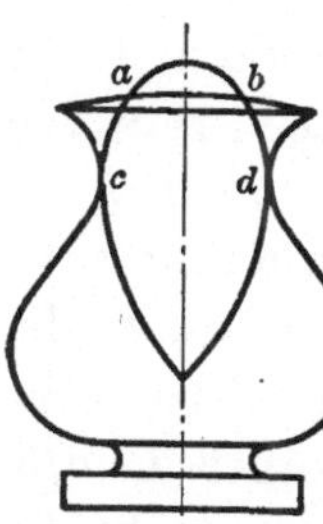

FIG. 181.

**1025. Surfaces of revolution having a common axis.** If two surfaces of revolution have a common axis and the surfaces intersect, tangentially or angularly, they do so all around in a circle which is common to the two surfaces of revolution. Thus, the two surfaces shown in Fig. 181 intersect, angularly, in a circle having **ab** as a diameter, and intersect, tangentially, in a circle having **cd** as a diameter.

**1026. Representation of the doubly curved surface of revolution.** Fig. 182 shows a doubly curved surface of revolution shown in two views. One view shows the same as that produced by a meridian plane cutting a meridian line and the other shows the same as concentric circles. When considered as a solid, no ground line is necessary as the distance from the principal planes is unimportant. Centre lines, **ab**, **cd** and **ef**

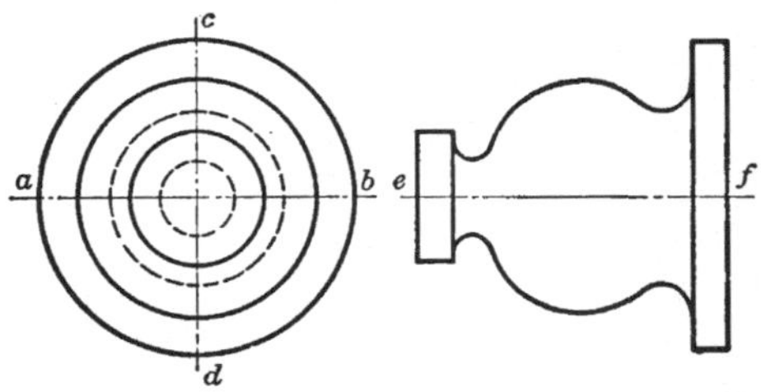


FIG. 182.

should be shown, **ab** and **ef** being represented as two lines, because both views are distinct from each other. The lines indicate that the object is symmetrical about the centre line as an axis.

**1027.** To **assume a point on a doubly curved surface of revolution.** Let **c**, Fig. 183, be assumed as one point on the surface.* With **oc** as a radius, draw the arc **ca**, **a** is, therefore, the revolved position of **c** when the meridian plane through **co** has been revolved to **ao**. Hence, **a** is at **a′** or **a″** in the corresponding view. On counter-revolution, **a′** describes a circle, the plane of which is perpendicular to the axis, and the plane is shown by its trace **a′c′**; in the other view, **a** returns to **c** and, hence, **c′** is the final position. It may also be at **c″** for the same reason, but then **c** is hidden in that view. If, on the other hand, **d** is chosen as one projection, its corre-

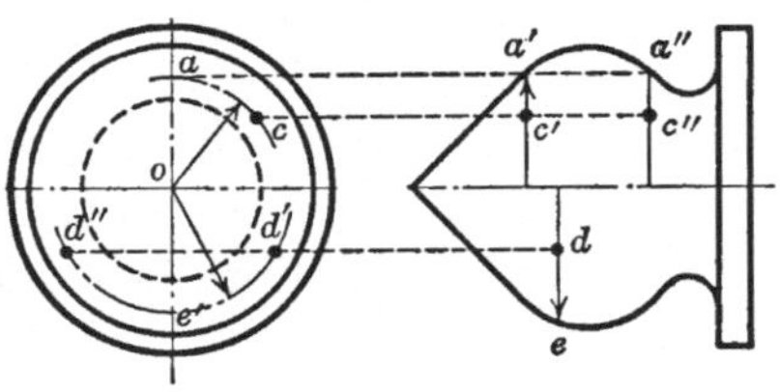


FIG. 183.

* These views bear third angle relation to each other.

sponding projection is **d′**, if **d** is visible; or, it is **d″**, if **d** is hidden.

**1028. Developable surface.** When a curved surface can be rolled over a plane surface so that successive elements come in contact with the plane and that the area of the curved surface can be made to equal the plane surface by rectification, the surface is a **developable** one. Hence, any singly curved surface, like a cylinder, can be rolled out flat or **developed.** A sphere cannot be rolled out as a flat surface because it has point contact with a plane, and is, therefore, incapable of development. If a sphere is to be constructed from flat sheets, it may be approximated by cutting it into the type of slices called **lunes,** resembling very much the slices made by passing meridian planes through the axis of a sphere. To approach more nearly the sphere, it would be necessary to take these lunes and hammer them so as to stretch the material to the proper curvature. Similarly, in the making of stove-pipe elbows, the elbows are made of limited portions of cylinders and cut to a wedge shape so as to approximate the doubly curved surface known as the **torus.**

**1029. Ruled surface.** Every surface on which a straight line may be drawn is called a **ruled surface.** A ruled surface may be plane, singly curved or doubly curved. Among the singly curved examples may be found the conical, cylindrical, convolute and helicoidal screw surfaces. The hyperboloid of revolution of one nappe furnishes a case of a doubly curved ruled surface (1023).

**1030. Asymptotic surface.** If a hyperbola and its asymptotes move so that their plane continually remains parallel to itself, and any point on the curve or on the asymptotes touches a straight line as a directrix, the hyperbola will generate a hyperbolic cylindrical surface and the asymptotes will generate a pair of **asymptotic** planes. Also, if the hyperbola revolves about the transverse or conjugate axis, the hyperbola will generate a hyperboloid of revolution and the asymptote will generate a conical surface which is asymptotic to the hyperboloid. In all cases, the **asymptotic surface** is tangent at two lines, straight or curved, at an infinite distance apart and the surface passes within finite distance of the intersection of the axes of the curve.

**1031. Classification of surfaces.**

- **Surfaces.**
  - **Ruled surfaces.** Straight lines may be drawn on the resulting surface.
    - **Planes.** Any two points when joined by a straight line lie wholly within the surface.
    - **Singly curved surfaces.** May be developed into a flat surface by rectification.
      - **Conical surfaces.** Rectilinear elements pass through a given point in space and touch a curved directrix.
      - **Cylindrical surfaces.** Rectilinear elements are parallel to each other and touch a curved directrix.
      - **Convolute surfaces.** Rectilinear elements tangent to a line of double curvature. Consecutive elements intersect two and two; no three intersect in a common point.
    - **Warped surfaces.** No two consecutive elements lie in the same plane; hence, they are non-developable.
  - **Doubly curved surfaces.** Tangent plane touches surface at a point.
    - **Doubly curved surfaces of revolution.** Generated by plane curves revolving about an axis in the plane of the curve. All meridian lines equal and all sections perpendicular to axis are circles.
    - **Unclassified doubly curved surfaces.** All others which do not fall within the foregoing classification.

## QUESTIONS ON CHAPTER X

1. How are surfaces generated?
2. What is a plane surface?
3. What is a rectilinear generatrix?
4. What is a directrix?
5. What is an element of a surface?
6. What is a conical surface?

7. What is the directrix of a conical surface?
8. What is the vertex of a conical surface?
9. Is it necessary for the directrix of a conical surface to be closed?
10. What is a nappe of a cone? How many nappes are generated in a conical surface?
11. What is a cone?
12. What is the base of a cone?
13. Must all elements be cut by the plane of the base for a cone?
14. What is a circular cone?
15. What is the axis of a cone?
16. What is a right circular cone? Is it a cone of revolution?
17. What is the altitude of a cone?
18. What is the slant height of a cone?
19. What is the an oblique cone?
20. What is a frustum of a cone?
21. How are the two bases of a frustum of a cone usually designated?
22. What is a truncated cone?
23. In the representation of a cone, why is the plane of the base usually assumed perpendicular to the plane of projection?
24. Is it necessary that the base of a cone should be circular?
25. Draw a cone in orthographic projection and assume the plane of the base perpendicular to the vertical plane.
26. Draw a cone in projection and show how an element of the surface is assumed in both projections. State exactly where the element is chosen.
27. Draw a cone in projection and show how a point is assumed on its surface. Locate point in both projections.
28. What is a cylindrical surface?
29. Define generatrix of a cylindrical surface; directrix; element.
30. Is it necessary that the directrix of a cylindrical surface be a closed curve?
31. How is a cylinder differentiated from a cylindrical surface?
32. How many bases must a cylinder have?
33. What is the axis of a cylinder?
34. Must the axis of the cylinder be parallel to the elements? Why?
35. What is an oblique cylinder?
36. What is a right circular cylinder? Is this cylinder a cylinder of revolution?
37. Is it necessary that a right cylinder have a circle for the base? Why?
38. Draw an oblique cylinder whose base lies in the horizontal plane.
39. In Question 38, assume an element of the surface and state which element is chosen.
40. Which elements are the limiting elements in Question 38?
41. Draw a cylinder in projection and then assume a point on the surface of it. Show it in both projections.
42. What is a convolute surface?
43. What is an oblique helicoidal screw surface? Give a prominent example of it.

44. What is a right helicoidal screw surface? Give a prominent example of it.
45. Show that the helicoidal screw surfaces are limiting helicoids as the inner helix becomes of zero diameter.
46. What is a warped surface? Illustrate by sticks.
47. What is a secant plane?
48. Show how a tangent plane is the limiting position of a secant plane to a conical surface.
49. Show how a tangent plane is the limiting position of a secant plane to a cylindrical surface.
50. Show that a tangent line to the surface is the limiting position of a secant drawn to a curve on the surface.
51. Show how two intersecting lines may be drawn on a curved surface and how the limiting positions of two secants drawn through this point of intersection determine a tangent plane to the surface.
52. Show how one element of a conical surface and one limiting position of a secant determine the tangent plane to the conical surface.
53. Show how one element of a cylindrical surface and one limiting position of a secant determine the tangent plane to the cylindrical surface.
54. Show how two intersecting lines may be drawn on the surface of a sphere and how the limiting positions of two secants drawn through the intersection determine a tangent plane to the sphere.
55. Define tangent plane in terms of the two intersecting tangent lines at a point on a surface.
56. Define normal plane.
57. How many normal planes may be drawn through a given point on a surface?
58. What is a normal (line) to a surface?
59. Define singly curved surface. Give examples.
60. Define doubly curved surface. Give examples.
61. Define singly curved surface of revolution. Give examples.
62. Define doubly curved surface of revolution. Give examples.
63. What is a doubly convex surface? Give examples.
64. What is a doubly concave surface? Give examples.
65. What is a doubly concavo-convex surface. Give examples.
66. Describe the surface of a torus. Is this a concavo-convex surface?
67. What surface is obtained when a pair of skew lines are revolved about one of them as an axis?
68. Construct the surface of Question 67.
69. What is a meridian plane?
70. What is a meridian line?
71. Why can any meridian line be assumed as a generatrix for its particular surface of revolution?
72. What curves are obtained by passing planes perpendicular to the axis of revolution?

73. When two surfaces of revolution have the same axis, show that the intersection is a circle whether the surfaces intersect tangentially or angularly.
74. Show how a doubly curved surface of revolution may be represented without the ground line. Draw the proper centre lines.
75. Assume a point on the surface of a doubly curved surface of revolution.
76. What is a developable surface?
77. Is development the rectification of a surface?
78. Are singly curved surfaces developable?
79. Are doubly curved surfaces developable?
80. Are warped surfaces developable?
81. What is a ruled surface? Give examples.
82. What is an asymptotic plane? Give an example.
83. If a hyperbola and its asymptotes revolve about the transverse axis, show why the asymptotic lines generate asymptotic cones to the resulting hyperboloids.
84. Show what changes occur in Question 83 when the conjugate axis is used.
85. Make a classification of surfaces.

# CHAPTER XI

## INTERSECTIONS OF SURFACES BY PLANES, AND THEIR DEVELOPMENT

**1101. Introductory.** When a line is inclined to a plane, it will if sufficiently produced, pierce the plane in a point. The general method involved has been shown (Art. 823), for straight lines, and consists of passing an auxiliary plane through the given line, so that it cuts the given plane in a line of intersection. The piercing point must be somewhere on this **line** of **intersection** and also on the **given line**; hence it is at their **intersection.**

In the case of doubly curved lines, the passing of auxiliary planes through them is evidently impossible. Curved surfaces, instead of planes, are therefore used as the auxiliary surfaces. Let, for example, Fig. 184 show a doubly curved line, and let the object be to find the piercing point of the doubly curved line on the principal planes. If a cylindrical surface be passed through the given line, the elements of which are perpendicular to the horizontal plane, it will have the curve **ab** as its trace, which will also be the horizontal projection of the curve **AB** in space. Similarly, the vertical projecting cylindrical surface will cut the vertical plane in the line **a′b′**, and will be the vertical projection of the curve **AB** in space. If a perpendicular be erected at **a,** where **ab** crosses the ground line, it will intersect the vertical projection of the curve at **a′,** the vertical piercing point of the curve. The entire process in substance consists of this: the surface of the horizontal projecting cylinder cuts the vertical plane in the line **aa′**; the piercing point of the curve **AB** must

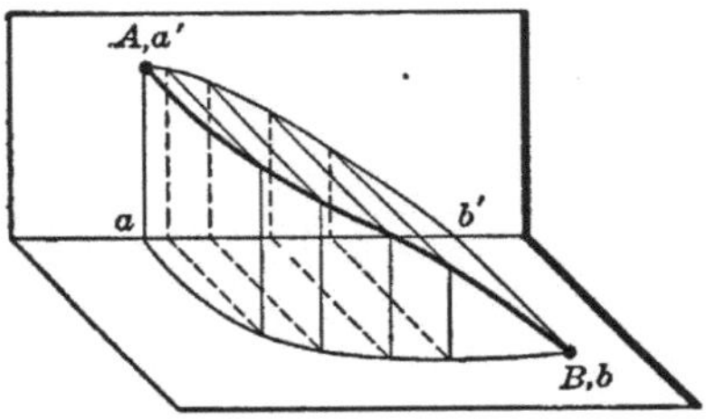

FIG. 184.

lie on **aa′** and also on **AB**, hence it is at their intersection **a′**. Likewise, **b**, the horizontal piercing point is found by a process identical with that immediately preceding.

**1102. Lines of intersection of solids by planes.** The extension of the foregoing is the entire scheme of finding the line of intersection of any surface with the cutting plane. Elements of the surface pierce the cutting plane in points; the locus of the points so obtained, determine the line of intersection.

A distinction must be made between a plane cutting a surface, and a plane cutting a solid. In the former case, the surface alone, gives rise to the line of intersection, whether it be an open surface, or a closed surface; the cutting plane intersects the surface in a line which is the line of intersection. In the latter case, the area of the solid, exposed by the cutting plane, is a section of the solid. This is the scheme of using section planes for the elucidation of certain views in drawing (313).

**1103. Development of surfaces.** The development of a surface consists of the rolling out or rectification of the surface on a plane, so that the area on the plane is equal to the area of the surface before development. If this flat surface be rolled up, it will regenerate the original surface from which it has been evolved (1028).

For instance, if a flat rectangular sheet of paper be rolled in a circular form, it will produce the surface of a cylinder of revolution. Similarly, a sector of a circle may be wound up so as to make a right circular cone. In both cases, the flat surface is the development of the surface of the cylinder or cone as the case may be.

**1104. Developable surfaces.** A prism may be rolled over a flat surface and each face successively comes in intimate contact with the flat surface; hence, its surface is developable. A cylinder may likewise be rolled over a flat surface and the consecutive elements will successively coincide with the flat surface, this, again, is therefore a developable surface. The surfaces of the pyramid and the cone are also developable for similar reasons.

A sphere, when rolled over a flat surface, touches at only one point and not along any one element; hence, its surface is not developable. In general, any surface of revolution which has a curvilinear * generatrix is non-developable.

A warped surface is also a type of surface which is non-developable, because consecutive elements even though rectilinear, are so situated that no plane can contain them.

Hence, to review, only singly curved surfaces, and such surfaces as are made up of intersecting planes, are developable. Doubly curved surfaces of any kind are only developable in an approximate way, by dividing the actual surface into a series of developable surfaces; the larger the series, the nearer the approximation.†

**1105. Problem 1.** To **find the line** of **intersection** of **the surfaces** of **a right** octa**gonal prism with a plane inclined to** its **axis.**

**Construction.** Let **abcd,** etc., Fig. 185, be the plan of the prism, resting, for convenience, on the horizontal plane. The elevation is shown by **a′b′c′**, etc. The plane T is perpendicular to the vertical plane and makes an angle $\alpha$ with the horizontal plane. In the supplementary view **S,** only half of the intersection is shown, because the other half is symmetrical about the line **a‴e‴.** Draw from **e′d′c′b′** and **a′**, lines perpendicular to **Tt′** and draw **a‴e⁗**, anywhere, but always parallel to **Tt′.** The axis of symmetry **ea,** shown in plan, is the projection of **e′a′** in elevation, and **e′a′** is equal to **e‴a‴**; the points **e‴** and **a‴** are therefore established on the axis. To find **d‴**, draw **dm,** perpendicular to **ea; dm** is shown in its true length as it is parallel to the horizontal plane. Accordingly, set off **m‴d‴ = md,** on a line from **d′**, perpendicular to **Tt′**, from **e‴a‴** as a base line. As **nb = md,** then **n‴b‴ = m‴d‴**, and is set off from **e‴a‴**, on a line from **b′**, perpendicular to **Tt′.** The final point **c‴** is located so that **o‴c‴ = oc** and is set off from **e‴a‴**, on a line from **c′**, perpendicular to **Tt.** The "half section" is

* If a curvilinear generatrix moves so that its plane remains continually parallel to itself and touches a rectilinear directrix, the surface generated is a cylindrical surface. Hence, this surface cannot be included in this connection.

† Maps are developments of the earth's surface, made in various ways. This branch of the subject falls under Spherical Projections. The student who desires to pursue this branch is referred to the treatises on Topographical Drawing and Surveying.

then shown completely and is sectioned as is customary. The line of intersection is shown by **e‴d‴c‴b‴a‴**; the half section is the area included by the lines **e‴d‴c‴b‴a‴n‴o‴m‴e‴**.

**1106. Problem 2.** To **find the developed surfaces in the preceding problem.***

**Construction.** As the prism is a right prism, all the vertical edges are perpendicular to the base; the base will develop into a straight line and the vertical edges will be perpendicular to it,

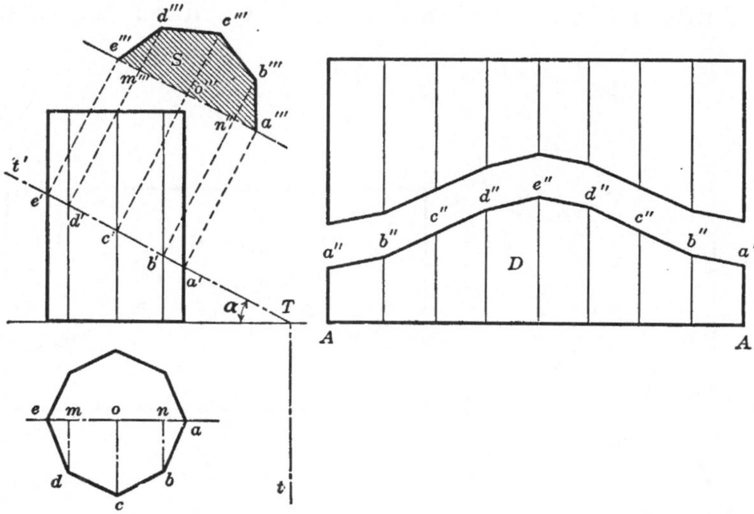


Fig. 185.

spaced an equal distance apart, because all faces are equal. Hence, on the base line **AA**, Fig. 185, lay off the perimeter of the prism and divide into eight equal parts. The distance of **a″** above the base line **AA** is equal to the distance of **a′** above the horizontal plane; **b″** is ablove **AA**, a distance equal to **b′** above the horizontal plane. In this way, all points are located. It will be observed that the development is symmetrical about the vertical through **e″**.

To prove the accuracy of the construction, the developed surface may be laid out on paper, creased along all the verticals

* In the problems to follow the bases are not included in the development as they are evident from the drawing.

and wound up in the form of the prism. A flat card will admit of being placed along the cut, proving that the section is a plane surface.

The upper and lower portions are both developed; the distance between them is arbitrary, only the cut on one must exactly match with the cut on the other.

**1107. Problem 3.** To **find the** line of **intersection of the surface** of **a right** circular **cylinder with a plane inclined to its axis.**

**Construction.** Let Fig. 186 show the cylinder in plan and

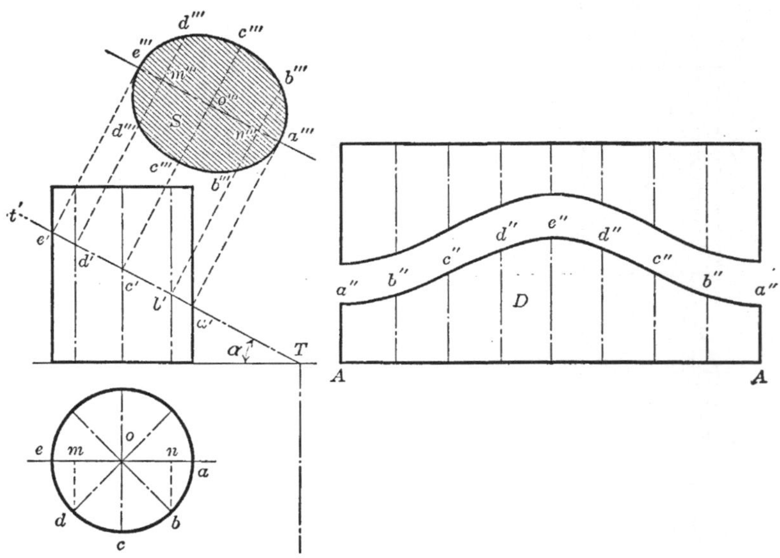


Fig. 186.

elevation. The plane cutting it is an angle $\alpha$ with the horizontal plane and is perpendicular to the vertical plane. It is customary, in the application, to select the position of the plane and the object so that subsequent operations become most convenient, so long as the given conditions are satisfied. Pass a series of auxiliary planes through the axis as **oe**, **od**, etc., spaced, for convenience, an equal angular distance apart. These planes cut rectilinear elements from the cylinder, shown by the verticals through **e′d′c′**, etc. Lay off an axis **e‴a‴**, parallel to **Tt′**, so that **e‴ e′** and **a‴a′** are perpendicular to **Tt′**. To find **d‴**, it is known that **md** is shown in its true length in the plan; hence, lay off $\mathbf{m'''d'''} = \mathbf{md}$ from the axis $\mathbf{e'''a'''}$, on a line from $\mathbf{d'}$, perpendicular to $\mathbf{Tt'}$. Also, make $\mathbf{o'''c'''} = \mathbf{oc}$ and $\mathbf{n'''b'''} = \mathbf{nb}$ in the same way. Draw a smooth curve through $\mathbf{e'''d'''c'''b'''a'''b'''c'''d'''e'''}$ which will be found to be an ellipse. The ellipse may be awn by plotting points as shown, or, the major axis $\mathbf{e'''a'''}$ and the minor axis $\mathbf{c'''c'''}$ may be laid off and the ellipse drawn by any method.* Both methods should produce identical results. The area of the ellipse is the section of the cylinder made by an oblique plane and the ellipse is the curve of intersection. As an example, a cylindrical glass of water may be tilted to the given angle, and the boundary of the surface of the water will be elliptical.

**1108. Problem 4. To find the developed surface in the preceding problem.**

**Construction.** As the cylinder is a right cylinder, the elements are perpendicular to the base, and the base will develop into a straight line, of a length, equal to the rectified length of the circular base. Divide the base **AA** Fig. 186, into the same number of parts as are cut by the auxiliary planes. Every element in the elevation is shown in its true size because it is perpendicular to the horizontal plane; hence, make $\mathbf{a''A}$ equal to the distance of $\mathbf{a'}$ above the horizontal plane; $\mathbf{b''A}$ equal to the distance of $\mathbf{b'}$ above the horizontal plane, etc. Draw a smooth curve through the points so found and the development will appear as shown at **D** in Fig. 186. Both upper and lower portions are shown developed, either one may be wound up like the original cylinder and a flat card placed across the intersection, showing, that the surface is plane.

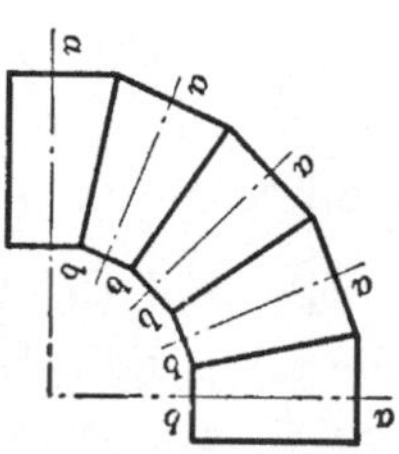

Fig. 187.

**1109. Application of cylindrical surfaces.** Fig. 187 shows an elbow, approximating a torus, made of sheet metal, by the use of short sections of cylinders. The ellipse is symmetrical about both axes, and, hence, the upper portion of the cylinder may be added to the lower portion so as to give an offset. Indeed in this way elbows

* See Art. 906.

are made in practice. The torus is a doubly curved surface, and, hence, is not developable, except by the approximation shown. To develop these individual sheets, pass a plane **ab,** perpendicular to the axis. The circle cut thereby will then develop into a straight line. Add corresponding distances above and below the base line so established and the development may be completed. Fig. 188 shows the sheets as they appear in the development.

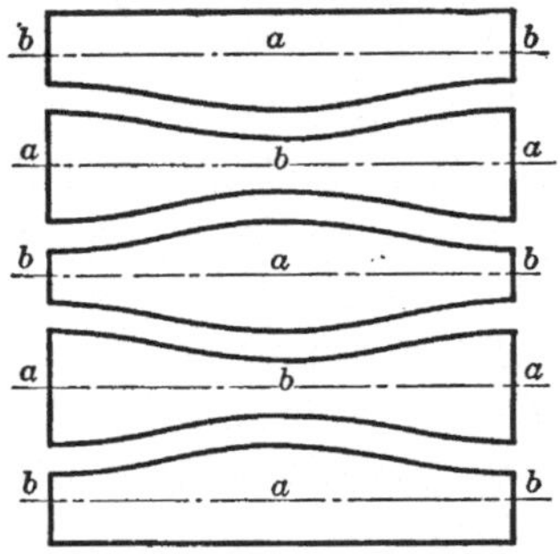


FIG. 188.

A sufficient number of points must always be found on any curve, so that no doubt occurs as to its form. In the illustration, the number of points is always less than actually required so as to avoid the confusion incident to a large number of construction lines.

**1110. Problem 5.** To **find the line of** intersection of **the surfaces of a right** octago**nal pyramid** with **a plane inclined to its** axis.

**Construction.** Let Fig. 189 represent the pyramid in plan and elevation, and let T be the cutting plane. The plane T cuts the extreme edge **o′e′** at **e′,** horizontally projected at **e,** one point of the required intersection. It also cuts the edge **o′d′** at **d′,** horizontally projected at **d,** thus locating two points on the required intersection. In the same way **b** and **a** are located. The point **c** cannot be found in just this way. If the pyramid be turned a quarter of a revolution, the point **c′** will be at **q′** and **c′q′** will be the distance from the axis where the edge **o′c′** pierces the plane T. Hence, lay off **oc = c′q′** and complete the horizontal projection of the intersection.

To find the true shape of the intersection, draw the supplementary view **S.** Lay off **e‴a‴** as the axis, parallel to **Tt′;** the length of the axis is such that **e′a′ = e‴a‴.** From the horizontal projection, **dm** is made equal to **d‴m‴** in the supplementary view, the latter being set off from the axis **e‴a‴,** and on a line from **d′,** perpendicular to **Tt′.** Also, **co = c‴o‴** and **bn = b‴n‴.** Thus, the true intersection is shown in the supplementary view **S.**

**1111. Problem 6. To find the developed surfaces in the preceding problem.**

**Construction.** The extreme element **o′s′**, Fig. 189, is shown in its true length on the vertical plane because it is parallel to that plane. Accordingly, with any point **o″** as a centre, draw an indefinite arc through **AA**, so that **o″A** = **o′s′**. Every edge of the pyramid meeting at the vertex has the same length and all are therefore equal to **o″A**. The base of each triangular face is shown in its true length in the plan, and, hence, with any one of them as a length, set the distance off as a chord on **AA**

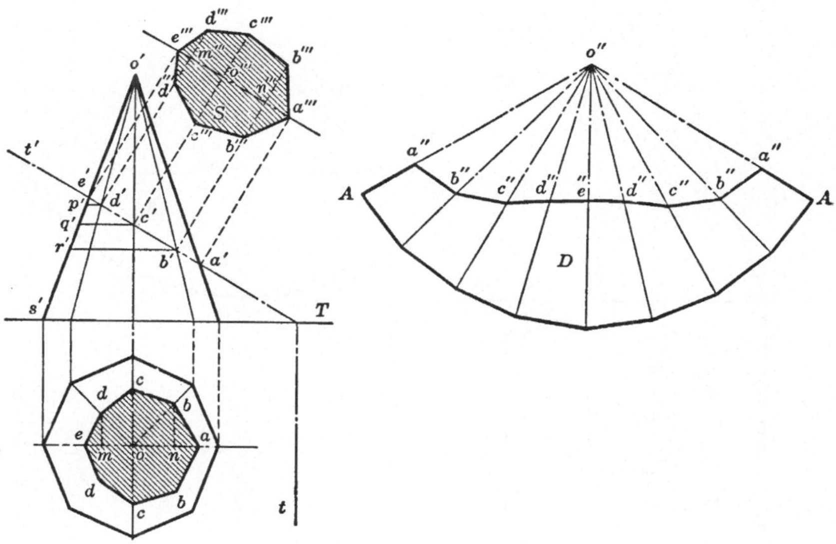


FIG. 189.

by the aid of a divider, so that the number of steps is equal to the number of faces. Draw these chords, indicate the edges, and it then remains to show where the cutting plane intersects the edges. The extreme edge **o′e′** is shown in its true length, hence, lay off **o″e″** = o′**e′**. The edge **o′d′** is not shown in its true length, but if the pyramid is revolved so that this edge reaches the position **o′s′**, then **d′** will reach **p′** and **o′p′** is the desired true length as it is now parallel to the vertical plane; therefore, set off **o′p′** = **o″d″**. In this way, **o′q′** = **o″c″**, and **o′r′** = **o″b″**. The edge **o′a′** is shown in its true length, therefore, **o′a′** = **o″a″**; and **a″A** on one side must equal **a″A** on the other, as, on rolling up, the edges must correspond, being the same initially. Join **a″b″**, **b″c″**, etc., to complete the development. The proof, as before, lies in the actual construction of the model and in showing that the cut is a plane surface.

**1112. Problem 7.** To **find the line of intersection** of **the surface** of **a right** circular cone **with a plane inclined to** its **axis.**

**Construction.** Let Fig. 190 show plan and elevation of the cone, and let T be the cutting plane. Through the axis, pass a

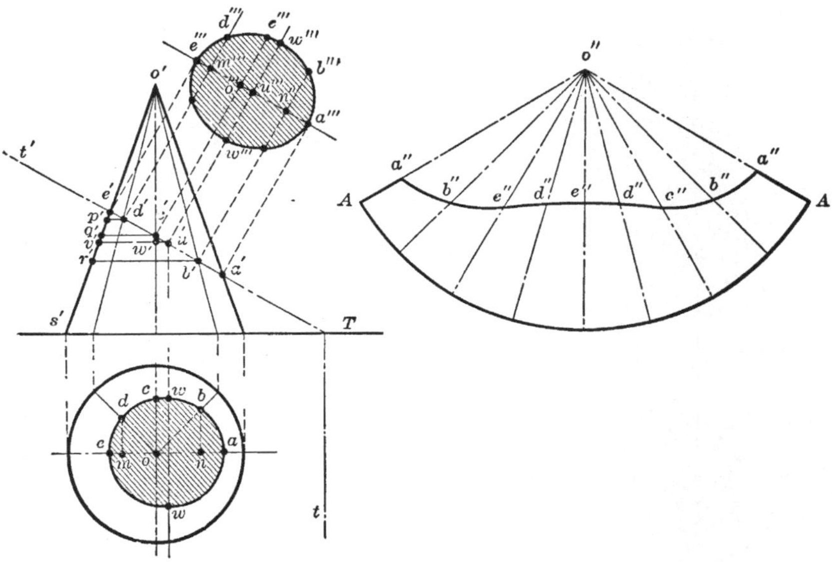


FIG. 190.

series of planes as **ao, bo,** co, etc. These planes cut rectilinear elements from the cone, shown as o′**a′**, **o′b′**, **o′c′**, etc., in the elevation. At first, it is a good plan to draw the horizontal projection of the line of intersection, as many points are readily located thereon. For instance, **e′** is the point where the extreme element **o′e′** pierces the plane T, horizontally projected at **e.** Similarly, the actual element **OD** pierces the plane so that **d** and **d′** are corresponding projections. The points **b** and **b′** and the points **a** and **a′** are found in an identical manner, but, as in the case of the pyramid, the point **c** cannot be located in the same way. If the cone be revolved so that the element **o′c′** occupies the extreme position **o′s′**, then c′ will be found at **q′** and **c′q′** will be the radius of the circle which the point **c′** describes; hence, make **oc = c′q′** and the resultant curve, which is an ellipse, may be drawn.

The true line of intersection is shown in the supplementary view **S.** As in previous instances, first the axis **e‴a‴** is drawn parallel to **Tt′**, and equal in length to **e′a′** so that **e‴e′** and **a‴a′** are both perpendicular to **Tt′**. From the axis, on a line from **d′**, lay off **d‴m‴ = dm;** also **o‴ c‴ = oc** and **b‴n‴ = bn.** A smooth curve then results in an ellipse.

If accuracy is desired, it is better to lay off the major and minor axes of the ellipse and then draw the ellipse by other methods,* since great care must be used in this construction. The major axis is shown as **e‴a‴**. To find the minor axis, bisect **e′a′** at **u′** and draw **u′v′**, the trace of a plane perpendicular to the axis of the cone. This plane cuts the conical surface in a circle, of which **w′v′** is the radius. The minor axis is equal to the length of the chord of a circle whose radius is **w′v′** and whose distance from the centre of the circle is **u′w′**.

**1113. Problem 8.** To **find the developed surface** in **the preceding problem.**

**Construction.** The extreme visible element **o′s′**, Fig. 190, is shown in its true length and is the slant height of the cone. All elements are of the same length and hence, any indefinite arc **AA**, drawn so that **o″A = o′s′** will be the first step in the development. The length of the arc **AA** is equal to the rectified length of the base, and, as such, is laid off and divided into any convenient number of parts. Eight equal parts are shown here because the auxiliary planes were chosen so as to cut the cone into eight equal parts. If the conical surface is cut along the element **OA,** then **o′a′** may be laid off on both sides equal to **o″a″** in the development. The elements **o′d′**, **o′c′** and **o′b′** are not shown in their true length, therefore, it is necessary to revolve the cone about the axis so as to make them parallel, in turn, to the vertical plane. The points will ultimately reach the positions indicated by **p,′ q′** and **r′**, and, hence, **o″b″ = o′r′**, **o″c″ = o′q′** and **o″d″ = o′p′**. The element **o′e′** is shown in its true length and is laid off equal to **o″e″**. A smooth curve through **a″b″c″d″**, etc., completes the required development.

* See Art. 906 in this connection.

When frustra of conical surfaces are to be developed the elements of the surface may be produced until they meet at the vertex. The development may then proceed along the usual lines.

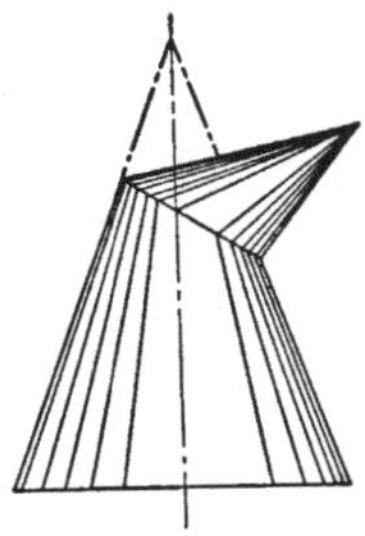

FIG. 191.

**1114. Application of conical surfaces.** As the ellipse is a symmetrical curve, the upper and lower portions of the cone may be turned end for end so that the axes intersect. The resultant shape is indicated in Fig. 191, used at times in various sheet metal designs, such as oil-cans, tea-kettles, etc.

**1115. Problem 9.** To **find the** line of **intersection** of **a** doubly **curved** surface **of revolution with a plane** inclined to **its axis.**

**Construction.** Let Fig. 192 show the elevation of the given surface of revolution.* Attention will be directed to the construction of the section shown in the plan. The highest point on the curve is shown at **a**, which is found from its corresponding projection **a′**, at the point where the plane T cuts the meridian curve that is parallel to the plane of the paper. The point **b** is directly under **b′** and the length **bb** is equal to the chord of a circle whose radius is **m′n′** and whose distance from the centre is **b′n′**. Similarly, cc is found by drawing an indefinite line under **c′** intersected by **op = o′p′** as a radius. As many points as are necessary are located, so as to get the true shape. One thing, however, must be observed: The plane **TT**

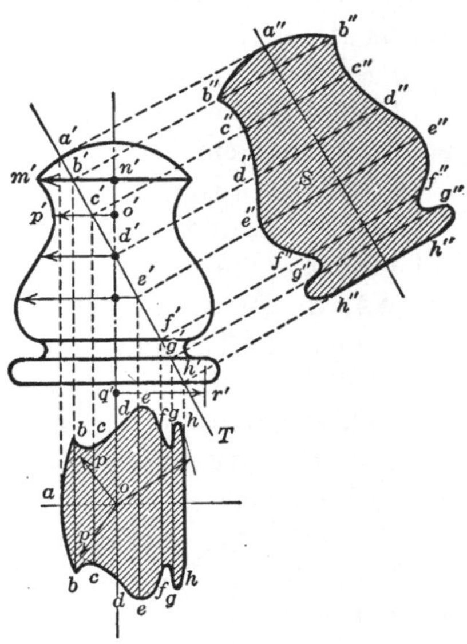

FIG. 192.

* Many of these constructions can be carried to completion without actually showing the principal planes. The operations on them are performed intuitively.

cuts the base of the surface of revolution at **h′** in the elevation and therefore **hh** is a straight line, which is the chord of a circle, whose radius is **q′r′** and which is located as shown in the plan.

The construction of the supplementary view resembles, in many respects, the construction in plan. The similar letters indicate the lengths that are equal to each other.

**1116. Problem 10.** To **find the line of intersection of a bell-surface with a plane.**

**Construction.** Fig. 193 shows the stub end of a connecting rod as used on a steam engine. The end is formed in the lathe by turning a bell-shaped surface of revolution on a bar of a

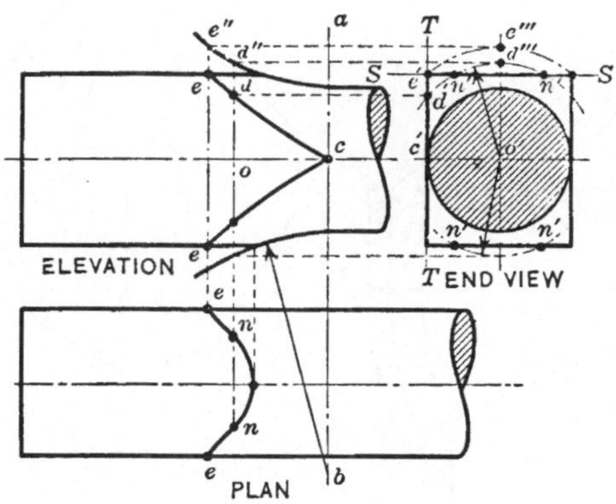


FIG. 193.

rectangular section, as shown in the end view, the shank being circular. The radius of curvature for the bell surface is located on the line **ab** as shown. The plane **TT** is tangent to the shank of the rod and begins to cut the bell-surface at points to the left of **ab**; hence, the starting point of the curve is at **c.** To find any point such as **d,** for instance, pass a plane through **d** perpendicular to the axis. It cuts the bell-surface in a circle (1024) whose radius is **od″ = o′d‴**. Where the circle intersects the plane **TT** at **d′**, project back to **d,** which is the required point on the curve. The scheme is merely this: By passing auxiliary planes perpendicular to the axis, circles are cut from the bell-surface which pierce the bounding planes in the required points of intersection. Attention might be directed to the piont **e** which is on both plan and elevation. This is true because the planes **TT** and **SS** intersect in a line which can pierce the bell-surface at only one point. The manner in which nn=n′n′ is located in the plan will be seen by the construction lines which are included in the illustration. To follow the description is more confusing than to follow the drawing.

**1117. Development by Triangulation.** In the developments so far considered, only the cases of extreme simplicity were selected. To develop the surface an oblique cone or an oblique cylinder requires a slightly different mode of procedure than was used

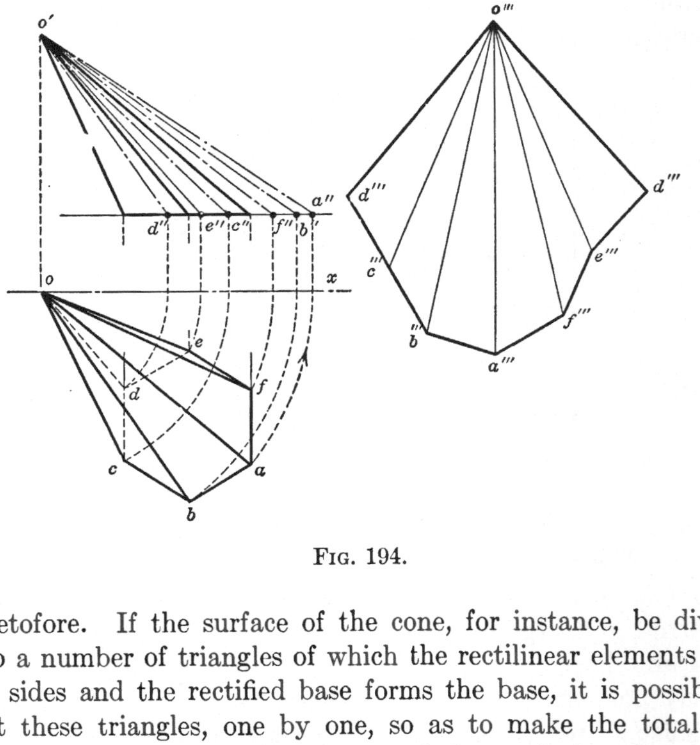


FIG. 194.

heretofore. If the surface of the cone, for instance, be divided into a number of triangles of which the rectilinear elements form the sides and the rectified base forms the base, it is possible to plot these triangles, one by one, so as to make the total area of the triangles equal to the area of the conical surface to be developed. The method is simple and is readily applied in practice. Few illustrations will make matters clearer.

**1118. Problem 11.** To develop the surfaces of an oblique hexagonal pyramid.

**Construction.** Fig. 194 shows the given oblique pyramid. It is first necessary to find the true lengths of all the elements of the surface. In the case of the pyramid, the edges alone need be considered. Suppose the pyramid is rotated about a perpendicular to the horizontal plane, through **o**, so that the base of the pyramid continually remains in its plane, then, when **oa** is parallel to the vertical plane, it is projected in its true length and is, hence, shown as the line **o′a″**. All the sides are thus brought para lel, in turn, to the plane and the true lengths are found. In most cases it will be found more convenient and less confusing to make a separate diagram to obtain the true lengths. To one with some experience, the actual lengths need not be drawn at all, but simply the distances a″; **b″**, **c″**, etc., laid off. Then from any point **o‴**, draw arcs **o′a″** = **o‴a‴**, **o′b″** = **o‴b‴**, **o′f″** =

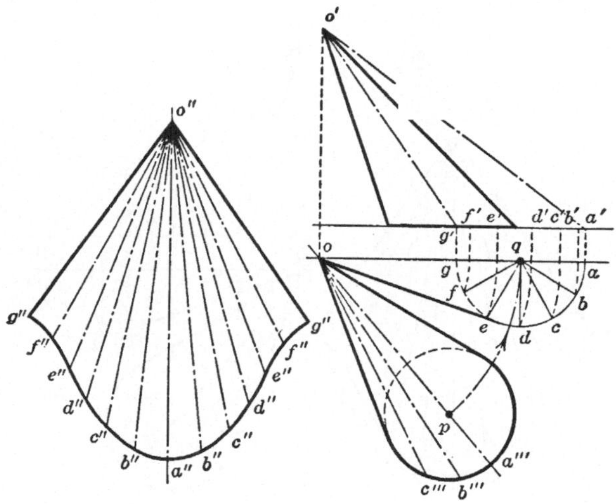


FIG. 195.

**o‴f‴**, etc. From **a‴**, lay off distances equal to the respective bases; in this case, **ab** = **bc** = **cd**, etc., and hence any one side will answer the purpose. Therefore, take that length on a divider and step off **ab** = **a‴b‴** = **b‴c‴** = **c‴d‴** = **a‴f‴**, etc. The development is then completed by drawing the proper lines.

The case selected, shows the triangulation method applied to a surface whose sides are triangles. It is extremely simple for that reason, but its simplicity is still evident in the case of the cone as will be now shown.

**1119. Problem 12. To develop the surface** of **an** o**bli**q**ue cone.**

**Construction.** Fig. 195 shows the given oblique cone. The horizontal projection of the axis is **op** and the base is a circle, hence, the cone is not a cone of revolution because the axis is inclined to the base. Revolve **op** to **oq**, parallel to the vertical plane. Divide the base into any number of parts **ab, bc, cd,** etc. preferably equal, to save time in subsequent operations. The element **oa** is parallel to the plane, hence, **o′a′** is its true length. The element **ob** is not parallel to the plane, but can be made so by additional revolution as shown; hence **o′b′** is its true length. From any point **o″**, draw **o″a″ = o′a′, o″b″ = o′b′, o″c″ = o′c′**, etc. On these indefinite arcs step off distances **a″b″ = b″c″ = c″d″**, etc., equal to the rectified distances **ab = bc = cd,** etc. A smooth curve through the points **a″b″c″**, etc., will give

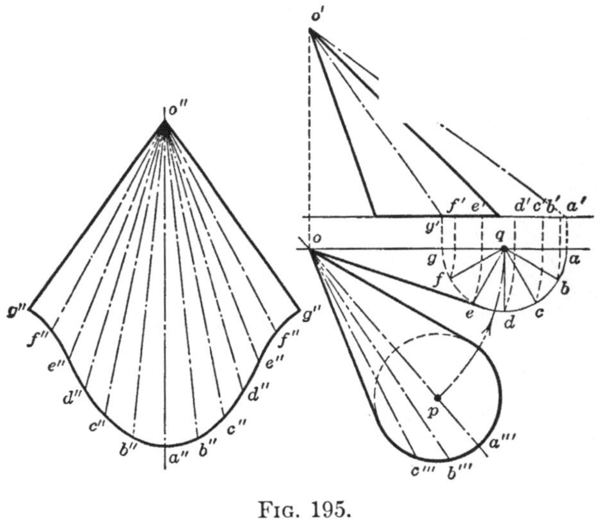


Fig. 195.

the development. As in previous problems, the cut is always made so as to make the shortest seam unless other requirements prevail.

**1120. Problem 13.** To develop the surface of an oblique cylinder.

**Construction.** In the case of the oblique cone, it was possible to divide the surface into a series of triangles which were plotted, one by one, and thus the development followed by the addition of these individual triangles. In the case of the cylinder, however, the application is somewhat different, although two cones may be used each of which has one base of the cylinder as its base. The application of this is cumbersome, an , the better plan will be shown.

Let Fig. 196 show the oblique cylinder, chosen, for convenience, with circular bases. Revolve the cylinder as shown, until it is parallel to the vertical plane. In the revolved position, ass a plane **T** through it, perpendicular to the axis. The curve so cut when rectified, will develop into a straight line and the elements of the surface will be perpendicular to it. The true shape of the section of the cylinder is shown by the curve **a″b″c″d″**, etc., and is an ellipse. Its construction is indicated in the diagram. Draw any base line **AA** and lay off on this the rectified portions

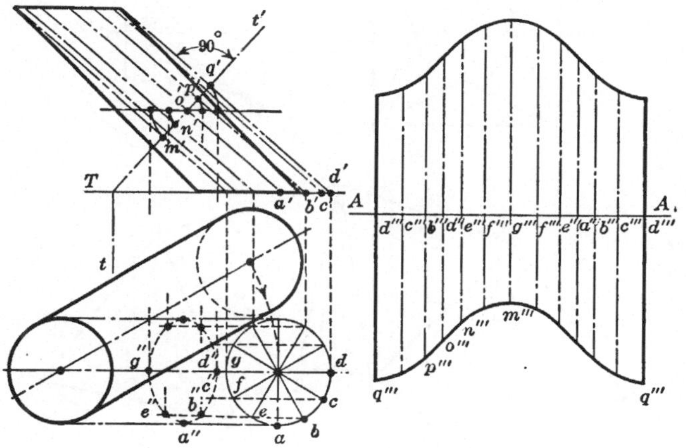


FIG. 196.

of the ellipse **a″b″ = a‴b‴**, **b″c″ = b‴c‴**, etc. The revolved positions of the elements shown in the vertical plane are all given in their true sizes because they are parallel to that plane. Hence, lay off **a‴o‴ = a′o′**, **b‴p‴ = b′p′**, etc., below the base line. Do the same for the elements above the base line and the curve determined by the points so found will be the development of the given oblique cylinder.

**1121. Transition pieces.** When an opening of one cross-section is to be connected with an opening of a different cross-section, the connecting piece is called a **transition piece.** The case of transforming a circular cross-section to a square cross-section is quite common in heating and ventilating flues, boiler flues and the like. In all such cases, two possible methods offer themselves as solutions. The two surfaces may be connected by a warped surface, the rectilinear elements of which are chosen so that the corners of the square are joined with the quarter points on the circle while the intermediate elements are distributed between them. A warped surface, however, is not developable, it is also difficult of representation and therefore commercially unsuited for application. The better method is to select some singly curved surface, or, a combination of planes and singly curved

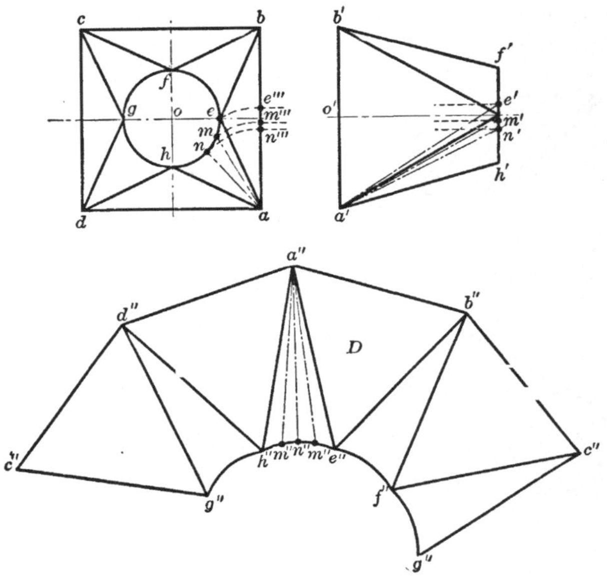


FIG. 197.

surfaces since these are developable. The application, which is quite a common one, is shown in the following problem.

**1122. Problem 14.** To **develop the** surface of **a transition piece** connecting **a circular opening with a square opening.**

**Construction.** Let the two upper views of Fig. 197 represent the transition piece desired. The square opening is indicated by **abcd** and the circular opening by **efgh.** The surface may be made up of four triangular faces **aeb, bfc, cgd, dha,** and four conical surfaces **hae, ebf, fcg, gdh,** whose vertices are at **a, b, c** and **d.**

The development is shown at **D,** on the same figure. The

triangle **a″b″e″** is first laid out so that the base **a″b″=ab;** and the true length of the sides are determined as found in the construction leading to the position **a′e′=a″e″=b″e″.** The conical surfaces are developed by triangulation. For example, the arc **he** is divided into any number of parts **em, mn,** etc.; and the true lengths of the elements of the surface are found

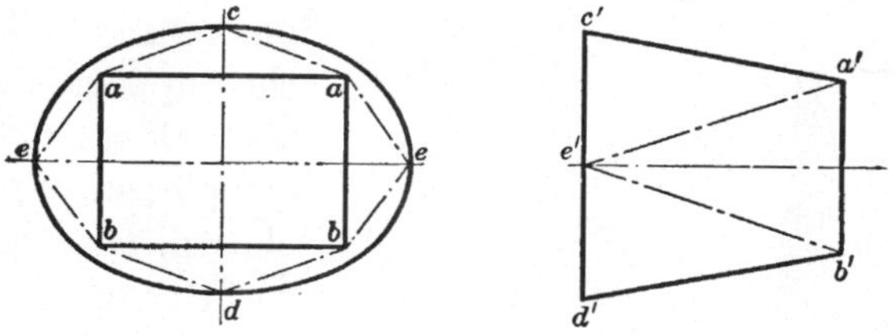


FIG. 198.

by the construction leading up to the positions **a′e′, a′m′, a′n′.** Hence, **a″e″=a′e′, a″m″=a′m′;** and **m″e″=me** is the rectified arc of the base of the conical surface. When four of these combinations of triangle and conical surface are laid out, in their proper order, the development is then complete.

If a rectangular opening is to be joined to an elliptical opening, the manner in which this may be accomplished is shown in Fig. 198.

**1123. Problem 15. To develop the surface a transition piece connecting two elliptical openings whose major axes are at right angles to each other.**

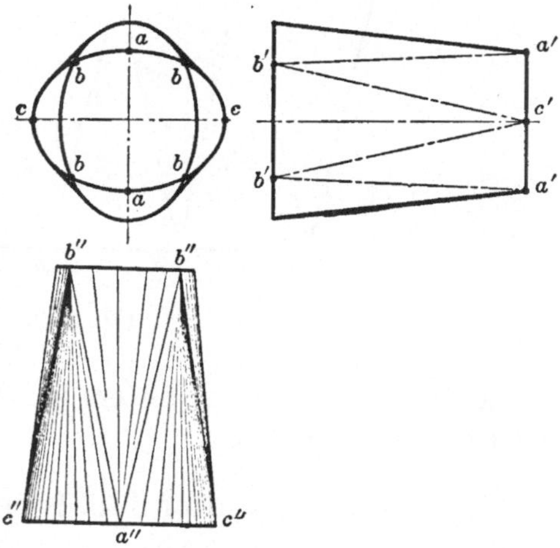


FIG. 199.

**Construction.** Fig. 199 shows three views of the elliptical transition piece. By reference to the diagram, it will be seen that the surface may be divided into eight conical surfaces, turned end for end; that is, four vertices are situated on one ellipse and four vertices are situated on the other. The shaded figure indicates the arrangement of the conical surfaces and the elements are shown as shade lines.

In all developments of this character, the arrangement of the surfaces has considerable effect on the appearance of the transition piece when completed. In the case chosen, the eight conical surfaces give a pleasing result. If the intersection of the eight alternate conical surfaces is objectionable then it is possible to use a still larger number of divisions.

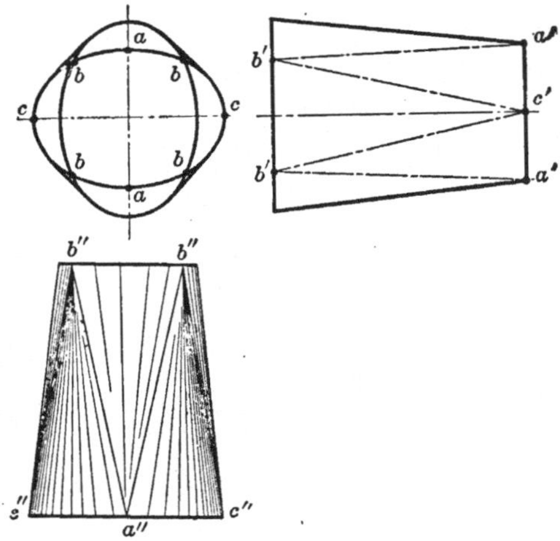

FIG. 199.

The development of the conical surfaces is performed by the triangulation method. When finished, its appearance is that

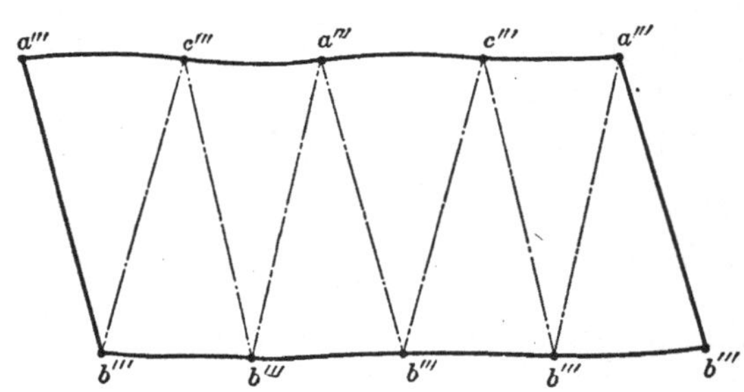

FIG. 200.

of Fig. 200. The similar letters indicate the order in which the surfaces are assembled.

**1124. Development of doubly curved surfaces by approximation.** Doubly curved surfaces are non-developable because successive elements cannot be made to coincide with a plane. It is possible, however, to divide the surface into a series of singly curved surfaces and then to develop these. By dividing the doubly curved surface into a sufficiently large number of parts, the approximation may be made to approach the surface as closely as desired.

For doubly curved surfaces of revolution, two general methods are used. One method is to pass a series of meridian planes through the axis and then to adopt a singly curved surface whose contour is that of the surface of revolution at the meridian planes. This method is known as the **gore** method.

The second method, known as the **zone** method, is to divide the surface into frusta of cones whose vertices lie on the axis of the doubly curved surface of revolution. The following examples will illustrate the application of the methods.

**1125. Problem 16.** To **develop the surface of a sphere by the gore method.**

**Construction.** Let the plan **P** of Fig. 201 show the sphere.

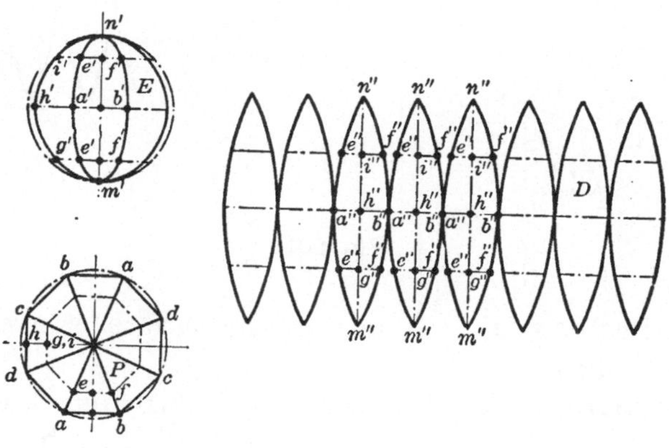


FIG. 201.

Pass a series of meridian planes **aa, bb, cc, dd,** through the sphere and then join **ab, bc, cd,** etc. From the plan **P** construct the elevation **E** and then pass planes through **i′** and **g′**, perpendicular to the axis of the sphere, intercepting equal arcs on the meridian circle, for convenience. Find the corresponding circles in the plan and inscribe an octagon (for this case) and determine **ef,** the chord length for that position of the cutting planes through i′ and **g′**. This distance may then be laid off as **e′f′** in the elevation **E** and the curve n′**e′a′e′m′** be drawn.

For the development **D**, it will be noted that **ab = a′b′ = a″b″**

and $\mathbf{ef = e'f' = e''f''}$. Also, the rectified distance $\mathbf{m'g' = m''g''}$, $\mathbf{g'h' = g''h''}$, $\mathbf{h'i' = h''i''}$, etc. A suitable number of points must be used in order to insure the proper degree of accuracy, the number chosen here is insufficient for practical purposes. By adding eight of these faces along the line $\mathbf{a''b''}$, the development is completed.

When this method is commercially applied, the gores may be stretched by hammering or pressing to their true shape. In this case they are singly curved surfaces no longer.

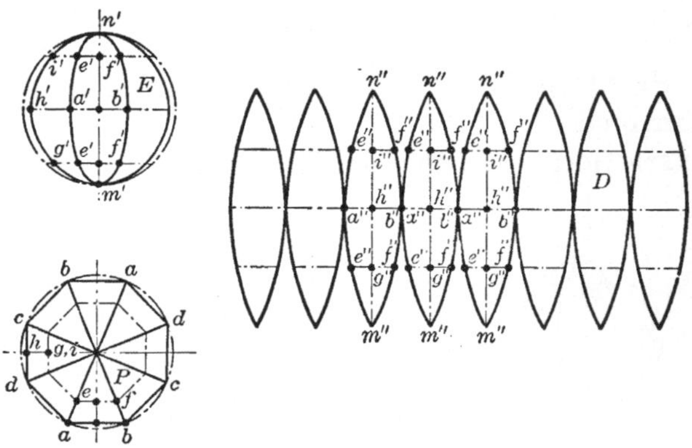


FIG. 201.

**1126. Problem 17.** To **develop the surface** of **a sphere by the zone method.**

**Construction.** Let **P**, Fig. 202, be the plan and **E**, the elevation of a sphere. Pass a series of planes $\mathbf{a'a'}$, $\mathbf{b'b'}$, $c'c'$ etc., perpendicular to the axis of the sphere. Join $\mathbf{a'b'}$, and produce to $h'$, the vertex of a conical surface giving rise to the frustum $\mathbf{a'b'b'a'}$. Similarly, join $\mathbf{b'c'}$ and produce to $\mathbf{g'}$. The last conical surface has its vertex $\mathbf{e'}$ in the circumscribing sphere.

The development **D** is s milar to the developnent of any frustum of a conical surface of revolution. That is, with $\mathbf{h''}$ as a centre, draw an arc with $\mathbf{h''a'' = h'a'}$ as a radius. At the centre line make $a''o'' = \mathbf{ao}$, $\mathbf{o''n''} = $ on etc. The radius $\mathbf{h''b'' = h'b'}$ so that the arc $b''\mathbf{b''b''}$ is tangent internally, to the similarly lettered arc. The radius for this case is $\mathbf{g''b'' = g' = b'}$. The development is completed by continuing this process until all the conical surfaces are developed.

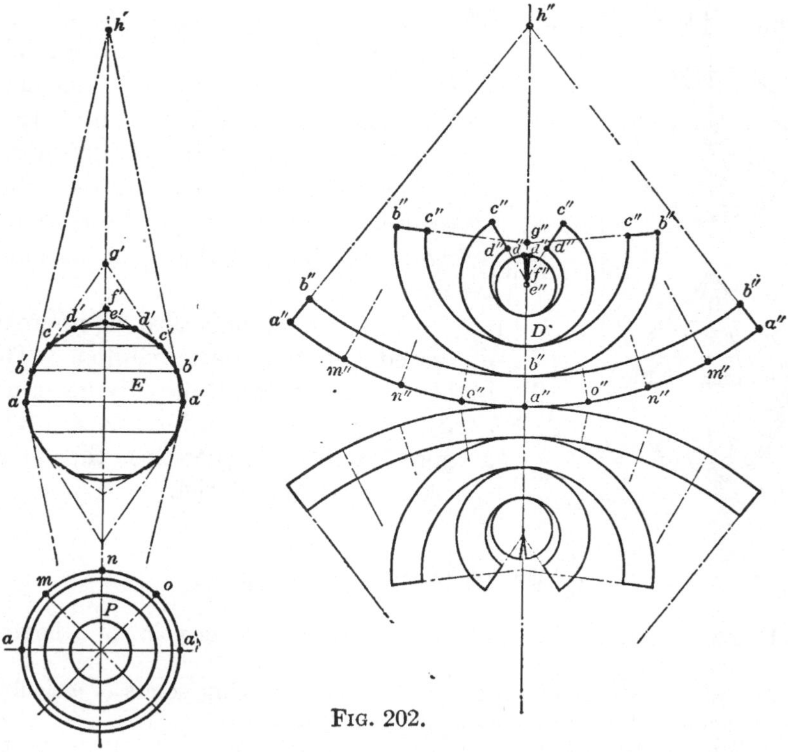


FIG. 202.

**1127. Problem 18.** To **develop a doubly-curved surface of revolution by the gore method.** Let Fig. 203 represent the doubly curved surface of revolution as finally approximated. Through the axis at **h** pass a series of equally spaced meridian planes, and then draw the chords, one of which is lettered as **dd.** In the elevation **E,** pass a series of planes **k′k′, l′l′, m′m′,** perpendicular to the axis. The lines **b′b′,** c′c′, **d′d′,** etc., are drawn on the resulting singly curved surface and are shown in their true length. The corresponding projections of these lines in the plan **P** are also shown in their true length.

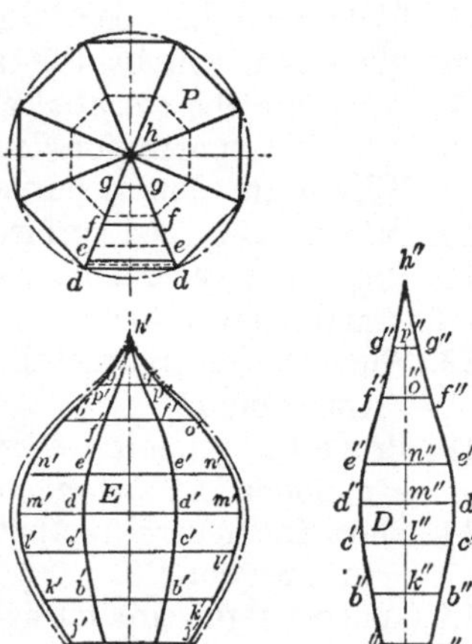


FIG. 203.

To develop the surface of one face lay off the rectified distance **j′k′ = j″k″**, **k′l′ = k″l″**, etc. At the points **j″**, **k″**, **l″**, etc., lay off **a′a′ = a″a″**, **b′b′ = b″b″**, etc., perpendicular to **h″j″** so that the resulting figure **D** is symmetrical about it. When eight of these faces (or gores) are joined together and secured along the seams, the resulting figure will be that shown in plan and elevation.

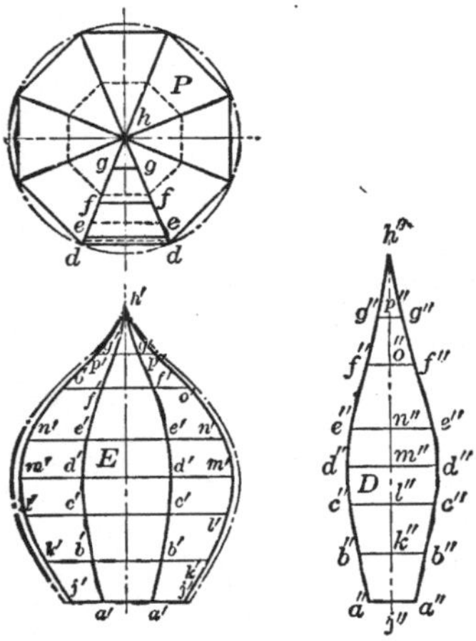

FIG. 203.

This surface may also be approximated by the zone method. The choice of method is usually governed by commercial considerations. The gore method is perhaps the more economical in material.

## QUESTIONS ON CHAPTER XI

1. State the general method of finding the piercing point of a line on a plane.
2. Show by an oblique projection how the piercing points of a doubly curved line are found on the principal planes.
3. Why is the projecting surface of a doubly curved line a projecting cylindrical surface?
4. What is a "line of intersection" of two surfaces?
5. Distinguish between "line of intersection" and "section" of a solid.
6. What is meant by the development of a surface? Explain fully.
7. What are the essential characteristics of a developable surface?
8. Why is a sphere non-developable?
9. Why is any doubly curved surface non-developable?
10. Why is a warped surface non-developable?
11. Prove the general case of finding the intersection of a right prism and a plane inclined to its axis.
12. Show the general method of finding the development of the prism in Question 11.
13. Prove the general case of finding the intersection of a right circular cylinder and a plane inclined to its axis.
14. Show the general method of finding the development of the cylinder in Question 13.
15. When a right circular cylinder is cut by a plane why must the ellipse be reversible?
16. How is the torus approximated with cylindrical surfaces?
17. Prove the general case of finding the intersection of a right pyramid and a plane inclined to its axis.

18. Show the general method of finding the development of the right pyramid in Question 17.
19. Prove the general case of finding the intersection of a right circular cone and a plane inclined to its axis.
20. Show the general method of finding the development of the right cone in Question 19.
21. Why is the ellipse, cut from a cone of revolution by an inclined plane, reversible?
22. Prove the general case of finding the intersection of a doubly curved surface of revolution and a plane inclined to the axis.
23. Is the surface in Question 22 developable? Why?
24. Prove the general case of finding the intersection of a bell-surface with planes parallel to its axis.
25. Is the bell-surface developable? Why?
26. What is development by triangulation?
27. Prove the general case of the development of the surface of an oblique pyramid.
28. Prove the general case of the development of the surface of an oblique cone.
29. Prove the general case of the development of the surface of an oblique cylinder.
30. What is a transition piece?
31. Why is it desirable to divide the surfaces of a transition piece into developable surfaces?
32. Prove the general case of the development of a transition piece which joins a circular opening with a square opening.
33. Prove the general case of the development of a transition piece which joins an elliptical opening with a rectangular opening.
34. Prove the general case of the development of a transition piece which joins two elliptical openings whose major axes are at right angles to each other.
35. What is the gore method of developing doubly curved surfaces?
36. What is the zone method of developing doubly curved surfaces?
37. Prove the general case of the development of a sphere by the gore method.
38. Prove the general case of the development of a sphere by the zone method.
39. Prove the general case of the development of a doubly curved surface of revolution by the gore method.
40. A right octagonal prism has a circumscribing circle of 2″ and is 4″ high. It is cut by a plane, inclined 30° to the axis, and passes through its axis, $1\frac{3}{4}$″ from the base. Find the section.
41. Develop the surface of the prism of Question 40.
42. A cylinder of revolution is $2\frac{1}{2}$″ in diameter and $3\frac{3}{4}$″ high. It is cut by a plane, inclined 45° to the axis and passes through its axis 2″ from the base. Find the section.
43. Develop the surface of the cylinder of Question 42.

44. A right octagonal pyramid has a circumscribing base circle of $2\frac{1}{4}''$ and is $4''$ high. It is cut by a plane, inclined $30°$ to the axis and passes through its axis $2''$ from the base. Find the section.
45. Develop the surface of the pyramid of Question 44.
46. A right circular cone has a base $2''$ in diameter and is $3\frac{3}{4}''$ high. It is cut by plane inclined $45°$ to the axis and passes through its axis $2\frac{1}{4}''$ from the base. Find the section.
47. Develop the cone of Question 46.
48. A $90°$ stove pipe elbow is to be made from cylinders $4''$ in diameter. The radius of the bend is to be $18''$. Divide elbow into 8 parts. The tangent distance beyond the quadrant is $4''$. Develop the surface to suitable scale.
49. Assume a design of a vase (a doubly curved surface of revolution) and make a section of it.
50. The stub end of a connecting rod of a steam engine is $4''\times6''$; the rod diameter is $3\frac{1}{2}''$. The bell-surface has a radius of $12''$. Find the lines of intersection. Draw to suitable scale.
51. An oblique pyramid has a regular hexagon for a base. The circumscribing circle for the base has a diameter of $2''$; the altitude is $3\frac{1}{2}''$ and the projection of the apex is $2\frac{1}{2}''$ from the centre of the base. Develop the surface of the pyramid.
52. An oblique cone has a circular base of $2\frac{1}{4}''$ in diameter and an altitude of $3''$. The projection of the vertex on the plane of the base is $1\frac{1}{4}''$ from the centre of the base. Develop the conical surface.
53. An oblique cylinder has a circular base $1\frac{3}{4}''$ in diameter; it is $2\frac{1}{2}''$ high and the inclination of the axis is $30°$ with the base. Develop the surface.
54. A transition piece is to be made joining a $3'$–$0''\times5'$–$6''$ opening with a $4'$–$0''$ diameter circle. The distance between openings $3'$–$6''$. Develop the surface. Use a suitable scale for the drawing.
55. A transition piece is to be made joining an opening having a $3'$–$0''$ $\times4'$–$0''$ opening to a $2'$–$0''\times6'$–$0''$ opening (both rectangular). The distance between openings is $4'$–$0''$. Develop the sheet and use suitable scale for the drawing.
56. A square opening $4''$–$0''\times4'$–$0''$ is to be joined with an elliptical opening whose major and minor axes are $5'$–$0''\times3'-0''$ respectively. The distance between openings is $3'$–$0''$. Develop the sheet. Use suitable scale in making the drawing.
57. A circular opening having a diameter of $3'$–$0''$ is to be connected with an elliptical opening whose major and minor axes are $4'$–$0''\times2'$–$6''$ respectively. The distance between openings is $6'$–$0''$. Develop the sheet. Use suitable scale in making the drawing.
58. An opening having two parallel sides and two semicircular ends has overall dimensions of $3'$–$0''\times5'$–$6''$. This opening is to be joined with a similar opening having dimensions of $3'$–$6''\times4'$–$6''$. The distance between openings is $3'$–$6''$. Develop the sheet. Use suitable scale in making the drawing.

59. A frustum of a cone has a base which is made up of two parallel sides and two semicircular ends and whose overall dimensions are 3′–6″×6′–0″. The height of the vertex above the base is 8′–6″; that of the upper base is 4′–0″ above the lower base. Develop the sheet and use suitable scale in making the drawing.
60. An elliptical opening having a major and minor axis of 5′–0″ and 4′–0″, respectively, is to be joined with a similar opening but whose major axis is at a right angle. Develop the sheet and use suitable scale in making the drawing.
61. An elliptical opening having a major and minor axis of 4′–6″ and 3′–6″, respectively, is to be joined with a similar opening but whose major axis is at an angle of 30°. Develop the sheet and use suitable scale in making the drawing.
62. An elliptical opening having a major and minor axis of 5′–0″ and 3′–6″, respectively, is to be joined with another elliptical opening whose major and minor axes are 4′–6″ and 3′–6″, respectively. Develop the sheet and use suitable scale in making the drawing.
63. A sphere is 6″ in diameter. Develop the surface by the gore method and divide the entire surface into sixteen parts. Use a suitable scale in making the drawing.
64. A sphere is 6″ in diameter. Develop the surface by the zone method and divide the entire surface into twelve parts. Use a suitable scale in making the drawing.
65. Assume some doubly curved surface of revolution and develop the surface by the gore method.
66. Assume some doubly curved surface of revolution and develop the surface by the zone method.

# CHAPTER XII

## INTERSECTIONS OF SURFACES WITH EACH OTHER, AND THEIR DEVELOPMENT

**1201. Introductory.** When two surfaces are so situated with respect to each other that they intersect, they do so in a line which is called the **line of intersection.** It is highly desirable in the conception of intersections to realize that certain **elements** of one surface **intersect** certain **elements** on the other surface, and that the locus of these intersecting elements is the desired line of intersection.

The line of intersection is found by passing auxiliary surfaces through the given surfaces. Lines will thus be cut from the given surfaces by the auxiliary surfaces, the intersections of which yield points on the desired line of intersection. The simplest auxiliary surface is naturally the plane, but sometimes cylindrical,* conical and spherical surfaces may find application. It is not necessary only to use a simple type of auxiliary surface, but also to make the surface pass through the given surfaces so as to cut them in easily determinable lines—preferably, in the elements. As illustrations of the latter, the case of a concial surface cut by a plane passing through the vertex furnishes an example. It cuts the surface in straight lines or rectilinear elements. Likewise, a plane passed through a cylindrical sur face parallel to any element will cut from it, one or more lines which are also rectiliner elements. For doubly curved surfaces of revolution, a plane passed through the axis (a meridian plane) cuts it in a meridian curve. When the plane is perpendicular to the axis, it cuts it in circles. An interesting and valuable

* A careful distinction must be made between solids and their bounding surfaces. The terms, cylinder and cylindrical surface are often used indiscriminately. The associated idea is usually obtained from the nature of the problem.

property of spheres is that all plane sections in any direction, or in any place, are all circles, whose radii are readily obtainable.

When prisms or pyramids intersect, auxiliary planes are not required to find their intersection, because the plane faces and the edges furnish sufficient material with which to accomplish the desired result. These types of surfaces are therefore exempt from the foregoing general method.

**1202. Problem 1. To find the line of intersection of the surfaces of two prisms.**

**Construction.** Let Fig. 204 represent the two prisms, one of which, for convenience, is a right hexagonal prism. The face **ABDC** intersects the right prism in the line **mn,** one line of the required intersection. The face **CDFE** is intersected by the edge of the right prism in the point **o,** found as shown in the construction. Hence, **mo** is the next line of the required intersection. Similarly, the edge **EF** pierces the faces of the right prism at **p,** and **op** is the continuation of the intersection. In this way, all points are found. The curve must be closed because the interpenetration is complete. Only the one end where the prism enters is shown in construction. The curve where it again emerges is found in an identical manner.

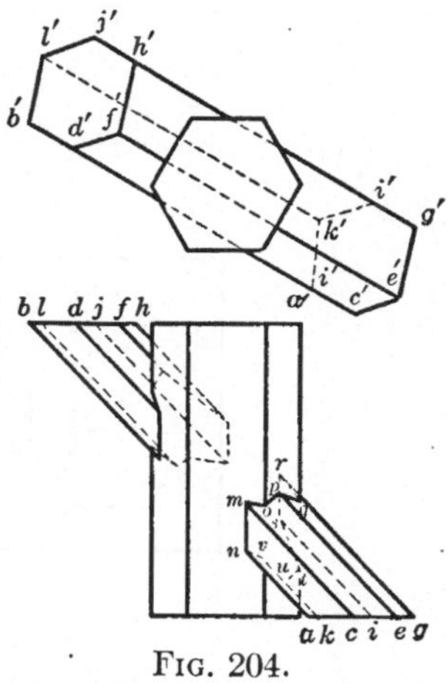

FIG. 204.

**1203. Problem 2. To find the developments in the preceding problem.**

**Construction.** The development of the right prism is quite simple and should be understood from the preceding chapter. The points at which the oblique prism intersects the right prism are also shown. Thus, it is only necessary to make sure on what element the point pierces, and this may be obtained from the plan view of the right prism.

In developing the oblique prism, **D′** of **Fig. 205**, the same general scheme is followed as was used in developing the oblique cylinder (1120). Revolve the prism of Fig. 204 so that the elements are parallel to the plane of projection; they are then shown in their true length. Pass a plane perpendicular to the edges and this line of intersection will develop into a straight line which is used as a base line. Find now the true section of the prism and lay off the sides perpendicular to the base line and at their proper distances apart. Lay off the lengths of the edges above and below the base line and join the points by lines to complete the development.

When actually constructing this as a model, it will be well to

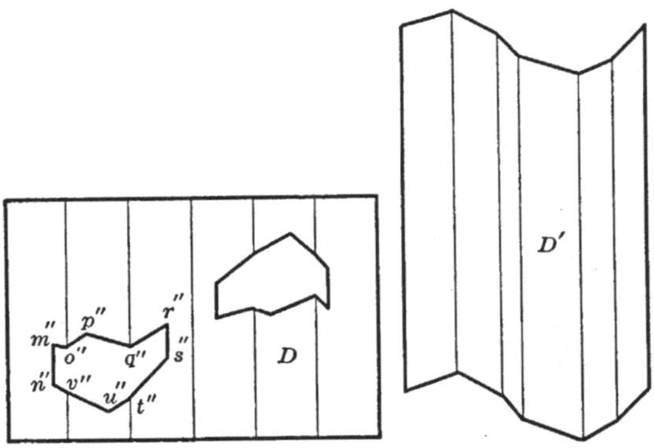


FIG. 205.

carry out the work as shown, and make the oblique prism in one piece. It may then be inserted in the opening provided for in the right prism, as indicated.

**1204. Problem 3. To find the line of intersection of two cylindrical surfaces of revolution whose axes intersect at a right angle.**

**Construction.** Let Fig. 206, represent the given cylindrical surfaces. Through **o′**, pass a series of planes a′**a′**, **b′b′**, **c′c′**, etc. The elements cut from the cylindrical surface by these planes interest the other cylindrical surface at the points **a, e, b,** d, c. The two upper views lead to the construct on of the lower view. It will be seen by this construction that the entire scheme of locating points on the curve lies in the finding of the successive intersections of the elements of the surfaces.

If the cylindrical surfaces have elliptical sections, instead of circular sections as shown, the method of procedure will be found to be much the same.

**1205. Problem 4. To find the developments in the preceding problem.**

**Construction.** As the elements of the surfaces depicted in Fig. 206 are parallel to the plane of the paper, they are therefore, shown in their true length. Hence, to develop the surfaces,

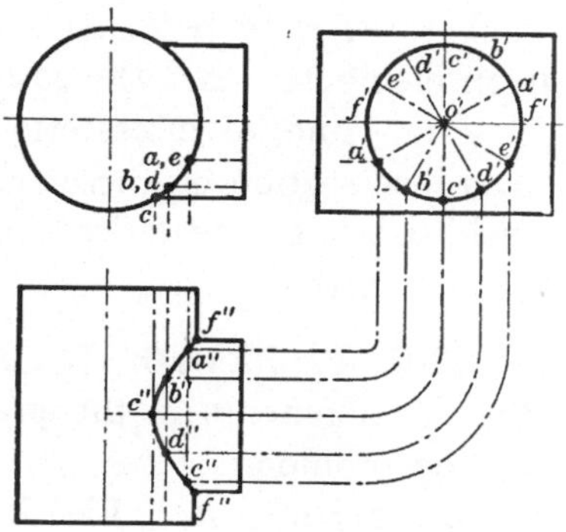

FIG. 206.

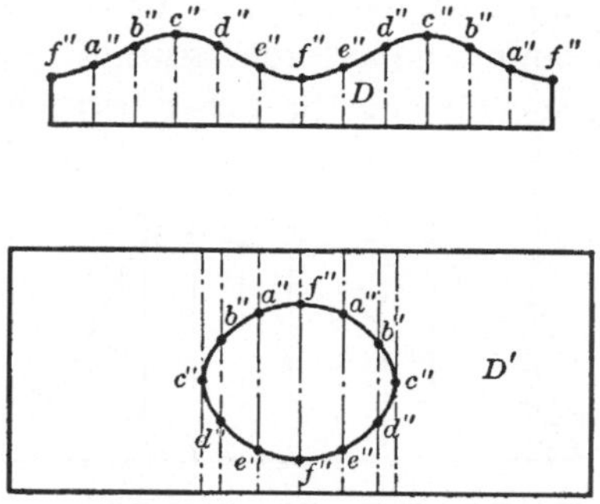


FIG. 207.

rectify the bases and set off the points at proper distances from the base line and also their rectified distance apart. The appearance of the completed developments are shown in Fig. 207.

This problem is similar to the development of the steam dome on a locomotive boiler.

**1206. Problem 5. To find the line of intersection of two cylindrical surfaces of revolution whose axes intersect at any angle.**

**Construction.** Fig. 208 shows the two cylindrical surfaces chosen. If a series of auxiliary planes be passed parallel to the plane of the intersecting axes they will cut the cylindrical surfaces in rectilinear elements. The elements of one surface will intersect the elements of the other surface in the required points of the line of intersection. The construction shown in the figure should be clear from the similar lettering for the similar points on the line of intersection.

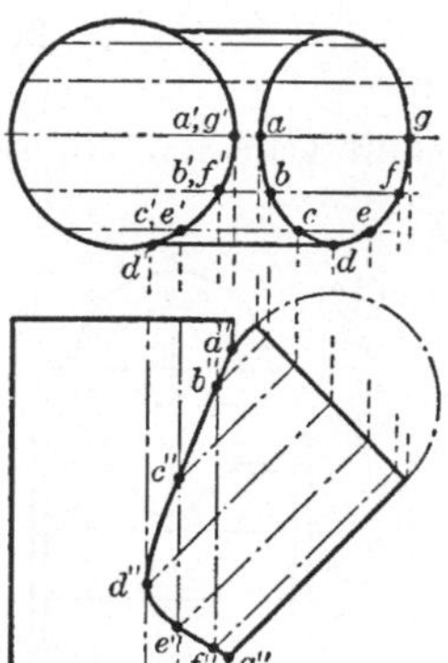

FIG. 208.

It may be desirable to note that this method of locating the required points on the curve is also applicable to the construction of Fig. 206, and vice versa.

If the plane of the intersecting axes is not parallel to the plane of the paper, the construction can be simplified by revolving the cylindrical surfaces until they become parallel. The method of procedure is then the same as that given here. If the axes cannot be made to lie in the same plane, then the construction is more difficult. The method in such cases is to pass a plane through one cylinder so as to cut in in elements; and the same plane will cut the other cylinder in some line of intersection. The intersection of these will yield points on the desired line of intersection.

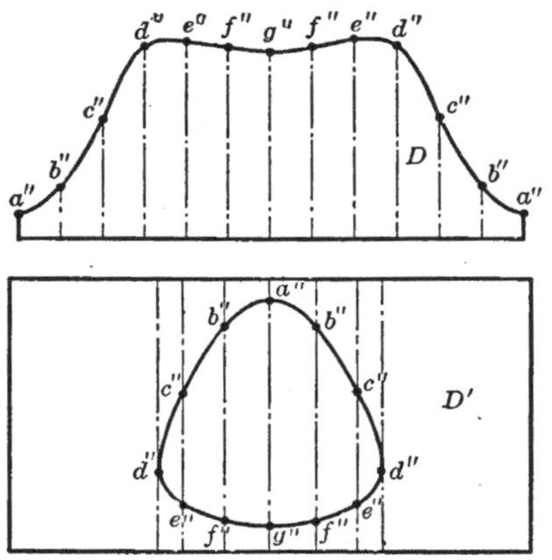


FIG. 209.

**1207. Problem 6. To find the developments in the preceding problem.**

**Construction.** Fig. 209 shows the development as it appears. If the plane of the base is perpendicular to the elements of the surface, the base will develop into a straight line. The elements will be at right angles to the base line and as they are shown in their true length, they may be laid off directly from Fig. 208.

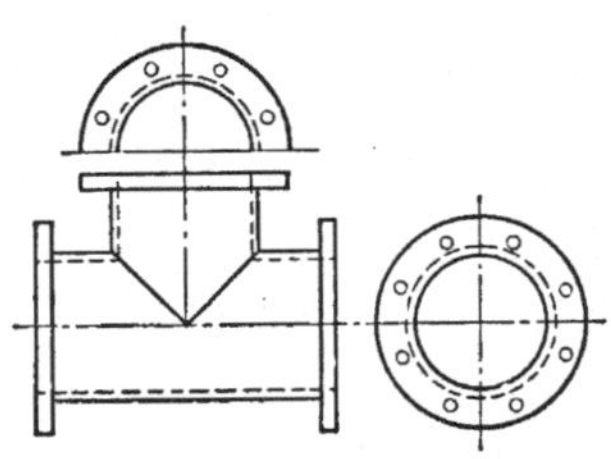

FIG. 210.

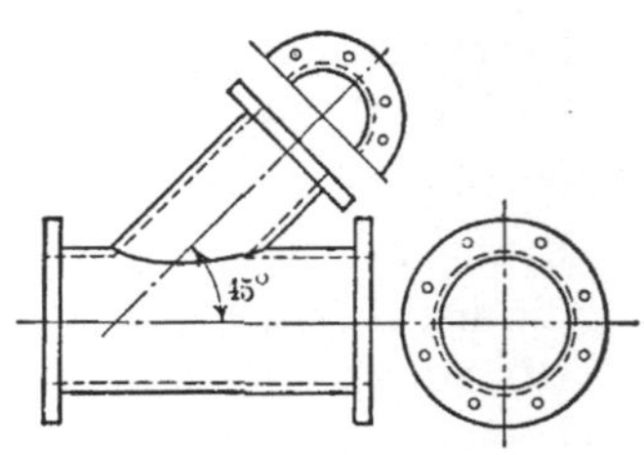


FIG. 211.

**1208. Application of intersecting cylindrical surfaces to pipes.** The construction of pipe fittings as commercially used furnish examples of intersecting cylindrical surfaces. Fig. 210

shows two cylindrical surfaces whose diameters are the same and whose axes intersect at a right angle. The line of intersection for this case will be seen to consist of two straight lines at right angles to each other. In Fig. 211, the cylindrical surfaces have their axes intersecting at an angle of 45° and have different diameters.

**1209. Problem 7. To find the line of intersection of two cylindrical surfaces whose axes do not intersect.**

**Construction.** Fig. 212 shows two circular cylindrical surfaces which are perpendicular to each other and whose axes are offset. Pass a series of planes **ab, cd, ef,** etc., through **o.** These planes cut the cylindrical surface in elements, which in turn, intersect elements of the other surface. As the construction lines are completely shown, the description is unnecessary.

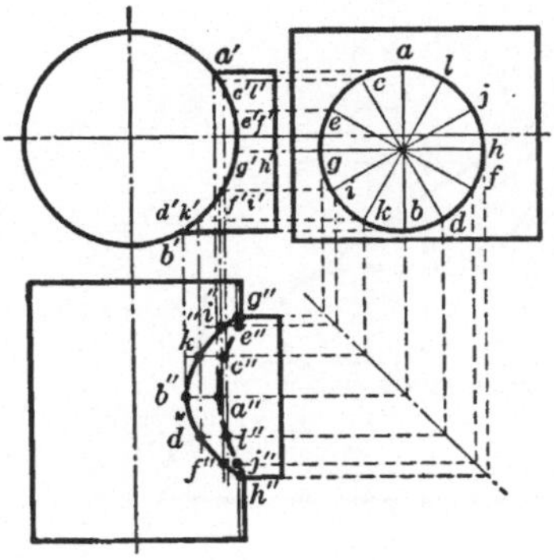

FIG. 212.

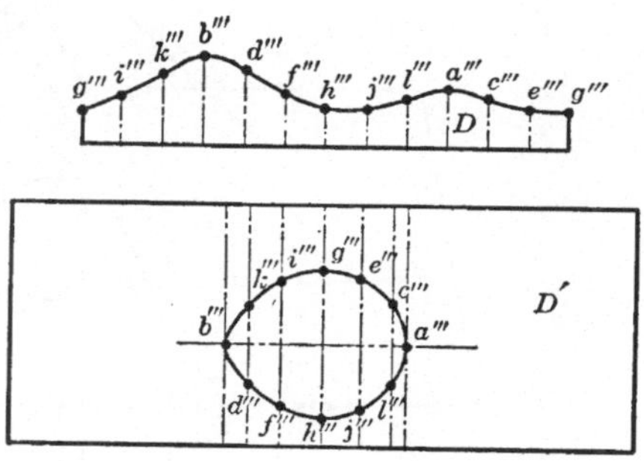


FIG. 213.

**1210. Problem 8. To find the developments in the preceding problem.**

**Construction.** First consider the larger cylindrical surface, **D′**, Fig. 213, which is cut along any element. With a divider, space off the rectified distances between elements; and on the proper elements, lay off $\mathbf{b'''}$ to correspond with $\mathbf{b''}$; $\mathbf{k'''d'''}=\mathbf{k''d''}$, $\mathbf{i'''f'''}=\mathbf{i''f''}$, etc.

For the smaller cylindrical surface, rectify the entire circle **ace . . . la** and divide into the number of parts shown. As the elements are shown parallel to the plane of projection in the side elevation, they may be directly plotted as indicated by the curve $\mathbf{g'''i'''k'''}$. . . $\mathbf{e'''g'''}$. This completes the final development.

**1211. Intersection of conical surfaces.** If a plane be passed through the vertex of a conical surface it cuts it in rectilinear elements if at all. When two conical surfaces intersect it is possible to pass a plane through the vertices of both. Thus, the plane may be made to intersect both surfaces in rectilinear elements, the intersections of which determine points on the required line of intersection.

Fig. 214 shows this pictorially. If the vertices **m** and n be joined by a line and its piercing point **o** be found, then, any line through **o** will determine a plane. Also, if **od** be the line chosen, the plane of the lines **mo** and **od** will cut the conical surfaces in

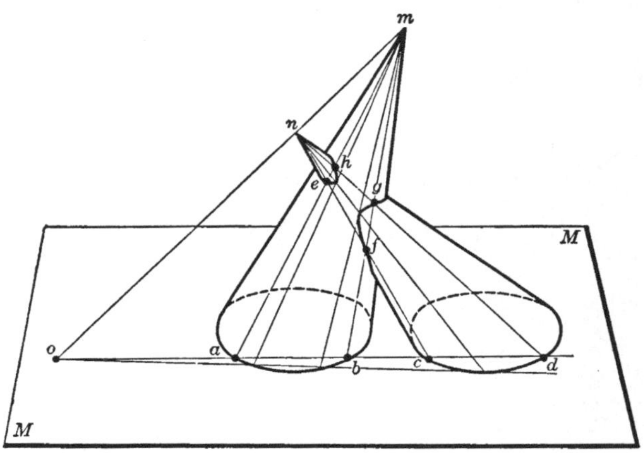


FIG. 214.

the elements **ma, mb, nc** and **nd.** These elements determine the four points **e,** f, **g,** h. Any other line through **o** will, if properly chosen, determine other elements which again yield new points on the line of intersection. The following problem will bring out the details more fully.

**1212. Problem 9.** To **find the line of** intersection **of the surfaces of two** cones, whose bases **may be made to lie** in **the same plane, and** whose altitudes differ.

**Construction.** Let **A** and **B,** Fig. 215 be the vertices of the two cones in question, whose bases are in the horizontal plane. If the bases do not lie in the principal planes, a new set of principal planes may be substituted to attain the result. Join **A** and **B** by a line and find where this line pierces the horizontal plane at c. Any line, through c, lying in the horizontal plane, in addition to the line **AB** will determine a plane, which may cut the conical surfaces in elements. Let, for instance, **cd** be such a line. This line cuts the bases at **d, e** and f, the points which will be considered. The elements in the horizontal projection are shown as **db, eb** and **fa;** in the vertical projection, they are **d′b′, e′b′** and **f′a′**. The element **f′a′** intersects the element **d′b′** at **g′**, and the element **e′b′** at **h′**, thus determining **g′** and **h′**, two points on the vertical projection of the required line of intersection. The corresponding projections **g** and **h** may also be found, which determine points on the horizontal projection

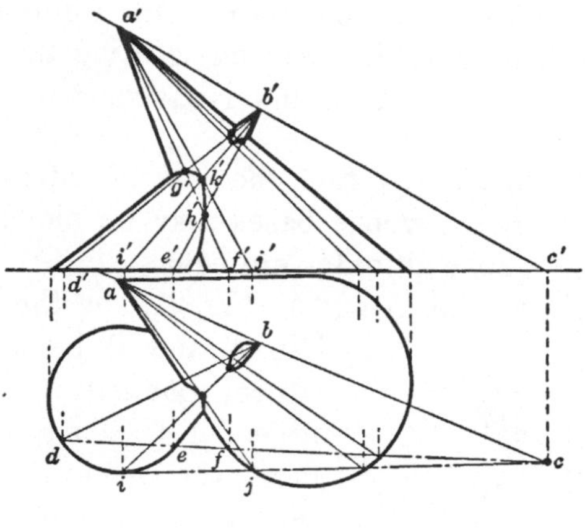


FIG. 215.

of the same line of intersection. Consider, now, the line ci, tangent to the one cone. Its element is **ib** in the horizontal projection and **i′b′** in the vertical projection; the corresponding element cut from the other cone is **ja** in the horizontal projection and **j′a′** in the vertical projection. The points **k** and **k′** are thus found, but they represent only one point **K** on the actual cones.

This process is continued until a sufficient number of points are determined, so that a smooth curve can be drawn through them. The cones chosen, have complete interpenetration, as one cone goes entirely through the other. Thus, there are two distinct curves of intersection. That, near the apex **B**, is found in an identical way with the preceding.

Attention might profitably be called to the manner in which points are located so as to miminize confusion as much as possible. To do this, draw only one element on each cone at a time, locating one, or two points, as the case may be; then erase the construction lines when satisfied of the accuracy. Several of the prominent points of the curve may be thus located and others estimated if considerable accuracy is not a prerequisite. If the surfaces are to be developed and constructed subsequently, however, more points will have to be established.

There is nothing new in the development of these cones, the case is similar to that of any oblique cone and is therefore omitted. One thing may be mentioned in passing however, and that is, while drawing the elements to determine the contour of the base, the same elements should be used for locating the line of intersection as thereby considerable time is saved.

**1213. Problem 10.** **To find the line of intersection of the surfaces of two cones, whose bases may be made to lie in the same plane and whose altitudes are equal.**

**Construction.** Let **A** and **B**, Fig. 216, be the desired cones. Join **A** and **B** by a line which is chosen, parallel to the planes of projection. Hence, this line cannot pierce the plane of the bases, and the preceding method of finding the line of intersection is thus inapplicable. It is possible, however to draw a line **cd** parallel to **ab.** These lines therefore determine a plane which passes through both vertices and intersects the surface in rectilinear elements. The completion of the construction becomes evident when the process which leads to the finding of **F** and **G** is understood.

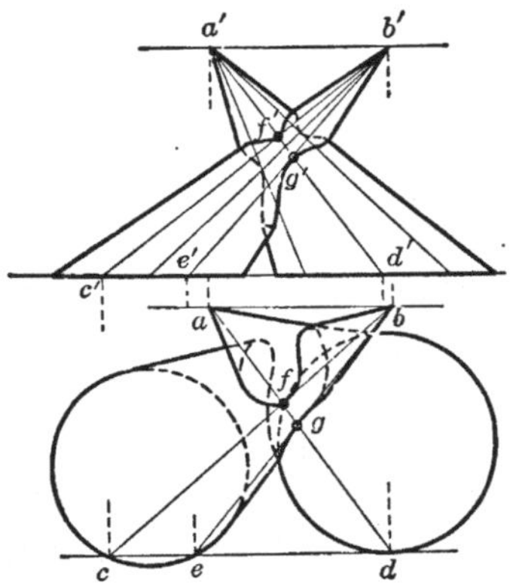

FIG. 216.

The cases of intersecting cones so far considered have been so situated as to have bases in a common plane. This may not always be convenient. Therefore to complete the subject, and to cover emergencies, an additional construction will be studied.

**1214. Problem 11.** To **find the** line **of intersection** of **the surfaces of two cones whose bases lie in different planes.**

**Construction.** Let **A** and **B,** Fig. 217, be the vertices of the two cones. The cone **A** has its base in the horizontal plane; **B** has its base in the plane T, which is perpendicular to the vertical plane. Join the vertices **A** and **B** by a line, which pierces the horizontal plane at c and the plane T in the point **d′** horizontally projected at **d.** Revolve the plane **T** into the vertical plane, and, hence, the trace **Tt** becomes **Tt″.** The angle **t′Tt″** must

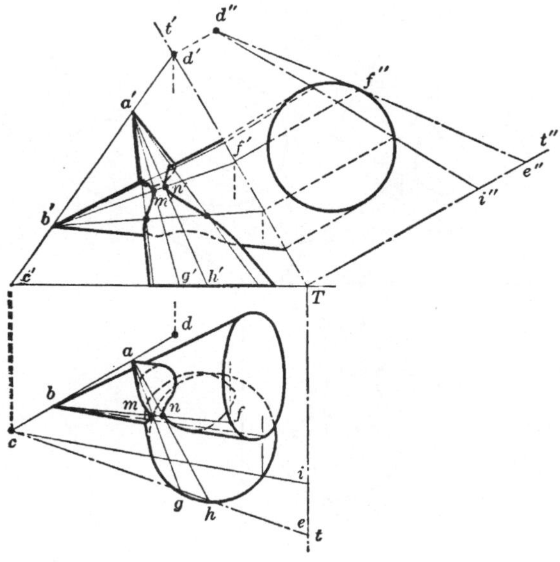


FIG. 217.

be a right angle, because it is perpendicular to the vertical plane, and, therefore cuts a right angle from the principal planes. The piercing point of the line **AB** is at **d″** in the revolved position, where **d′d″** is equal to the distance of **d** from the ground line. In the revolved position of the plane T, draw the base of the cone B and from it **accurately** construct the horizontal projection of the base. Draw a line **d″e″** tangent to the revolved position of the base of the cone **B** at f″. From it, find **f,** the horizontal, and f′, the vertical projection of this point, and draw the elements **fb** and **f′b′.** Lay off **Te″=Te,** and draw **ce.** The lines **CD** and **DE** determine a plane which cuts the horizontal projection of the base of the cone **A** in **g** and **h,** and thus, also, the two elements **ag** and **ah** which are horizontal projections, and **a′g′** and **a′h′** the corresponding vertical projections of the elements. The element **BF** intersects the elements **AG** and **AH** in the points **M** and **N** shown, as usual, by their projections. **M** and **N** are therefore two points of the required curve, being prominent points because the elements are tangent at these points. To obtain other points, draw a line **d″i″** and make Ti″ = Ti. Where **ci** cuts the cone **A,** draw the elements as shown, also the correspond-

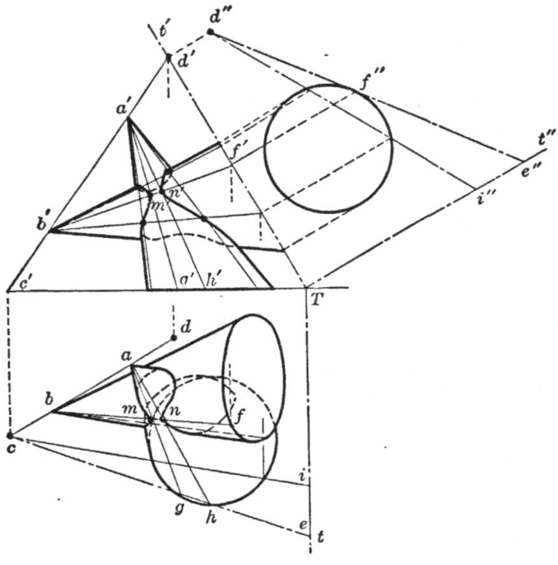


FIG. 217.

ing elements of the cone **B.** The points of the curve of intersection are therefore as indicated.

One fact is to be observed in this and in similar constructions. Auxiliary planes are passed through the vertices of both cones, cutting, therefore, elements of the cones whose intersection determine points on the curve. All planes through the vertices of both cones must pass through c in the horizontal plane and through **d″** in the plane T. Also, such distances as **Te″** must equal **Te** because these auxiliary planes cut the horizontal plane and the plane T on their line of intersection **Tt;** the revolution of the plane T into the vertical plane does not disturb the location of any point on it. Hence such distance as **Te** will be revolved to **Te″** where **Te = Te″**.

When applying this problem to a practical case, it would be better to select a profile plane for the plane T, as then **Tt″** would coincide with the ground line and all construction would be simplified. It has not been done in this instance, in order to show the generality of the method, and its adaptation to any condition.

**1215. Types of lines of intersection for surfaces of cones.** When the surfaces of two cones are situated so that there is **complete interpenetration,** the line of intersection will appear as **two** distinct closed **curves.** Fig. 215 is an example.

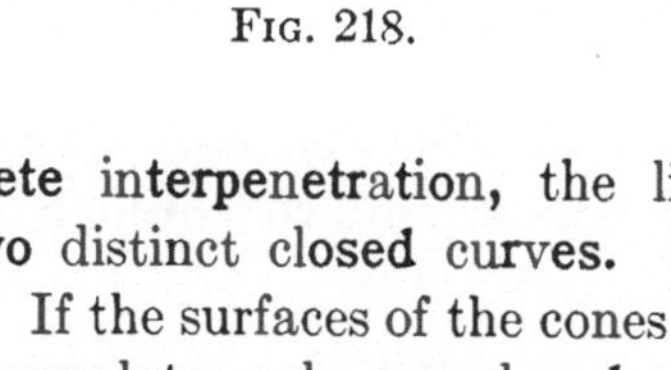

FIG. 218.

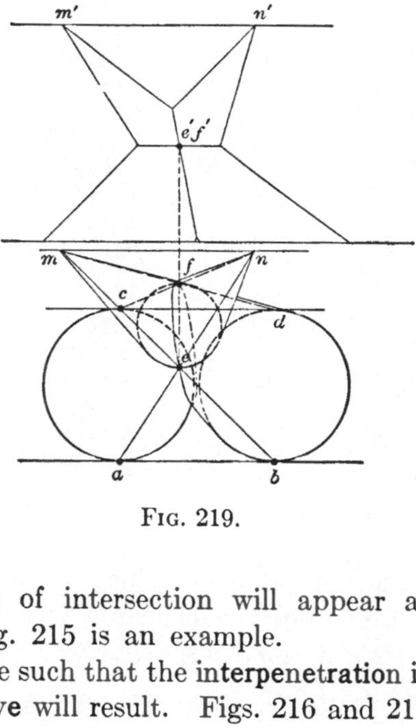


FIG. 219.

If the surfaces of the cones are such that the **interpenetration** is **incomplete,** only **one** closed **curve** will result. Figs. 216 and 217 are examples of this case.

When the surfaces of two cones have a **common tangent plane** then the **curve** is **closed** and **crosses** itself **once.** An example under this heading is given in Fig. 218.

It is possible to have two cones the surfaces of which have **two common tangent planes.** In this case there are **two closed curves** which **cross** each other **twice.** This illustration appears in Fig. 219.

**1216. Problem 12. To find the line of intersection of the surfaces of a cone and a cylinder of revolution when their axes intersect at a right angle.**

**Construction.** Let Fig. 220 represent the cone and the cylinder. Through the cone, pass a series of planes perpendicular to its axis. If the planes are properly chosen, they will cut the conical surface in circles and the cylindrical surface in rectilinear elements, the intersection of which determine points on the line of intersection. A reference to Fig. 220 will show this in construction. As a check on the accuracy of the points on the curve, it is possible to draw elements of the conical surface through some point; the corresponding projections of the elements must contain the corresponding projections of the points. In the illustration, the elements **OA** and **OB** are drawn through the points **E** and **J** respectively.

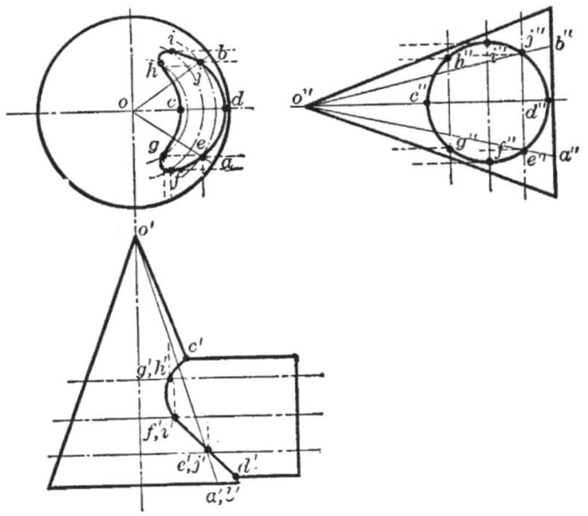

FIG. 220.

**1217. Problem 13. To find the line of intersection of the surfaces of a cone and a cylinder of revolution when their axes intersect at any angle.**

**Construction.** The given data is shown in Fig. 221. In this case it is inconvenient to pass planes perpendicular to the axis of the cone, since ellipses will be cut from the cylinder. A better plan is to find **m**, the intersection of their axes, and use this as a centre for auxiliary spherical surfaces. The spherical surfaces intersect the surfaces of revolution in circles (1025).

The details of the construction are shown in Fig. 221. To check the accuracy of the construction it is possible to draw an element of one surface through some point and then find the corresponding projection of the element; the corresponding projection of the point must be located on the corresponding projection of the element. Two elements **OF** and **OG** are shown in the figure. The points determined thereby are shown at **D**.

**1218. Problem 14. To find the line of intersection of the surfaces of an oblique cone and a right cylinder.**

**Construction.** Let Fig. 222 illustrate the conditions assumed.

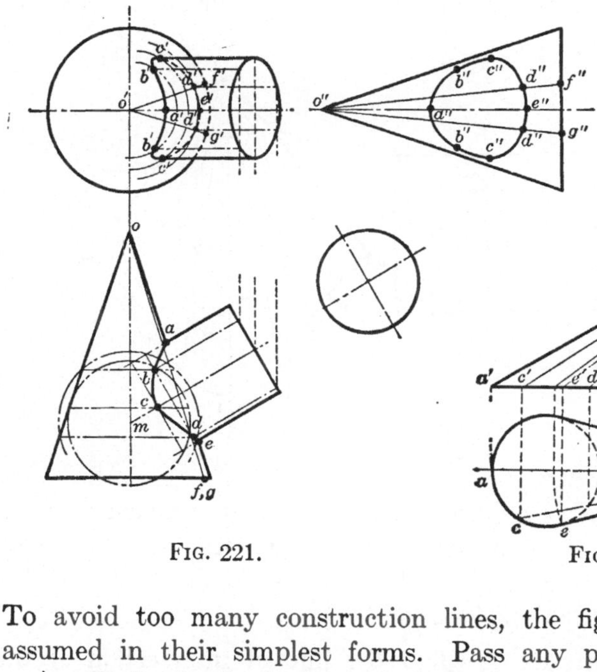

FIG. 221.

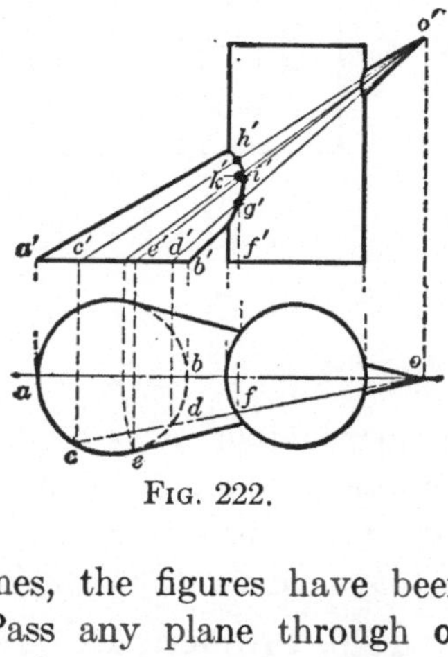

FIG. 222.

To avoid too many construction lines, the figures have been assumed in their simplest forms. Pass any plane through **o,** perpendicular to the horizontal plane; it cuts elements **DO** and **CO** from the cone and the element from the cylinder which is horizontally projected at **f** and vertically at **f′g′**. In the vertical projection, the elements **c′o′** and **d′o′** intersect the element **f′g′** at **g′** and **h′**, two points of the required curve. The extreme element **OE** determines the point i by the same method. There are two distinct lines of intersection, in this case, due to complete interpenetration. The points on the line of intersection near the vertex are located in a manner similar to that shown.

**1219. Problem 15. To find the developments in the preceding problem.**

**Construction.** The oblique conical surface is developed by triangulation. In Figs. 222 and 223, the lines **o′a′** and **o′b′** are shown in their true length in the vertical projection; hence, lay off $o'a' = o''a''$, and $o'b' = o''b''$. If the element **oe** be revolved so that it is parallel to the vertical plane, the point i′, in the vertical projection, will not change its distance above the horizontal plane during the revolution. Hence it moves from i′ to **k′**, the revolved position. Accordingly, lay off $o''i'' = o'k'$ and one point of the intersection on the development is obtained. Other points, of course, are found in absolutely the same manner.

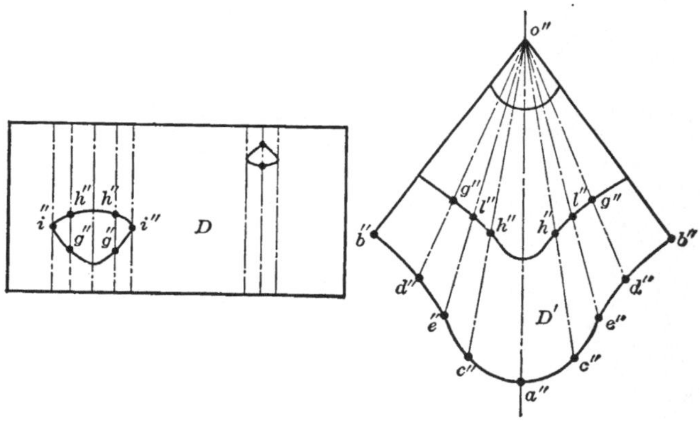


Fig. 223.

Extreme accuracy is required in most of these problems. Constructions like this should be laid out to as large a scale as convenient. The development of the cylinder is also shown and is perhaps clear without explanation.

**1220. Problem 16. To find the line of intersection of the surfaces of an oblique cone and a sphere.**

**Construction.** Let Fig. 224 represent the cone and sphere in question. The general scheme is to pass planes through the vertex of the cone perpendicular to the horizontal plane. These planes cut the cone in rectilinear elements and the sphere in circles; the intersection of the elements and the circles so cut will determine points on the curve.

Thus, through **o**, draw a plane which cuts the cone in **a** and **b** and the sphere in **d** and **e**. The elements cut are shown as **o′a′**

and **o′b′** in the vertical projection. Attention will be confined to the determination of **g′**, one point on the lower curve, situated on the element **OA.** The circle cut from the sphere by the plane through **oa** and **ob** has a diameter equal to **de.** If **pc** is a perpendicular to **de** from **p** the centre of the sphere, then **c** is the horizontal projection of the centre of the circle **de,** and **cd** and **ce** are equal. If the cutting plane is revolved about a perpendicular through **o** to the horizontal plane, until it is parallel to the vertical plane, **a** will move to **a″** and **o′a‴** will be the revolved position of this element. The centre of the circle will go to **h** in the horizontal projection and **h′** in the vertical projection, because, in this latter case, the distance of **h′** above the horizontal plane does not change in the revolution. The element and the centre of the circle in a plane parallel to the vertical plane are thus determined. Hence, with **cd** as a radius and **h′** as a centre, describe an arc, cutting **o′a‴** in f′. On counter revolution, **f′** goes to **g′** on **o′a′,** the original position of the element. The point **g′** is therefore one point on the curve. Every other point is found in the same way.

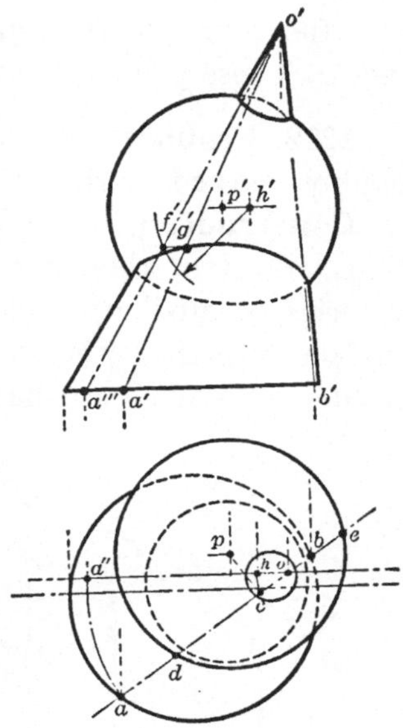


FIG. 224.

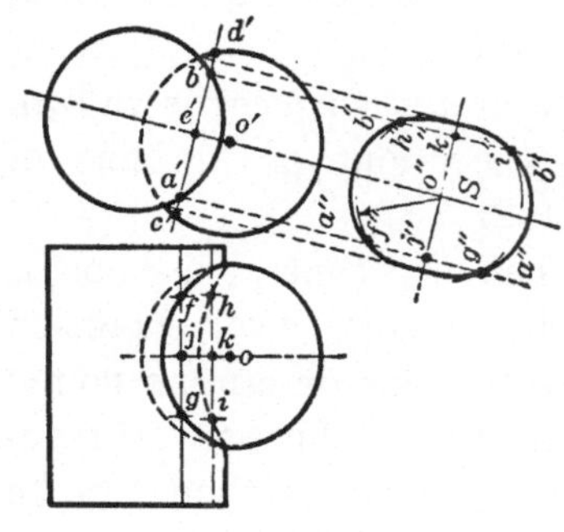


FIG. 225.

**1221. Problem 17. To find the line of intersection of the surfaces of a cylinder and a sphere.**

**Construction.** Fig. 225 pictures the condition. Pass a series of planes, through the cylinder and the sphere, perpendicular to the plane of the base of the cylinder. One position of the cutting plane cuts the cylinder in **a′b′** and the sphere in **c′d′.** Construct a supplementary view **S** with the centre of the sphere at o″ as shown. The elements appear as **a″a″** and **b″b″.** The diameter of the circle cut from the sphere is **c′d′** and with c′**e**′ as a radius, (equal to one-half of **c′d′**), draw an arc cutting the elements at **f″g″h″** and i″. Lay off **f″j″=fj; g″j″=gj,** etc., and the four points f, **g,** h, **i** are determined on the required view. These points are on the required line of intersection.

**1222. Problem 18.** To **find the** line of intersection of **two** doubly curved **surfaces of revolution** whose axes **intersect.**

**Construction.** Let Fig. 226 represent the surfaces in question. With **o,** the intersection of the axes, as a centre, draw a series of auxiliary spherical surfaces. One of these spherical surfaces cuts the surface whose axis is **on** in a circle whose diameter is **cd.** This same auxiliary sphere cuts the surface whose axis is

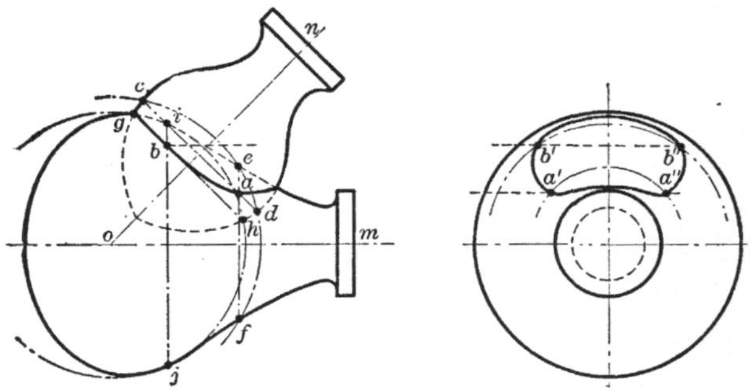


FIG. 226.

**om** in a circle projected as **ef.** Hence cd and **ef** intersect at **a,** a point on the required line of intersection.

In the view on the right, only one of the surfaces is shown. The location of the corresponding projections of the line of intersection will be evident from Art. 1027.

When the axes do not intersect then the general method is to pass planes so as to cut circles from one surface of revolution and a curve from the other. The intersections determine points on the curve. It is desirable in this connection to chose an arrangement that gives the least trouble. No general method can be given for the mode of procedure.

**1223. Commercial application** of **methods.** In practice, it is always desirable as a matter of time to turn the objects so that the auxiliary surfaces may be passed through them with the least effort. Frequently, many constructions may be carried out without any special reference to the principal planes.

There is no harm in omitting the principal planes, but the student should not go to the extreme in this ommission. With the principal planes at hand, the operations assume a familiar form, which will have a tendency to refresh the memory as to the basic principles involved. All the operations in the entire subject have a remarkable simplicity in the abstract; the confusion that sometimes arises is not due to the principles involved, but solely to the number of construction lines required. It, therefore, seems proper to use such methods as will lead to the least confusion, but it should always be borne in mind that accuracy is important at all hazards.

## QUESTIONS ON CHAPTER XII

1. State the general method of finding the intersection of any two surfaces.
2. When the surfaces are those of prisms or pyramids, is it necessary to use auxiliary planes as cutting planes? Why?
3. Prove the general case of finding the line of intersection of the surfaces of two prisms.
4. Show the general method of finding the development of the prisms in Question 3.
5. Prove the general case of finding the line of intersection of two cylindrical surfaces of revolution whose axes intersect at a right angle.
6. Show the general method of finding the development of the surfaces in Question 5.
7. Prove the general case of finding the line of intersection of two cylindrical surfaces of revolution whose axes intersect at any angle.
8. Show the general method of finding the development of the surfaces in Question 7.
9. Prove the general case of finding the line of intersection of two cylindrical surfaces whose axes do not intersect.

Show the general method of finding the development of the cylindrical surfaces in Question 9.

. State the general method of finding the line of intersection of two conical surfaces.

Prove the general case of finding the line of intersection of the surfaces of two oblique cones whose bases may be made to be in the same plane and whose altitudes differ.

Show the general method of finding the developments of the surfaces of the cones in Question 12.

Prove the general case of finding the line of intersection of the surfaces of two oblique cones whose bases may be made to lie in the same plane and whose altitudes are equal.

15. Show the general method of finding the developments of the surfaces of the cones in Question 14.
16. Prove the general case of finding the line of intersection of the surfaces of two oblique cones whose bases lie in different planes.
17. Show the general method of finding the developments of the cones in Question 16.
18. When the surfaces of two cones have complete interpenetration, discuss the nature of the line of intersection.
19. When the surfaces of two cones have incomplete penetration, discuss the nature of the line of intersection.
20. When the surfaces of two cones have a common tangent plane, discuss the nature of the line of intersection.
21. When the surfaces of two cones have two common tangent planes, discuss the nature of the line of intersection.
22. Prove the general case of finding the line of intersection of the surfaces of a cone and a cylinder of revolution when their axes intersect at a right angle.
23. Show the general method of finding the developments of the surfaces in Question 22.
24. Prove the general case of finding the line of intersection of the surfaces of a cone and a cylinder of revolution when their axes intersect at any angle.
25. Show the general method of finding the developments of the surfaces in Question 24.
26. Prove the general case of finding the line of intersection of the surfaces of an oblique cone and a right cylinder.
27. Show the general method of finding the developments in Question 26.
28. Prove the general case of finding the line of intersection of the surfaces of an oblique cone and a sphere.
29. Show the general method of finding the development of the cone in Question 28.
30. Develop the surface of the sphere in Question 28 by the gore method.
31. Prove the general case of finding the line of intersection of the surfaces of a sphere and a cylinder.
32. Show the general method of finding the development of the cylinder in Question 31.
33. Develop the surface of the sphere in Question 31 by the zone method.
34. Prove the general case of finding the line of intersection of two doubly curved surfaces of revolution whose axes intersect.
35. Develop the surfaces of Question 34 by the gore method.
36. Develop the surfaces of Question 34 by the zone method.
37. State the general method of finding the line of intersection of two doubly curved surfaces of revolution whose axes do not intersect.
38. What items are to be considered when applying the principles of intersections and developments to commercial problems?
39. Is it always necessary to use the principal planes when solving problems relating to intersections and developments?

40. Find the intersection of the two prisms shown in Fig. 12–A. Assume suitable dimensions.
41. Develop the prisms of Question 40.
42. Two cylinders of 2″ diameter intersect at a right angle. Find the line of intersection of the surfaces. Assume suitable dimensions for their lengths and position with respect to each other.
43. Develop the surfaces of Question 42.
44. Two cylinders of 2″ diameter and 1¾″ diameter intersect at a right angle. Find the line of intersection of the surfaces. Assume suitable dimensions for their lengths and position with respect to each other.
45. Develop the surfaces of Question 44.

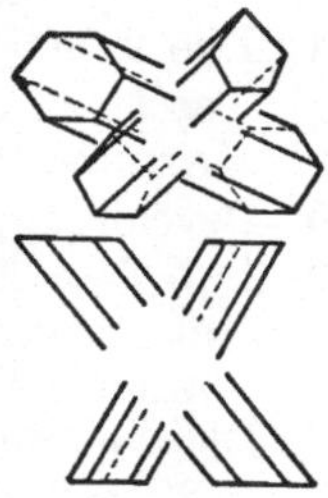

FIG. 12–A.

46. Two cylinders of 2″ diameter intersect at an angle of 60°. Find the line of intersection of the surfaces. Assume suitable dimensions for their lengths and position with respect to each other.
47. Develop the surfaces of Question 46.
48. Two cylinders of 2″ diameter intersect at an angle of 45°. Find the line of intersection of the surfaces. Assume suitable dimensions for their lengths and position with respect to each other.
49. Develop the surfaces of Question 48.
50. Two cylinders of 2″ diameter intersect at an angle of 30°. Find the line of intersection of the surfaces. Assume suitable dimensions for their lengths and position with respect to each other.
51. Develop the surfaces of Question 50.
52. Two cylinders of 2″ diameter and 1¾″ diameter intersect at an angle of 60°. Find the line of intersection of the surfaces. Assume suitable dimensions for their lengths and position with respect to each other.
53. Develop the surfaces of Question 52.
54. Two cylinders of 2″ diameter and 1¾″ diameter intersect at an angle of 45°. Find the line of intersection of the surfaces. Assume suitable dimensions for their lengths and position with respect to each other.
55. Develop the surfaces of Question 54.
56. Two cylinders of 2″ diameter and 1¾″ diameter intersect at an angle of 30°. Find the line of intersection of the surfaces. Assume suitable dimensions for their lengths and position with respect to each other.
57. Develop the surfaces of Question 56.
58. Two cylinders of 2″ diameter intersect at a right angle and have their axes offset ½″. Find the line of intersection of the surfaces. Assume the additional dimensions.
59. Develop the surface of one of the cylinders of Question 58.
60. A 2″ cylinder intersects a 1¾″ cylinder so that their axes are offset ⅜″ and make a right angle with each other. Find the line of intersection of the surfaces. Assume the additional dimensions.

61. Develop the surfaces of Question 60.
62. Two 2″ cylinders have their axes offset $\frac{1}{2}$″. The elements intersect at an angle of 60°. Find the line of intersection of the surfaces. Assume the additional dimensions.
63. Develop the surfaces of Question 62.
64. Two 2″ cylinders have their axes offset $\frac{1}{2}$″. The elements intersect at an angle of 45°. Find the line of intersection of the surfaces. Assume the additional dimensions.
65. Develop the surfaces of Question 64.
66. Two 2″ cylinders have their axes offset $\frac{1}{2}$″. The elements intersect at an angle of 30°. Find the line of intersection of the surfaces. Assume the additional dimensions.
67. Develop the surfaces of Question 66.
68. A 2″ cylinder intersects a 1$\frac{3}{4}$″ cylinder at an angle of 60°. Their axes are offset $\frac{1}{4}$″. Find the line of intersection of the surfaces. Assume the additional dimensions.
99. Develop the surfaces of Question 68.

Fig. 12–B.

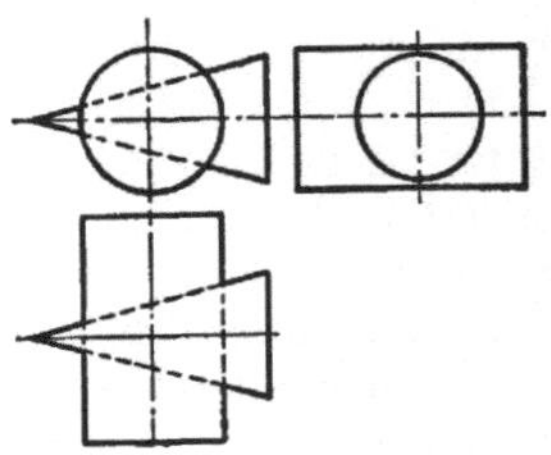

Fig. 12–C.

70. A 2″ cylinder intersects a 1$\frac{3}{4}$″ cylinder at an angle of 45°. Their axes are offset $\frac{1}{4}$″. Find the line of intersection of the surfaces. Assume the additional dimensions.
71. Develop the surfaces of Question 70.
72. A 2″ cylinder intersects a 1$\frac{3}{4}$″ cylinder at an angle of 30°. Their axes are offset $\frac{1}{4}$″. Find the line of intersection of the surfaces. Assume the additional dimensions.
73. Develop the surfaces of Question 72.
74. Find the line of intersection of the surfaces of the two cones shown in Fig. 12–B. Assume suitable dimensions.
75. Develop the surfaces of Question 74.
76. Assume a pair of cones similar to those shown in Fig. 12–B, but, with equal altitudes. Then, find the line of intersection of the surfaces.
77. Develop the surfaces of Question 76.
78. Assume a cone and cylinder similar to that shown in Fig. 12–C. Then, find the line of intersection of the surfaces.
79. Develop the surfaces of Question 78.

80. Assume a cone and cylinder similar to that shown in Fig. 12–C, but, have the cylinder elliptical. Then, find the line of intersection of the surfaces.
81. Develop the surfaces of Question 80.
82. Assume a cone and cylinder similar to that shown in Fig. 12–C, but, have the cone elliptical. Then, find the line of intersection of the surfaces.
83. Develop the surfaces of Question 82.
84. Assume an arrangement of cone and cylinder somewhat similar to that of Fig. 12–C, but, have both cone and cylinder elliptical. Then, find the line of intersection of the surfaces.
85. Develop the surfaces of Question 84.
86. Assume a cylinder and cone of revolution, whose general direction of axes are at right angles, but, which are offset as shown in Fig. 12–D. Then, find the line of intersection of the surfaces.
87. Develop the surfaces in Question 86.

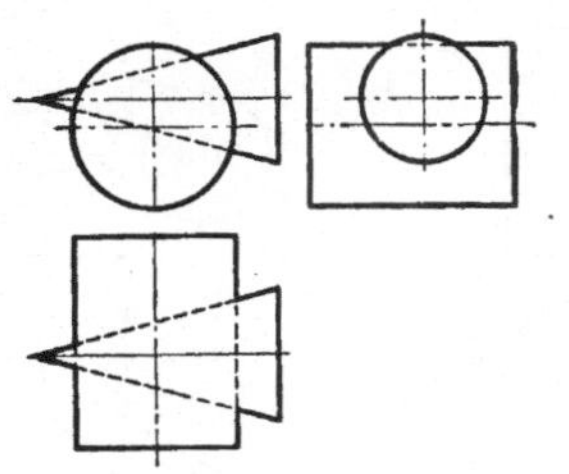

FIG. 12–D.

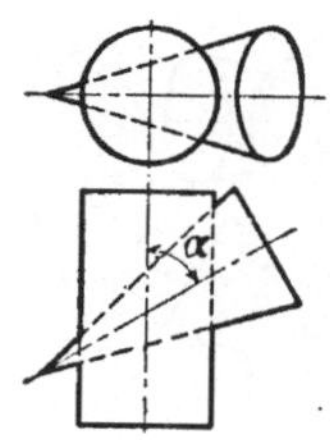


FIG. 12–E.

88. Assume an elliptical cylinder and a cone of revolution, whose general direction of axes are at right angles to each other, but, which are offset as shown in Fig. 12–D. Then, find the line of intersection of the surfaces.
89. Develop the surfaces of Question 88.
90. Assume a circular cylinder of revolution and an elliptical cone, whose general direction of axes are at right angles to each other, but, which are offset as shown in Fig. 12–D. Then, find the line of intersection of the surfaces.
91. Develop the surfaces of Question 90.
92. Assume an elliptical cylinder and an elliptical cone, whose general direction of axes, are at right angles to each other, but, which are offset, as shown in Fig. 12–D. Then, find the line of intersection of the surfaces.
93. Develop the surfaces of Question 92.
94. Assume a cylinder and cone of revolution, similar to that of Fig. 12–E, and make angle $\alpha = 60°$. Then, find the line of intersection of the surfaces.
95. Develop the surfaces of Question 94.

96. Assume a clyinder and cone of revolution, similar to that of Fig. 12–E, and make angle $\alpha = 45°$. Then, find the line of intersection of the surfaces.
97. Develop the surfaces of Question 96.
89. Assume a cylinder and a cone of revolution, similar to that of Fig. 12–E, and make angle $\alpha = 30°$. Then, find the line of intersection of the surfaces.
99. Develop the surfaces of Question 98.
100. Assume an elliptical cylinder and a cone of revolution arranged similar to that of Fig. 12–E, and make the angle $\alpha = 60°$. Then, find the line of intersection of the surfaces.
101. Develop the surfaces of Question 100.
102. Assume a cylinder of revolution and an elliptical cone, arranged similar to that of Fig. 12–E, and make the angle $\alpha = 45°$. Then, find the line of intersection of the surfaces.
103. Develop the surfaces of Question 102.

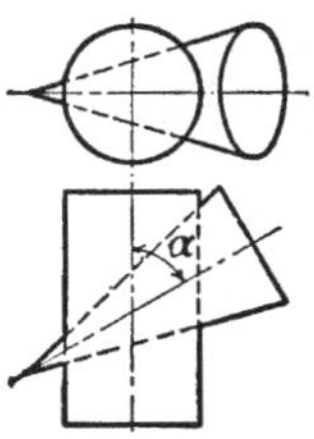

FIG. 12–E.

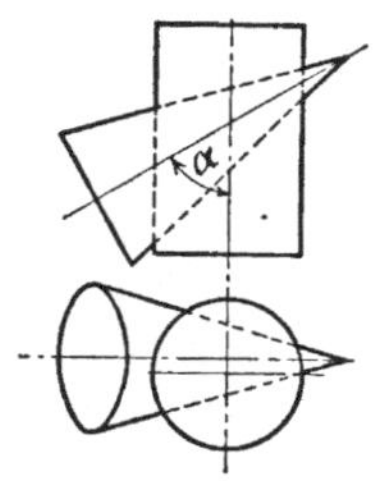

FIG. 12–F.

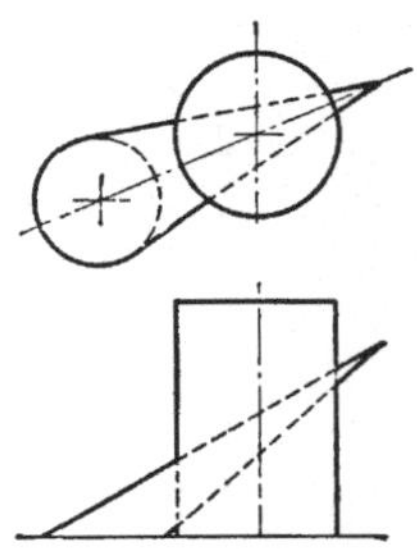

FIG. 12–G.

104. Assume an elliptical cylinder and an elliptical cone arranged similar to that of Fig. 12–E, and make the angle $\alpha = 60°$. Then find the line of intersection of the surfaces.
105. Develop the surfaces of Question 104.
106. Assume a cylinder and cone of revolution as shown in Fig. 12–F, and make angle $\alpha = 60°$. Then, find the line of intersection of the surfaces.
107. Develop the surfaces of Question 106.
108. Assume a cylinder and a cone of revolution as shown in Fig. 12–F, and make angle $\alpha = 45°$. Then, find the line of intersection of the surfaces.
109. Develop the surfaces of Question 108.
110. Assume a cylinder and a cone of revolution as shown in Fig. 12–F, and make angle $\alpha = 30°$. Then, find the line of intersection of the surfaces.
111. Develop the surfaces of Question 110.
112. Assume an elliptical cylinder and a cone of revolution, arranged similar to that shown in Fig. 12–F, and make angle $\alpha = 60°$. Then find the line of intersection of the surfaces.

113. Develop the surfaces of Question 112.
114. Assume a cylinder of revolution and an elliptical cone, arranged similar to that shown in Fig. 12–F, and make angle $\alpha = 45°$. Then, find the line of intersection of the surfaces.

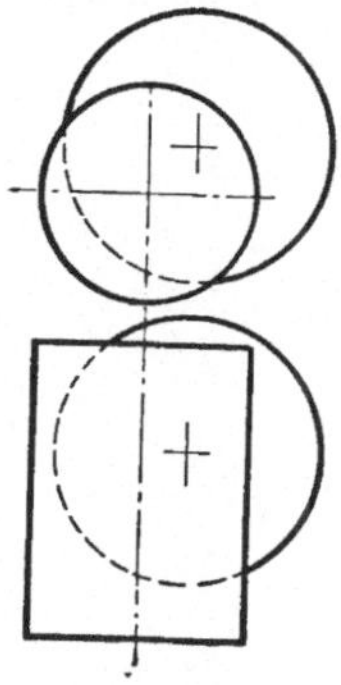

FIG. 12–H.

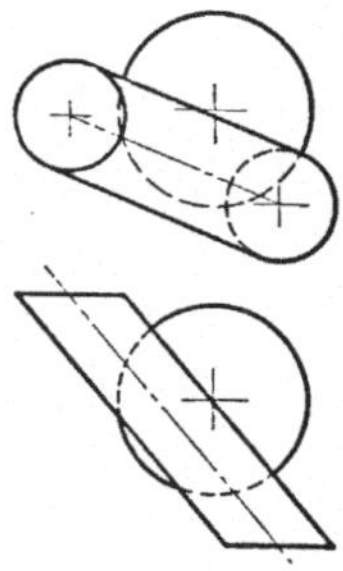

FIG. 12–I.

115. Develop the surfaces of Question 114.
116. Assume an elliptical cylinder and an elliptical cone, somewhat similar to that shown in Fig. 12–F, and make angle $\alpha = 60°$. Then find the line of intersection of the surfaces.
117. Develop the surfaces of Question 116.
118. Assume a cone and cylinder as shown in Fig. 12–G. Then, find the line of intersection of the surfaces.
119. Develop the surfaces of Question 118.
120. Assume a cylinder and a sphere as shown in Fig. 12–H. Then, find the line of intersection of the surfaces.
121. Develop the surface of the cylinder of Question 120.
122. Develop the surface of the cylinder of Question 120, and, also, the surface of the sphere by the gore method.
123. Assume a cylinder and sphere as shown in Fig. 12–I. Then, find the line of intersection of the surfaces.
124. Develop the surface of the cylinder in Question 123.

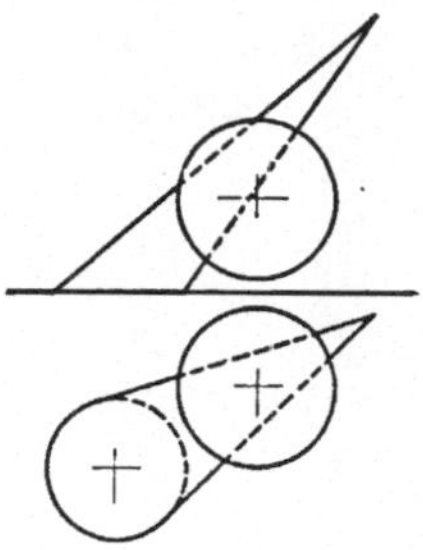

FIG. 12–J.

125. Develop the surface of the cylinder in Question 123, and, also, the surface of the sphere by the zone method.
126. Assume a cone and a sphere as shown in Fig. 12–J. Then, find the line of intersection of the surfaces.
127. Develop the surface of the cone in Question 126.
128. Develop the surface of the cone in Question 126, and, also, the sphere by the gore method.

129. Assume two doubly curved surfaces of revolution, whose axes intersect. Then, find the line of intersection of the surfaces.
130. Develop the surfaces of Question 129 by the gore method.
131. Develop the surfaces of Question 129 by the zone method.
132. Assume two doubly curved surfaces of revolution whose axes do not intersect. Then, find the line of intersection of the surfaces.

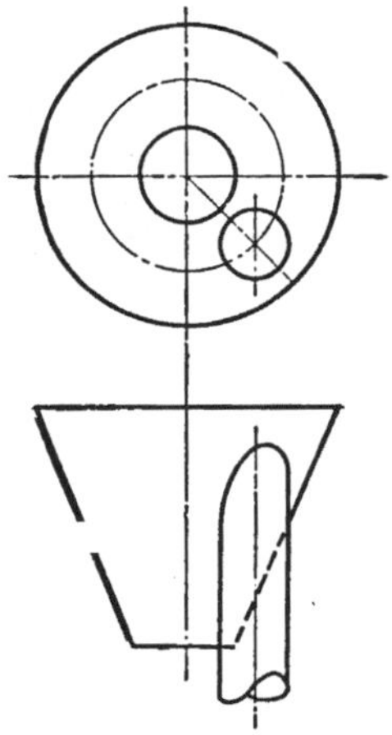

FIG. 12–K.

133. Develop the surfaces of Question 132 by the gore method.
134. Develop the surfaces of Question 132 by the zone method.
135. Assume a frustum of a cone as shown in Fig. 12–K. A circular cylinder is to be fitted to it, as shown. Develop the surfaces.
   HINT.—Find vertex of cone before proceeding with the development.

# PART III

## *PRINCIPLES OF CONVERGENT PROJECTING-LINE DRAWING*

## CHAPTER XIII

### PERSPECTIVE PROJECTION

**1301. Introductory.** Observation shows that the apparent magnitude of objects is some function of the distance between the observer and the object. The drawings made according to the principles of parallel projecting-line drawing, and treated in Part I of this book, make no allowance for the observer's position with respect to the object. In other words, the location of the object with respect to the plane of projection has no influence on the size of the resultant picture, provided that the inclination of the various lines on the object, to the plane of projection, remain the same. Hence, as the remoteness of the object influences its apparent size, then, as a consequence, parallel projecting-line drawings must have an unnatural appearance. The strained appearance of drawings of this type is quite noticeable in orthographic projection wherein two or more views must be interpreted simultaneously, and is less noticeable in the case of oblique or axonometric projection. On the other hand, the rapidity with which drawings of the parallel projecting-line type can be made, and their adaptability for construction purposes, are strong points in their favor.

**1302. Scenographic projection.** To overcome the foregoing objections, and to present a drawing to the reader which corrects for distance, **scenographic** projections are used. To make these, convergent projecting lines are used, and the observer is located at the point of convergency. The surface on which scenographic projections are made may be spherical, cylindrical, etc., and find their most extensive application in decorative painting.

**1303. Linear perspective.** In the decoration of an interior of a dome or of a cylindrical wall, the resulting picture should be of such order as to give a correct image for the assumed location of the eye. In engineering drawing, there is little or no use for projections on spherical, cylindrical, or other curved surfaces. When scenographic projections are made on a plane, this type of projection is called **linear perspective.** A linear perspective, therefore, may be defined as the drawing made on a plane surface by the aid of convergent projecting lines, the point of convergency being at a finite distance from the object and from the plane. The plane of projection is called the **picture plane,** and the position of the eye is referred to as the **point of sight.**

**1304. Visual rays and visual angle.** If an object—an arrow for instance—be placed a certain distance from the eye, say in the position ab (Fig. 227) and **c** be the point of sight, the two extreme rays of light or **visual rays, ac** and **ab,** form an angle which is known as the **visual angle.** If, now, the arrow be moved to a more remote position **de,** the limiting visual rays **dc** and **ec** give a smaller visual angle. The physiological effect of this variation in the visual angle is to alter the apparent size of the object. If one eye is closed during this experiment, the distance from the eye to the object cannot be easily estimated, but the apparent magnitude of the object will be some function of the visual angle. In binocular vision, the muscular effort required to focus both eyes on the object will, with some experience, enable an estimate of the distance from the eye to the object; the mind will automatically correct for the smaller visual angle and greater distance, and, thus, to an experienced observer, give a more or less correct impression of the actual size of the object. This experience is generally limited to horizontal distances only, as very few can estimate correctly the diameter of a clock on a church steeple unless they have been accustomed to making such observations. As the use of two eyes in depicting objects in space causes

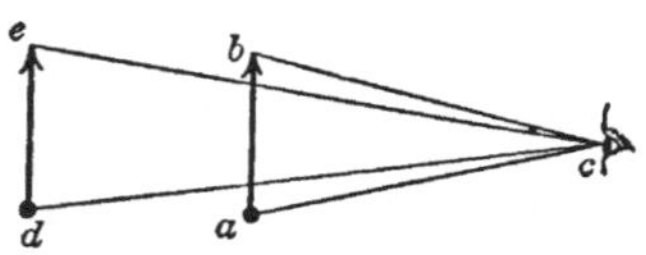

FIG. 227.

slightly different inpressions on different observers, the eye will be assumed hereafter as a single point.

**1305. Vanishing point.** When looking along a stretch of straight railroad tracks, it may be noted that the tracks apparently vanish in the distance. Likewise, in viewing a street of houses of about the same height, the roof line appears to meet the sidewalk line in the distance. It is known that the actual distances between the rails, and between the sidewalk and roof is always the same; yet the visual angle being less in the distant observation, gives the impression of a **vanishing point,** which may, therefore, be defined as the point where parallel lines seem to vanish. At an infinite distance the visual angle is zero, and, hence, the parallel lines appear to meet in a point. The lines themselves do not vanish, but their perspective projections vanish.

**1306. Theory of perspective projection.** The simplest notion of perspective drawing can be obtained by looking at a distant house through a window-pane. If the observer would trace on the window-pane exactly what he sees, and locate all points on the pane so that corresponding points on the house are directly behind them, a true linear perspective of the house would be the result. Manifestly, the location of each successive point is the same as locating the **piercing point** of the **visual ray** on the **picture plane,** the picture plane in our case being the window-pane.

**1307. Aerial perspective.** If this perspective were now colored to resemble the house beyond, proper attention being paid to light, shade and shadow, an **aerial perspective** would be the result. In brief, this aerial perspective would present to the eye a picture that represents the natural condition as near as the skill of the artist will permit. In our work the linear perspective will alone be considered, and will be denoted as the " perspective," aerial perspective finding little application in engineering.

**1308. Location of picture plane.** It is customary in perspective to assume that the picture plane is situated between the eye and the object. Under these conditions, the picture is smaller than the object, and usually this is necessary. The eye is assumed to be in the first angle; the object, however, is generally in the second angle * for reasons noted above. The vertical plane is thus the picture plane. A little reflection will show that this is in accord with our daily experience. Observers stand on the ground and look at some distant object; visual rays enter the eye at various angles; the mean of these rays is horizontal or nearly so, and, therefore, the projections naturally fall on a vertical plane interposed in the line of sight. The window-pane picture alluded to is an example.

**1309. Perspective of a line.** Let, in Fig. 228, **AB** be an arrow, standing vertically as shown in the second angle; the point of sight **C** is located in the first angle. The visual rays pierce the picture plane at a″ and **b″**, and **a″b″**, in the picture plane, is the perspective of **AB** in space. The similar condition

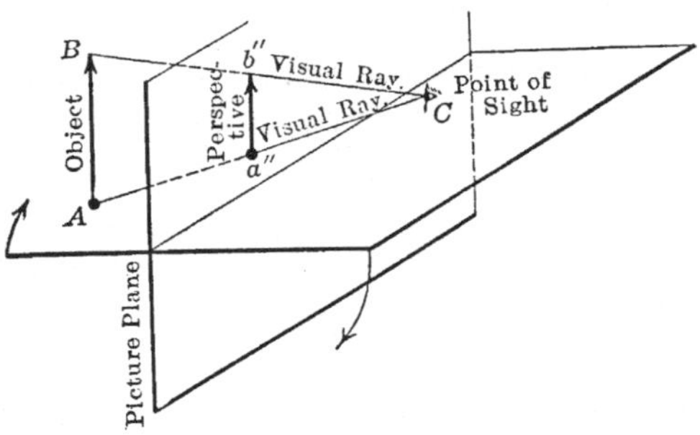


FIG. 228.

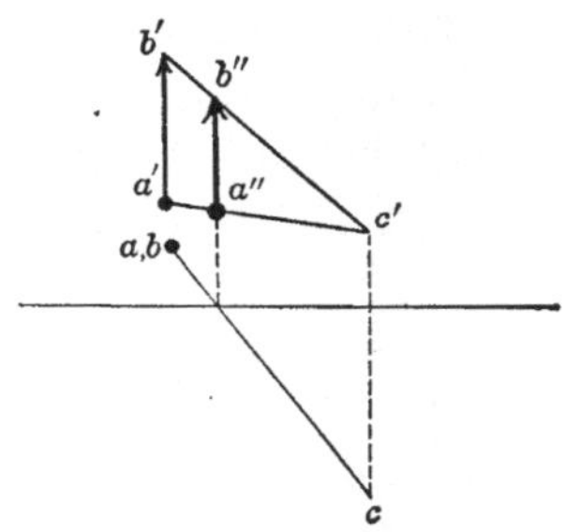


FIG. 229.

of Fig. 228 in orthographic projection is represented in Fig. 229. The arrow and the point of sight are shown by their projections on the horizontal and vertical planes. The arrow being perpendicular to the horizontal plane, both projections fall at the same point ab; the vertical projection is shown as **a′b′**; the point of sight is represented on the horizontal and vertical planes as **c** and c′, respectively. Any visual ray can likewise be represented by its projections, and, therefore, the horizontal projection of the point of sight is joined with the horizontal pro-

* The object may be located in any angle; the principles are the same for all angles. It is perhaps more convenient to use the second angle, as the lines do not have to be extended to obtain the piercing points as would be the case for first-angle projections.

jections. Similarly, the same is true of the vertical projections of the arrow and point of sight.

It is now necessary to find the piercing points (506,805) of the visual rays on the picture plane (vertical plane); and these are seen at **a″** and **b″**. Therefore, **a″b″** is the perspective of **AB** in space.

**1310. Perspectives of lines perpendicular to the horizontal plane.** In Fig. 230, several arrows are shown, in projection, all of which are perpendicular to the horizontal plane. Their perspectives are **a″b″, d″e″, g″h″.** On observation, it will be noted that all the perspectives of lines perpendicular to the horizontal plane are vertical. This is true, since, when a plane

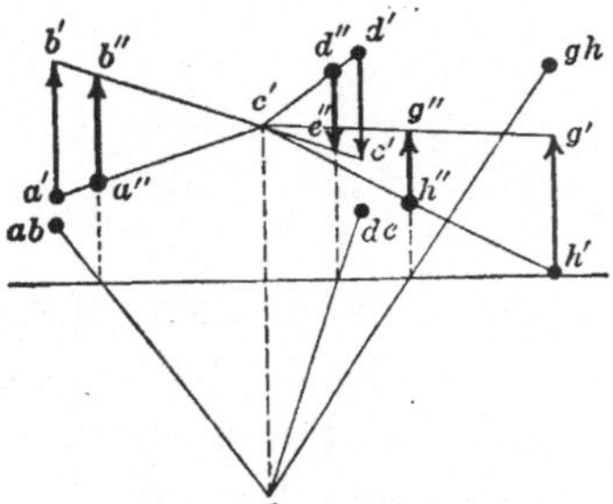


FIG. 230.

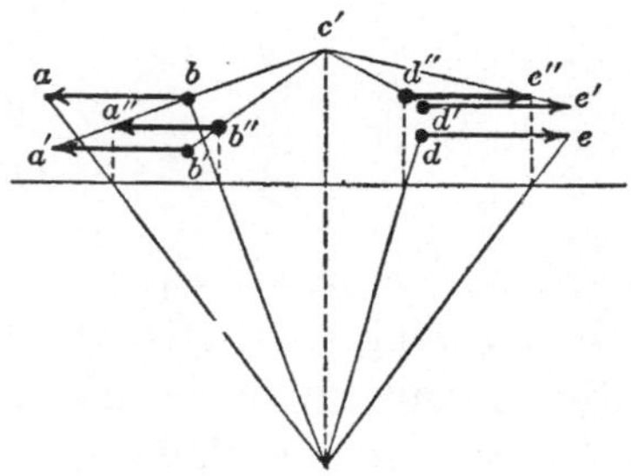


FIG. 231.

is passed through any line and revolved until it contains the point of sight, the **visual plane** (as this plane is then called) is manifestly perpendicular to the horizontal plane, and its vertical trace (603) is perpendicular to the ground line.

**1311. Perspectives of lines parallel to both principal planes.** Fig. 231 shows two arrows parallel to both planes, the projections and perspectives being designated as before. This case shows that all perspectives are parallel. To prove this, pass a plane through the line in space and the point of sight; the vertical trace of the plane so obatined will be parallel to the ground line * because the line is parallel to the ground line.

* If the line in space lies in the ground line, the vertical trace will coincide with the ground line. This is evidently a special case.

**1312. Perspectives of lines perpendicular to the picture plane.** Suppose a series of lines perpendicular to the vertical plane is taken. This case is illustrated in Fig. 232. The perspectives are drawn as before and designated as is customary. It may now be observed that the perspectives of all these lines

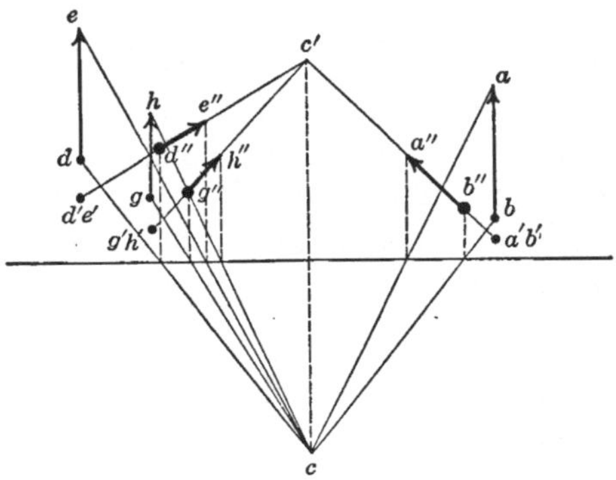


FIG. 232.

(or arrows) vanish in the vertical projection of the point of sight. This vanishing point for the perspectives of all perpendiculars to the picture plane is called the **centre of the picture.** The reason for this is as follows: It is known that the visual angle

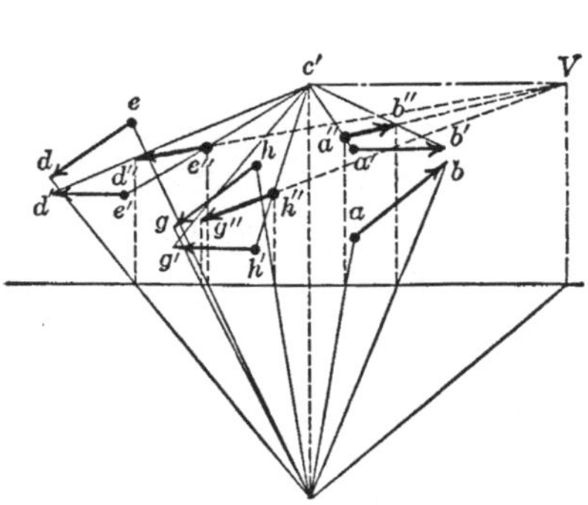


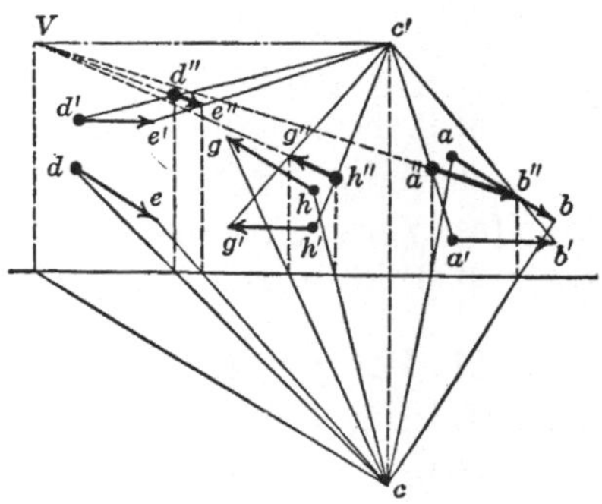


FIG. 233. FIG. 234.

becomes less as the distance from the point of sight increases; at an infinite distance the angle is zero, the perspectives of the lines converge, and, therefore, in our nomenclature vanish.

**1313. Perspectives of parallel lines, inclined to the picture plane.** Assume further another set of lines, Fig. 233, parallel to each other, inclined to the vertical plane, but parallel to the horizontal plane. Their orthographic projections are parallel and their perspectives will be seen to converge to the point V. Like the lines in the preceding paragraph, they vanish at a point which is the vanishing point of any number of lines parallel only to those assumed. The truth of this is established by the fact that the visual angle becomes zero (1304) at an infinite distance from the point of sight and, hence, the perspectives vanish as shown. To determine this vanishing point, draw any line through the point of sight parallel to the system of parallel lines; and its piercing point on the vertical or picture plane will be the required vanishing point. It amounts to the same thing to say that the vanishing point is the perspective of any line of this system at an infinite distance.

A slightly different condition is shown in Fig. 234. The lines are still parallel to each other and to the horizontal plane, but are inclined to the vertical plane in a different direction. Again, the perspectives of these lines will converge to a new vanishing point, situated, however, much the same as the one just preceding.

**1314. Horizon.** On observation of the cases cited in Art. 1313, it can be seen that the vanishing point lies on a horizontal line through the vertical projection of the point of sight. This is so since a line through the point of sight parallel to either system will pierce the picture plane in a point somewhere on its vertical projection. As the line is parallel to the horizontal plane, its vertical projection will be parallel to the ground line and, as shown, will contain all vanishing points of all systems of horizontal lines. Any one system of parallel lines will have but one vanishing point, but as the lines may slope in various directions, and still be parallel to the horizontal plane, every system will have its own vanishing point and the horizontal line drawn through the vertical projection of the point of sight will be the locus of all these vanishing points. This horizontal line through the vertical projection of the point of sight is called the **horizon.**

As a corollary to the above, it may be stated, that all planes parallel to the horizontal plane vanish in the horizon. As before, the visual angle becomes less as the distance increases, and, hence, becomes zero at infinity.

There are an unlimited number of systems of lines resulting in an unlimited number of vanishing points, whether they are on the horizon or not. In most drawings the vertical and horizontal lines are usually the more common. The lines perpendicular to the picture plane are horizontal lines, and, therefore, the centre of the picture (vanishing point for the perspectives of the perpendiculars) must be on the horizon.

**1315. Perspective of a point.** The process of finding the perspective of a line of definite length is to find the perspectives

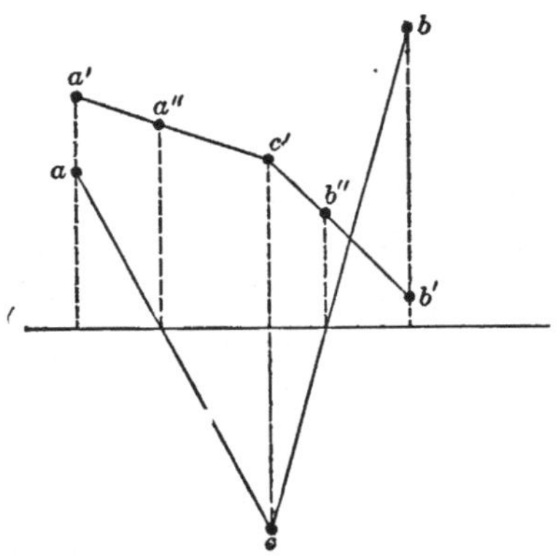


FIG. 235.

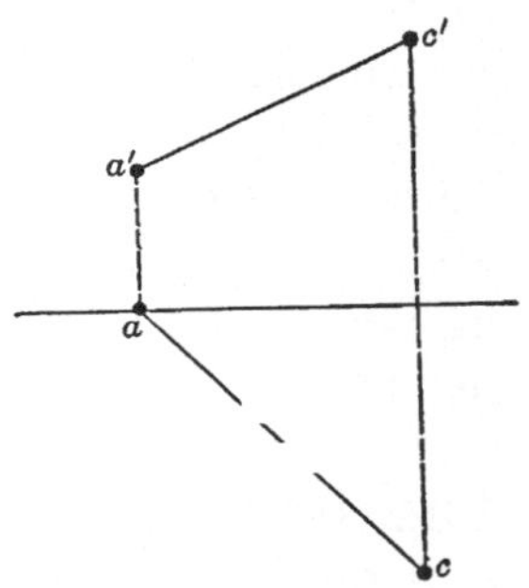


FIG. 236.

of the two extremities of the line. When the perspectives of the extremities of the line are found, the line joining them is the perspective of the given line. In Fig. 235, two points **A** and **B** are chosen whose perspectives will be found to be **a''** and **b''**.

When the point lies in picture plane it is its own perspective. This is shown in Fig. 236, where **a'** is the vertical projection and **a** is therefore in the ground line; hence, the perspective is **a'**.

In the construction of any perspective, the method is to locate the perspectives of certain points which are joined by their proper lines. The correct grouping of lines determine certain surfaces which, when closed, determine the required solid.

**1316. Indefinite perspective of a line.** Let **AB**, Fig. 237, be a limited portion of a line **FE**. Hence, by obtaining the piercing points of the visual rays **AC** and **BC**, the perspective **a″b″** is determined. Likewise, **DE** is another limited portion of the line **FE** and its perspective is **d″e″**. If a line be drawn through the point of sight **C**, parallel to the line **FE**, then, its piercing point **g′** on the picture plane will be the vanishing point of the perspectives of a system of lines parallel to **FE** (1313). Also, as **FE** pierces the picture plane at **f′**, then **f′** will be its own perspective (1315). Therefore, if a line be made to join **f′** and **g′**, it will be the perspective of a line that reaches from the picture plane out to an infinite distance. And, also, the perspective of any limited portion of this line must lie

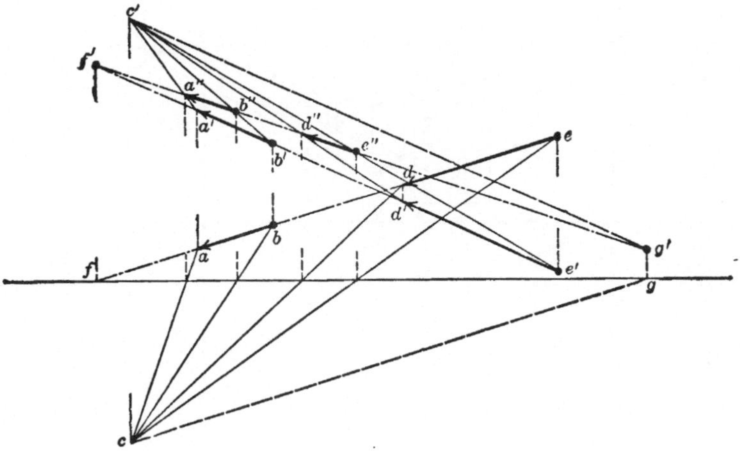


Fig. 237.

on the perspective of the line. From the construction in Fig. 237, it will be observed that **a″b″** and **d″e″** lie on the line **f′g′**.

Consequently, the line **f′g′** is the indefinite perspective of a line **FE** which reaches from the picture plane at **f′** out to an infinite distance. Thus, the **indefinite perspective** of a line may be defined as the perspective of a line that reaches from the picture plane to infinity.

Before leaving Fig. 237, it is desirable to note that **g′** is the vanishing point of a system of lines parallel to **FE**. It is not located on the horizon because the line **FE** is not parallel to the horizontal plane.

**1317. Problem 1. To find the perspective of a cube by means of the piercing points of the visual rays on the picture plane.**

**Construction.** Let **ABCDEFGH,** Fig. 238, be the eight corners of the cube, and let **S** be the point of sight. The cube is in the second angle and therefore both projections are above the ground line (315, 317, 514, 516). The horizontal projection of the cube is indicated by **abcd** for the upper side, and **efgh** for the base. The vertical projections are shown as **a′b′c′d′** for the upper side, and **e′f′g′h′** for the base. The cube is located in the second angle so that the two projections overlap. The point of sight is in the first angle and is shown by its horizontal projection **s** and its vertical projection **s′**. Join **s** with **e** and

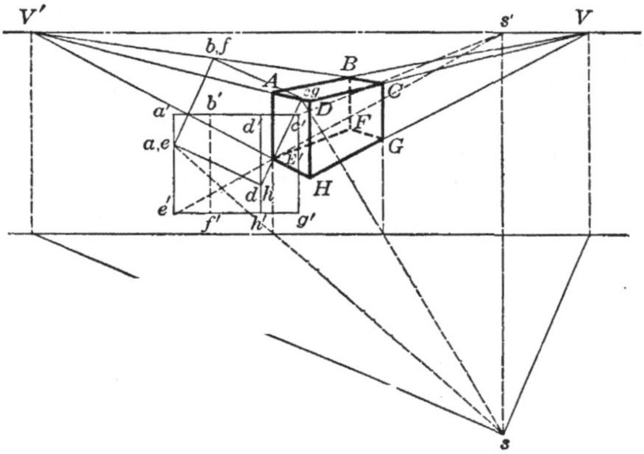


FIG. 238.

obtain the horizontal projection of the visual ray **SE** in space; do likewise for the vertical projection with the result that **s′e′** will be the visual ray projected on the picture plane. The point where this pierces the picture plane is **E,** and this is one point of the required perspective. Consider next point **C.** This is found in a manner similar to point **E** just determined. The horizontal projection of the visual ray **SC** is **sc** and the vertical projection of the visual ray is **s′c′** and this pierces the vertical or picture plane in the point **C** as shown. In the foregoing manner, all other points are determined. By joining the correct points with each other, a linear perspective will be obtained.

It will be noticed that **CG, BF, DH,** and **AE** are vertical because the lines in space are vertical (1310), and hence their perspectives are vertical. This latter fact acts as a check after locating the perspectives of the upper face and the base of the cube. It will be noticed, further, that the perspectives of the horizontal lines in space meet at the vanishing points **V′** and **V** (1313, 1314).

**1318. Perspectives of intersecting lines.** Instead of locating the piercing point of a visual ray by drawing the projections of this ray, it is sometimes found desirable to use another method. For this purpose another principle must be developed.

If two lines in space intersect, their perspectives intersect, because the perspective of a line can be considered as being made up of the perspectives of all the points on the line. As the intersection is a point common to the two lines, a visual ray to this point should pierce the picture plane in the intersection of the perspectives. Reference to Fig. 239 will show that such is the case. **CG** is the visual ray in space of the point of intersection of the two lines, and its perspective is **g″**, which is the intersection of the perspectives **a″b″** and **d″e″**.

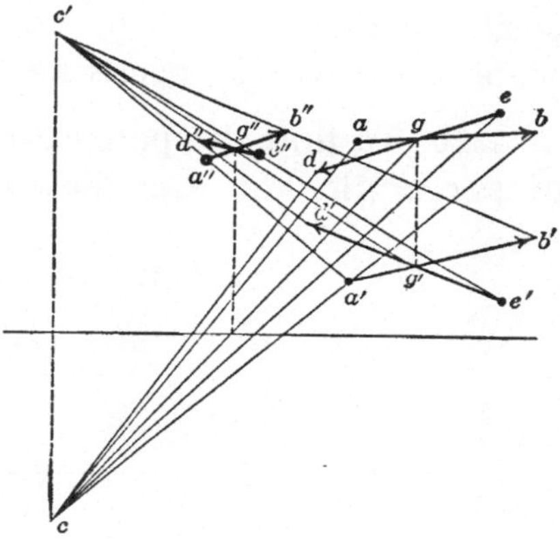

Fig. 239.

**1319. Perpendicular and diagonal.** Obviously, if it is desired to find the perspective of a point in space, two lines can be drawn through the piont and the intersection of their perspectives found. The advantage of this will appear later. The two lines generally used are: first, a **perpendicular,** which is a line perpendicular to the picture plane and whose perspective therefore vanishes in the vertical projection of the point of sight (1312); and second, a **diagonal** which is a **horizontal** line making an angle of 45° with the picture plane, and whose perspective vanishes somewhere on the horizon (1313). As the perpendicular and diagonal drawn through a point are both parallel to the horizontal plane, these two intersecting lines determine a plane which, like all other horizontal planes, vanish in the horizon. Instead of using a diagonal making 45°, any other angle may be used, provided it is less than 90°. This latter line would be parallel to the picture plane and therefore would not pierce it.

It can also be observed that there are two possible diagonals through any point, one whose perspective vanishes to the left of the point of sight and the other whose perspective vanishes to the right of the point of sight.

It is further known that the perspectives of all parallel lines vanish in one point and therefore the perspectives of all parallel diagonals through any point must have a common vanishing point. With two possible diagonals through a given point in space, two vanishing points are obtained on the horizon.

**1320. To find the perspective of a point by the method of perpendiculars and diagonals.** Let **a** and **a′**, Fig. 240,

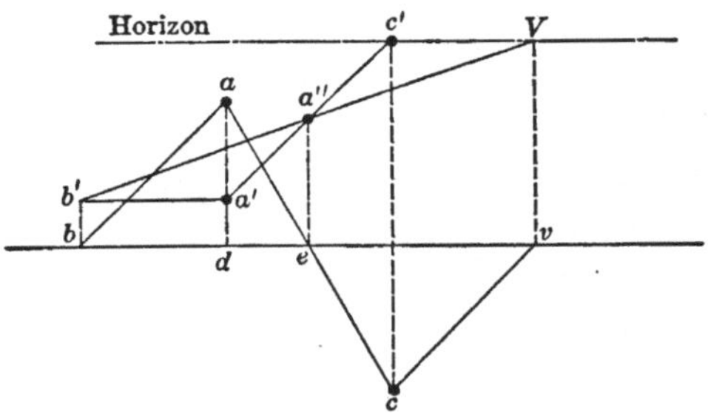


FIG. 240.

represent the projections of a point in the second angle, and let **c** and **c′** be the projections of the point of sight. By drawing the visual rays **ac** and **a′c′** the piercing point **a″** is determined by erecting a perpendicular at **e** as shown. Although the perspective **a″** is determined by this method, it may also be determined by finding the intersections of the perspectives of a perpendicular and a diagonal through the point **A** in space.

Thus, by drawing a line ab, making a 45° angle with the ground line, the horizontal projection of the diagonal is found. As the diagonal is a horizontal line, its vertical projection is **a′b′**. This diagonal pierces the picture plane at **b′**, which point is its own perspective. Its perspective also vanishes at **V**, the vanishing point of all horizontal lines whose inclination to the picture plane is at the 45° angle shown and whose directions are parallel to each other. The point **V** is found by drawing a line

**cv** parallel to **ab, c′V** parallel to **a′b′**, and then finding the piercing point **V.** The horizontal projection of a perpendicular through **A** is **ad;** its vertical projection is evidently **a′**, which is also its piercing point on the picture plane and as it lies in the picture plane, it is hence its own perspective. The vanishing point of the perspective of the perpendicular is at **c′**, the centre of the picture.

Since the perspective of a given point must lie on the perspectives of any two lines drawn through the point, then, as **b′V** is the indefinite perspective of a diagonal, and **a′c′** is the indefinite perspective of a perpendicular, their intersection **a″** is the required perspective of the point **A.** The fact that **a″** has already been determined by drawing the visual ray and its

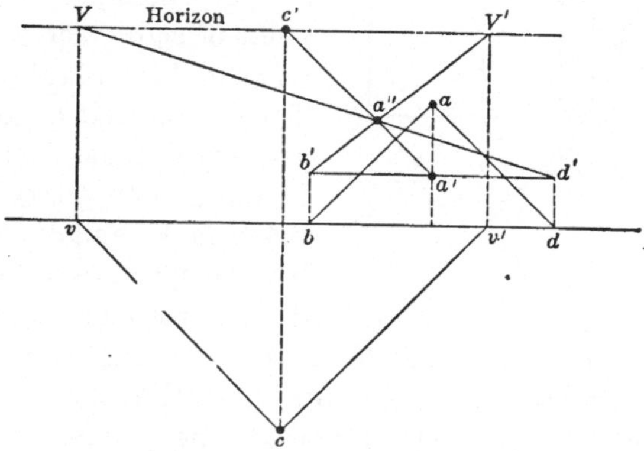


FIG. 241.

piercing point found shows that the construction is correct, and that either method will give the same result.

In Fig. 241, a similar construction is shown. The points V and V′ are the vanishing points of the left and right diagonals respectively. The perspective **a″** may be determined by the use of the two diagonals without the aid of the perpendicular. For instance **ab** and **a′b′** are corresponding projections of one diagonal; **ad** and **a′d′** are corresponding projections of the other diagonal. Hence **b′V′** is the indefinite perspective of the right diagonal (since **cv′** is drawn to the right) and **d′V** is the indefinite perspective of the left diagonal. Their intersection determines **a″,** the required perspective of the point **A.** The indefinite perspective of the perpendicular is shown as **a′c′** and passes through the point **a″** as it should.

Any two lines may be used to determine the perspective and should be chosen so as to intersect as at nearly a right angle as possible to insure accuracy of the location of the point. The visual ray may also be drawn on this diagram and its piercing point will again determine **a″**.

**1321.** To **find the perspective of a line by the method of perpendiculars and diagonals.** Suppose it is desired to construct the perspective of an arrow by the method of perpendiculars and diagonals. Fig. 242 shows a case of this kind. **AB** is an arrow situated in the second angle; **C** is the point of sight. A perpendicular through the point of sight pierces the picture plane in the vertical projection **c′**. The two possible diagonals whose horizontal projections are given by **cm** and **cn** pierce the picture plane in **V′** and **V** respectively. The perspective of any diagonal drawn through any point in space will vanish in either of these vanishing points depending upon whether the diagonal is drawn to the right or to the left of the point in question. Likewise, the perspective of a perpendicular drawn through any point in space will vanish in the centre of the picture.

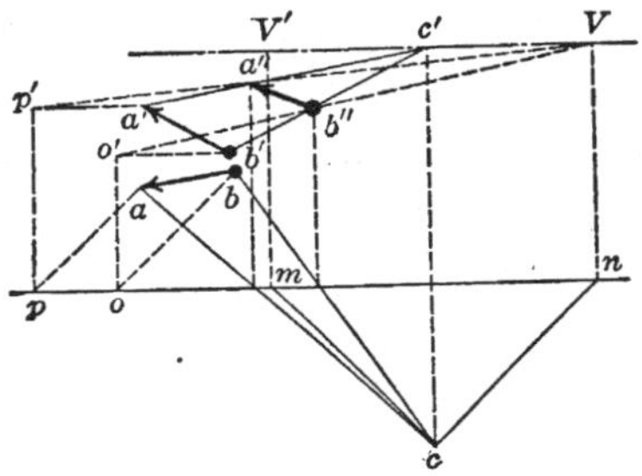

FIG. 242.

In the case at issue, the horizontal projection of a diagonal through **b** is **bo** and its vertical projection is **b′o′**; the piercing points is at **o′**. As the perspectives all lines parallel to the diagonal have a common vanishing point, then the perspective of the diagonal through **B** must vanish at **V** and the perspective of the point **B** must be somewhere on the line joining **o′** and **V**. Turning attention to the perpendicular through **B**, it is found that its vertical projection corresponds with the vertical projection of the point itself and is therefore b′. The perspectives of all perpendiculars to the vertical or picture plane vanish in the centre of the picture; and, hence, the perspective of **B** in space must be somewhere on the line **b′c′**. It must also be somewhere on the perspective of the diagonal and, hence, it is at their intersection **b″**. This can also be shown by drawing the visual ray through the point of sight **C** and the point **B**. The horizontal and vertical projections of the visual ray are **cb** and **c′b′** and they pierce the picture plane at **b″**, which is the same point obtained by finding the indefinite perspectives of the perpendicular and the diagonal.

By similar reasoning the perspective **a″** is obtained and, therefore, **a″b″** is the perspective of **AB**.

**1322. Revolution of the horizontal plane.** The fact that the second and fourth angles are not used in drawing on account of the conflict between the separate views has already been considered (315, 317). This is again shown in Fig. 238. The two views of the cube overlap and make deciphering more difficult. To overcome this difficulty the horizontal plane is revolved

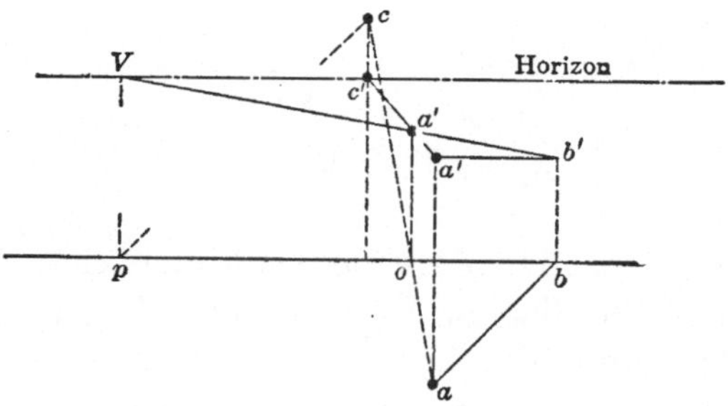


FIG. 243.

180° from its present position. This brings the horizontal projections below the ground line and leaves the vertical projections the same as before. Now the diagonals through any point slope in the reverse direction, and care must therefore be used in selecting the proper vanishing point while drawing the indefinite perspective of the diagonal.

**1323.** To **find the perspective of a point when the horizontal plane is revolved.** Let Fig. 243 represent the conditions of the problem. The vertical projection of the given point is **a′** and its corresponding horizontal projection is at a, below the ground line due to the 180° revolution of the horizontal plane. The vertical projection of the point of sight is at **c′** and its corresponding horizontal projection is at c, now above the ground line. The conditions are such that the given point seems like a first angle projection and the point of sight seems like a second angle projection, whereas the actual conditions are just the reverse of this.

Through **a,** draw **ab** the horizontal projection of the diagonal; the corresponding vertical projection is **a′b′** with **b′** as the piercing point. As **ab** is drawn to the right, the indefinite perspective of the diagonal must vanish in the left vanishing point at **V,** Hence, draw **Vb′**, the indefinite perspective of the diagonal.

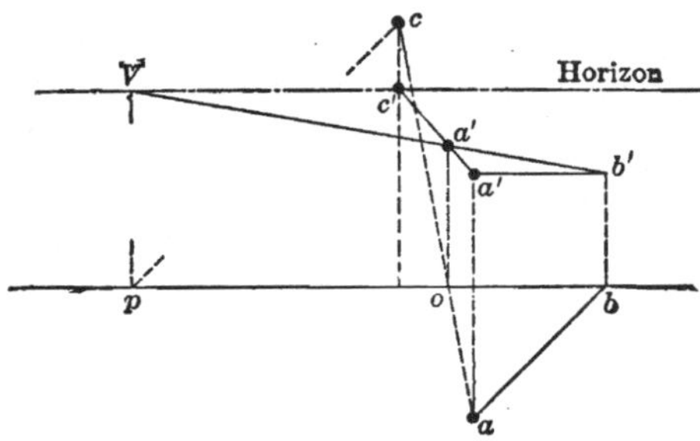


FIG. 243.

The indefinite perspective of the perpendicular remains unchanged and is shown in the diagram as **a′c′.** Therefore the intersection of **Vb′** and **a′c′** determine **a″,** the required perspective of the point **A.** The accuracy of the construction is checked by drawing the visual ray **ca** and then erecting a perpendicular at **o,** as shown, which passes through **a″** as it should.

**1324. To find the perspective of a line when the horizontal plane is revolved.** The point **B** in space will again be located in Fig. 244 just as was done in Fig. 242. The horizontal projection of the diagonal is **bo** and its vertical projection is **b′o′;** the piercing point, therefore, is o′. The horizontal projection of the point of sight **c** is now above the ground line instead of below it, due to the 180° revolution of the horizontal plane; the original position of this point. is marked **c″.** A diagonal through the point of sight, parallel to

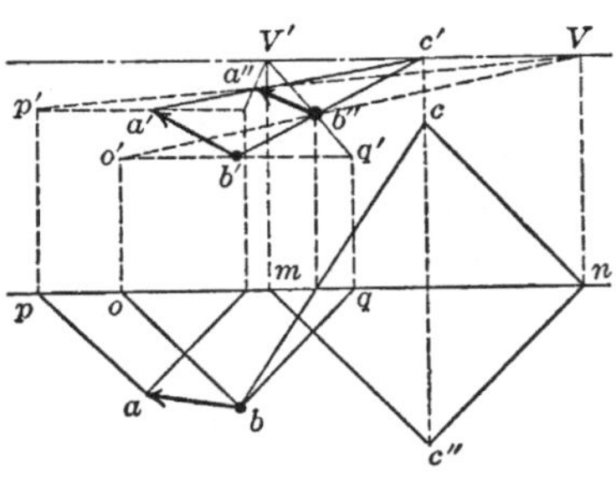


FIG. 244.

the diagonal through the point **B**, is shown as **cn** and pierces the vertical plane at **V** and, therefore, **o′V** is the indefinite perspective of the diagonal. The indefinite perspective of the perpendicular, as before, is **b′c′**, vanishing in the centre of the picture. The intersection of these two indefinite perspectives determines **b″**, the perspective of the point **B** in space.

Instead of using the left diagonal **bo**, through b, it is possible to use the right diagonal **bq**, and this pierces the picture plane at **q′**, and vanishes at **V′** which (as must always be the case) again determines the perspective **b″**. It must be observed that it matters little which diagonal is used with a perpendicular, or, whether only the diagonals without the perpendicular are used. In practice such lines are selected as will intersect as nearly as possible at right angles since the point of intersection is thereby more accurately determined than if the two lines intersected acutely. Whatever is done the principal points can always be located by any two lines, and the other may be used as a check. Still another check can be had by drawing the horizontal projection of the visual ray **cb** whereby **b″**, the perspective, is once more determined. The point **A** in space is located in an identical manner.

**1325. Location of diagonal vanishing points.** On observation of Figs. 242 and 244, it is seen that the distance **V′** to **c′** and **V** to **c′** is the same as the distance of the point of sight is from the vertical plane. This is true because a 45° diagonal is used and these distances are the equal sides of a triangle so formed. The use of any other angle would not give the same result, although the distance of the vanishing points from the centre of the picture would always be equal.

All the principles that are necessary for the drawing of any kind of a linear perspective have now been developed. The subsequent problems will illustrate their uses in a variety of cases. Certain adaptations required for commercial application will appear subsequently.

**1326. Problem 2. To find the perspective of a cube by the method of perpendiculars and diagonals.**

**Construction.** Let **ABCDEFGH** in Fig. 245 represent the cube. A case has been selected that is identical to the one shown in Fig. 238, in order that the difference between the two methods may be clearly illustrated. Suppose it is desired to locate the perspective of the point **E.** Draw from **e,** in the horizontal projection, the diagonal **eo,** the vertical projection is **e′o′** with **o′** as a piercing point. Join o′ with **v,** and the indefinite perspective of the diagonal is obtained. The perpendicular from **e** pierces the vertical plane at **e′** and **e′s′** is the indefinite perspective. The intersection **E** of these indefinite perspectives is the required perspective of the point. This point can also be checked by drawing the other diagonal which pierces the picture plane at **p′**, thereby making **p′v′** the indefinite perspective of the latter diagonal, which passes through **E,** as it should.

The point **C** is located by drawing the perpendicular and

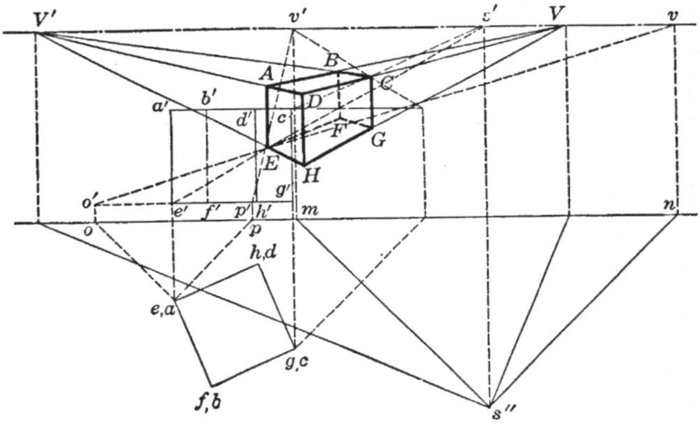


FIG. 245.

diagonal in the same way as was done for the point **E.** The rest of the construction has been omitted for the sake of clearness. As in Fig. 242, the vanishing points **V′** and **V** are laid out by drawing a line through the point of sight parallel to the system of lines. Fig. 245 does not show the construction in this way because the horizontal projection of the point of sight is now above the ground line, due to the 180°-revolution of the horizontal plane. Instead, the lines have been drawn from the original horizontal projection shown as **s″** and care has been taken to see that the lines are parallel to the reversed position of the horizontal projection. A reference to both Figs. 238 and 245 will make this all clear.

In Fig. 245 two vanishing points v′ and v will be noted which are (as has already been shown to be) the vanishing points of the perspectives of all diagonals. It is also known that the centre of the picture **s′** is the vanishing point of the perspectives of all perpendiculars. **A**ltogether, there are five vanishing points; the points **V** and **V′** are the vanishing points of the perspectives of the horizontal lines on the cube.

**1327. Problem 3.** **To find the perspective of a hexagonal prism.**

**Construction.** Reference to Fig. 246 shows that one edge of the prism lies in the picture plane while the base is in the horizontal plane.* The diagonals used to determine the vanishing points are here chosen to be 30°, as in this way they are also parallel to some of the lines of the object and, therefore, have

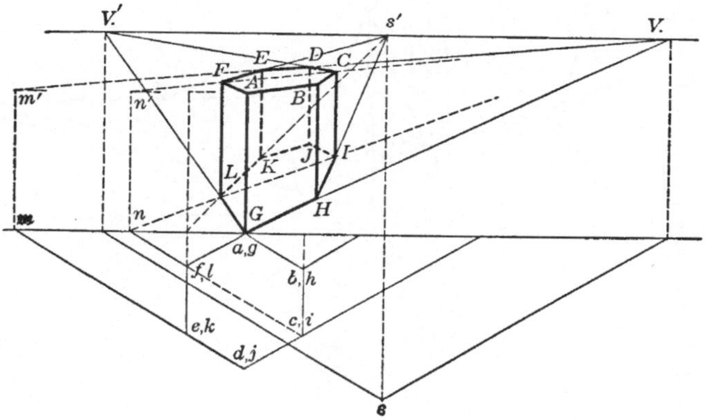


FIG. 246.

common vanishing points. **V′** and **V** are the vanishing points of the diagonals, and of those sides which make an angle of 30° with the picture plane. The centre of the picture is at **s′** and, therefore, the vanishing point of the perspectives of all perpendiculars. The edge **AG** lies in the picture plane, and, therefore, is shown in its actual size. The indefinite perspectives of the diagonals from the extremities **A** and **G** will give the direction of the sides **FA** and **AB** for the top face and **LG** and **GH** for the base. The points F and **L** are located by drawing a diagonal and perpendicular through f and **l** in the horizontal projection. The distance **mm′** and **nn′** is equal to **AG,** the height of the prism.

* This picture has a strained appearance due to the selection of the point of sight. See Art. 1331 in this connection.

**1328. Problem 4. To find the perspective of a pyramid superimposed on a square base.**

**Construction.** In Fig. 247, the edge **GK** is shown in the picture plane, a fact which enables the immediate determination of the direction of **JK, KL, FG** and **GH** by joining **G** and **K** with the vanishing points **V′** and **V.** It is only necessary to show the points **J** and **L** to determine the verticals **FJ** and **HL.** The method for this has already been shown. One other important point to locate is the apex **A.** This is shown by drawing a diagonal and perpendicular through **a.** The line **AO,** in space, pierces the

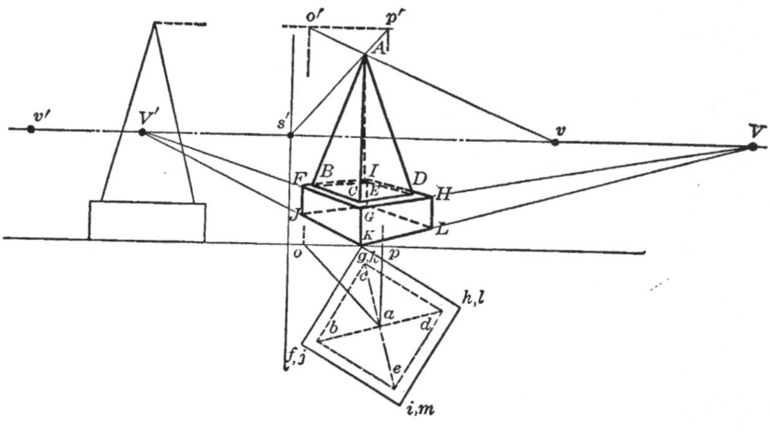


FIG. 247.

picture plane at **o′,** and **AP** at **p′** at a height **oo′** equal to the height of the apex above the horizontal plane. Joining **p′** with **s′**, the indefinite perspective of the perpendicular is obtained. At its intersection with the indefinite perspective of the diagonal **oa,** locate **A,** the perspective of the apex. The horizontal projection of the point of sight is not shown as the location of **v′** from **s′** and **v** from **s′** also gives the distance of the point of sight from the picture plane (1325).

**1329. Problem 5. To find the perspective of an arch.**

**Construction.** Fig. 248 shows plan and elevation of the arch. The corner nearest to the observer is in the picture plane, and therefore the lines in the plane are shown in their true length.

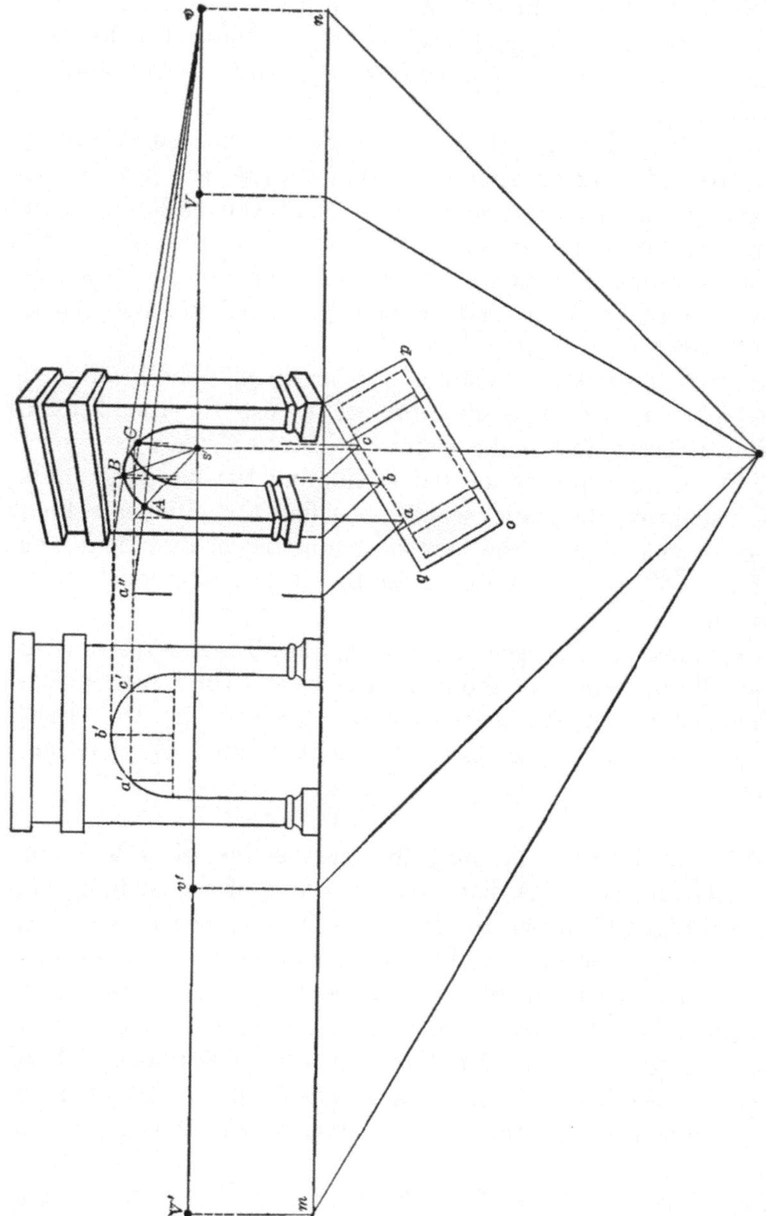


FIG. 248.

This length need not be in actual size but may be drawn to any scale desired. From the extremities of these lines, others are drawn to the vanishing points **V′** and **V,** as these are the vanishing points of the perspectives of the parallels to the sides of the arch.

It is to be remembered that through **s,** a line **sm** is drawn parallel to the reversed direction of **op,** because the plan would ordinarily be above the ground line. This convention may or may not be adopted. In Fig. 249 it is shown in another way and perhaps this may seem preferable. The matter is one of personal choice, however, and to the experienced, the liability to error is negligible.

The most important feature of this problem is the location of points on the arch.* The advantage of the use of perpendiculars and diagonals, to locate the points **A, B** and **C,** may be shown here. Were these points located by finding the piercing points of the visual ray, the reader would soon find the number of lines most confusing, due to the lack of symmetry of direction; the use of the 45° and 60° triangles for the diagonals is much more convenient.

In commercial perspective drawing, the draftsman estimates such small curves as are shown at the base. Only such points are located which are necessary for guides. In this case, the verticals and their limiting position are all that are required.

**1330. Problem 6.** To **find the perspective of a building.**

**Construction.** The plan and elevations of the building are shown on Fig. 249 drawn to scale. In drawing the perspective, the plan only is necessary to locate the various lines. Continual reference must be made to the elevations for various points in the height of the building. Considerable work can be saved by having one corner of the building in the picture plane. Thus, that corner is shown in its true length even though it may not be the actual length. In the case shown, it is drawn to scale.

The vanishing points of the horizontal lines on the building have been located from the horizontal projection of the point

* This arch may also be drawn by craticulation. See Art. 1331.

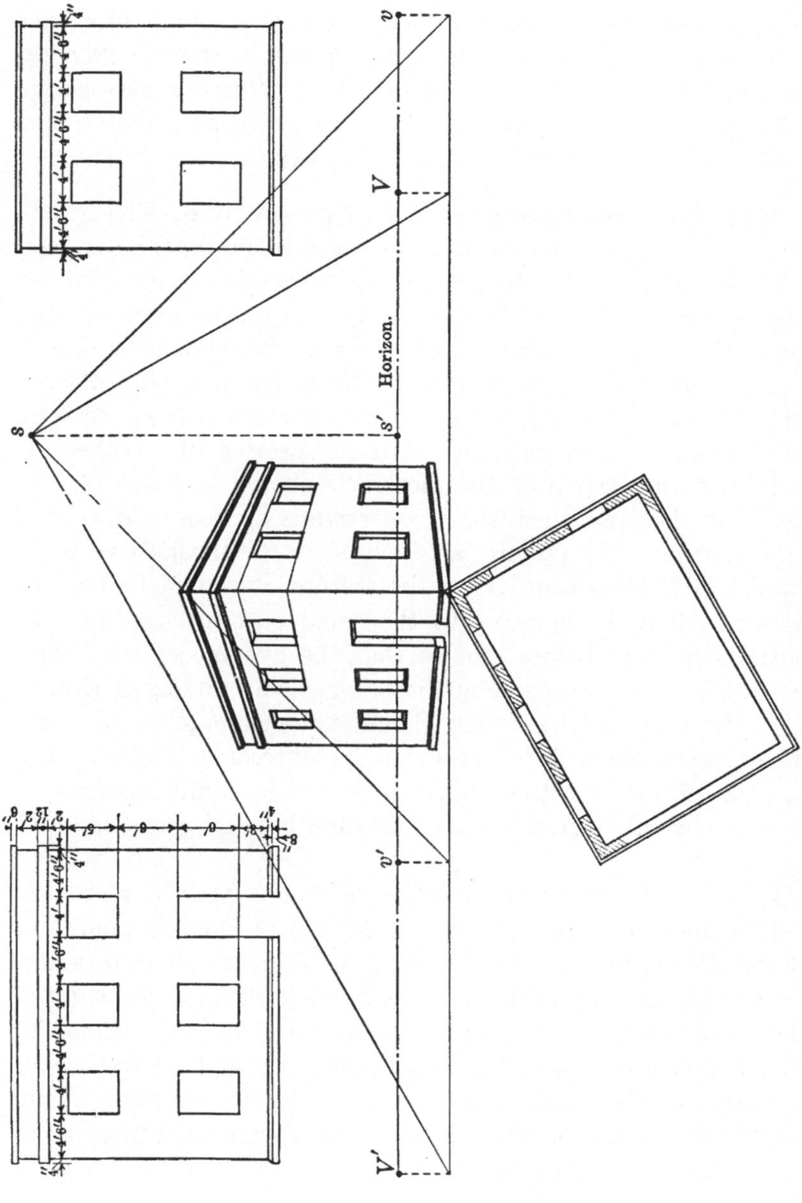


FIG. 249.

of sight, above the ground line. The construction lines are therefore drawn parallel to the sides of the building. The distances of the window lines may be laid out to scale on the corner of the building which lies in the picture plane, as shown. Strictly speaking, the term "scale" cannot be applied to perspective drawing, as a line of a given length is projected as a shorter line as the distance from the observer increases.

**1331. Commercial application of perspective.** The artistic requirement of perspective involves some choice in the selection of the point of sight. In general, the average observer's point of sight is about five feet above the ground, unless there is some reason to change it. The center of the picture should be chosen so that it is as nearly as possible in the centre of gravity of area of the picture and this may modify the selection of the observer's point of sight. For instance, if a perspective of a sphere is made and the centre of the picture is chosen in the centre of gravity of the area, then the perspective is a circle. Otherwise, if the centre of the picture is to one side, the perspective is an ellipse,* and, to properly view the picture, it should be held to one side. This is contrary to the usual custom; an observer holds the picture before him so that the average of the visual rays is normal to the plane of the paper. On building or similar work, the roof and base lines should not converge to an angle greater than about 50°. This can be overcome by increasing the distance between the vanishing points, or, what amounts to the same thing, increasing the distance between observer and object.

It is also desirable to choose the position of the observer so as to show the most attractive view of the object most prominently. Where a building has two equally prominent adjacent sides, it is a good plan to adjust the observer's position to present the sides approximately in proportion to their lengths. That is, when one side of a building is 200 feet long and 50 feet wide, the length of the building should appear on the drawing about four times as long as the width (these recommendations have been purposely ignored in Fig. 249).

* The limiting rays from the sphere are elements of the surface of a cone of revolution; hence, its intersection with a plane inclined to its axis will be an ellipse.

When impressions of magnitudes of objects are to be conveyed, it can be done by placing men at various places on the drawing. A mental estimate of the height of a man will roughly give an estimate of the magnitude of the object.

When curves are present in a drawing, the use of bounding figures of simple shape again finds application (210, 408). Architects know this under the name of **craticulation.** Fig. 250

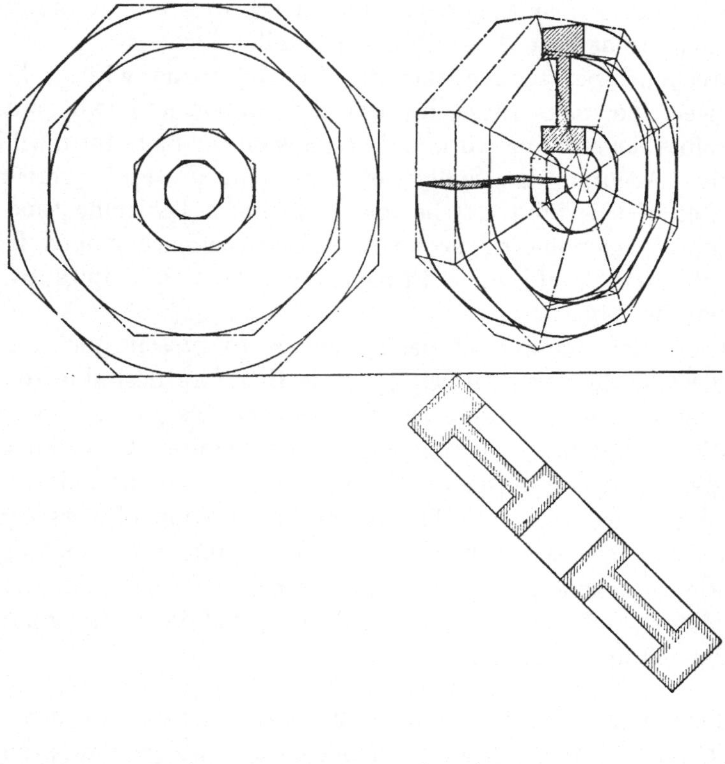

Fig. 250.

shows an example as applied to the drawing of a gas-engine fly-wheel. A slightly better picture could have been obtained by giving the wheel a tilt so as to show the " section " more prominently. This would also bring the centre of the picture nearer to the centre of gravity of the area. If the reader will study a few photographs, keeping these suggestions in mind he will note the conditions which make certain pictures better than others.

To make large perspectives is sometimes inconvenient due to the remoteness of the vanishing points. This requires a large drawing board and frequently the accuracy is impaired by the unwieldiness of the necessary drawing instruments. To overcome these objections, it is possible to make a small drawing of the object and then to redraw to a larger one by means of a proportional divider or by a pantograph. Only the more important lines need be located on the drawing. Such details as windows, doors, etc., can usually be estimated well enough so as to avoid suspicion as to their accuracy. The artist, with a little practice, soon accustoms himself to filling in detail.

Freehand perspective sketches can be made with a little practice. To make these, lay out the horizon and two vanishing points for building work and perhaps one or more for machine details. Accuracy is usually not a prerequisite, and, therefore, sketches of this kind can be made in almost the same time as oblique or axonometric sketches. The experience gained from this chapter should have furnished sufficient principles to be applied directly.

The chief function of perspective is to present pictures to those unfamiliar with drawing. It is therefore desirable to use every effort possible to present the best possible picture from the artistic viewpoint. The increased time required to make perspectives is largely offset by the ease with which the uninitiated are able to read them. The largest application of perspective is found in architect's drawings to clients, and in the making of artistic catalogue cuts. With perspective is usually associated the pictorial effect of illumination so as to call on the imagination to the minimum extent.

**1332. Classification of projections.*** When drawings are made on a plane surface then there are two general systems employed: those in which the projecting lines are parallel to each other and those in which the projecting lines converge to a point.

* See Art. 413 in this connection.

- Projections on plane surfaces
  - Parallel projecting lines
    - Orthographic
      - Showing two dimensions
        - Commonly called orthographic projections or Mechanical drawings.
      - Showing three dimensions and known as axonometric projections.
        - Isometric
        - Dimetric
        - Trimetric
    - Oblique
  - Convergent projecting lines
    - Linear perspective
      - Outline alone is shown
    - Aerial perspective
      - Color and illumination added to linear perspective

## QUESTIONS ON CHAPTER XIII

1. What is a scenographic projection?
2. What is a linear perspective?
3. Define visual rays.
4. Define visual angle.
5. What is the physiological effect of a variation in the visual angle?
6. How does binocular vision afford a means of estimating distance?
7. Why is the eye assumed as a single point in perspective?
8. What is a vanishing point? Give example.
9. Is the vanishing point the vanishing point of the line or of its perspective?
10. Show the theory of perspective by a window-pane illustration.
11. What is an aerial perspective?
12. What is the picture plane?
13. How is the picture plane usually located with respect to the object and the observer?
14. Show by an oblique projection how the perspective of a line is constructed.
15. Show how the perspective of a line is constructed in orthographic projection.
16. Prove that all perspectives of lines perpendicular to the horizontal plane have vertical perspectives.
17. Prove that all perspectives of lines parallel to both principal planes have perspectives parallel to the ground line.
18. What is the centre of the picture?
19. Prove that the perspectives of all lines perpendicular to the picture plane vanish in the centre of the picture.

20. Is the centre of the picture the vertical projection of the point of sight?
21. What is a system of lines?
22. Prove that the perspectives of all systems of lines have a common vanishing point.
23. How is the vanishing point of a system of lines found?
24. What is the horizon?
25. Prove that the perspectives of all horizontal systems of lines have a vanishing point on the horizon.
26. Why is the centre of the picture on the horizon?
27. Find the perspective of a point which is located in the second angle, by means of the piercing point of the visual ray on the picture plane.
28. Find the perspective of a point which is located in the first angle, by means of the piercing point of the visual ray on the picture plane.
29. Show that the vertical projection of a point which is situated in the picture plane is its own perspective.
30. Show that the vertical projection of a line which is situated in the picture plane is its own perspective.
31. What is the indefinite perspective of a line? Give proof.
32. Find the perspective of a cube by means of the piercing points of the visual rays on the picture plane.
33. Prove that if two lines in space intersect, their perspectives intersect in a point which is the perspective of the point of intersection on the lines.
34. What is a perpendicular when applied to perspective?
35. Where does the perspective of a perpendicular vanish?
36. What is a diagonal when applied to perspective?
37. How many diagonals may be drawn through a given point?
38. Where do the diagonals vanish? Why?
39. What angle is generally used for the diagonals? What other angles may be used?
40. Find the perspective of a second angle point, by the method of perpendiculars and diagonals.
41. Find the perspective of a second angle point, by drawing two diagonals through it. Check by drawing the perpendicular.
42. Find the perspective of a first angle point, by the method of perpendiculars and diagonals.
43. Find the perspective of a first angle point, by drawing two diagonals through it. Check by drawing the perpendicular.
44. Find the perspective of a second angle line, by the method of perpendiculars and diagonals.
45. Find the perspective of a second angle line, by drawing the diagonals only. Check by drawing the perpendicular and visual rays.
46. Find the perspective of a first angle line, by the method of perpendiculars and diagonals.
47. Find the perspective of a first angle line, by drawing the diagonals only. Check by drawing the perpendiculars and visual rays.

48. What is the object of revolving the horizontal plane in perspective?
49. What precaution must be used in perspective with reference to the diagonals, when the horizontal plane is revolved?
50. Find the perspective of a second angle point, by the method of perpendiculars and diagonals, when the horizontal plane is revolved.
51. Find the perspective of a first angle point, by the method of perpendiculars and diagonals, when the horizontal plane is revolved.
52. Find the perspective of a second angle line, by the method of perpendiculars and diagonals, when the horizontal plane is revolved.
53. Find the perspective of a first angle line, by the method of perpendiculars and diagonals, when the horizontal plane is revolved.
54. When the diagonals make an angle of 45° with the picture plane, how far are the vanishing points from the centre of the picture?
55. Find the perspective of a cube by means of perpendiculars and diagonals.
56. Why should the centre of the picture be chosen as near as possible to the centre of gravity of the perspective?
57. What is the perspective of a sphere, when the centre of the picture is in the centre of gravity of the perspective?
58. What is the perspective of a sphere, when the centre of the picture does not coincide with the centre of gravity of the perspective?
59. What should be the approximate angle of convergence of the roof and base lines of a building on a perspective?
60. If the roof and base lines of a building converge to an angle considered too large, what remedy is there for this condition?
61. When adjacent sides of a building are equally attractive, what should be their general relation on the perspective?
62. How may impressions of magnitude be conveyed on a perspective?
63. What is craticulation?
64. How may large perspectives be made when the drawing board is small?
65. When perspective is commercially applied, is it necessary to locate every point on the details or can it be drawn with sufficient accuracy by estimation?
66. Make a complete classification of projections having parallel and convergent projecting lines.

**Note.** In the following drawings, keep the centre of the picture as near as possible to the centre of gravity of the drawing.

67. Make a perspective of Fig. 1 in text.
68. Make a perspective of Fig. 10 in text.
69. Make a perspective of Fig. 17 in text.
70. Make a perspective of Fig. 2*A*. (Question in Chap. II.)
71. Make a perspective of Fig. 2*B*. (Question in Chap. II.)
72. Make a perspective of Fig. 21 in text.
73. Make a perspective of Fig. 3*A*. (Question in Chap. III.)
74. Make a perspective of Fig. 3*B*. " " "
75. Make a perspective of Fig. 3*C*. " " "

76. Make a perspective of Fig. 3*D*. (Question in Chap. III.)
77. Make a perspective of Fig. 3*E*. " " "
78. Make a perspective of Fig. 3*F*. " " "
79. Make a perspective of Fig. 3*G*.
80. Make a perspective of Fig. 3*H*.
81. Make a perspective of Fig. 3*I*.
82. Make a perspective of Fig. 3*J*.
83. Make a perspective of Fig. 3*K*. " " "
84. Make a perspective of Fig. 3*L*. "
85. Make a perspective of Fig. 40 in text.
86. Make a perspective of Fig. 41 in text.
87. Make a perspective of Fig. 42 in text.
88. Make a perspective of a pyramid on a square base.
89. Make a perspective of an arch.
90. Make a perspective of a building.

# PART IV

## *PICTORIAL EFFECTS OF ILLUMINATION*

---

## CHAPTER XIV

### PICTORIAL EFFECTS OF ILLUMINATION IN ORTHOGRAPHIC PROJECTION

**1401. Introductory.** The phenomena of illumination on objects in space is a branch of the science of engineering drawing, which aims to give the observer a correct imitation of the effect of light on the appearance of an object. In the main, it is desired to picture reality. The underlying principles of llumination are taken from that branch of physics known as Optics or Light. The application of these principles to graphical presentation properly forms a part of drawing.

It is needless to say that the subject borders on the artistic; yet it is sometimes desirable to present pictures to those who are unfamiliar with the reading of commercial orthographic projections. The architect takes advantage of perspective in connection with the effects of illumination, and in this way brings out striking contrasts and forcibly attracts attention to the idea expressed in the drawing.

It is not always essential, however, to bring out striking effects, as occasion often arises to picture the surfaces of an object. This is done by pictorially representing the effects of illumination.

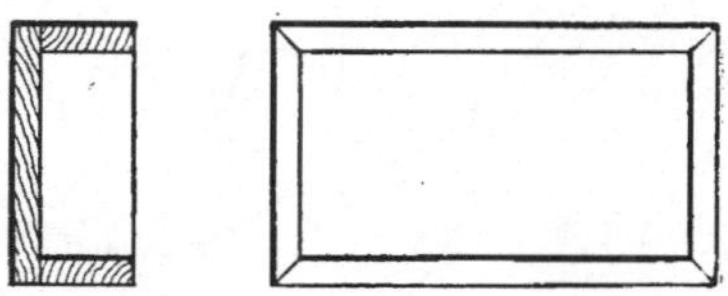

FIG. 251.

**1402. Line shading applied to straight lines.** The simplest application of **line shading** is shown in Fig. 251; the object is a rectangular cover for a box. In the illumination, it is assumed that the light comes in parallel lines, from the upper left-hand corner of the drawing. The direction is downward, and to the right, at an angle of 45°. The illuminated surfaces are drawn with any thickness (or, as is commercially termed, "weight") of line; the surfaces not in the light are made heavier as though the line or surface actually cast a shadow. Irrespective of the location on the sheet, the drawing would always be represented in the same way since the light is assumed to come in parallel lines.

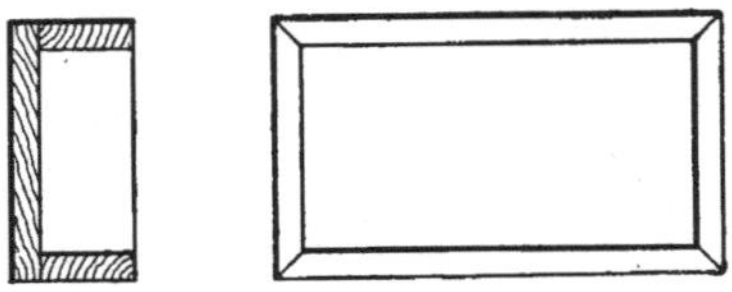

FIG. 251.

Evidently there is (strictly speaking) no underlying theory in this mode of shading, the process being merely a convention adopted by draftsmen, thus its extended use merely is the necessary recommendation for its value.

**1403. Line shading applied to curved lines.** In Fig. 252

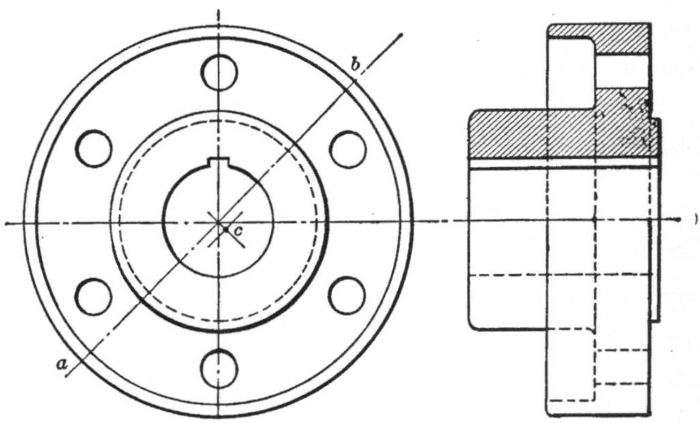


FIG. 252.

is shown one part of a flange coupling, the illustration being chosen to show the application of **line shading** to the drawing of curves. In this latter application all is given that is necessary to make drawings using this mode of representat on.

As before, the light comes from the upper left-hand corner

of the drawing. By the aid of the two views (one-half of one being shown in section) such surfaces as will cast a shadow are easily distinguished. The shade lines of the circles are shown to taper gradually off to a diagonal line **ab.** In drawing the shade line of a circle, for instance, draw the circle with the weight of line adopted in making the drawing; with the same radius and a centre located slightly eccentric (as shown much exaggerated at **c** in Fig. 252), draw another semicircle, adding thickness to one side of the circle or the other, depending upon whether it is illum'nated or not.

It will be seen that this second circle will intersect the first somewhere near the diagonal ab. For instance, the extreme outside circle casts a shadow on the lower right-hand side, whereas the next circle is shaded on the upper left-hand side. These two shaded circles indicate that there is a projection on the surface. In the same manner the drawing is completed. It makes no difference whether the surface projects much or little, the lines are all shaded in the same way and with the same weight of shade line.

Notice should be taken that for all concentric circles, the **eccentric centre** is always the same. The six bolt holes are also shown shaded, and each of which has its own eccentric centre.

Many cases arise in practice where there are projections or depressions in the surface. This convention helps to interpret, rapidly and correctly, such drawings. The time taken to use this method is more than offset by the advantages thereby derived; only in extremely simple drawings does it become unnecessary.

**1404. Line shading applied to sections.** It makes no difference whether the outside view is shown, or whether the object is shown in section (Fig. 252) the shade lines are drawn as though the supplementary planes actually cut the object so as to expose that portion. This is done for uniformity only.

**1405. Line shading applied to convex surfaces.** Occasionally, curved surfaces must be contrasted with flat surfaces, or, perhaps, the effect of curvature brought out without an attempt to contrast it with flat surfaces. Fig. 253 shows a cylinder shaded. The heavier shade is shown to the right as the light is supposed to come from the left; the reason for this will be shown later. The effect of shading and its graduation is produced by gradually altering the space between the lines, however, keeping the weight of line the same. A somewhat better effect is produced by also increasing the weight of the line in connection with the decrease in the spacing, but the custom is not general.

**1406. Line shading applied to concave surfaces.** A hollow cylinder is shown shaded in Fig. 254. Again, the light comes from the left and the heavier shade falls on the left, as shown.

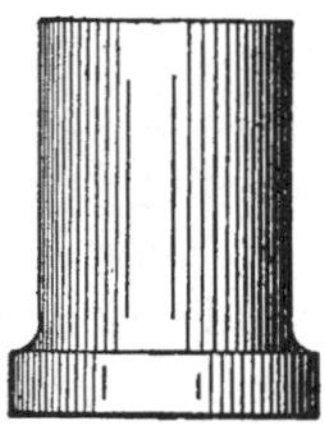

FIG. 253.

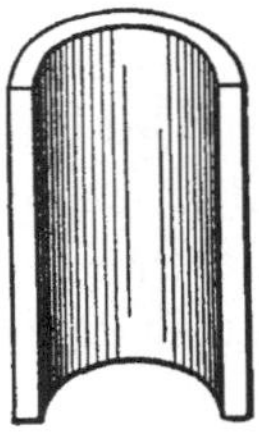

FIG. 254.

A comparison between Figs. 253 and 254 shows how concave and convex surfaces can be indicated.

**1407. Line shading applied to plane surfaces.** Flat surfaces are sometimes shaded by spacing lines an equal distance apart. The effect produced is that of a **flat shade.** The method is used when several surfaces are shown in one view whose planes make different angles with the planes of projection, like an octagonal prism, for instance.

PHYSICAL PRINCIPLES OF LIGHT.

**1408. Physiological effect of light.** Objects are made evident to us by the reflected light they send to our eyes. The brain becomes conscious of the form of the object due to the physiological effect of light on the retina of the eye. The locality from which the light emanates is called the **source.** Light travels in straight lines, called **rays,** unless obstructed by an opaque body. If the source of light is at a considerable distance from the object, the light can be assumed to travel in parallel lines.

The chief source of light is the sun and its distance is so great (about 93,000,000 miles) that all rays are practically parallel.

**1409. Conventional direction of light rays.** The source of light may be located anywhere, but it is usual to assume that it comes from over the left shoulder of the observer who is viewing an object before him. The projections of the rays on the horizontal and vertical plane make an angle of 45° with the ground line. The problems to follow will be worked out on this assumed basis.

**1410. Shade and shadow.** The part of the object that is not illuminated by direct rays is termed the **shade.** The area from which light is excluded, whether on the object itself or on any other surface, is called the **shadow.** As an example, take a building with the sun on one side; the opposite side is evidently in the shade. A cornice on this building may cast a shadow on the walls of the building, while the entire structure casts a shadow on the ground, and sometimes on neighboring buildings.

**1411. Umbra and penumbra.** When the source of light is chosen near the object, two distinct shadows are observable, one within the other. Fig. 255 shows a plan view of a flat gas flame **ab** and a card **cd.** Rays emanate from every point of the flame in all directions. Consider the point **a,** in the flame. The two rays **ac** and **ad** will determine a shadow cast by the card the area of which is located away from the flame and limited to that behind **fcdh.** Similarly, from the point **b,** the two rays **bc** and **bd** cast a shadow, limited by the area behind **ecdg.** These two areas overlap. From the position of **fcdg,** no part of the flame can be seen by an observer standing there; but from any one of the areas behind **eof** or **gdh,** a portion of the flame can be seen. The effect of this is that the shadow in **fcdg** is much more pronounced and therefore is the darker.

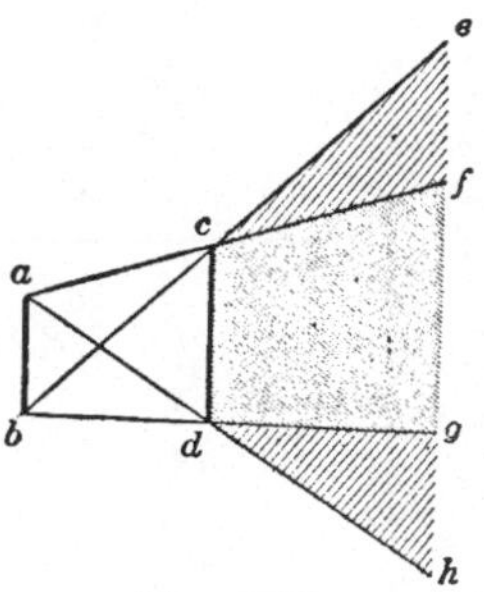

FIG. 255.

That portion of the shadow from which the light is totally excluded (**fcdg**) is called the **umbra;** that portion from which the light is partly excluded (**ecf** or **gdh**) is called the **penumbra.**

This effect is easily shown by experiment, and is sometimes seen in photographs taken by artificial illumination when the source of light is quite near the object. In passing, it may also be mentioned that if there are two sources of light, there may be two distinct shadows, each having its own umbra and penumbra, but such cases are not usually considered in drawing.

When applying these principles to drawing, the shadow is limited to the **umbra**, and the penumbra is entirely neglected. The light is supposed to come from an infinite distance, and, therefore, in parallel rays. So little in the total effect of a drawing is lost by making these assumptions, that the extra labor involved in making theoretically correct shadows is uncalled for.

## GRAPHICAL REPRESENTATION

**1412. Application of the physical principles of light to drawing.** In the application of the physical principles enumerated above, it is merely necessary to draw the rays of light to the limiting lines of the object, and find their piercing points with the surface on which the shadow is cast. This is the entire theory.

**1413. Shadows of lines.*** Fig. 256 exhibits the shadow cast by an arrow **AB** shown by its horizontal projection **ab** and its

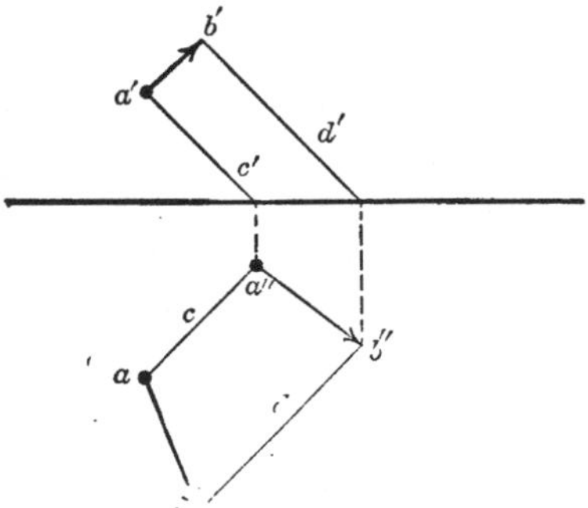


FIG. 256.

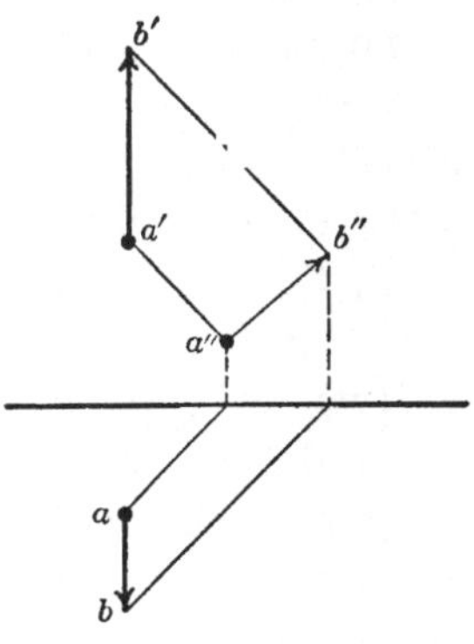


FIG. 257.

vertical projection **a′b′**. The rays of light come, as assumed,

* Lines are mathematical concepts and have no width or thickness. They can, therefore, strictly speaking, cast no shadow.

in lines whose horizontal and vertical projections make an angle of 45° with the ground line. A ray of light to **A** is shown as **ca** in the horizontal projection and **c′a′** in the vertical projection. The ray of light to B is shown by the similar projection **db** and **d′b′**. These two rays pierce the horizontal plane at **a″** and **b″** and **a″b″** is therefore the shadow of the arrow **AB** in space.

If the arrow is as shown in Fig. 257, then the shadow is on the vertical plane. A similar method is used for drawing the projections of the rays on the horizontal and vertical planes. Instead, however, the piercing points on the vertical plane are found, and these are shown as **a″b″**, which again is the shadow of **AB** in space.

In Fig. 256 the rays pierce the horizontal plane before they pierce the vertical plane and the shadow is therefore on the horizontal plane. Since the plane is assumed o**paque** there is no vertical shadow. Fig. 257 is the reverse of this. A vertical shadow and no horizontal shadow is obtained. Cases may occur where the shadow is partly on both planes, similar to a shadow cast partly on the floor and partly on the wall of a room. Fig. 258 shows this in construction. It differs from the preceding in so far as the two horizontal and the two vertical piercing points of the rays are obtained, and thus the direction of the shadow is determined on both planes. If the construction is carried out accurately, the projections will intersect at the ground line, and the shadow will appear shown as **a″b″**.

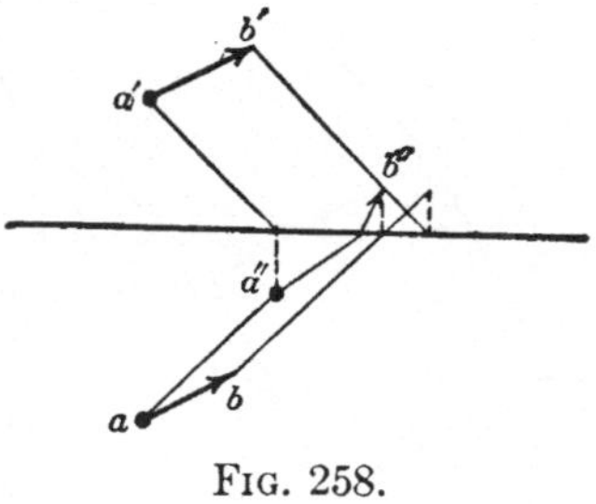

FIG. 258.

**1414. Problem 1. To find the shadow cast by a cube which rests on a plane.**

Let, in Fig. 259, **abcd** be the horizontal projection of the top of the cube and **a′b′c′d′** be the vertical projection of the top of the cube. The three points in space **A, B** and **C** will be sufficient to determine the shadow and, as a consequence, the projections of these rays are drawn an angle of 45°, as shown. The horizontal projections of the rays are accordingly **ae, bf** and **cg;** the vertical projections are likewise **a′e′, b′f′** and **c′g′**. The piercing points (506, 805) of these rays are **e,** f and **g.** The shadow is therefore determined because the cube rests on the horizontal plane, and the base must necessarily be its own shadow.

**1415. Problem 2.** To **find the shadow cast, by a pyramid, on the principal planes.**

In order to show a case where the shadow is cast on both planes, the pyramid must be located close to the vertical plane. The pyramid, **ABCDE,** Fig. 260, is shown in the customary way

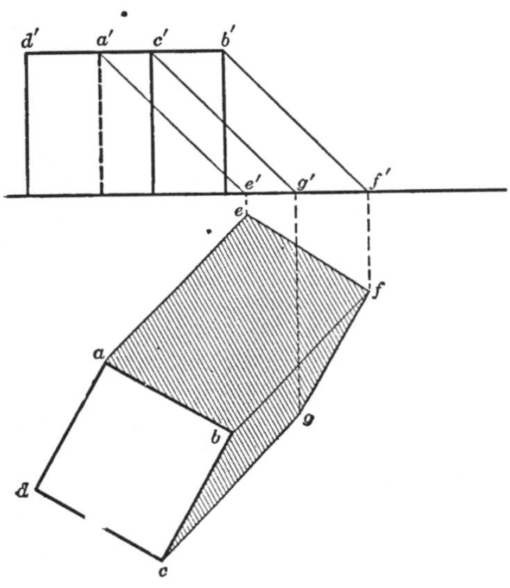


FIG. 259.

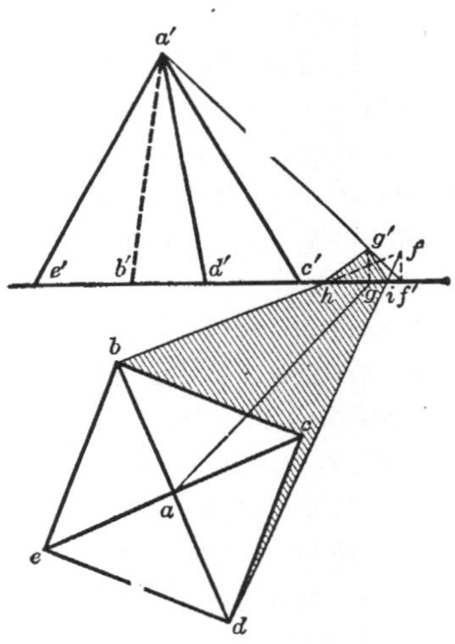


FIG. 260.

as **abcde** or the horizontal projection, and **a′b′c′d′e′** for the vertical projection. The horizontal piercing point of what would be the shadow of the apex must be located in order to determine the shadow of the side **BA,** even though it forms no part of the actual shadow. Locate also the vertical piercing point **g′** which is the actual shadow of the apex. It will be noticed that the shadow of **BA** only continues until it meets the vertical plane and is therefore limited by the projection **bh.** Similarly, the shadow is limited by **di,** a portion of the line **df.** Where these two lines meet the ground line, join the points with the actual shadow of the apex and the shadow is then completed. It may be observed that the limiting lines of an object determine the shadow in all cases, and that the interior lines do not influence the figure unless they project above the rest of the object in any way.

**1416. Problem 3.** To **find the shade and shadow** cast by **an** octagonal **prism having a superimposed octagonal cap.**

Let Fig. 261 represent the object in question. Confine attention at present to the shadow on the horizontal plane. Consider, first, the shadow cast by the line **GH** in space. It will be seen that the rays of light from **G** and H pierce the horizontal plane at points **g″** and **h″** and that these points are found by drawing the projections of the rays from the points **G** and H in space. If the construction is correct so far, then **g″h″** should be parallel to **gh,** as **GH** is parallel to the horizontal plane and as **its** shadow must be parallel both to the line itself and also to **its** horizontal projection. Similarly, locate **a″** and **f″**. Thus, three lines of the shadow are determined.

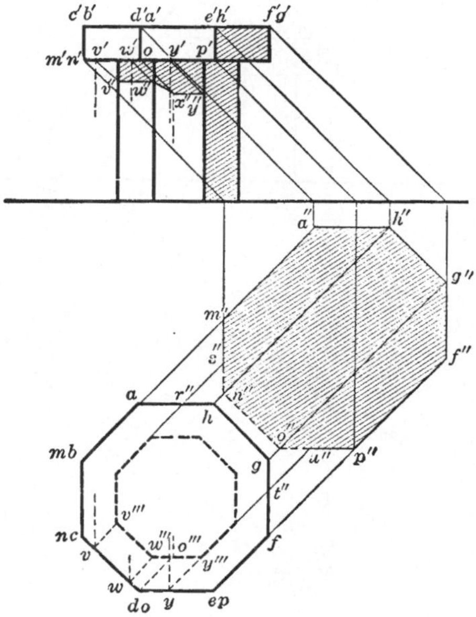

FIG. 261.

It is now necessary to observe carefully that the shadow of

the superimposed cap is not only due to the top face, as the points **m″n″o″p″** are the piercing points of rays that come from the points **MNOP,** in space, and that they are on the lower face of the cap. The shadow of the points **BCDE** fall within the area **a″h″g″f″p″o″m″n″** and therefore need not be located. The shadow is completed by drawing **r″s″** and **t″u″** which are a part of the shadow cast by the octagonal prism below. It is unnecessary to determine the complete outline of the shadow of the

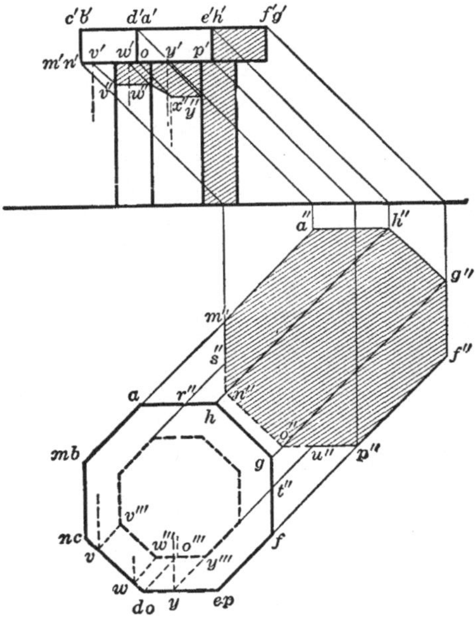

FIG. 261.

prism as it merges into that cast by the cap. The shadow on the horizontal plane is thus completely determined.

Consider, in addition, the shadow cast on the prism due to the superimposed cap. The shadow limited by the line **v″w″** is due to the limited portion of the lower face of the cap shown horizontally projected at **vw** and vertically as **v′w′**. The shadow of the point **O** in space is shown as x″ and that of **Y** in space as y″. All these latter points are joined by straight lines as they are shadows of straight lines cast upon a plane surface and may be considered as the intersection of a plane of rays through the line forming the outline of the object.

The right of the face of the prism and of the cap is shaded entirely, because it is in the shade, and since it receives no direct illumination, it is represented as shown.

**1417. Problem 4. To find the shade and shadow cast by a superimposed circular cap on a cylinder.**

Fig. 262 shows the cylinder with its superimposed cap. The shadow cast by the cap will be some form of curve, and attention will be directed at present, to the location points on this curve. From **a′**, in the vertical projection, draw a ray whose projection makes an angle of 45° with the ground line, and locate it so that it impinges on the surface of the cylinder at the extreme visible element to the left. The corresponding horizontal projection of **a′** is **a,** and the point where this ray impinges is **a,″** one point of the required shadow. Consider point **b,** vertically projected at **b′**. The projections of its ray will intersect the surface of the cylinder at the point **b″** along an element shown vertically projected at **b‴**. Select another point **c′** in the vertical projection, so that the ray **c′d′** will be tangent to the cylinder. The element is horizontally projected at **c″d** and the ray impinges at **c″** which is still another point of the shadow.

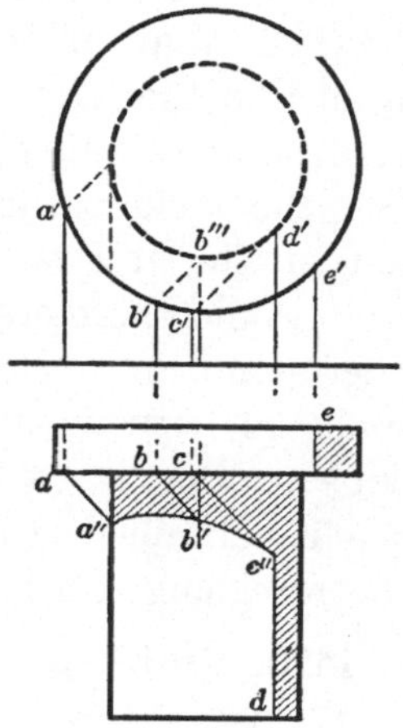


FIG. 262.

In practice, several more points are determined, but they are omitted here for the sake of clearness. The portion of the cylinder away from the source of light must be in the shade and **d′** shows the vertical projection of one element from which the illuminated portion is separated from the shade. Accordingly, the portion of the cylinder to the right of **c″d** is shaded entirely. The same effect occurs on the superimposed cap, and, hence, from the element **e,** to the right, the entire remaining area is shaded, being unilluminated from rays having projections which make an angle 45° with the ground line.

**1418. High-light.** When a body, such as a polished sphere, is subjected to a source of light, one spot on the sphere will appear much brighter than the rest of the sphere. This spot is called the **brilliant point,** or, more commonly, the **high-light.** The effect is that due to the light being immediately reflected to the eye with practically undiminished intensity.

**1419. Incident and reflected rays.** It is a principle in optics * that the incident ray and the reflected ray make equal angles with the normal to the surface on which the light impinges. The tangent plane at the point where the light impinges must be perpendicular to the normal; the incident ray and the reflected ray also lie in the same plane with the normal and therefore this plane is perpendicular to the tangent plane. It may be observed that if a line be drawn through any point in space parallel to the ray of light or incident ray, and through the same point, another line be drawn parallel to the reflected ray, then the included angle will be the same irrespective of the location of the arbitrary point chosen. The normal through this point would therefore be parallel to a normal drawn through any other point in space, and a plane perpendicular to one normal would be perpendicular to all. By choosing the perpendicular plane so that it touches the surface a tangent plane to the surface is obtained; the point of contact is then the **high-light.** The foregoing can best be illustrated by an example.

**1420. Problem 5.** To **find the high-light on a sphere.**

To use a simple illustration, the high-light on the vertical projection only will be determined. Fig. 263 shows this construction. Assume that the eye is directed perpendicularly to the vertical plane. The light comes in a direction whose projections make an angle of 45° with the ground line. For convenience, take a ray through the centre of the sphere **o′**; the incident ray is therefore **m′o′.** The line through the point of sight is perpendicular to the plane of the paper, and is therefore projected at **o′**. Revolve the plane of

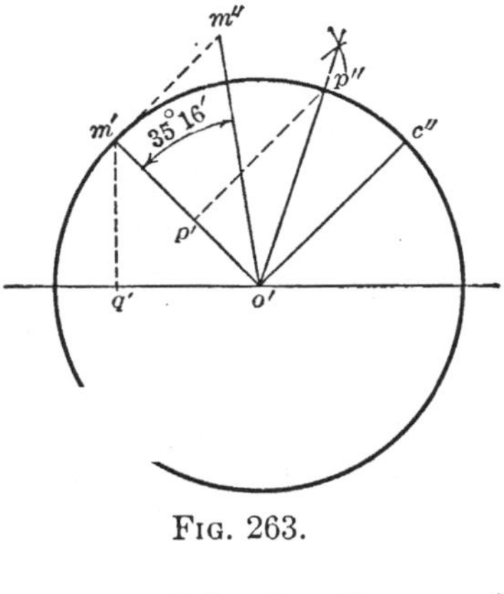


Fig. 263.

* See a text-book on Physics.

these incident and reflected rays about **m′o′** until it coincides or is parallel with the vertical plane. The perpendicular to the plane of the paper through **o′** will fall to **c″** and the revovled angle will be **c″o′m″**; the angle **m′o′m″** being numerically * equal to 35° 16′ for rays whose projections make an angle of 45° with the ground line. The point **m″** is graphically located as follows: Assume that a horizontal plane is passed through **o′**, the centre of the sphere. The distance of the point **m′** from this new horizontal plane is **m′q′** and this distance does not change in the revolution. Hence, the point **M** in space falls at **m″**, **om″** being the revolved position of the actual ray of light.

The bisector of the angle **m″o′c″** is the normal to the surface and a plane tangent to the revolved position of the sphere will be tangent at the point **p″**. It is unnecessary to draw the plane in this case as the normal readily determines **p″**. The counter revolved position of **p″** is **p′**; therefore, **p′** is the required high-light.

**1421. Multiple high-lights.** Before leaving this subject it must be noted that with several sources of light on an object, there may be several high-lights, although it is usual to assume only one on a surface like the sphere. A corrugated surface will have several high-lights for any one position of the eye and a single source of light.

**1422. High-lights of cylindrical or conical surfaces.** A cylinder or a cone can have only one high-light for any one position and direction of vision of the eye. If the surface is highly polished, it will be the only point visible; the object itself cannot be distinguished as to the details of its form. As the eye is directed anywhere along the surface, a new high-light is observed for each direction of vision and the locus of these points forms approximately a straight line.

**1423. Aerial effect of illumination.** The foregoing principles are true for the conditions assumed. In nature, however, it is impossible to receive light from only one source in directly parallel rays, to the total exclusion of any other light. Modifications must be introduced because the surfaces are not optically true

* Computed by trigonometry.

in the first instance. This means that a cylinder, although made round as carefully as possible, very slight deviations hardly discernible by measuring instruments are readily detected by their appearance in the light. The reflected light augments the imperfections, so that to the experienced eye the effect is noticeable. Other equally important facts are those due to the reflection from the walls of the room, and from other objects; the diffusion caused by the light being transmitted through the window-pane, and that reflected from dust particles suspended in the air. All these disturbing influences tend to illuminate certain other portions of the object and actually do so to such an extent that cognizance of this **aerial effect of illumination** must be taken.

**1424. Graduation of shade.** The effect on a highly polished sphere can be brought out by holding one in a room whose walls are a dull black, similar to a room used for photometric testing. Even this photometer room does not fulfil the requirements to the last degree, as there is no surface which does not reflect at least some light. Observing this sphere by aid of a ray of light coming through any opening in the room, the high-light will alone be visible. If there were no variation in the amount of light sent to the eye from the various points on the object, due to the aerial effect of illumination, it would be impossible to recognize its form. Hence no light can come to the eye except from the high-light unless the aerial effect is present.

With these difficulties to contend with, it may seem that the foregoing principles become invalid. Such is not the case, however, as the principles are true, in the main, but the proper correction is made for diffused light and a graduation in shade is introduced so as make the observer conscious of the desired idea to be conveyed.

**1425. Shading rules.** At times it may even be necessary to strain a point in order to bring out some detail of the object drawn. This latter is a characteristic of the skill of the artist. The rules for the representation of shades are here inserted, being taken from Mahan's Industrial Drawing:

"1. Flat tints should be given to plane surfaces, when in the light, and parallel to the vertical plane; those nearest the eye being lightest.

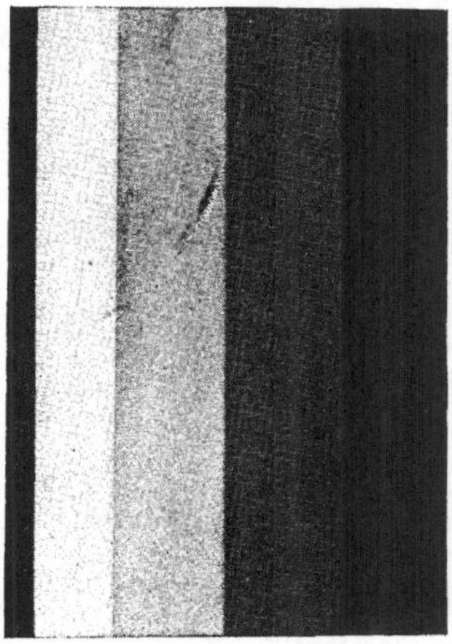

Fig. 264.

Fig. 265.

Fig. 266.

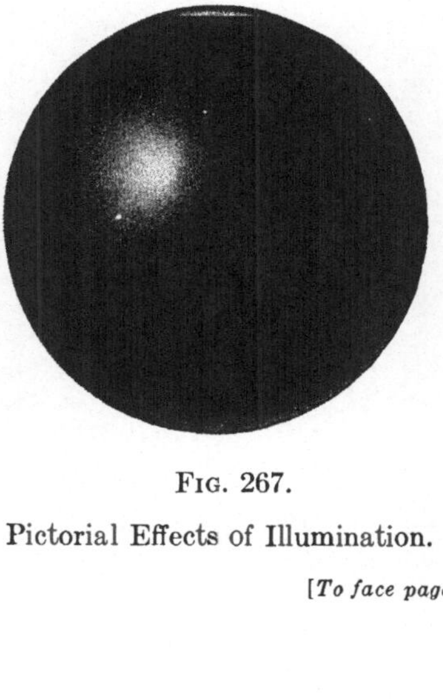

Fig. 267.

Examples of Graduated Shades in Pictorial Effects of Illumination.

[*To face page 278*

"2. Flat tints should be given plane surfaces, when in the shade, and parallel to the vertical plane; those nearest the eye being darkest.

"3. Graduated tints should be given to plane surfaces, when in the light and inclined to the vertical plane; increasing the shade as the surfaces recede from the eye; when two such surfaces incline unequally the one on which the light falls most directly should be lightest.

"4. Graduated tints should be given to plane surfaces, when in the shade, and inclined to the vertical plane; decreasing the shade as the surfaces recede from the eye."

**1426. Examples of graduated shades.** In Figs. 264, 265, 266 and 267 are shown a prism, cylinder, cone and sphere shaded in accordance with the above rules. It will be seen that no mistake can occur as to the nature of the objects, thus certifying to the advisability of their adoption.

## QUESTIONS ON CHAPTER XIV

1. What is the purpose of introducing the pictorial effects of illumination?
2. What is meant by line shading?
3. How are the straight lines of an object line shaded? Give example.
4. How are the curved lines of an object line shaded? Give example.
5. How are the "sections" line shaded? Give example.
6. How are convex surfaces line shaded? Give example.
7. How are concave surfaces line shaded? Give example.
8. How are plane surfaces line shaded? Give example.
9. How are objects made evident to us?
10. What is the source of light?
11. What are light rays?
12. What conventional direction of ray is adopted in shading drawings?
13. What is the shade on an object?
14. What is the shadow of an object?
15. What is the umbra? Give example.
16. What is the penumbra? Give example.
17. Why is only the umbra used on drawings?
18. What is the fundamental operation of finding the shadow of an object?
19. Construct the shadow of a line that is situated so as to have a shadow on the horizontal plane.
20. Construct the shadow of a line that is situated so as to have a shadow on the vertical plane.

21. Construct the shadow of a line that is situated so as to have a shadow on both principal planes.
22. What is a high-light? Explain fully.
23. What is the incident ray?
24. What is the reflected ray?
25. What angular relation is there between the normal and the incident and reflected rays?
26. Do the normal, the incident ray and the reflected ray lie in one plane?
27. Find the high-light on a sphere.
28. How are multiple high-lights produced?
29. What is the aerial effect of illumination?
30. What is meant by graduation of shade?
31. To what is the graduation of shade due?
32. Shade a sphere with lead pencil so as to show the high-light and the graduation of the shade.
33. Shade a cylinder with lead pencil so as to show the high-light and the graduation of the shade.
34. Shade a cone with lead pencil so as to show the high-light and the graduation of the shade.
35. Shade an octagonal prism with lead pencil so as to show the high-light and the graduation of the shade.
36. Construct the horizontal shadow of a cube resting on the horizontal plane.
37. Construct the horizontal shadow of a cube which is some distance above the horizontal plane.
38. Construct the horizontal shadow of a triangular prism which rests on the horizontal plane.
39. Construct the horizontal shadow of a hexagonal prism which rests on the horizontal plane.
40. Construct the horizontal shadow of a pyramid which rests on the horizontal plane.
41. Construct the shade and horizontal shadow cast by a cylinder with a superimposed circular cap.
42. Construct the shade and horizontal shadow cast by a cylinder with a superimposed square cap.
43. Construct the shade and horizontal shadow cast by a cylinder with a superimposed octagonal cap.
44. Construct the shade and horizontal shadow cast by an octagonal prism with a superimposed circular cap.
45. Construct the shade and horizontal shadow cast by an octagonal prism with a superimposed square cap.
46. Construct the shade and horizontal shadow cast by an octagonal prism with a superimposed octagonal cap.
47. Construct the shade and horizontal shadow cast by a cone which rests on a square base.
48. Construct the shade and horizontal shadow cast by an octagonal pyramid which rests on a square base.

49. Construct the shadow cast by a cone which is situated so as to cast a shadow on both principal planes.
50. Construct the shadow cast by an octagonal pyramid which is situated so as to cast a shadow on both principal planes.
51. Construct the shadow cast by an octagonal prism which is situated so as to cast a shadow on both principal planes.
52. Construct the shadow cast by a superimposed cap on the inside of a hollow semi-cylinder.

# CHAPTER XV

## PICTORIAL EFFECTS OF ILLUMINATION IN PERSPECTIVE PROJECTION

**1501. Introductory.** The fundamental principles of the pictorial effects of illumination are best studied in orthographic projection. Their ultimate use, however, is usually associated with perspective. Thus, in one color, an attempt is made to picture reality, whether it be used for engineering purposes, as catalogue illustrations, or whether it be used for general illustrating purposes. The principles, established here, hold equally well when color is added to the perspective (making it an aerial perspective) and its illumination; but, as this is recognized as a distinct field, it will not be considered in this book.

**1502. Problem 1. To draw the perspective of a rectangular prism and its shadow on the horizontal plane.**

The first step in this case is to draw the object and its shadow orthographically. The object is shown in the second angle as has been the custom in perspective; the shadow is on the horizontal plane and its construction is carried out in accordance with principles previously discussed (Chap. XIV). The shaded area in Fig. 268 shows the shadow so constructed. The advisability of the 180° revolution of the horizontal plane has been given (1322), and carrying this into effect in the present instance, the effect shown in Fig. 269 is obtained. The horizontal projection of the prism and the shadow of the prism are then shown below the ground line. The perspective of the prism

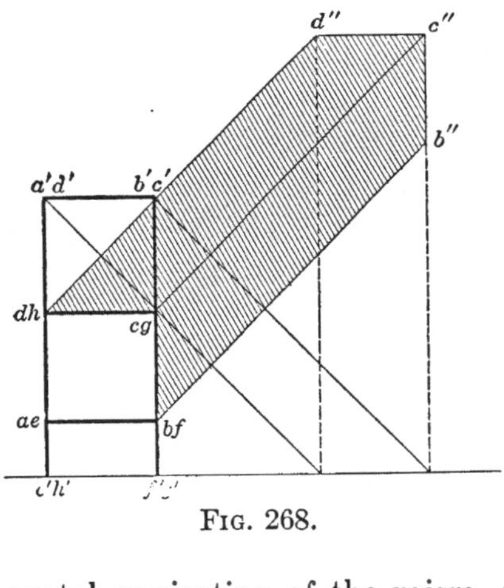

FIG. 268.

will perhaps be clear from the illustration in Fig. 269 as all the necessary construction lines have been included. The steps necessary for the construction of the perspective of the shadow, however, will be considered.

The point of sight is at **S**, shown horizontally projected at **s** and vertically projected at s′. The vanishing points of the diagonals are shown as v and v′; the distance of **v** and v′ from **s′** are equal to the distance **s** above the ground line (1325). A

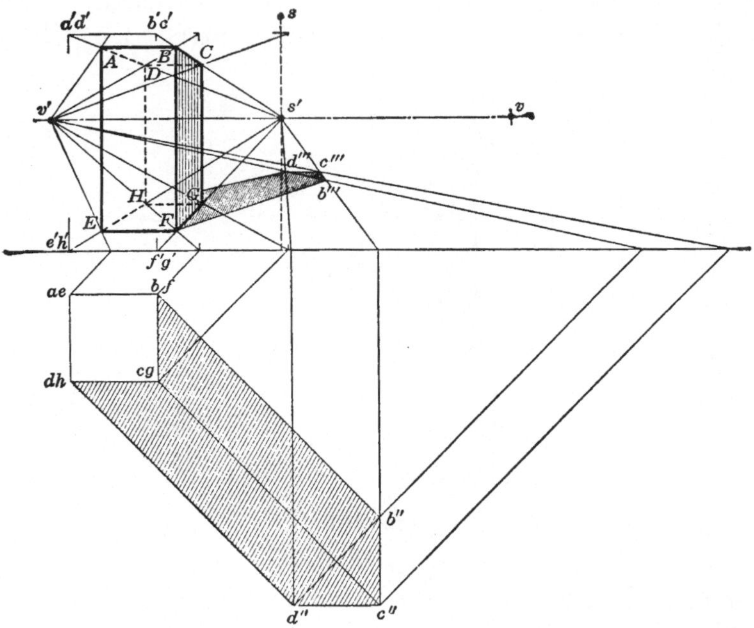


Fig. 269.

perpendicular and a diagonal through the point d″ (the shadow of **D** in space) will intersect at **d‴** which is the required perspective of the shadow of this point. The same procedure will locate **c‴** and **b‴**. The corners F and **G** are the perspectives of those points in space, and as they rest on the horizontal plane, they are also the perspectives of their shadows. By joining **Fb‴c‴d‴** and H with lines the complete outline of the shadow is obtained, except in so far as the limited portion behind the prism from **H** which is hidden from the observer is concerned.

**1503. General method of finding the perspective of a shadow.*** The above method of constructing the perspectives of shadows is perfectly general, although lengthy. It is possible to economize time, however, by taking advantage of the method of locating the perspective of the shadow directly. The shadow of a point in space on any surface is the piercing point of a ray of light through the point on that surface; the perspective of that shadow must therefore lie somewhere on the perspective of the ray of light. It will also lie on the line of intersection of the plane receiving the shadow with a plane containing the ray of light. The perspective of this line of intersection will also

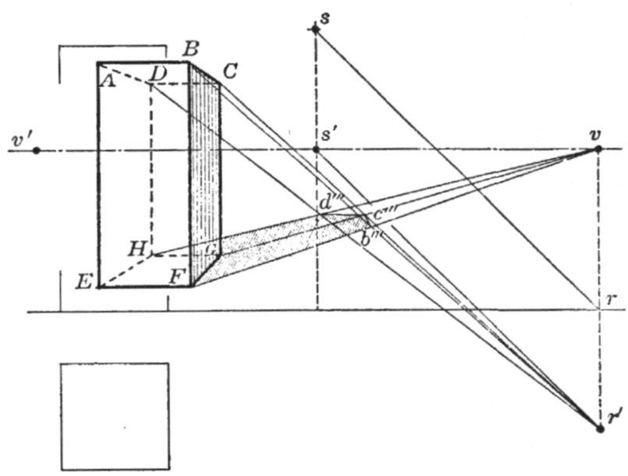


Fig. 270.

contain the perspective of the shadow. Hence, the perspective of the shadow of the point will lie on the intersection of these two perspectives (1318).

**1504. Perspectives of parallel rays of light.** The rays of light are assumed as coming in parallel lines; being parallels, they therefore have a common vanishing point. To find this vanishing point (1313) draw through the point of sight, a line parallel to these rays; and the piercing point of this line on the picture plane will be the required vanishing point. In Fig. 270, if a ray be drawn through the point of sight, then the vertical

* This method is similar, in general, to the finding of the piercing point of a given line on a given plane. See Art. 823.

projection of the ray will be **s′r′**; the horizontal projection of the ray will be **sr** (a careful note being made of the 180° revolution of this plane and hence the revolved direction of the ray) and the piercing point on the picture plane will therefore be at **r′**.

**1505. Perspective of the intersection of the visual plane on the plane receiving the shadow.** The line of intersection of the plane receiving the shadow and the plane containing the ray of light (or **visual plane** as this latter plane is called) is in our case a horizontal line, as the plane receiving the shadow is the horizontal plane. If the horizontal projecting plane of the ray be taken, it is known that the trace makes an angle of 45° with the ground line, and that this horizontal line must vanish in the horizon at v. It will be observed that this same point (v) is also the vanishing point of all diagonals drawn to the right of the point of sight. A further note may be taken of the fact that if the perspective of the horizontal projection of the point be joined with the right vanishing point of the diagonal, the perspective is identical with the perspective of the intersection of the horizontal plane and the visual plane, because the perspectives of the horizontal projection of the point and the vanishing point are common to the two.

**1506. Application of the general method of finding the perspective of a shadow.** The foregoing can be applied to the finding of the shadow of Problem 1. A reference to Fig. 270 in addition to what follows, will indicate the application. Suppose the perspective of the shadow of **D** is under consideration. The perspective of the visual ray is **Dr′**; the perspective of the horizontal projection of the ray is **Hv**; their intersection is **d‴**, the perspective sought. Likewise, **c‴** is similarly located, and it is the perspective of the shadow of **C**, found by the intersection of the **Cr′** (perspective of the ray) and **Gv** (perspective of the horizontal projection of the ray). The point **B** has its shadow at **b‴**, and its location is clearly shown in the figure.

The shadow is completed by joining the proper points with lines. In every way it is identical with the shadow determined in Problem 1.

**1507. Problem 2.** To **draw the perspective of an obelisk with its shade and shadow.**

Let **AFGHK** be the obelisk (Fig. 271) and **S** the point of sight. The perspective is drawn in the usual way. The problem is of interest in so far as the rays of light make an angle of 30° with the ground line, thus causing a longer shadow than when the 45° ray is used.

Through the horizontal and vertical projections of the point of sight, draw a ray parallel to the conventional ray adopted. This ray pierces the picture plane at **r′** the vanishing point of all the rays in space. The horizontal projections of all rays vanish

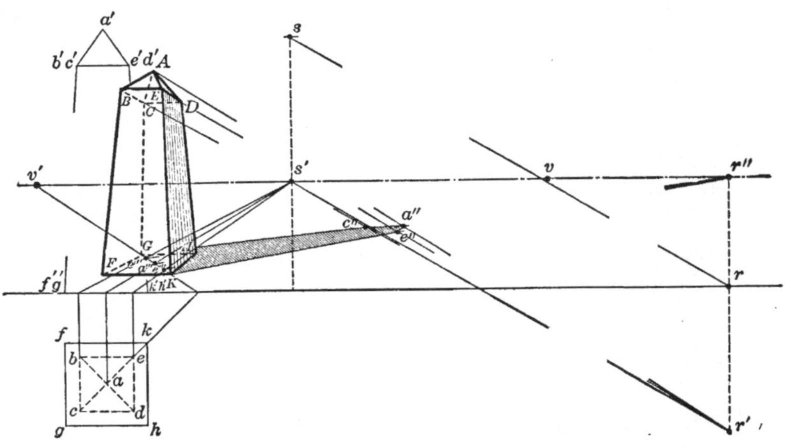

FIG. 271.

at **r″** on the horizon, as all lines should that are parallel to the horizontal plane and at the same time belong to the system of lines parallel to the rays of light.

Inspection of Fig. 271 will show that the lines **GC, CA, AE,** and **EK** affect the shadow, and that the only points to be located for the shadow are **C, A,** and **E**. To locate c″, the shadow of point **C**, draw the perspective of the ray through **C**; **Cr′** is this perspective. The perspective of the horizontal projection is **c‴r″**; **c‴** is the perspective of the horizontal projection of **C**, the necessary construction lines being shown in the figure. The intersection of these two perspectives is **c″**, the required perspective of the shadow of **C** in space.

The point **A** has the perspective of its shadow at **a″** which,

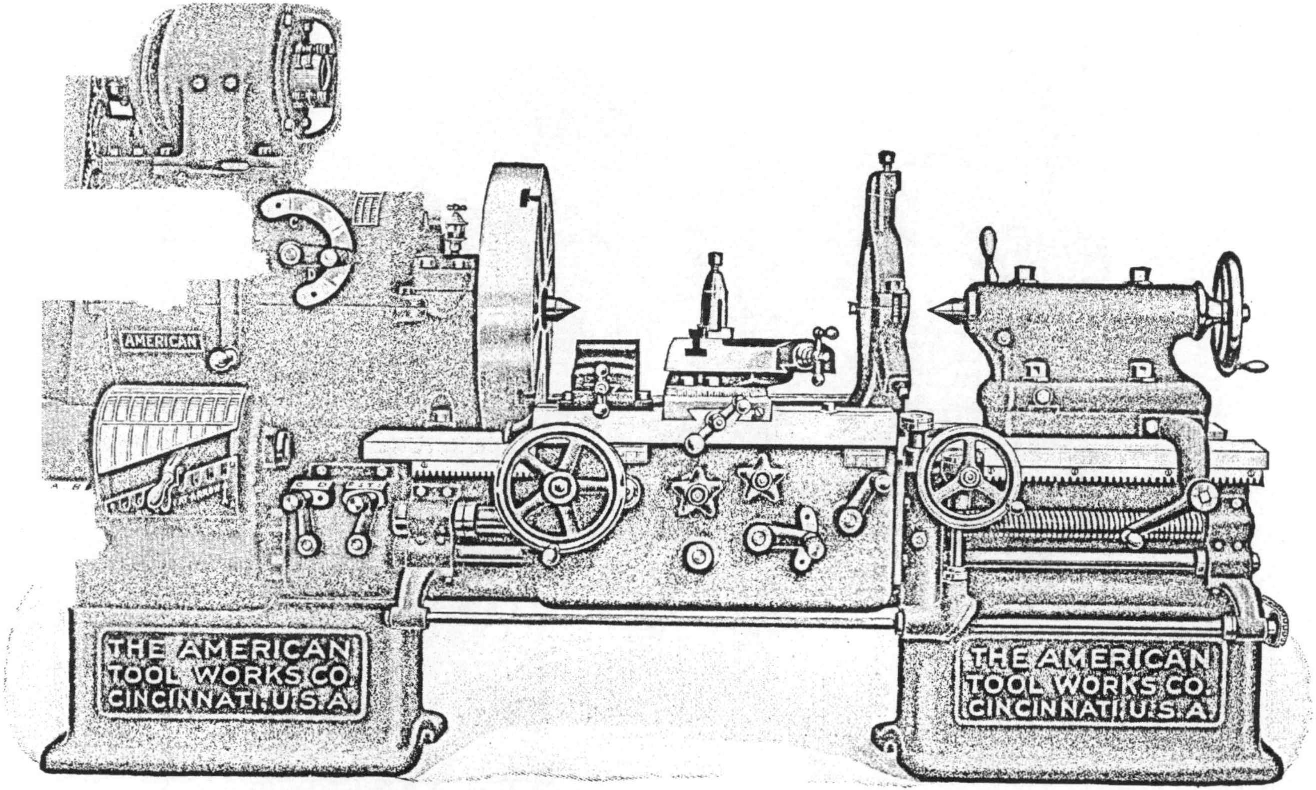


FIG. 272.—Commercial Application of the Pictorial Effects of Illumination in Perspective.

[*To face page 286*

IG. 273.—-Commercial Application of the Pictorial Effects of Illumination in Perspect

[*To face page 287*]

as before, is the intersection of the perspective **Ar′** (of the ray) and **a‴r″** (of the horizontal projection of the ray). The point **E** has its shadow **e″** located in an identical manner as the preceding points **c″** and **a″**.

As the obelisk is resting on a plane (the horizontal in this case) the base is its own shadow, and it is only necessary to join the shadow of **C** with **G** and the line of the shadow **c″G** is determined. Likewise, join c″ with **a″**, **a″** with **e″**, and, finally, **e″** with **K**.

**1508. Commercial application of the pictorial effects of illumination in perspective.** A few general remarks, in cases where the shadow falls on itself or nearby objects, may not be amiss. The draftsman usually has some choice in the selection of the direction of the rays, and, sometimes, in the location of nearby objects.

Where the shadow is cast on the object itself or on neighboring objects, it will, in general, be found much easier to find the shadow, orthographically, and then to proceed with the making of a perspective from it. When the shadow is cast on a horizontal surface only, the general method outlined in Arts. 1503, 1504, and 1505 will find ready application.

The application of the pictorial effects of illumination in perspective in general, requires some consideration of the time required to make the drawings. The principles developed serve as a useful guide, so that the draftsman does not picture impossible shadows, even though the correct outline is not given. In fact, it is a difficult matter exactly to determine the assumed direction of the light from the picture itself. For artistic reasons, certain portions of an object are purposely subdued in order more strongly to emphasize some particular feature. The largest application of these principles lies in making illustrations for high-class catalogues, particularly for machinery catalogues. Figs. 272 and 273 give examples of this kind of work. It will be observed that the presented principles are ignored in many respects, yet, the effect is pleasing notwithstanding. After all, the theory indicates correct modes of procedure, but the time required to make such drawings is frequently prohibitive. Hence, common sense, based on mature judgment, must be used as a guide.

## QUESTIONS ON CHAPTER XV

1. When rays of light are parallel, do their perspectives have a common vanishing point on the picture plane? Why?
2. How is the vanishing point of the perspectives of a parallel system of lines found?
3. What is a visual plane?
4. Show that the perspective of the intersection of a visual plane and the horizontal plane vanishes on the horizon.
5. If the conventional direction of rays is used, show that the perspectives of their horizontal projections vanish in the right diagonal vanishing point.
6. State the general method of finding the perspective of a shadow without first constructing it orthographically.
7. Show that the method of Question 6 is an application of finding the perspectives of intersecting lines.
8. A rectangular prism rests on the horizontal plane. Find its shadow on that plane by constructing it orthographically and then make a perspective of it.
9. Take the same prism of Question 8 and construct its horizontal shadow directly.
10. An obelisk rests on the horizontal plane. Find its shadow on that plane by constructing it orthographically and then make a perspective of it.
11. Take the same obelisk of Question 10 and construct its horizontal shadow directly.

**Note.** In the following problems construct the shade and shadow orthographically and then find its perspective.

12. A square-based pyramid rests on a square base. Construct the shadow.
13. A square-based pyramid rests on a circular base. Construct the shadow.
14. A square-based pyramid rests on a hexagonal base. Construct the shadow.
15. A cone rests on a hexagonal base. Construct the shadow.
16. A rectangular prism rests on two square bases (stepped). Construct the shadow.
17. A rectangular prism rests on two circular bases (stepped). Construct the shadow.
18. A rectangular prism rests on two hexagonal bases (stepped). Construct the shadow.
19. A cylinder has a superimposed square cap. Construct the shadow.
20. A cylinder has a superimposed circular cap. Construct the shadow.
21. A cylinder has a superimposed hexagonal cap. Construct the shadow.
22. A cylinder has a superimposed square cap and rests on a square base. Construct the shadow.

23. A cylinder has a superimposed circular cap and rests on a circular base. Construct the shadow.
24. A cylinder has a superimposed hexagonal cap and rests on a hexagonal base. Construct the shadow.
25. A hollow semi-cylinder has a superimposed cap. Construct the shadows on the inside of the cylinder and on the horizontal plane.

# INDEX

## A

## D

## E

## I

## L

## M



## N



## O

## P

## T